Praise for *The Sociology of Islam*

A brilliant, pioneering effort to explain the cosmopolitan ethos within Islamicate civilization, *The Sociology of Islam* encompasses all the terminological boldness of Marshall Hodgson, making the Persianate and Islamicate elements of civic cosmopolitanism, across the vast Afro-Eurasian ecumene, accessible to the widest possible readership in both the humanities and the social sciences. **Bruce B. Lawrence,** *author of Who is Allah? (2015)*

Sociologists of religion have long been awaiting a successor volume to Brian Turner's pathbreaking but now dated *Weber and Islam* (1974). Armando Salvatore's new book provides just this update and much more. Ranging across a host of critical case studies and theoretical issues, Salvatore provides a masterful account of religious ethics, rationalization, and civility across the breadth of the Muslim world, from early times to today. The result is a book of deep intellectual insight, important, not just for the sociology of Islam, but for scholars and students interested in religion, ethics, and modernity in all civilizational traditions. **Robert Hefner,** *Boston University*

The sociology of Islam has been a late and controversial addition to the sociology of religion. This field of research has been the principal target of the critique of Orientalism and after 9/11 the study of Islam became heavily politicized. Terrorist attacks in Paris and Beirut have only compounded the long-standing difficulties of objective interpretation and understanding. In the first volume of what promises to be a major three-volume masterpiece, Armando Salvatore steers a careful and judicious course through the various pitfalls that attend the field. The result is an academic triumph combining a sweeping historical vision of Islam with an analytical framework that is structured by the theme of knowledge–power. One waits with huge excitement for the delivery of the remaining volumes. **Bryan Turner,** *City University of New York*

THE SOCIOLOGY OF

ISLAM

KNOWLEDGE, POWER AND
CIVILITY

ARMANDO SALVATORE

WILEY Blackwell

This edition first published 2016
© 2016 John Wiley & Sons Ltd

Registered Office
John Wiley & Sons Ltd, The Atrium, Southern Gate, Chichester, West Sussex, PO19 8SQ, UK

Editorial Offices
350 Main Street, Malden, MA 02148-5020, USA
9600 Garsington Road, Oxford, OX4 2DQ, UK
The Atrium, Southern Gate, Chichester, West Sussex, PO19 8SQ, UK

For details of our global editorial offices, for customer services, and for information about how to apply for permission to reuse the copyright material in this book please see our website at www.wiley.com/wiley-blackwell.

Library of Congress Cataloging-in-Publication Data

Names: Salvatore, Armando, author.
Title: The sociology of Islam : knowledge, power and civility / Armando Salvatore.
Description: 1 | Hoboken, N.J. : Wiley, 2016. | Includes bibliographical references and index.
Identifiers: LCCN 2016005808 (print) | LCCN 2016006680 (ebook) | ISBN 9781118662649
    (hardback) | ISBN 9781119109976 (paper) | ISBN 9781118662625 (pdf) |
    ISBN 9781118662632 (epub)
Subjects: LCSH: Islamic sociology. | Civil society–Islamic countries. | BISAC: RELIGION / Islam /
    General.
Classification: LCC BP173.25 .S34 2016 (print) | LCC BP173.25 (ebook) | DDC 306.6/97–dc23
LC record available at http://lccn.loc.gov/2016005808

A catalogue record for this book is available from the British Library.

Cover image: Khaju bridge, Esfahan, Iran. © Aurora Photos / Alamy

Set in 10.5/13pt Minion by Aptara Inc., New Delhi, India

Printed in Singapore by C.O.S. Printers Pte Ltd

1   2016

CONTENTS

Conclusion 271

PREFACE AND ACKNOWLEDGMENTS

The sociology of Islam is an emerging, strategic field of inquiry, teaching, and debate located at the delicate intersection of a variety of disciplines, including sociology, history, Islamic Studies, anthropology, comparative religion, and comparative civilizational analysis. It deals both with conceptual questions and historical interpretations as they originated back in the 1970s, particularly in the pioneering work of Bryan S. Turner and his commentary on Marshall Hodgson's monumental trilogy *The Venture of Islam*. Covering this field of study is a longer-term undertaking that cannot be completed in one volume. This is why this book was born with an introductory intent and use value.

While the beginnings of the sociology of Islam should be traced back to Bryan S. Turner's *Weber and Islam* (Turner 1974), my own entry into the field as a scholar goes back to the early 1990s and coincides with the beginning of my PhD dissertation, which I completed at the European University Institute, Florence in 1994 and published in 1997 (Salvatore 1997). Yet my baptism of fire into the sociology of Islam occurred when I taught my first graduate seminar, in the winter of 1995, at Humboldt University, Berlin. The seminar was titled, in a kind of self-indulgent provocation, 'Is a Sociology of Islam Possible?'

Clearly, whatever the sociology of Islam was by the mid-1990s, it still appeared fragile, dependent on scattered contributions and intermittent collaborations among individual scholars. Still absent, or at best latent, was the sense of a nexus between historical and empirical work, on the one hand, and whatever we happen to call 'theory,' on the other. In the summer prior to that graduate seminar, right after my arrival in Berlin, I convened a small panel on the sociology of Islam at an international conference sponsored by the leading social science journal *Theory, Culture and Society*. The event took place, by sheer coincidence, in Berlin. The journal editor, Mike Featherstone, had months earlier suggested to me that I invite Bryan Turner and Georg Stauth as speakers to the panel. I had never met them before, though I had read a lot of what they had published, including their co-authored works. These included *Nietzsche's Dance* (Stauth and Turner 1988) which, though devoted to a philosopher, was largely an alternate reading of the genesis of sociology which was to have an impact on my own understanding of the sociology of Islam. During the panel, I was struck by the difference between Bryan's and Georg's papers (and, more generally, approaches), since I had until then strictly associated their names as scholars with each other, and both of them together with the sociology of Islam. Even more, from that point onward, I admired what they had accomplished together, by being able to build powerful synergies and by combining their different sociological geniuses. Twenty years later, I am still profoundly attracted to the scholarship of both Bryan Turner and Georg Stauth and my debt to them in my own venture into and across the sociology of Islam is correspondingly high.

Since the summer of 1995, Georg Stauth has been an invited speaker at every institution I have worked for. His assiduous presence and our serial conversations have fed into my endeavors to develop an original yet balanced approach to the sociology of Islam. Georg has consistently responded to my cultivation of his rich and complex scholarship by offering me the chance to co-edit with him the *Yearbook of the Sociology of Islam* until it ceased publication in 2008, and by inviting me to be a member of the research group he directed at the Institute for Advanced Study in the Humanities, Essen, on 'Islam and Modernity' between 2003 and 2006.

This trajectory of twenty years culminated in a conference that took place in June 2015, just a few weeks before this manuscript went into production. The conference's topic was quite straightforward, 'Sociology of Islam: Reflection, Revision, & Reorientation' and I contributed to it a paper on "The Sociology of Islam and the Rise of China." It was convened by the Sociology of Religion section of the German Sociological Association and took place at the Center for Religious Studies (CERES) of Ruhr University, Bochum. The event was inaugurated by a keynote given by Bryan Turner which looked back at forty years of development in the field. Georg Stauth was not present and we missed his critical mind. His absence was for us a healthy warning on how the incessant, climactic politicization of Islam-related themes within the global public sphere presents a serious challenge to the sociology of Islam.

Yet this politicization is also a major reason why a viable sociology of Islam is urgently needed. As Bryan Turner reminded us in his introductory keynote, this field of study, born in the 1970s parallel to—yet independent from—the critique of Orientalism, was propped up by 9/11, alongside other academic fields dealing with Islam from the angle of modernity. The sociology of Islam should avoid being suffocated by this politicization while aiming to retain a scholarly significance and contemporary relevance by also speaking to the concerns of colleagues and students within political science and international relations, as much as it entertains key dialogues with scholars from history and anthropology. Not by chance does this introductory volume address the key dimension at stake in the majority of such conversations, namely power. I hope that this book, due to the consistent interdisciplinary porousness of the sociology of Islam from its beginnings, will attract the attention of practitioners of all academic disciplines concerned with power as well as that of a lay public interested in what—with a crude shorthand similar to those I tried to deconstruct in my PhD thesis more than twenty years ago—we often call 'political Islam.' This construct increasingly depends on Western—and more recently Chinese— perceptions and interests more than on the inner and outer complexities of the diverse social dynamics variably associated with Islam. The sociology of Islam does not ignore this interpretive syndrome but works to shield its object—namely the nexus of religion and civility produced by social forces associated with Islam—from the risk of a preventive, and potentially devastating politicization determined by the interests of powerful observers more than by the concerns of embattled actors.

In pursuing the goal of investigating the nexus of religion and civility, this introductory volume adopts a combined historical, theoretical, and comparative perspective, while it privileges key entanglements that push forward the classic boundaries of comparison. Historical references in the book are of crucial importance, yet by necessity selective. They reflect key periods, characters, or formations and illuminate particularly significant, long-term, and transregional processes of transformation. The main emphasis is on how social relations produce associational bonds and institutional configurations: therefore I opted to explore the unfolding of what I call 'the knowledge–power equation' and the way it produces patterns of civility. The book refers most consistently to the core 'Nile-to-Oxus' area of the Islamic ecumene and to its Central Asian and Mediterranean extensions.

While absolute comprehensiveness is unrealistic in a single, introductory volume, the trilogy that it intends to introduce (also in association with the forthcoming *Wiley Blackwell History of Islam*, a textbook that I have been editing together with Roberto Tottoli and Babak Rahimi over the last few years) will rebalance such initial regional and thematic foci. Ideally, the present volume should be followed by one dedicated to *The Law, the State, and the Public Sphere* and by a concluding study on *Transnationalism, Transculturalism, and Globalization.*

The book is primarily addressed to the same type of audiences and thematic discussions that generated it in the first place: classes of advanced undergraduate and graduate students on the one hand, and interdisciplinary explorations and debates with fellow scholars on the other. Social activists and policy analysts might also find inspiration in the proposed sociology of Islam for facilitating an understanding of Islam as a longer-term force providing a socio-cultural nexus and an institutional glue to a variety of relations and arrangements.

The Introduction situates the sociology of Islam in its historical and disciplinary context and provides a first discussion of the basic concepts used in the volume. Chapters 2 and 3 refer to the epoch that Marshall Hodgson (whose majestic historical trilogy provides the main source of inspiration for the sociology of Islam) called the Middle Periods (mid-10th to mid-15th centuries). Chapters 5 and 6 embrace early modernity and the colonial stage of late modernity. Chapters 1 and 7 discuss theoretical questions directly relevant to the analysis, while Chapter 4 adopts an explicitly comparative perspective. The Conclusion summarizes the results of the exploration while also providing an initial bridge to future studies and volumes.

Thanking all the colleagues who have directly or indirectly enriched my path through the sociology of Islam would appear as a replica of my email inbox of the last twenty and more years. In what follows, I remember as many as I can among my key interlocutors and I apologize for those omitted due to lapses of memory. I owe thanks to Setrag Manoukian, Fabio Vicini, Tom Troughton, Johann Arnason, Dale Eickelman, Klaus Eder, Arpad Szakolczai, Hatsuki Aishima, Benoit Challand, Khalid Masud, Gianfranco Poggi, James Piscatori, Şerif Mardin, Prasenjit Duara, Bruce Lawrence, Volkhard Krech, Levent Tezcan, Recep Şentürk, Michael Feener, Faisal Devji, Mark LeVine, Fabio Petito, Massimo Galluppi, Gennaro Gervasio, Enrico De Angelis, Andrea Teti, Mohammed Bamyeh, Jeanette Jouili, Schirin Amir-Moazami, Michael Gilsenan, Reinhard Schulze, Jamal Malik, Shmuel Eisenstadt, Alessandro Pizzorno, Charles Hirschkind, Ruth Mas, Sami Zubaida, Kathryn Spellman, Pnina Werbner, Chiara Bottici, Ian Chambers, Talal Asad, Jose Casanova, Craig Calhoun, Ali Zaidi, Meena

Sharifi-Funk, Werner Schiffauer, Bob Hefner, Michael Gasper, Amyn Sajoo, Rouzbeh Parsi, Mohammad Tabishat, Joel Kahn, Aziz Al-Azmeh, Agnes Horvath, Alexander Caeiro, Tommaso Trevisani, Linda Herrera, Asef Bayat, Saba Mahmood, John Bowen, John Esposito, John Voll, Badouin Dupret, Hussein Agrama, Irfan Ahmad, Satoshi Ikeuchi, Ruba Salih, Margot Badran, Mona Abaza, Sigrid Nökel, Valerie Amiraux, Irene Becci, Nadia Fadil, Said Samir, Riem Tisini, Emilio Spadola, Frederic Volpi, Gabriele Marranci, Rouzbeh Parsi, Benjamin Soares, Martin van Bruinessen, Luca Mavelli, Abdulkader Tayob, Ebrahim Moosa, Filippo Osella, Pnina Werbner, Caroline Osella, Massimo Campanini, Albrecht Hofheinz, Georges Khalil, Jörn Thielmann, Michelangelo Guida, Claudio Lojacono, Mara Tedesco, Bo Stråth, Stefano Allievi, Vincenzo Pace, Olivier Roy, Andreas Christmann, Naveeda Khan, Brinkley Messick, Dyala Hamzah, and Behrooz Ghamari-Tabrizi. I am also grateful to all the students who attended my classes, seminars, and summer schools over the last twenty years at various institutions and who contributed to the exploration and discussion of key transformations within the Islamic ecumene.

I should not forget to show my appreciation of the endeavors of the editors and administrators of a cluster of new academic initiatives within the sociology of Islam. Right after the cessation of the publication of the previously mentioned *Yearbook of the Sociology of Islam* an increasingly successful listserv and newsletter on the sociology of Islam saw the light, followed more recently by an academic journal, published by Brill, entitled *Sociology of Islam*. These fora have provided an uninterrupted supply of fresh fuel igniting kaleidoscopic debates and corroborating the contemporary relevance and transdisciplinary scope of the sociology of Islam.

In conclusion, I would like to offer my special thanks to the institution that has hosted me during my last year of mostly integrative endeavors on the manuscript, namely McGill University. I remember here in particular Ellen Aitken, the painfully missed Dean of Religious Studies, and I thank all the colleagues from the Institute of Islamic Studies, particularly Rob Wisnovsky and the Institute's Director, Rula Jurdi Abisaab, who have been consistently supportive from the first minute. I have always associated the Institute with the teachings of two towering scholars who have influenced my scholarly trajectory since I was working on my PhD dissertation, namely Wilfred Cantwell Smith and Toshihiko Izutsu. Even more, I thank the Keenan Foundation and particularly Barbara Keenan for believing in the idea of reviving and renewing the heritage of those seminal teachings at McGill, whose significance clearly transcends the study of Islam to embrace the multiple entanglements between various religious traditions and their nexus with cultures, societies, and politics.

Armando Salvatore
Montreal, September 2015

References

Salvatore, Armando. 1997. *Islam and the Political Discourse of Modernity.* Reading: Ithaca Press.
Stauth, Georg and Bryan S. Turner. 1988. *Nietzsche's Dance: Resentment, Reciprocity and Resistance in Social Life.* Oxford: Blackwell.
Turner, Bryan S. 1974. *Weber and Islam: A Critical Study.* London and Boston: Routledge & Kegan Paul.

Introduction

Knowledge and Power in the Sociology of Islam

The project of the sociology of Islam is first indebted to the main paradigms of sociology. Sociology is, in several ways, the queen of the social sciences, but also a discipline interfacing with several crucial subdivisions and dimensions of the humanities, most notably with philosophy and history. One key trait of sociology is its rise as a scholarly reflection of (and on) modernity and its constitutive and transformative processes. It is the discipline not only inquiring into but also theorizing about modern society and its genesis. How we understand modernity probably depends more on sociologists' understandings and definitions of the term than on the work of historians or philosophers. While sociology is characterized by such a strong focus (sometimes bordering on obsession) on modernity, the discipline has often allowed for waves of transdisciplinary opening toward other horizons of scholarship. At a more recent stage of its development, sociology has also shown a capacity to question the supposed Western monopoly on the definition and management of modernity and ultimately some of its own certainties, or at least paradigms (see e.g. Eisenstadt 2000; 2003). This step has coincided with a reflexive turn within sociology led by the initiative of rereading several key authors both within the heart of sociology as an academic discipline and at its margins, often with a view to better contextualizing their works and intellectual biographies (Bourdieu & Wacquant 1992; Szakolczai 2000). While this 'reflexive turn' cannot be considered representative of the discipline as a whole, it has certainly affected the trajectory, if not the genesis, of the sociology of Islam.

The Sociology of Islam: Knowledge, Power and Civility, First Edition. Armando Salvatore.
© 2016 John Wiley & Sons, Ltd. Published 2016 by John Wiley & Sons, Ltd.

The reason why the sociology of Islam dovetails with the reflexive turn is also due to the initial challenge that the study of Islam has presented to solidified sociological categories, including, if not mainly, modernity. During the 19th century a wide array of academic disciplines targeting an increasingly comparative study of religions, cultures (primarily languages), and civilizations have constructed Islam as a powerful yet sinister counter-model representing a potential of resistance, both in history and the present, to how Western modernity tamed and appropriated the force of religious traditions (Masuzawa 2005: 179–206). This process occurred prior to the rise of sociology, which only saw the light as an academic discipline between the end of the 19th and the beginning of the 20th century. Yet sociology inherited this biased view of Islam for the simple reason that as a new discipline it initially depended on the findings and ideas of linguistic, textual, and historical disciplines. This is particularly evident in the German case, which also witnessed a continuous role of philosophers in mapping the global relations between cultural and religious traditions (Stauth 1993; Johansen 2004). However, the idea that Islam simply does not fit into modernity, though still popular among Western media professionals and policy-makers today, could not hold for too long once sociology took over. Yet Islam's full normalization and its folding into the 'sociological normal' did not work either. Thus Islam was bound to remain a force able to permanently unsettle sociology's never-renounced ambitions to explain the factors and impediments of social transformations and social cohesion on a global scale. It goes without saying that the quality and weight of this purportedly ambivalent role of Islam, along with the extent to which this characterization embarrassed rather than bolstered sociological paradigms during the 20th century, are themselves manifestations of the initial paradigmatic limitations of Western sociology.

Sociology is too often (and rather wrongly) perceived as a strongly self-entrenched discipline, whose main internal cleavage is merely a tension between quantitative vs. qualitative methods. Against such simplified views, we should see sociology's limits as potentially productive of new openings. The sociology of Islam takes such limitations as a resource. Let us first consider the way one of the fathers of sociology, Max Weber (1864–1920), championed the idea of a specifically Western path of rationalization of life conduct as the potentially universal key of access to the modernity of capitalism and of state bureaucracies. He essentially viewed power as the basic engine of instrumental human relations. Correspondingly, he understood modernity as the stage of human development at which the instrumentalization of power relations reaches a particularly high sophistication and also a point of no return. This instrumentalization is particularly evident in a process that he called 'rationalization.' The process, whose cradle was North-Western Europe, embraced both economic production in the form of capitalism and political rule in the guise of bureaucratic steering. The primary tool of sophistication of this instrumental rationalization consists in a reliance on calculative reason. This yielded an unprecedented optimization of instrumental power, measured in terms of the output of economic production and the effectiveness of the legal order.

What remained largely undetermined, though not ignored, by Weber was the extent to which this modern triumph of power obliterated earlier dynamics. He was interested in the process through which the sheer power commanded by the social elites who controlled wealth and violence has been resisted and largely tamed in various societies since antiquity. This resistance was associated with the cultural production of knowledge and meaning via intellectual and scholarly elites. It is here that religious traditions enter the center stage of Weberian sociology. Teachings and practices providing instructions on human salvation and/or liberation from pain and suffering have offered a foremost example of such a counter-dynamics to sheer power, and have ushered in the creation of forms of immaterial, knowledge-based, alternate power. This latter process should also be understood, according to Weber, as a rationalization, albeit one oriented to perfecting what he called cultural values rather than to maximizing sheer power. One main channel through which cultural elites tame power is by defining its legitimate exercise through enacting religious and cultural values. In this manner the elites, often acting as counter-elites, have been able to acquire a power of definition of patterns and forms of socially and politically acceptable authority. They have legitimized themselves and acquired weapons of conditional legitimation of rulers. Cultural elites (better defined as the elites in charge of knowledge production) might not have understood this process in terms of rationalization, which is indeed a conceptual label it acquired through the categories of Weber, the sociologist. Yet it seems plausible that the elites of knowledge played the game of legitimization of power by taking a leading role—in a quite conscious way— in its authoritative definition.

One particular modern turn of religion, which Weber condensed in his famous (or infamous) Protestant Ethic Thesis, has religion, in the shape of Calvinist Christianity, working as the very engine of the transformation of rationalization processes from value oriented into instrumental within

European modernity (Weber 1986 [1920]: 17–206). Calvinism, i.e. the most radical and successful expression of the Protestant Reformation, was credited with providing key impulses to shaping the self-propelling dynamism of capitalist enterprise. However, one would grossly misunderstand Weber's thesis if one did not relate it to his wider argument. He intended to explain the advances in the rationalization of sheer power as an autonomous social factor similar to those we associate with modernity in general. This applies in particular to the modern, increasingly secular state and to the type of capitalist development that the state itself promoted. But the core of Weber's explanation intended to highlight a coincident, and to some extent prior, development, or rather metamorphosis. This process unfolded at the cultural and more specifically religious level. It consists of the ways the early modern Protestant Ethic, while rooted in the search for salvation, led to a sharp maximization of the purposive rationality of religious traditions by breaking through the idea itself of value reflecting a purpose. The consequence of this breakthrough was the folding of the originally value-oriented rationality into an ultimately autonomous and instrumental type of rationality. This occurred because salvation, which the Calvinists saw as absolutely depending on God's grace, could only be ascertained through success in a brave new enterprising world and therefore depended on a rigorously calculative chase of profit. This triumphing model of rationality is now almost exclusively guided by the pursuit of pure wealth (which we could see as a more liquid, yet also symbolically effective, form of power), via calculation (capitalism) and regulation (bureaucracy).

Once such rationalization dynamics have been set in motion, the originally religious impulse gives way to secularization. The "spirit of capitalism" theorized by Weber as the product of the Protestant Ethic no longer needs religious virtue in order to unfold. However, the Weberian distinction between a modern and a premodern pattern of rationalization (an instrumental one vs. one oriented to the creation of cultural values) remained a major resource for dealing with the broader process to whose explanation sociology remained committed more than any other modern social science, namely the transformation of human society from a stage dominated by tradition to a phase characterized by modernity. Clearly tradition and modernity work as polar opposites within sociological discourse. A key arrow of tradition is commonly identified with religious practice and doctrine and sociologists have been no exception in primarily collapsing religion into tradition. Yet they also saw their relation as dynamic, not static. Two other founding fathers of sociology, namely Emile Durkheim (1858–1917) and

Georg Simmel (1858–1918), passionately dealt with religion's crossing the purported boundary between tradition and modernity (Salvatore 2009). Rooted in the traditional construction of knowledge-based cultural values, religion is transformed and transmitted to modern societies in ways that make it an indispensable resource within modern patterns of rationalization themselves, even when there is no specific intervention of a Weberian type of religious ethic (Protestant or otherwise). Far from erasing religion, modern society, while resting on an increasingly rational and complex social division of labor, facilitates a human appropriation of religion's pristine force in altered, increasingly secular, civic forms, which have often cohered into what has been dubbed a 'civil religion' (Bellah and Hammond 1980). The quintessentially modern form of religion is therefore less its disappearance than its manifestations as a key ingredient of civility, as a provider of what Durkheim called 'civic morals' (Turner 1992). In other words, religion is not merely on the resisting side to the rise of modern instrumental rationality, of modern individualization, and modern solidarity. Secularity itself appears to be the continuation of religion with other (and more powerful) means, to the extent it has to draw on, and transform, the pristine cohesive form of religion in order to produce responsible individuals committed to a rational, social division of labor and corresponding patterns of solidarity.

It is sociology's dynamic, rather than static, view of religion that ultimately compels to complexify the relation between tradition and modernity, in ways that transcend what the founding fathers of the discipline were able to do. This complexification should help reframe and elasticize the very notion of religion in a perspective that overcomes the merely comparative analysis of its role in a variety of (Western and non-Western) societies. The sociology of Islam contributes to this larger task through addressing the specificities of Islamic commitments in history and in the present as being both rooted in religious teachings and practices and by necessity transcending the horizon of faith. The birth of the sociology of Islam might be traced back to the publication of *Weber and Islam* by Bryan S. Turner in 1974 (Turner 1974). This occurred in the middle of the decade that saw the breakdown of modernization theory, the rise of theorems of reislamization, and the global critique of Orientalism, which in the 1960s had been restricted to intellectual interventions quite rigorously framed within the anti-colonial and liberation discourse. An increasing part of Turner's work on the sociology of Islam dealt with these overlapping developments in Weberian terms. However, and from the beginning, the idea was not so much to merely apply Weberian categories to Islam (Weber's references to Islam are scant and scattered: see Nafissi 1998 and Schluchter 1999 [1987]) but rather to redress them (or their trivialization via 'Weberist' orthodoxies) by studying the complexities themselves of Islam as a religion, a civilization, and a complex matrix of social and institutional arrangements. Within this trajectory Turner also published, in the same year as Said's *Orientalism* (1978), the often-neglected *Marx and the End of Orientalism* (Turner 1978).

It is at this juncture that inserting Islam's diversity into sociological questions and paradigms becomes a potential instrument for renewing sociology's ever unfulfilled universal ambitions. The sociology of Islam was born through the way Bryan Turner almost singlehandedly connected the historical study of Islam—most notably the work of Marshall G.S. Hodgson, whose monumental trilogy *The Venture of Islam* was published posthumously in 1974 (Hodgson 1974, I–III), the same year as Turner's *Weber and Islam* (Turner 1974)—to key transversal questions inherited (and left unsolved) by the fathers of sociology. However, what emerged from this tour de force was not just the need to review some paradigmatic concepts of sociological theory, like charisma, social cohesion, social development, and rationalization. The pioneering endeavors of Turner also revealed latent questions connected to how some defective conceptualizations within Weber's corpus might derive from the skewed ways the Heidelberg sociologist coped with the conceptual heritage of earlier key thinkers like Karl Marx (Turner 1978) and Friedrich Nietzsche (Stauth and Turner 1988). In both cases, the interactions between the globally hegemonic, modern West—whose bourgeois cultures and ideologies Marx and Nietzsche had famously criticized from different angles—and the closest part of the hegemonized non-West, represented by the Islamic ecumene, started to be seen as a crucial terrain for theoretical critiques and revisions.

This preliminary work on the sociology of Islam acquired a strong relevance throughout the 1980s, a decade that witnessed serious interpretive contentions (often through the opaque prism of 'reislamization') on the nature of the relations between religion, society, and politics in Muslim contexts. The dissertation I started in 1990 and which led to the publication of my *Islam and the Political Discourse of Modernity* in 1997 (Salvatore 1997) also originated from the quite rapid opening of a field of contentious reflections. The contours of a 'mission' for the sociology of Islam started to take shape: helping sociology to emancipate itself from a particularly weighty 'original sin,' namely a reluctance to recognize the social and civil dynamism of non-Western articulations of religion. While after the Iranian revolution of 1979 Henry Kissinger had pontificated that modernization theory does not work, now the sociology of Islam could help in raising the issue of an 'Islamic modernity' as a research question to pursue and no longer as an oxymoron. Not by chance a leading thinker of the age like Michel Foucault (1926–1984) had visited Iran during the revolution and suggested that the engine of historical transformations, the 'spirit' of revolutions, had left the West and moved East, adopting an Islamic vocabulary (Salvatore 1997: 145–55). In a coincident development, a collection of translated writings by the Iranian Islamic intellectual Ali Shari'ati, who passed away shortly before the revolutionary events in his country, was published under the title *The Sociology of Islam* (Shari'ati 1979). One started to take seriously the possibility of seeing the emergence of a truly transformative potential of Islam vis-à-vis society, even in the absence of those precise factors of modern rationalization that had been at work in the Western trajectory. Islam was no longer static but 'in movement.'

The sociology of Islam thus started to help sociology in general, and the sociology of religion in particular, gain a much richer and less Eurocentric notion of religion. The key to reappraising religion as a compound of knowledge and power articulated through the prism of civility (be it the source of social cohesion or mobilization) is to distinguish between a rather institutional notion of religion, which ultimately coincides with its authorities, creeds, and practices, and its rather creative, and in this sense eminently rational (following Weber's sense of value rationality), meta-institutional impetus. This creative power is manifest in forms of social knowledge that have the capacity to invent and initiate (or reconstruct and collate) new types of human institutions serving a variety of social needs. This richer notion of religion cannot simply consist of emphasizing the plurality and often syncretic dimension of religions (their authorities, practices, and creeds) found among the non-Western other but should rather focus on religion as a potentially universalizable, meta-institutional, and knowledge-based type of power. As we will see, studying Islam facilitates this step to the extent that in the Islamic case (or rather cases) the relation between tradition and modernity can no longer be streamlined in easy functional terms as was the case within the original parameters of Western sociology summarized above. Less functionalization means a greater focus on both the regularities and the unpredictabilities of what I will call 'the knowledge–power equation,' which substantiates the meta-institutional, creative, and 'constellating' power of religion.

Therefore the sociology of Islam should not be reduced to a mere application to Muslim-majority societies of standardized Western sociological approaches to the way religion is first constituted and then transformed in the modern world. The sociology of Islam has rather to treasure the tensions and antinomies that underlie the originally Western, yet over time global, sociological project of modernity and the ambivalent role of religion therein (see Milbank 1990; Heilbron 1995 [1990]; Kilminster 1998)]. The most crucial among such tensions are strictly related to yet unsolved dilemmas of sociology's coping with Islam's challenge. For example, from the viewpoint of Western historic experiences of modernity, sociology produced, particularly in the second half of the 20th century, by going beyond its own classics, key ideas of secularization that were part of a wider theory of modernization—only to radically question this 'secularization theory' in the latter quarter of the century. Yet from a perspective inspired by the specific weight and richness of historic Muslim practices and interpretations of religion, a full-fledged theory predicting either the privatization or disappearance of religion is quite problematic in sociological terms. This is the case even if we reformulate the idea of secularization in terms of religion's confinement to a specific field of society. This is the 'religious field,' in the terminology of one of the leading sociologists of the last part of the 20th century, Pierre Bourdieu (1971).

The difficulty in endorsing either an outright privatization or a rigorous confinement of religion in the case of Islam does not disprove the existence of secular trends and processes of differentiation of religious authority within Muslim-majority societies at several stages of their transformations, as we will see in this volume. This difficulty rather disqualifies Western binaries of religious vs. secular spaces and practices from being adopted as universal standards of analysis and comparison. Thus the increasing acknowledgment since the end of the 1990s, in several branches of the social sciences, that the 'secular' and religion are closely intertwined in their becoming (most exemplarily and influentially, see Asad 2003), is much more of a given from the viewpoint of a sociology of Islam. It is also in this sense that a sociology of Islam is not just the sociology of a specific religion or civilization but a channel of intervention into key questions and concepts of sociology, the social sciences at large (particularly anthropology), and the humanities as a whole (especially history). The sociology of Islam should be the trigger that can make the sociological project both more dialogical and more useful to account for the emerging multiverse of civility patterns in the world. By integrating Islam, sociology, along with a host of key concepts it successfully produced and disseminated (from charisma through secularization to modernity itself), does not look the same.

An important and growing portion of original research, in both historical and contemporary perspectives, on a variety of aspects of Islam since the end of the 1980s has established significant links to wider conceptual debates in social theory and cultural studies. The *Yearbook of the Sociology of Islam*, published between 1998 and 2008 (launched by Georg Stauth, and which I co-edited for several years), was instrumental in linking the sociological recontextualization of the study of Islam with the main research program through which sociology has tried to deparochialize itself by escaping the grip of 'Westernist' assumptions. I am referring to the adoption of an increasingly reflexive, theoretically informed, yet also historically conscious, perspective on the interaction between ideas and practices of modernity in the West, in South, East, and Southeast Asia, and in the Islamic ecumene. This approach has animated a research field that happened to be labeled, perhaps reductively, 'civilizational analysis' (for seminal contributions within this trajectory see Arnason 2003; Arjomand and Tiryakian 2004).

Yet while the sociology of Islam certainly benefits from adopting a comparative perspective (in this volume still largely focused on a comparison with Western Christendom) and a theoretical focus (which here is still crucially determined by a critical dialogue with sociological classics like Max Weber and Norbert Elias), it cannot be completely satisfied by both. To the extent that it studies Islam as a devotional commitment, as an idea of moral and social order, and as an historical ecumene that transcends civilizational boundaries, the sociology of Islam is bound to unsettle those evolutionist postulates which see modern life and modern society as emerging out of poorly defined 'traditions' (see Salvatore 2007). Such postulates have proved resistant in providing benchmarks for societal and civilizational comparisons. In this sense, a sociology of Islam defies common wisdom and unquestioned assumptions about key concepts of sociology and in so doing also questions the value of comparison as a panacea against Eurocentrism. In small doses comparison can have a heuristic potential by helping open up new horizons of meta-institutional analysis oriented to understand the workings of knowledge and power and with it of what we call religion. In heavy doses comparison risks entrenching the analysis within solidified categories.

Throughout the volume, I am consciously referring to Islam as an 'ecumene.' This term is hardly used within sociology and should be considered distinct both from civilization (a concept dear to the humanities) and community (which usually denotes within sociology the traditional background of modern societies). If a translation of the protean Islamic concept of *umma*, intended as a rather 'an-organic' collective body that can constellate into cohesive groups at local, translocal, and global levels, is afforded, it would be 'ecumene.' By 'an-organic' I refer to a dimension of the social bond producing cohesion through a rather rhizomatic replication of connectedness, more than via the 'organic' dimension of solidarity within modern societies, particularly as theorized by Durkheim. The *umma* is farther from being quintessentially unmodern since built on rather fluid, connective patterns of sociability and cohesion. As a correction to the bias describing the *umma* as a traditional, particularistic, unmodern community, the term 'ecumene' represents the overlapping, both religious and civil dimensions of a potentially global, cohesive nexus. As such, it has the potential to absorb, desaturate, and dynamize the sociological meaning of both civilization (now understood as an ongoing 'civilizing process') and community (intended as an incessant process of knowledge–power 'constellation'). Ecumene also denotes the process of map-making that is necessary to the constitution of this global nexus, in view of the fact that it is difficult to consider an ecumene as gravitating on an exclusive center. The Islamic ecumene should be then understood as an extremely mobile set of patterns of normativity and civility providing both cohesion and orientation to translocal networks and a variety of locales. Such an ecumene nurtures social life by facilitating and legitimizing modes to build flexible institutions that provide for a variety of social needs, from cooperation to education, from health to the production of meaning, from provision for the poor to the encoding of high culture, including court culture. The latter in turn can work as a tool for selecting, instructing (or advising) elites, and implementing blueprints of governance.

While new approaches to comparisons between societies and civilizations (as well as to their definitions) have provided initial impulses to the sociology of Islam, their limitation is due to their strong anchoring within 'post-classic' views of societal evolution and underlying assumptions about tradition and modernity (or, in the plural, traditions and modernities). On the other hand, it should also be acknowledged that even immanent critiques of one-sided and ultimately self-celebratory ideas of (Western or Western-centered) modernity within sociology, social theory, and philosophy, like those produced within postcolonial and cultural studies, have not fared much better in revising established, yet weak and lopsided, conceptualizations in ways that could benefit the sociology of Islam. Such limits become apparent to the extent that postcolonial and cultural studies too often take on Western hegemonic views of modernity and disarticulate them, without seriously enquiring whether completely different entry points into binaries like tradition and modernity or knowledge and power can be gained from non-Western perspectives. Such alternate angles would not only unsettle Western theory but also the need for purported critiques and deconstructions thereof from reiterated (and badly disguised) Western-centric perspectives.

A radical deconstruction of Western categories often leads to the decentering of power with its related production of knowledge, without questioning whether such a deconstruction really challenges the notions themselves of knowledge and power or, as I will suggest, the articulation itself of the knowledge–power equation as seen from a Western hegemonic perspective. Most prominent here is the work of Michel Foucault, the inspirer of several such critiques and the author of popular reformulations of modern Western definitions of how knowledge is folded into power without residues. Foucault framed the knowledge–power equation through the prism of the historical force of the Western disciplinary, institutional, and subjective powers which he uncovered in a series of brilliant 'archaeologies' and 'genealogies' (for a synthetic view, see Foucault 1991). However, the limits of such a type of work for a critique of the Western knowledge of Islam are revealed by the largely self-enclosed (and, through a proliferating fandom, self-complacent) critique of Orientalism performed by Edward Said and based on revised Foucaultian postulates. This critique has proved embarrassingly unable (even to attempt) to uncover alternative Islamic perspectives on the articulation of the knowledge–power equation and thus on the attendant relation between tradition and modernity. It should be nonetheless acknowledged that by shaking the self-confidence of Western Orientalism such critiques have indirectly provided key stimuli for such a parallel and distinct enterprise as the sociology of Islam. These endeavors have also, admittedly and thankfully, benefited from traversing an intermediate, poststructuralist stage in the 1990s (nonetheless, an earlier critical recontextualization of Foucault's and Said's work from the viewpoint of an embryonic sociology of Islam was already central at that stage of transition: see Salvatore 1997: 133–55).

Ultimately, the sociology of Islam not only has the potential to provide coherence to the new, postorientalist wave of historical and contemporary studies on Islam, but also and even more to disturb the conventional wisdom of sociology itself as the harbinger of an enlightened self-understanding of modern society. The sociology of Islam can perform this task by going beyond the critique of sociological notions of modernity performed by debates on postmodernism and postcolonialism. The critical angle opened up by the sociology of Islam within the body of sociological enquiry and theory allows us to not only look at Western modernity as if from its margins but also to critique the idea itself of a fixed core of modernity within a rapidly evolving global order. This is possible since Islam provides, in its historical trajectory of 'map-making' as an increasingly transcivilizational ecumene, a bundle of alternate perspectives on such an order. In this way, Western modernity can free itself from its illusions of having authored an incomparably original rupture with tradition via a unique yet (paradoxically) universal type of (individual and collective) subjectivity. Through the path initiated by the sociology of Islam, Western modernity itself can open itself up to more genuinely pluralistic and crosscivilizational conceptions of modern society and agency therein which are more suitable to meet global challenges, including the obvious, albeit slow, eclipse of the geopolitical centrality of the West. The undeniable peculiarities of the Western subject and attendant conceptions of modern political order (impinging on the trajectory and plasticity of notions and practices of religion) are then susceptible to be reframed within a wider horizon of ruptures and reassemblages within the historic Afro-Eurasian civilizational realm (also known as the 'Eastern hemisphere') than would be allowed within a strictly Foucaultian framework of immanent (Western) critique.

However, the most immediately relevant backgrounds to the emerging field of the sociology of Islam are not the slippery scholarly battlefields within social theory and cultural studies but the tectonic (though often overly dramatized) shifts in the reimagination and practice of Islam that occurred at a variety of levels in recent decades. Such background transformations include, since the 1970s, a deep restructuring of the post-World War order both at the level of capitalist development and of interstate relations, and the increasing centrality of the Near and Middle East within global affairs, due to critical issues of energy supply and price, alongside an array of regional conflicts. This development has been matched by the emergence of Southeast Asia as a major pole of economic growth and political change. Such a major restructuring of fragile global and inner-Islamic balances has deeply affected the way an inherently diverse, long-term Islamic perspective on the fit between religion and civility can alter global articulations of the production of knowledge and the accumulation of power. In this context, the increasingly tense coexistence of Western hegemony (which is conceptual before it is practical) and a variety of non-Western challenges has inevitably revived the significance of Islam as a force capable of shaping social relations at a variety of local and translocal levels. This capacity does not necessarily reside in the rather totalizing way propagated by the Islamist groups that have raised the exclusive banner of the implementation of *shari'a* (Islamic normativity, imperfectly translated as 'Islamic law'). It more commonly manifests itself through what I have defined as the longer-term, meta-institutional articulation of the knowledge–power equation through civil patterns of organization and governance.

This crystallization of civility will be the main object of analysis in this volume. A meta-institutional force shapes social reality not via a ready-made institutional solution (such as a *shari'a* frequently misconstrued as a legal code ready to be applied) but by empowering social actors to draw on a civilizational reservoir to creatively shape solutions to social problems based on the specific circumstances of a locale and of the age. An initial mapping and analysis of the meta-institutional power of Islam is provided in this Introduction and in the following chapters. If the map is that of the Islamic ecumene and of its wider Afro-Eurasian civilizational environment, the meta-institutional power of Islam is the force that draws and redraws the map. The sociologist of Islam, being herself a product of the long waves of modernization and globalization, can only sit on the border of the map in order to observe and diagnose regularities and volatilities within the movements of the square compasses represented by this Islamic power.

If we relate recent developments within Islamic movements to the above-mentioned novelties within sociological theory and those set in motion by the critique of Orientalism, we can improve our understanding of the imperative to shift the study of Islam away from predominantly text-oriented methodologies toward analyzing it as a continual 'mapping' process. This process was set in motion by aspirations, attritions, and conflicts generated by social complexification and geopolitical expansion, drawing from a rich discursive reservoir that we easily associate with just one, largely reified (yet still inherently dynamic) word, namely *islam*/Islam. Being a verbal noun of the fourth form and as such possessing a marked inchoative force, *islam* as the keyword denoting surrender to Allah/God does not signify an accomplishment, but a new, continual beginning. The contemporary attention paid by observers to the increasingly complex social entanglements of Islamic movements, groups, and associations, of their programs and visions, allows us to see just the tip of the iceberg of the historic and contemporary dynamism manifested by the meta-institutional power of Islam.

In the context of the global constraints of economic restructuring, liberalization, and commodification, diverse types of strictly or loosely Islamic associational networks (i.e. with a stronger or weaker relation to the historic waves of Islam's meta-institutional power) have taken form. These are largely independent from the traditional religious establishment that represents just one historic pattern of institutional crystallization of that power. Rather than signing up to the wholesale image of an 'Islamic revival' or 'awakening,' practitioners of the sociology of Islam should acknowledge the highly ambivalent place of Islamist movements within much more complex upheavals occurring within Muslim-majority societies. It has been increasingly recognized since the 1980s that such groups and movements, even if and while they reconstruct a kernel of supposedly immutable, God-given, fundaments of knowledge and truth, at the same time partake in processes of social innovation which often decisively shape their direction as movements. This typically occurs via a direct or indirect confrontation with (or, alternately, selective assimilation of) the norms of what is conventionally (yet also reductively) called neoliberal globalization (see e.g. Tugal 2009). However, against a rising tide of academic discourse claiming that contemporary Islamism is largely to be explained as an accommodative folding of Islam's force into the creases of neoliberal globalization, I suggest in this book that the long-term impetus of the meta-institutional power of Islam cannot be (at least up until the present) seen as having exhausted its autonomy and creativity. Such an exhaustion would only be warranted if we were to diagnose Islam's ineluctable submersion within an allegedly alien, overwhelming, quintessentially modern and global force of history (called modern capitalism).

By uncovering such complex entanglements where confrontation meets assimilation, the sociology of Islam can play a crucial role in developing a study of multiple traditions and entangled modernities as it takes into account alternative, non-Western genealogies and articulations of the knowledge–power equation. This angle alters the comparative perspective and facilitates a reflexive dealing with religion, politics, and secularity, now considered not just as solidified fields but as contentious arenas of knowledge and power. In the process, Islam as an innerly diversified religious, meta-institutional matrix, as a civilizational idea and as a blueprint of life conduct facilitating individual devotion and collective aspirations, does not disappear from the modern stage (as predicted by modernization theorists of the 1950s and 1960s: Masud and Salvatore 2009). It rather undergoes multiple and often unpredictable metamorphoses. The sociologist of Islam reads the ongoing meta-institutional mapping (and the narratives that continually nurture it) as if from the border of the map drawn by the compasses of historical manifestations of Islamic power. This posture of the sociologist of Islam should not be equated with blindly espousing the view of Muslim actors but rather with opening up an angle adequately informed by Islam's own venture into history, as taught to us by the historian of Islam Marshall Hodgson. Starting in this Introduction and for the rest of the volume I will invoke at several points his extraordinarily prescient and forward-looking approach. Working on Islam as a map-making venture proves crucial for enlivening the project of the sociology of Islam in ways that do not subvert sociology and social theory per se but push them into a direction more in tune with the weakening centrality of Western social thought on a global scale. This approach is also better aligned with the emerging consciousness that Western universalism has represented the temporary submersion of an earlier multiverse of globalizing perspectives on human agency in world history. The importance of such a move within the sociology of Islam should be compared with the coincidental emergence of different brands of a challenging 'Southern theory' (Connell 2007; Patel 2010), some of which adopt an Asian if not an explicitly Islamic perspective (Alatas 2006; 2010). It remains that the significance of the idea and practice of the sociology of Islam cannot be reduced to such, certainly welcome, emerging trends, since we will argue that Islam's diversity and complexity are largely transversal to North and South, East and West, and cannot be diluted into any vision of a 'global South.'

Rather than a specific sociology of religion applied to Islam, the sociology of Islam explores the way knowledge and power interact to shape Islamic traditions and their transformations via patterns of sociability, manners, and civility that 'constellate' into mostly malleable institutional forms. These patterns and the resulting forms are analyzed as civilizationally specific on the one hand, but also as contributing to and sharing in an emerging global civility, on the other. Therefore the sociology of Islam can be seen as innervating a comparative sociology of religion-*cum*-civility that explores modes of constructing and inhabiting the socio-cultural world. Such modes exist alongside (and therefore are not contradicted but often fed by) a strong sense of transcendence, which is undeniably one of the key traits of what we call religion. This view of civility should immunize us from thinking in terms of civilizations as trivial cultural monoliths. Civilizations are the contingent, intersecting, and competing arenas of civilizing processes, intended as the transformations through which patterns of civility are formed and unsettled. Hereby religious traditions often play a decisive role in equipping practitioners with a type of knowledge that decisively nurtures—even though not always smoothly—wider civilizing processes.

Particular attention should be paid to the notions of knowledge and power as the key coordinates of civility, which results from their mutual impingement. Knowledge is as ubiquitous as power, since knowledge is within power and vice versa. They are not, to use a social science terminology, distinct variables or contending forces within the making of the social and civic bonds. They are rather imperfect metaphors of an ongoing human dialectic between material coercion and symbolic cohesion. These two realms cannot be neatly demarcated in each case analyzed. One should rather be aware that what constitutes a distinctive civilizational constellation is in the first instance the specific way knowledge defines power. This often occurs by distinguishing sheer, brute power from legitimate power (which is often called, with a shorthand, authority). This process of definition of power is reflected in the relation between rulers and administrators on the one hand and scholars and religious specialists on the other. Thus the ultimate foil of a civilizational program is the specific way knowledge delimits (or contains) power and power organizes (or subjugates) knowledge.

The approach of comparative civilizational analysis spelled out in the work of leading historical sociologists and social theorists like Shmuel N. Eisenstadt and Johann P. Arnason is helpful here. It primarily consists in exploring civilizationally specific interplays of knowledge and power within a timeframe ranging from antiquity to modernity, a *longue durée* that provides the necessary background to the present introductory volume (Eisenstadt 2003; Arnason 2003). This approach can be further expanded into the study of the vexed relations between the law, the state, and the public sphere, which I wish to explore in volume II of a trilogy on the sociology of Islam which the present volume intends to inaugurate. The program can also embrace the tense interfacing between nationalist programs of reconstruction of society and the transnational (and 'transcultural') openings and trajectories of escape from national boundaries: trajectories that have been often, though not necessarily, tied to the notion of an Islamic *umma* (ideally to constitute the subject of volume III within the same trilogy).

As shown by Arnason, the idea of civilization in the singular and the analysis of civilizations in the plural became the object of attention among some of the fathers of sociology. This is scarcely surprising, to the extent that civilizational analysis "is very much about taking seriously the idea of diverse ways of being-in-the-world" (Arnason 2003: 357). In this sense, the approach can facilitate the exploration of the interpretive prisms and practical orientations of social agents, along with their intrinsic diversity. Arnason primarily refers to Emile Durkheim, the main theorist of an integrated and organic notion of modern society, and to his nephew Marcel Mauss (1872– 1950). The latter author is particularly important for having bridged the concerns of sociology and anthropology in researching the fundaments of the social bond also through exploring such essential features, variously related to what we generally intend with 'religion,' as sacrifice, gift, and techniques of the body (Mauss 1950). The two French scholars pioneered a concept of civilization that could provide a corrective device to the unilateral and mono-dimensional notion of society as coincident with the nation and its boundaries. Mauss added to this idea a strong sense that civilizations cannot grow organically out of a supposed gravitational center but result from the deployment of local and translocal networks. Therefore the key sociological significance of the process is not the formation of self-enclosed civilizational blocks but resides in the process itself.

Civilization appeared to them as a convenient tool "to identify the most comprehensive and self-contained forms of social life" (Mauss 1950: 70), while society, the most direct object of sociology, provided a much too integrated view of discrete and differentiated logics of action, becoming too quickly entrenched (and often institutionalized) in a nation-state framework (Mauss 1950: 78). Freed from such strictly sociological straitjackets, civilizational analysis facilitates a vivid insight into the cultural (including, if not mainly, religious) traditions which provide a meta-institutional capacity to impact frames of social action and to shape matrices and codes innervating a variety of institutions. This type of approach, clearly not extraneous to the concerns of the classics of sociology, allows for exploring knowledge (often with religion at its core) with a sensibility as to how it defines power. It is important to keep in mind this essential fluidity of the knowledge–power equation and not to succumb to the impression that power necessarily tends to congeal (as it mostly occurs in modernized or modernizing settings) into a largely autonomous factor of social cohesion and/or conflict: namely as the power intrinsic to the often rationalizing agency of specific actors, whether individual or collective, institutional or movement based. The idea itself of Islam as an eminently meta-institutional force should inoculate us against any view of power as essentially impermeable to knowledge and culture at large.

Knowledge/Charisma vs. Power/Wealth: The Challenge of Religious Movements

Both Arnason and, before him, Eisenstadt have had the merit to conceive of civilizational analysis within a framework that has treasured and substantially revised key ideas and arguments of Weber's sociology. The origin of the values carried by cultural elites was explained by Weber by reference to the outbursts represented by collective movements initiated by what he famously called the 'charisma' of exceptional personalities. Weber's idea of charisma has been very influential, although (or perhaps because) it has remained shrouded in a cloudy conceptual frame. For sure, as we saw, he considered the dynamics of value rationalization through knowledge as ultimately giving way to the dominance of instrumental rationalization, represented by the maximization of power and wealth per se. We also remarked that according to Weber the latter process might be culturally legitimized via religious change, as exemplified by the already visited Protestant Ethic Thesis that Weber formulated to explain the origin of modern capitalist entrepreneurship (Weber 1986 [1920]: 17–206).

Eisenstadt largely relied on Weber but also attempted to tackle some of the most controversial nodes within the approach of the German father of sociology. For Eisenstadt, referring to the dynamics of knowledge and power is a convenient way to describe a phenomenon of discursive contention and social transformation. This phenomenon does not necessarily entail viewing knowledge and power as ontologically distinct in the way Weber seemed to view them, at least as far as in premodern societies cultural and political elites were often engaged in tense contentions. Eisenstadt was more explicit than Weber in stating that within the conceptual doublet of knowledge and power the component that triggers the contentious process is actually knowledge itself. This is true to the extent that in premodern societies the cultural elites are the group that wields the most formidable and enduring form of societal power itself. This is due to the fact that they produce and almost inhabit knowledge (or, as Eisenstadt still prefers to say, culture) as a dense net of promulgated codes, values, and regulations affecting all social fields, from the family level through education and leisure to politics proper.

According to Eisenstadt, at the very moment this preeminence of cultural elites, which ultimately justifies their social prestige, provides legitimation to the power holders and to the power establishment itself, it also creates the possibility (and sometimes necessity) of its contestation by potentially emerging counter-elites. Here we see that the mysterious dynamics of the eruption of creative charisma on the social and cultural stage are at root a response to cracks in the system itself of cultural hegemony. Rather than seeing essentially creative charismatic outbursts and subsequent phases of routinization of transformational charisma in the form of new institutions, as Weber suggested, Eisenstadt instructed us to appreciate a more balanced dynamics of innovation and conservation in the social circulation of that distinctive form of immaterial, cultural power that we call charisma. Accordingly, charisma is usually produced and wielded by fragments of the intellectual elites who break away from consensus or complicity with the political establishment, thus initiating periodic, often highly transformative, upheavals (Eisenstadt 1968).

Discursive contestation and the pressure for social change therefore occur thanks to the fact that the cultural order of society, in spite of all rituals that support it (from the individual level to the collective dimension of society as a whole), is inherently fragile and exposed to, as it were, charismatic challenges. In a theological vocabulary such challenges are often stigmatized as 'heterodox', since they defy the dominant, correct *doxa*, i.e. the institutionalized and legitimate doctrine or code, the 'orthodoxy'. Rituals are often thought of as being necessarily supportive of a correct doctrine. They are necessary indeed. But it is through the necessary rituals supporting the periodic reconstitution of the order that the fragility of a *doxa* is revealed. This exposure occurs to the potential benefit less of the commoners, who in premodern societies are seldom the promoters of large-scale contestations of the dominant order, than of segments of potentially competing, emerging elites. These counter-elites can profit from the order's fragility and challenge the ruling elites. However sacred the order may be as constructed by the ruling elites and supported by regulations and rituals, it is ultimately arbitrary and exposed to challenges. Such movements of contestation are the breeding ground for emerging forms of what Weber saw as a charismatic type of leadership that can shatter the fragile balances of tradition and present a challenge to established powers.

The arbitrariness of both an order pinpointed by legitimate power that rests on tradition and of its charismatic challenge that creates potentially new cultural values is a typical Weberian motif. The German sociologist largely inherited this 'nihilistic' idea of power as arbitrariness from his compatriot, the philosopher Friedrich Nietzsche (1844–1900). Eisenstadt's clarification of Weber's approach is here particularly precious, to the extent that it unveils the necessarily continuous reconstruction of the cultural and symbolic order beyond arbitrariness. Under normal circumstances this order is aligned with the political one and legitimizes it. The cultural order itself is not innocent of social inequality, since it includes the legitimation of measures or rules that usually entail a discrimination in the allocation of resources among the members of a given community (the most extreme of such discriminatory rules being the religious justification of the division of community into castes). It is this practical dimension of the symbolic order that reveals and exacerbates its intrinsic arbitrariness and keeps it potentially vulnerable to contestations. These are legitimized by cultural formulas ultimately resting on recombining the same codes through which arbitrary order is itself legitimized. This is a particularly crucial argument, since it entails that the cultural formulas that secure cohesion and those that unleash conflict are basically mirror-like: they are just prone to completely different, potentially opposite, types of politicization. As I will try to show in this volume (and possibly demonstrate even better in a second volume more specifically focused on the political sociology of Islam), these dynamics are certainly a major leitmotif of Islamic history and society, up to the present time. Yet the reformulation by Eisenstadt of Weber's argument also shows that charisma, far from being a different source of legitimacy to tradition, is ultimately resting on (often radical) reinterpretations or reconstructions of tradition itself.

Going one step further, we could see the factor that we call knowledge as consisting in essence of the more or less 'charismatic,' mostly innovative and inventive, capacity to devise justifications and formulas to convince and galvanize a constituency by constructing the legitimacy of a challenge to established authority. Knowledge is in this sense a type of know-how that originates from a capacity to intervene on culture itself. This type of intervention consists primarily in constructing an alternate view of the social order by drawing from the same resources represented by the dominant codes, values, and their underlying symbolic underpinnings with which wider sectors of society are familiar. Undoubtedly the challenge, based on an innovative recombination of knowledge, can manifest itself in radical or moderate terms, therefore appearing alternately as a revolution or reform. Such a modulation does not unsettle the dense way through which knowledge and power interact. The distinction between 'radical' and 'moderate' challenges to the dominant order (as also reflected in contemporary talk about moderate vs. radical Islam) is not a primary one from the viewpoint of the sociology of Islam. It only becomes meaningful at the level of a political sociology that takes into account the 'opportunity cost structure' of mobilizing knowledge/charisma through different types of inflection of the challenge posed. The meta-institutional power of Islamic knowledge (of Islam as 'religion') is beyond any such differentiation as it prefigures a large spectrum of options. As we will see toward the end of this volume (and even more in future ones), the mother of all cost-opportunity structures that have altered the balance between moderate and radical options has been Western colonial hegemony and its postcolonial extension.

This process of stepping out of the cultural order is the condition itself for social unrest and political protest, change, and ultimately revolutions. Yet any group that intends to contest the established order has to play with the available cultural frames and resources. This view makes the protest not merely destructive of the order but potentially reconstructive of it, and ultimately essential to the order's long-term maintenance and renewal. Ruling codes are not just transgressed; they are often reformulated and occasionally subverted. Yet such challenges do not destroy the social order itself but provide an alternate one that bears some key resemblances to the older. This capacity to contest and protest often originates from latent, antinomian tendencies that are nested (often invisibly) within the social order itself, whereby the ruling cultural and religious code (or *doxa*) is perpetually challenged but never erased.

This is particularly evident in religious movements that contest the dominant, correct *doxa*, i.e. the orthodoxy, and that are consequently dubbed as 'heterodox.' Such movements provide a different, sometimes opposite, interpretation to dominant rules or symbols. Protest movements can thus evidence and exploit antinomian tendencies already latent in dominant codes, often affecting delicate spheres, like family relationships and sexuality. Contravening rules in such spheres can be pushed up in diametrically opposed directions: e.g. one can subvert marriage through a more or less ritualized extramarital intercourse or into a rigorous abstention that forbids procreation. Yet even the contravention is not just lived out as a carnivalesque transgression that releases the anxiety produced by the rigor of the disciplining orders: it can be constructed as a religious obligation and even as a condition for true salvation. Starting at the level of knowledge (which obviously includes religion, often at its core), such protest movements have the potential to alter the balance of power, the structuring of elites, and ultimately the political order itself. All dimensions of the order are potentially affected.

In order to attain such a comprehensive goal, however, there is a long transformative way to go, which is seldom accomplished in a fully revolutionary fashion. The cultural system often inoculates itself and society against such a radical dissent by incorporating and legitimizing, as it were preventively, the possibility of alternate patterns of life conduct. This possibility occurs not just through rituals that periodically (e.g. once a year) mimic and reverse the dominant order but through coopting and institutionalizing potentially challenging roles. This integration of alternate patterns of life conduct is most typically seen in the insulated, yet highly respected, spaces provided for practicing ascetic life ideals in a variety of forms of so-called monasticism (or its equivalents and alternatives) within several traditions. Yet the possibility of a radical dissent that claims to reinterpret the true and pure essence of the *doxa* because of its corruption via the currently dominant institutionalized forms remains latent. Its chance to be turned into an open challenge increases in times of social distress, when the arbitrariness of the order and of the corresponding distribution of resources becomes more evident and painful to wider social groups. The risk is higher if economic hardship and the shrinking of the resources available add to social strains. The 'heterodox' challenge to the order (something that is not confined to the fold of 'Abrahamic' religions, as shown by recurring, popular, often messianic movements in the history of China inspired by Daoism, Buddhism, or combinations thereof) can be expressed in such cases as an attempt to restore pristine blessing and justice. Movements of rebellion can then target quite directly the social stratification that justifies specific patterns of the social division of labor and the attendant power hierarchies.

Within this broader analytical framework that is applicable to the civilizations of the West and East alike, knowledge is to be analyzed in conjunction with power, as the forging ground of those notions of legitimacy through which power becomes socially pervasive and politically legitimate. Yet the working itself of power depends on how power is conceptualized and put to work within specific civilizational contexts, which are in turn influenced by cultural and religious traditions (Arnason 2003). According to this approach, behind the apparent rebus of how knowledge can justify power and how power can reproduce knowledge without their mutual, principled autonomy being unsettled, lies a hidden interpretive key. This key opens the door to an understanding of how formulas of legitimation of a given order, in spite of primarily working to support that order, might cause some fissures to the same order. Such rifts then invite the formulation and channeling of challenges to the order. Far from indefinitely securing the legitimacy of the ruling order and the power of the elites, patterns and formulas of legitimation hide hardly visible cracks in the fabric of society and nourish invisible seeds of change. Paradoxically, the game of legitimation is the harbinger itself of social transformations.

Civility as the Engine of the Knowledge–Power Equation: Islam and 'Islamdom'

The notion of 'civilization' thrived in Europe from the age of the Enlightenment to the era of the birth of sociology and anthropology (often in parallel with the notion of civility: see Mazlish 2001; 2004). We should not hide the fact that the concept itself of civilization is decisively invested into a modern, Western, and largely colonial imagination. From the 19th century onward it has been inherited and reshaped within several branches of the humanities and the social sciences (including the previously mentioned classics of sociology). As a result, it has perpetually oscillated between a singular articulation, in the form of envisioning Western Europe as the sole contemporary carrier of the light of civility on a global scale, and a plural declination, through the view of extra-European civilizations as not only the depositories of past treasures but also as the cradles of what in the 1950s and 1960s happened to be called the 'new nations,' and therefore as the harbingers of future developments of global society.

If we do not want to throw the baby out with the bath water, we should risk a theoretical upgrading of such a politically saturated, yet for too long scarcely reflected-upon, concept of civilization. Johann P. Arnason's civilizational theory is of incommensurable help in this respect. His approach strikes a balance between civilization in the singular, i.e. modernity as a global civilizing process—a process that also configures the program to overcome civilizational differences—and civilization in the plural, i.e. a world of diverse civilizations allowing for multiple modernities (Arnason 2003). A civilization always combines power and knowledge in original ways; therefore the constitution of, and mutual relations between, political and cultural elites are crucial to the formation and transformation of civilizations. A civilization transcends the closed boundary of a specific, national society and articulates across time (epochs) and space (geo-cultural units) the spectrum of possibilities of societal organization allowed within culturally specific definitions of power and within power-determined configurations of cultural traditions. The way power is exercised and legitimized is in turn dependent on such traditions: i.e. on the codes of legitimacy elaborated by cultural elites, but also on the concrete, everyday judgment of the citizens (earlier, of the 'commoners,' which I would define as the social groups excluded from privileges and basing a large part of their socio-economic and power resources on forms of common—both material and immaterial—property). The dialectic of power and knowledge is therefore specific to each civilizational cluster.

The macro-sociological dimension of tradition becomes the cultural kernel of a specific civilization or, as I will try to reformulate it for our sociological purposes (particularly in Chapters 1 and 7), of a discrete form of civility. Traditions are not power-neutral or blind, since they also provide orientation to the shaping of patterns of power and the legitimacy of power holders. This principled openness (though not neutrality) of tradition vis-à-vis power creates occasions and provides justifications for a contestation of authority by practitioners of a given tradition (religious or otherwise). This occurs when they protest the extent to which power is unwarranted by authority, or authority is exaggeratedly upheld by the sheer exercise of untamed power. Authority itself should not be overinflated as a concept, since it ultimately consists in the art of knowing how to go further in practicing a tradition and especially how to instruct other practitioners about how to go further (MacIntyre 1988).

While looking at cultural and religious traditions, we should consider the mechanisms through which their transmission and absorption immunizes their practitioners from seeing power as an end of social action in itself. It is such mechanisms, and the connectedness that supports them, which encourage practitioners to see the legitimacy of the exercise of power as based on knowledge: particularly the type of knowledge or know-how that consists in 'how to go further.' Authority, which for Weber would be simply jellied, routinized charisma, is here nothing more than a secondary or intermediate variable within the larger knowledge–power equation and can be ignored without any sensible loss in the analysis. Ultimately authority is simply the mastering of such a know-how and the respect gained by those who excel in such mastering. Further than that, there is no sense of legitimate authority that can be securely immunized against the practitioners' vigilance over any excess in the self-perpetuation of a power not based on excellence and mastering. Any such attempt at immunization would collapse authority into sheer power. Anything exceeding a recognition of excellence in mastering would constitute a form of sacralization of power: a recurrent feature of human history and society, and probably the opposite of what Weber envisioned with his view of original, not routinized charisma.

This is namely a type of charisma that challenges not only established power but also authority and tradition.

This is not to idealize the power of knowledge against sheer power. Quite the opposite. It is to prepare the terrain for the analysis of a domain that takes shape very much at the confluence of both, through their inevitable interaction, combination, and even convergence. It is convenient for our reconstruction of the foundations of a sociology of Islam to conceptualize the intermediate crystallization of the fragile order of the social bond through a dense interaction of knowledge and power delimiting a realm that we can ascribe to 'civility.' Arnason's work integrates and specifies Eisenstadt's analysis of knowledge and power by explicitly introducing civility as the third key component of the sociological approach here proposed. Civility represents the dimension through which the inertia of daily sociability is nourished less by an open contestation of power than by 'bracketing out' power gaps and cultural differences among agents and groups. This property of civility should not be equated with the ideological suppression of such inequalities by the elites. Civility appears then as a game of modulating the tensions in the knowledge–power equation without any need to postulate an 'original' charisma that is then rigidified, routinized, and ultimately neutralized by extinguishing the transgressive dimension of the challenge it originally represented. Civility can only thrive under the conditions that social agents share in some common or at least overlapping idiom, allowing for a modulation of underlying social conflicts, pending their eruptions in crisis times.

Civility might appear as a 'weak' socially cohesive force if compared, for example, with much more organic forms of solidarity (like those Durkheim saw expressed in the social division of labor within modern societies, or those emanating from class consciousness in a Marxian sense). Yet civility is as essential to the fabric of society (traditional or modern) as gravitation (considered the weakest among the interaction forces in physics) is to the physical world. The type and quality of the social bond can be best recognized in the mostly unspectacular modulations of civility within everyday life, rather than in the full-fledged institutionalized forms of social organization and governance. The sociology of Islam intends to build its axis along the way the Islamic traditions produce and modulate patterns of civility without necessarily passing through eruptive forms of 'original' charisma such as those postulated by Weber. Civility works in this sense as an important field of decompression of the meta-institutional creativity of religious traditions. Civility in many ways arbitrates whether a given meta-institutional potential of religion (e.g. one demanding from the individual a strong commitment to the welfare of the other) can be successfully institutionalized and in which forms.

We will see the extent to which Islam has historically provided (or has even been mainly identified with) such a common, yet locally and timely diversified, idiom of civility, over the long term, across widening geographic distances and shifting cultural, linguistic, and religious barriers. Through referring to a shared normative idiom provided not just by Islamic jurisprudence but also by overlapping (though locally differentiated) customs, the civil habitus of bracketing out differences of status, wealth and, not least, virtuosity and religiosity could also apply, albeit to a limited extent, to power differences. On the other hand, the dimension of contention that is inherent in the complex management of the social and cultural order is not preempted or repressed by civility, but, so to speak, policed from the inside out and tamed through codes of self-restraint. This typically occurs through the ways a variety of interactants learn similar or comparable patterns of tact and manners which can regulate exchange and even, within certain limits, conflict.

Viewing civility as a key outcome of the knowledge–power equation is essential to articulate our sociological study of the Islamic civilizational ecumene in a global perspective. As much as the sociology of Islam can at its root be articulated as exploring an extraordinarily effective (in the long term) set of patterns of civility, it is also a sociology of its two key components, namely knowledge and power. The interaction between these three elements does not neatly reflect a principled differentiation between religion and the social. This differentiation is at best contingent, superficial, and collateral to the civilizing process, to the extent that religion is not just a set of specific institutions but is primarily a meta-institutional matrix. We will need to pay attention to other, subtler patterns of differentiation than those postulated by a roughly Western-centered sociology of religion.

The notion of civility promoted by Ibn Khaldun (1332–1406) in his *Muqaddimah* is extraordinarily useful here for spelling out more fine-tuned levels of differentiation (see Chapters 3 and 4). It also, at the same time, dovetails nicely with the idea of civility cultivated within civilizational analysis as a strategy to counter the inherent reductionism of social sciences in general and of sociology in particular. It offsets particularly well the sociological obsession with rigidly differentiated spheres within an organically structured ensemble called 'society' and the attendant socio-centric patterns of its alleged self-organization. This was exactly the concern that, as we saw, pushed Durkheim and Mauss to work on a notion of civilization. Interestingly, Ibn Khaldun, although a premodern author, did not refrain from using a concept of society, which is the same word employed in contemporary Arabic (*ijtima'*), but tended to view it as a contingent crystallization of civility (*'umran*). Revealingly, as shown by Arnason and Stauth, Ibn Khaldun's *'umran* highlighted how

> a discontinuous but unending development of human abilities—set out in detailed analyses of arts, crafts and sciences in the concluding books of the *Muqaddimah*—lends itself to comparison with Durkheim's conception of the human being as a product of a civilization (which was also his explicit reason for accepting Comte's definition of sociology as a 'science of civilization').
>
> (Arnason and Stauth 2004: 32)

Marshall Hodgson's three-volume *The Venture of Islam* (1974), his posthumously published *magnum opus*, had the merit not only of framing Islamic history in the context of an integrated intercivilizational vision but also of problematizing sociological notions of religion, civilization, civility, tradition, and institution. Hodgson was also well aware of how much the inherited conceptualizations related to Islam came to depend on the Western historic experience and in particular on the hegemony of Western modernity. Long before Edward Said, he was acutely critical of orientalist generalizations and bias. As maintained by Edmund Burke III, "Marshall Hodgson clearly saw that Islamic history was a strategic point from which to undertake a critique of the discourse on Western civilization" (Burke III 1993: xv).

On the other hand, Hodgson enjoyed the double advantage of working closely both with representatives of world history and of modernization theory. He also responded to philosophical views of the epoch-making eruption of new types of transcendence-based religious traditions in the genesis of civilizations. Such visions were most cogently exemplified by Karl Jaspers (1883–1969) in the so-called Axial Age theory, which reformulated earlier civilizational approaches rooted in the German philosophical and sociological traditions, including the work of Max Weber (Salvatore 2013). By developing in an integrated intercivilizational (and even, embryonically, transcivilizational) perspective the type of historical breakthrough that creates a principled differentiation between power holders and cultural carriers, Axial Age theory envisaged a crucial breakthrough in human history occurring in the middle centuries of the first millennium BCE. As depicting the age of the sages and prophets (from Pythagoras and Plato through Zoroaster and Isaiah to the Buddha Shakyamuni and Laozi), this approach provided a major inspiration and various themes to the sociological program of civilizational analysis, thanks especially to the seminal work of the already mentioned Shmuel N. Eisenstadt (1982; 1986).

Based on such a rich and original combination of historical knowledge and theoretical insights, the nature of Islamic civilization, as one legitimate and particularly dynamic heir of the breakthroughs of the Axial Age, appeared to Hodgson as *sui generis*. This was particularly true if comparing Islam with China, India, or the West, a comparison from which Islam emerged as being uniquely able to set in motion a new type of transcivilizational dynamics across the Afro-Eurasian landmass. Hodgson even coined a term, "Islamdom," to represent the specific "complex of social relations" or "the milieu of a whole society" (both definitions being emphasized by Hodgson) produced by Islamic civilization. Islamdom reflects the link to Islam's cultural and religious traditions, and adds to them the value represented by a strong dimension of transcivilizational circulation and exchange (Hodgson 1974, I: 58):

> In the mid-Arid Zone … the pressures toward a cosmopolitan dissolution of local legitimations could be unusually strong. Perhaps on this account, in that region the compensating institutions proved to be the less tightly structured. They were highly flexible, for agrarian times; but they also, more than in either India or the Occident, did tend to leave the individual relatively insecure in status, and face to face with society at large—as his religion left him face to face with the supreme God—with a minimum of buffering intermediaries.
>
> (Hodgson 1974, II: 63)

This uniqueness, formulated in terms of cosmopolitan opening and institutional flexibility, was also due to the fact that according to Hodgson Islam was the civilization that inherited and creatively recombined the cultural characters and the political specificities of a vast and more ancient geo-cultural unit, the Irano-Semitic civilizational area. In particular he stressed that "the post-Cuneiform Irano-Semitic tradition between Nile and Oxus, from Syria to Khurasan," one of the four civilizational realms of Jaspers' Axial Age (the others being the Hellenic, the Indic, and the Sinitic civilizations), was taken over by Islam. In this, as it were, friendly takeover, Islam had the specific merit of bringing prophetic monotheism "to a certain culmination," also by exalting the "communal articulation" of the town commoners most exposed to the lures of prophetic monotheism, "while overcoming its divisiveness" (Hodgson 1993: 107).

To mark both the idiosyncrasies and the continuities characterizing the emergence and unfolding of Islamic civilization, Hodgson's idea of Islamdom was also suited to transcend the static notion of a generic and monolithic civilization. It effectively described the unstable crystallization of an ecumene comparable in principle with Latin Christendom. The latter is usually considered the cradle of what came to be identified first as Western Europe and later as simply the 'West' and its modernity. Yet Hodgson kept Islamdom distinct from Islam also for its potential to create synergies among previously distinct cultural worlds and religious traditions. As put by him,

> the Islamic tradition itself was largely the product of the cosmopolitan and mercantile bias of society from Nile to Oxus. Both with its *Shari'a* and … in its Sufi orders, it reinforced, in the face of temporary attempts at a more hierarchical or parochial structuring, the sort of free open social structuring to which it had itself responded. Yet even Islam could be made to serve a different tendency when that became strong.
>
> (Hodgson 1974, II: 85)

Therefore Hodgson depicted Islamdom as the outcome of that "different tendency" that grew out of Islam's own cosmopolitan impetus. This is manifest in the ensemble of social and institutional patterns that inherited and creatively recombined the cultural characters and the political specificities of the Irano-Semitic civilizational realm, with its mostly town-based and mercantile-biased prophetic traditions. On the one hand, Islamic civilization revealed a strong rooting within this specific cultural world. On the other, by virtue of the articulation itself of Islam as a religious tradition that sealed the chain of Semitic prophecy while also integrating, at a very early stage of its development (basically from its onset), the rich and complex heritage of Persianate culture (including religion) and statecraft, it was particularly porous to intercivilizational exchange. This is why Islam quickly acquired a uniquely expansive potential in cultural, as well as political, terms. I would propose that Hodgson's articulation of Islam and Islamdom be seen as a uniquely suitable instance of the dynamics of religion (Islam) and civility (Islamdom). In other words, Hodgson's Islamdom provides a suitable conduit for covering the ensemble of Islamic articulations of patterns of civility.

Islam, as just specified in its inner complexity and outer projection, quickly became an expanding ecumene continually nourished by the strong impulse to imprint culturally, before politically, the depths of the Afro-Eurasian macro-civilizational realm. The process reached its peak in what Hodgson depicted as the "Middle Periods" of Islamic history (10th to 15th centuries), which Orientalists before (but also, though in decreasing measure, after) Hodgson have too often and too easily downgraded to a phase of decadence and lack of creativity if not of socio-cultural and political disintegration. It was the epoch that roughly stretched from the decline of the Abbasid Caliphate to the rise of the early modern "gunpowder empires": the Ottoman, the Safavid, and the Mughal. During this era, cut in the middle by the Mongol invasion, political domination was weak and fragmented. Yet precisely for these reasons the cultivation of the relationship between human government and the normative idiom keeping together the Islamic ecumene entered a phase of particularly intense, sometimes mutual, problematization and elaboration. The main keyword for human government happened to be *siyasa*, a term appearing quite early, though sporadically, in the two main genres of normative literature, the *hadith* (including the sayings and deeds of Muhammad), and court literature (*adab*), and which became significantly related to the later 'secular turn' determined by Mongol rule in the Later Middle Period and after. The principal term for Islamic normativity was *shari'a*, too often mistranslated and misconceived as 'Islamic law,' and designating a normative ideal more than a body of laws or rulings.

We are not dealing here with a unique case of an almost one-to-one relation between a religion and a civilization, as suggested by the quite lazy visions conveyed to us by several generations of Orientalists. The uniqueness of Islam highlighted by Hodgson (as doubling up into 'Islamdom' being not quite the same as Islam) should rather encourage a critical review of the alleged universality and clarity of the hardened concepts of religion and civilization themselves. This binary conceptualization, if intended too rigidly, does not work too well in the case of Islam because of the rather entropic character of its expansion and especially due to its institutional nesting in a variety of civilizational contexts, across conventional civilizational borders (also within 'Europe,' 'India,' and 'China'). Yet more than in a one-to-one relation between sclerotized notions of religion and civilization, the uniqueness of Islam lies in its capacity—most notably manifested in the Middle Periods, even after the so-called Mongol invasion—to probe the porousness of the boundaries of rather self-contained civilizations like Western

Christendom, India, and, though to a lesser extent, even China. Islam proved able to infiltrate diverse civilizational constellations via a particularly versatile alchemy of the knowledge–power crucible inscribing patterns of civility into the social bond. The winning formula consisted most of the time in keeping loyal to a flexible yet solid normative idiom while allowing for culturally diverse, local and regional articulations of the knowledge-power equation and attendant patterns of civility. This capacity also came to extraordinarily good fruition in the relatively late, yet until now tremendously successful, insertion of Islam into the already rich and uniquely complex civilizational dynamics of Southeast Asia, which came to maturation toward the end of the Middle Periods.

The chance to reread Hodgson through the lenses of civilizational analysis has made more plausible his key insight that Islam reassembled and gave an unprecedented impetus to the heritage of a number of civilizational components. He thought that Islam brought to a new and particularly powerful synthesis the cosmopolitan and largely egalitarian orientation of the Irano-Semitic traditions. Yet it also gave them a new transcivilizational spin by investing their expansive orientation into the depths of the Afro-Eurasian hemisphere. This impetus has been so forcefully stressed by Hodgson that Islam could be correspondingly identified as a decisive, ongoing trigger of intercivilizational processes and transcivilizational encounters producing distinctive patterns of civility more than as a compact 'civilization.' Paradoxically yet crucially, therefore, the crossfertilization of comparative civilizational analysis and the sociology of Islam has contributed to deflate the controversial, essentializing traits of the notion of civilization. Civilizations are at best contingent crystallizations of an open-ended civilizing process within Afro-Eurasia, to which Islam was for long epochs central and not, as it later became under the hegemony of Western-centered colonial modernity, eccentric (see Lawrence 2010).

The inner key but also the outer symptom of this expansive adaptability that makes of Islam a transcivilizational ecumene more than a self-contained civilizational monolith lies precisely in its capacity to promote a particularly open and semi-formal approach to the institutional consecration of connective bonds and collective identities. We are all keenly aware that this is exactly the opposite of the dominant image conveyed by global (not just Western) media and policy-making. This versatility was in turn favored by a particularly open recombination of religious sources and inputs. This is evident in the meta-institutional matrices represented by the body of Muhammad's normative traditions (the *hadith*), the pious foundation that funded a wide variety of social and educational services (the *waqf*), and the Sufi brotherhood (the *tariqa*), a crucial hub of sociability and networking. All such meta-institutions took shape over several centuries and happened to be fully legitimized and in full gear (particularly the *tariqa*) during the Middle Periods. The resulting institutional patterns, far from representing hardened models of Islamic civility exactly matching religious visions, reflected a rather contractual model of articulating the underlying, enabling norms.

This rather flexible model is an important historical alternative to the prevalence, in late-medieval Europe, of autonomous offices and statutes, like those acquired by municipalities and kingdoms as they gradually emancipated themselves from feudal structures of authority distribution and transmission. As this book will try to show both conceptually and historically, the Islamic patterns of civility stood out for warranting a quite strong (and conscious) immunization against consecrating any institution in the form of a corporation. They implied a refusal of such entrenched institutional demarcations as those represented in other civilizations by caste, estate, municipality, and corporate guild. More than any other institution, the aforementioned Islamic matrices entailed the refusal of a Church-like structuring of religious authority. The Islamic *umma* was never modeled on the *ekklesia*, a consecrated gathering of the faithful, but rather remained an inchoate, an-organic, yet connective (more than simply collective), body of the faithful. The mosques themselves, those located in urban centers and close to the ruling authority and the innumerable more peripheral ones—both in the cities and in the countryside—were unconsecrated, rather multifunctional places of prayer and gathering.

Hodgson's approach by necessity entailed a sustained criticism of the provincialism of Western orientalist views on Islam. These have often privileged its Mediterranean projection, most notably due to the heritage of the long-drawn-out rivalry of Latin Christendom with the Ottoman Empire, and the resulting perception (and construction) of a 'Turkish Threat' being so central to the fears of early modern Europe. Even more, orientalist views have obsessively revolved around Islam's Arabian origin. The consequence has been to disregard a key fact in the long-term evolution of Islam as an increasingly transcivilizational ecumene: namely that right from its inception not just its expansive flourishing but also its intrinsic vitality presupposed substantial, and not just decorative, crosscultural borrowings from other civilizational realms (Hodgson 1993: 104). It is also important to add, following Hodgson, that the implications for Islam's unfolding of wider Afro-Eurasian entanglements became ever more visible in the postcaliphal era. Thus rather than the Hijaz (the crucial yet narrow region of the Arabian peninsula where Mecca and Medina are located), the cradle of Islam and the platform from which its hemisphere-wide expansion originated should be seen in the wider area that Hodgson defined as the "Nile-to-Oxus region": "when Islam was announced there, the new doctrine did not seem strange" (Hodgson 1993: 105), since it was quite well aligned with earlier developments in this civilizational area, namely the Irano-Semitic realm. This applied particularly well to the aspirations of townspeople facing agrarianate dominance over societies strongly stratified in classes or castes through their moral egalitarian ethos. This dominance remained instead virtually unchallenged in all other civilizations from the Axial Age well into the modern era.

Yet the fact that Islam brought to maturation a longer-term combination of the egalitarianism and cosmopolitanism sown within the Irano-Semitic civilizational realm should not lead us to neglect the extent to which it also valorized key components of the Greek and Hellenistic heritage. Hodgson's flexible model of Islam/Islamdom is not a dual one matching a hardened religion with a self-entrenched civilization but rather a synthesis of several cultural and religious traditions originating within, yet also transcending, the porous borders of the Irano-Semitic area. For example, the pre-Islamic closeness of key components of the Iranian heritage to the Sanskritic stock—not just linguistically but also religiously and anthropologically—was later integrated into the interfacing of Iranic and Turkic nomadism beyond the Oxus. The circle was finally sealed by the way Alexander the Great's conquests through that region and into the Indus valley left enduring traces on the Irano-Semitic imagination, which could be later retrieved through the Islamic and Persianate lore, irrespective of whether his identification with the mysterious, apocalyptic character of Dhul-Qarnain appearing in the Qur'an is correct or not. In Indo-Persian figurative art, the Macedonian empire-builder and disciple of Aristotle was often depicted in front of the mythic fountain of life together with al-Khidr, a key saintly character of Islamic lore, particularly of Sufism. More in general, it is possible to argue that the eastward trajectory of conquest of Alexander, whose cultural impact outlasted his colossal but fragile empire, prefigured the longer-term expansive trajectory of Islam into Central and South Asia.

Hodgson's geographically, historically, and culturally complex and nuanced characterization of Islam's beginning and trajectory can also help in desaturating the overloaded debates on the revisionist model concerning the origins of Islam, often associated with the names of Patricia Crone and Michael Cook (1977). These discussions have been particularly controversial over the last three decades for their insistence on addressing the relation between aspects of Judaism and of the new Islamic faith. Such issues, however settled or left unsettled, appear at best as confined within a little province within the much larger and more complex intercultural and trans-civilizational field highlighted by Hodgson. With all due respect owed to the work of historians and philologists on the matter, the sociology of Islam maintains a distance from this orientalist battlefield and focuses on long-term trends revolving around the notion of an ongoing civilizing process affecting the way knowledge infuses power, enlivens religion, and produces patterns of civility.

This perspective is necessary in order to revise and subvert teleological assumptions concerning why the Islamic civilization finally succumbed to the hegemonic power of the 'West.' Hodgson convincingly demonstrated how by the dawn of the epoch that we conventionally identify as the modern era this civilizing process writ Islamic had generated the most vital and probably the best articulated civilization in the world. More than a self-enclosed civilization, Islam resembled a transcivilizational ecumene with a hegemonic potential over both the Eastern and the Western parts of the Afro-Eurasian landmass, soon to be designated as the 'Old World.' According to Hodgson, at exactly this time Islam reached the zenith not only of its political power but also of its cultural creativity, in spite of emerging factors of self-limitation caused by its geographical overstretching. These factors depended on socio-political more than on sheer religious reasons and configured a deficit not of religious vision and civilizing potential but rather of the capacity to administer the gained complexity. Geographical overstretching and cultural complexification in turn favored conservative reentrenchments of the Islamic normative ideals and practices (Hodgson 1993: 100).

Yet in spite of this latter trend diminishing Islam's longer-term openness and inventiveness, Hodgson demonstrated in *The Venture of Islam* that there was nothing inherently at odds between Islam and advanced artic-ulations of the knowledge–power equation. This conviction is condensed in the following, famous statement: "In the sixteenth century of our era, a visitor from Mars might well have supposed that the human world was on the verge of becoming Muslim" (Hodgson 1993: 97). With his approach,

Hodgson challenged head-on the dominant orientalist bias which alleged a culturally rooted incapacity of Islamic civilization to evolve into ever new modes of civility and culture (von Grunebaum 1964). This prejudice is still popular today, particularly after being revived by the leading British orientalist Bernard Lewis (2002) after 9/11. In many ways, however, this distorted perception of Islam by the West is rooted in the ambivalent character of Western modernity itself, which has proved incapable of consistently aligning its will to power with its universalistic openings (Salvatore 1997).

Hodgson knew Weber all too well, including the fact that Weber, in his rather thin dealing with Islam, had not only got wrong some basic facts about its origin and development but had also raised lopsided questions about it. Islam and Islamdom simply did not fit Weber's contrasting Western rational puritan asceticism with purportedly Eastern mystical paths (Turner 2013: 23). Back in the 1970s Bryan Turner criticized Hodgson for reducing Islam to inner faith and conscience (Turner 1976). Yet in more recent writings by the British sociologist, Hodgson has been rehabilitated for having been able to show, for the first time and in vivid terms, Islam's original cosmopolitan imagination as rooted not in military imperialism but in a rather inclusive type of piety. In this way Hodgson, a committed Quaker, exposed, in the name of a pacifist ethics, the admixture of Western historic provincialism and colonial arrogance in missing how Islam (supposedly a 'religion') smoothly turned into Islamdom, a social nexus and civilizational matrix manifest in networks of local and translocal connectedness and attendant normative patterns (Turner 2013: 13).

In Hodgson's work, we can detect key ingredients for a sociological analysis of the doublet Islam/Islamdom as constituting both more and less than a self-entrenched civilization: rather a transcivilizational ecumene producing strong patterns of translocal civility (Hodgson 1974, I and II; 1993; for an earlier analysis of mine, see Salvatore 2009). Arnason particularly appreciated Hodgson's sensitivity to the interplay between civilizations and the underlying cultural traditions (Arnason 2006). As a result of the rich insights we can gain from studying Hodgson, we now have the chance to become better equipped to flesh out the analytical potential and the interactive purview of the conceptual cluster on which a sociology of Islam should be based. The Islam sociologically analyzed in this volume is not just a privileged field for testing a conceptual enrichment of the sociological arsenal of concepts and analyses but also a cumulative historical venture whose interpretation can and should be invested into the task of sociological self-reflection and enrichment.

References

Alatas, Syed Farid. 2006. *Alternative Discourses in Asian Social Science: Responses to Eurocentrism*. New Delhi: Sage.

Alatas, Syed Farid. 2010. "Religion and Reform: Two Exemplars for Autonomous Sociology in the Non-Western Context." In *The ISA Handbook of Diverse Sociological Traditions*, edited by Sujata Patel, 29–40. London: Sage.

Arjomand, Said Amir and Edward Tiryakian, eds. 2004. *Rethinking Civilizational Analysis*. London: Sage.

Arnason, Johann P. 2003. *Civilisations in Dispute: Historical Questions and Theoretical Traditions*. Leiden: Brill.

Arnason, Johann P. 2006. "Marshall Hodgson's Civilizational Analysis of Islam: Theoretical and Comparative Perspectives." In *Islam in Process: Historical and Civilizational Perspectives*, edited by Johann P. Arnason, Armando Salvatore, and Georg Stauth, 23–47. Bielefeld: Transcript; New Brunswick, NJ: Transaction (*Yearbook of the Sociology of Islam* VII).

Arnason, Johann P. and Georg Stauth. 2004. "Civilization and State Formation in the Islamic Context: Re-reading Ibn Khaldun." *Thesis Eleven*, 76: 29–47.

Asad, Talal. 2003. *Formations of the Secular: Christianity, Islam, Modernity*. Stanford, CA: Stanford University Press.

Bellah, Robert N. and Philip E. Hammond, eds. 1980. *Varieties of Civil Religion*. San Francisco: Harper & Row.

Bourdieu, Pierre. 1971. "Genèse et structure du champ religieux." *Revue française de sociologie*, 12/3: 295–334.

Bourdieu, Pierre and Loïc J.D. Wacquant. 1992. *An Invitation to Reflexive Sociology*. Chicago: University of Chicago Press.

Burke, Edmund III. 1993. "Introduction: Marshall G.S. Hodgson and World History." In *Rethinking World History: Essays on Europe, Islam and World History*, edited, and with Introduction and Conclusion, by Edmund Burke III. Cambridge: Cambridge University Press.

Connell, Raewyn. 2007. *Southern Theory: Social Science and the Global Dynamics of Knowledge*. Cambridge: Polity Press.

Crone, Patricia and Michael Cook. 1977. *Hagarism: The Making of the Islamic World*. Cambridge: Cambridge University Press.

Eisenstadt, Shmuel N. 1968. "Introduction: Charisma and Institution Building: Max Weber and Modern Sociology." In *Weber on Charisma and Institution Building*, edited and with an Introduction by Shmuel N. Eisenstadt, ix–lvi. Chicago and London: University of Chicago Press.

Eisenstadt, Shmuel N. 1982. "The Axial Age: The Emergence of Transcendental Visions and the Rise of Clerics." *European Journal of Sociology*, 23/2: 294–314.

Eisenstadt, Shmuel N. 1986. "Introduction: The Axial Age Breakthroughs: Their Characteristics and Origins." In *The Origins and the Diversity of Axial Age Civilizations*, edited by Shmuel N. Eisenstadt, 1–25. New York: SUNY Press.

Eisenstadt, Shmuel N. 2000. "Multiple Modernities." *Daedalus*, 129/1: 1–29.

Eisenstadt, Shmuel N. 2003. *Comparative Civilizations and Multiple Modernities: A Collection of Essays*. Leiden: Brill.

Foucault, Michel. 1991. "Governmentality." In *The Foucault Effect: Studies in Governmentality*, edited by Graham Burchell, Colin Gordon, and Peter Miller, 87–104. Chicago: University of Chicago Press.

Heilbron, Johan. 1995 [1990]. *The Rise of Social Theory*. Cambridge: Polity Press.

Hodgson, Marshall G.S. 1974. *The Venture of Islam: Conscience and History in a World Civilization, I–III*. Chicago and London: University of Chicago Press.

Hodgson, Marshall G.S. 1993. *Rethinking World History: Essays on Europe, Islam and World History*, edited, with Introduction and Conclusion, by Edmund Burke III. Cambridge: Cambridge University Press.

Johansen, Baber. 2004. "Islamic Studies: The Intellectual and Political Conditions of a Discipline." In *Penser l'Orient*, edited by Youssef Courbage and Manfred Kropp, 65–93. Beirut: IFPO & Orient-Institut.

Kilminster, Richard. 1998. *The Sociological Revolution: From the Enlightenment to the Global Age*. London and New York: Routledge.

Lawrence, Bruce B. 2010. "Islam in Afro-Eurasia: A Bridge Civilization." In *Civilizations in World Politics: Plural and Pluralist Perspectives*, edited by Peter J. Katzenstein, 157–76. London: Routledge.

Lewis, Bernard. 2002. *What Went Wrong? Western Impact and Middle Eastern Response*. Oxford and New York: Oxford University Press.

MacIntyre, Alasdair. 1988. *Whose Justice? Which Rationality?* London: Duckworth.

Masud, M. Khalid and Armando Salvatore. 2009. "Western Scholars of Islam on the Issue of Modernity." In *Islam and Modernity: Key Issues and Debates*, edited by Muhammad Khalid Masud, Armando Salvatore, and Martin van Bruinessen, 36–53. Edinburgh: Edinburgh University Press.

Masuzawa, Tomoko. 2005. *The Invention of World Religions: Or How European Universalism Was Preserved in the Language Pluralism*. Chicago: University of Chicago Press.

Mauss, Marcel. 1950. *Sociologie et anthropologie*. Paris: Presses Universitaires de France.

Mazlish, Bruce. 2001. "Civilization in an Historical and Global Perspective." *International Sociology*, 16/3: 293–300.

Mazlish, Bruce. 2004. *Civilization and its Contents*. Stanford, CA: Stanford University Press.

Milbank, John. 1990. *Theology and Social Theory: Beyond Secular Reason*. Oxford: Blackwell.

Nafissi, Mohammad. 1998. "Reframing Orientalism: Weber and Islam." *Economy and Society*, 27/1: 97–118.

Patel, Sujata, ed. 2010. *The ISA Handbook of Diverse Sociological Traditions*. London: Sage.

Salvatore, Armando. 1997. *Islam and the Political Discourse of Modernity*. Reading: Ithaca Press.

Salvatore, Armando. 2007. *The Public Sphere: Liberal Modernity, Catholicism, and Islam*. New York: Palgrave Macmillan.

Salvatore, Armando. 2009. "Tradition and Modernity within Islamic Civilisation and the West." In *Islam and Modernity: Key Issues and Debates*, edited by Muhammad Khalid Masud, Armando Salvatore, and Martin van Bruinessen, 3–35. Edinburgh: Edinburgh University Press.

Salvatore, Armando. 2013. "The Sociology of Islam: Precedents and Perspectives." *Sociology of Islam*, 1/1–2: 7–13.

Schluchter, Wolfgang. 1999 [1987]. "Hindrances to Modernity: Max Weber on Islam." In *Max Weber & Islam*, edited by Toby Huff and Wolfgang Schluchter, 53–138. New Brunswick, NJ and London: Transactions.

Shari'ati, Ali. 1979. *On the Sociology of Islam*, translated by Hamid Algar. Berkeley, CA: Mizan Press.

Stauth, Georg. 1993. *Islam und Westlicher Rationalismus. Der Beitrag des Orientalismus zur Entstehung der Soziologie*. Frankfurt and New York: Campus.

Stauth, Georg and Bryan S. Turner. 1988. *Nietzsche's Dance: Resentment, Reciprocity and Resistance in Social Life*. Oxford: Blackwell.

Szakolczai, Arpad. 2000. *Reflexive Historical Sociology*. London and New York: Routledge.

Tugal, Cihan. 2009. *Passive Revolution: Absorbing the Islamic Challenge to Capitalism*. Stanford, CA: Stanford University Press.

Turner, Bryan S. 1974. *Weber and Islam: A Critical Study*. London and Boston: Routledge & Kegan Paul.

Turner, Bryan S. 1976. "Conscience in the Construction of Religion: A Critique of Marshall G.S. Hodgson's The Venture of Islam." *Review of Middle East Studies*, 2: 95–111.

Turner, Bryan S. 1978. *Marx and the End of Orientalism*. London: George Allen and Unwin.

Turner, Bryan S. 1992. *"Preface" to Emile Durkheim, Professional Ethics and Civic Morals*, 2nd ed. London: Routledge.

Turner, Bryan S. 2013. "Introduction to Section I: Classical Approaches—Understanding Islam." In *The Sociology of Islam: Collected Essays of Bryan*

S. Turner, edited by Bryan S. Turner and Kamaludeen Mohamed Nasir, 11–21. Farnham and Burlington, VT: Ashgate.

Von Grunebaum, Gustave E. 1964. *Modern Islam: The Search for Cultural Identity*. New York: Vintage.

Weber, Max. 1986 [1920]: *Gesammelte Aufsätze zur Religionssoziologie*, I: J.C.B. Mohr (Paul Siebeck): Tübingen.

PART I
PATTERNS OF CIVILITY

1

THE LIMITS OF CIVIL SOCIETY AND THE PATH TO CIVILITY

The Origins of Modern Civil Society

In order to pursue the exploration sketched in the Introduction, the sociology of Islam should perform a preliminary step. It should contribute to replace a politically overloaded idea of civil society reflecting Western aspirations and postulates with a more malleable, yet historically sound and transculturally plausible, concept of civility. We should distill an adequate notion of civility out of the waves that have recurrently pushed up the banner of civil society, until the end of the 20th century.

The idea of civility binds together and, as it were, balances knowledge and power, innovative potential and institutional crystallization, against each other. However, we cannot ignore that civility, however reformulated here with a view to its usefulness for the sociology of Islam, comes to us heavily filtered through the more specific, integrated, and therefore strongly one-sided articulation and theorization of the historic Western concept of civil society. Due to the genealogy itself of Western social sciences, civility appears as first integrated into a full-fledged, and to a large extent modern, concept of society. This concept has been in turn modeled on specific, hegemonic Western trajectories, most notably those originating from North-Western Europe.

Surely in order to reconstruct a rather transversal notion of civility and emancipate it from its dependence on a unilateral Western heritage one needs to take into account non-Western experiences and trajectories. The inevitable tension between the need to start from an integrated Western

The Sociology of Islam: Knowledge, Power and Civility, First Edition. Armando Salvatore.
© 2016 John Wiley & Sons, Ltd. Published 2016 by John Wiley & Sons, Ltd.

model (or, as we will see, 'dream') of civil society and the goal of achieving a transculturally more suitable concept of civility is reflected in the fact that, as stated by Şerif Mardin, civil society "does not translate into Islamic terms. Civility, which is a latent content of civil society, does, but these two are not interchangeable terms" (Mardin 1995: 279). Translated into operational terms, this means that we need to explore the extent to which a transversal idea of civility can be extracted or redeemed, as it were, from the hegemonic model of civil society and put to the service of a more global vision, and specifically to a non-Eurocentric approach to Islam. The fact that since the end of the 18th century the Western notion of civil society has been gradually ingrained into the hegemonic processes that allowed for a climax in the Western exercise of power and knowledge over the non-Western world makes this move even more necessary, though also difficult.

Let us start by recalling that although first theorized by different branches of the European Enlightenment, civil society experienced a strong and sudden revival during the 1990s (most representative of it, Cohen and Arato 1992). It rapidly became a privileged tool, both conceptually and practically, for covering the emerging aspirations to democratic transformations within the Muslim world. In introducing his seminal two-volume *Civil Society in the Middle East*, Augustus Norton defined civil society as the icon of democracy:

> If democracy has a home, it is in civil society, where a mélange of associations, clubs, guilds, syndicates, federations, unions, parties and groups come together to provide a buffer between state and citizen … The functioning of civil society is literally and plainly at the heart of participant political systems.
>
> (Norton 1995: 7)

This strategic opening to the concept of civil society in the study of both Muslim-majority societies and of transnational forms of Islam occurred in the wake of the collapse of the authoritarian regimes of Eastern and East-Central Europe belonging to the so-called Soviet bloc. The idea of civil society was quite swiftly adopted by movements within Muslim-majority societies, from the Arab world to Southeast Asia, in the popular struggles against overtly autocratic or pseudo-democratic regimes, variably associated with the ongoing neoliberal globalization (Hefner 2000). In cases like that of Egypt, where the regime claimed a democratic legitimacy by holding parliamentary elections curtailed by state violence, intimidation, and fraud, the act of raising the banner of civil society pointed out that democratization can never be a top-down concession of autocratic cliques. Democratization rather needs—so the message goes—a bottom-up process that starts at the level where associations, unions, parties, but also informal groups (the ensemble of which, it was remarked, constitutes civil society), are formed in order to represent citizens' grievances and claims to distant and exploitative state authorities.

This surging enthusiasm for civil society as a panacea against corruption and authoritarianism in the Muslim world and particularly in the Middle East was clearly misplaced. This was partly due to the fact that many of the same Western governments and donors that were ostensibly supportive of the ideal were in fact undermining it through the continued support of authoritarian regimes. Yet there was an even deeper contradiction to this facile operationalization of civil society that was revealed by the ways through which much too often aid policies weakened rather than strengthened the associational bonds of basically spontaneous cooperation (Salvatore 2011). In this context, civil society, which had been reconceived as the privileged arena for preparing democratic transformations, shrank into a mere logo impressed on the business cards of a new generation of professionally staffed non-governmental organizations committed to public advocacy around often narrow questions of good practices and policy optimization (Challand 2011). The encompassing idea initially written on the banner proved hardly suitable to enable activists and citizens to grapple with the larger questions surrounding the essentially undemocratic and inequitable nature of regimes and their political economies. Yet while the promise of civil society, increasingly identified with Western-certified NGOs, became less obviously regenerative, other potentially formative (and transformative) patterns of civility were still latent in the process. As Mardin warned, the one-sided and not seldom fraudulent nature of an imitative politicization of Western civil society—a notion that, as we will see, is already in itself (due to its origin and history) a hardly coherent platform of change—did not exclude that more complex and less streamlined artic-ulations of civility through Islamic idioms could be gradually and honestly unveiled.

In the post-9/11 trajectory of the Muslim-majority world up to the Arab Spring, also due to the petering out of the latter's initial impetus, popular responses to oppressive state systems have become more nuanced. In this context, the extent to which ideas and practices of civility can facilitate democratic transformations beyond the one-sidedness of European models of civil society's functional interactions with modern, Westphalian states has been subject to reappraisal (Gervasio 2014). In parallel, there have been attempts to critically reframe ideas of the civic glue of the social bond in a historically more diversified perspective that has shown the inherent limits of a sheer application of the civil society model to potentially every locale on a global scale (Challand 2011; Volpi 2011). Particularly, the 2000s have been important for inflicting a dystopian twist to the more specifically Western 'dream' of civil society, due to its slipping toward thin conceptions of market democracy often forcefully married to the rhetoric on the War on Terror. Let us, in this chapter, take stock and analyze the historical precedents and ideological bias that make the construct of civil society a far cry from being a limpid, universally extendable site of societal self-empowerment.

In order to understand the lopsided effects of the mere extension of a revived notion of civil society on the Muslim-majority world since the 1990s, it is important to fully grasp how the weakness of the theory is coextensive to its potential strength in depicting an exceptional development in parts of Western Christendom across the epoch conventionally dubbed the Enlightenment. The idea of civil society envisions a society whose constituting ties are shaped by the prevalence of politeness and affection rather than violence and fear. This notion is not the innocent pleonasm that it appears at first sight. The concept imbues the construction itself of society, which can be hardly taken for granted, with the no less problematic attribute of civility. This, in turn, is intended as both the outcome and the engine of a continual social process that tames violence by facilitating the inculcation of proper codes of behavior and cooperation in the members of society. While society and civility appear in themselves as contested concepts, predicating society through civility construes the former as a stable, functional, and cohesive entity almost by default. This is true to the extent that society appears organized in a civil way, namely according to modalities that restrict and ultimately prevent recourse to arbitrary violence. On the positive side, a society thus made civil provides, according to the theory, agency, rights, and ultimately the benefits and entitlements of citizenship to its members. Ernest Gellner, one of the major theorists of civil society throughout its late 20th-century revival, maintained that the red thread unfolding through a variety of Western definitions of civil society is a "highly specific," and in this sense not easily replicable view of the social bond among individuals as "unsanctified, instrumental, revocable." According to Gellner, civil society is a highly modern construct to the extent that it relies on ad hoc associations and cooperations which overcome any traditional, indissoluble bonds and dependences among individuals (Gellner 1995: 42).

The process underlying what appears as a well-rounded conception of civil society reflects quite immediately the experience of modern transformations in North-Western Europe, most notably of Scotland, particularly in the 18th century. According to this conception, society can be sufficiently civilized only under quite exceptional conditions like the prevalence of secure frameworks for the implementation of the law and the guarantee of contracts. Ultimately, in the words of Gellner, this condition is reflected in the acceptance of the "tyranny of kings" over the "tyranny of cousins." Through this suggestive formula he emphasized the Westphalian regimes' capacity to effectively overcome bonds of kin and build an (even if initially despotic) enlightened, centralized rule. It clearly emerges from this formula that, paradoxically perhaps, civil society is premised on the prevalence of a political regime over the autonomy of the social bond. It is also important to stress that the interests and aspirations of an emerging commercial and industrial bourgeoisie were decisive in supporting the process. To prevail in the process is exactly the type of modern power (first absolutist, then liberal, finally democratic) that enables the individual to pursue her interests. This can only occur within a legal framework gravitating around a law of contract ultimately secured by the Westphalian state's monopolization of force, operating alongside the administration of society through a well-functioning bureaucracy. This monopolization purportedly extinguishes tribal or clan-based forms of social power and control (the "tyranny of cousins"). These indeed provide the allegedly premodern socio-political background against which Scottish views of civil society took form.

Mardin (1995) echoes Gellner (1995) in evidencing the specificity, even the peculiarity, of the Western dream of civil society. The Turkish scholar stressed that what needs to be carefully analyzed are not only the factors that make society civil. One also needs to focus on what habilitates society itself to provide the cohesive yet innerly differentiated macro-dimension of the social bond. Mardin agrees with Gellner in seeing civil society as the foil of the prevalence of forms of cohesiveness transcending bonds of kin and locality. Underneath the formulaic emphasis on individuals and rights, the genie in the lamp of civil society is in the empowerment of agents to autonomous action and the pursuit of their interests via benefiting from a legal frame that does not fully absorb, and so risk to hijack, individual creativity and freedom.

Nonetheless, this view is a dream, according to Mardin, in that it presupposes that the state can steadily project a protective shadow on individual interactants without degenerating into becoming an intrusive despot. This condition is not necessarily matched by the way modern bureaucracies work. Yet it is even more of a dream since the factors of cohesion which allow individuals to be bound to each other socially while pursuing their particular interests are assumed to reside in factors other than the law or the individual rights that they exercise. Civil law can be an instrument of civil society, but the latter cannot be collapsed into the former, since it presupposes a type of agency that is non-legal or prelegal. There seems to be a mysterious factor that matches right with liberty: a factor so evanescent that Mardin can locate it only at the level of aspirations, if not wishful thinking (Mardin 1995).

As shown by Adam Seligman (1992; 2002), the crux of the idea of civil society lies in the fact that it presupposes ties of trust that it cannot actually produce or explain. This evanescence is reflected by the vague and even naïvely sounding postulation by the thinkers belonging to the so-called 18th-century Scottish Enlightenment of a natural sympathy or a 'moral sense' spontaneously binding even heterogeneous individuals, across class identities and status ascriptions. Individual interests are matched by reciprocal affections and ultimately mutual trust among individuals. According to Seligman it is particularly evident that the notion of trust underlying this view overstates the individual moral agency of social actors or at least its unitary character (see Silver 1997).

This reconstruction of the nature of the social bond goes back in particular to 18th-century Scottish thinkers like Shaftesbury, Hutcheson, and Ferguson. The individual social agent is depicted as knowing her own interest and possessing a capacity to act autonomously, while also sharing a sense of affection and sympathy toward other individuals/agents. This nexus of sympathy between *ego* and *alter* provides the kernel to the type of bond that, if replicated on a macro-scale, constitutes civil society. If the agency presupposed by the model is overstated, the notion (and the glue) of civil society crumbles. As remarked by Alasdair MacIntyre, the trouble with this conception owes much to the fact that the theorized "moral sense," and its accompanying trust, are quite unexplainable in sociological terms. The activation of the mysterious sense requires a largely unilateral act of trust on the part of the social agent. Thus interaction presupposes individual agency, which however in turn requires trust. Since trust cannot be explained through interaction, it depends on a unilateral act, which looks like pure faith in disguise (MacIntyre 1984 [1981]: 229).

The key to civil society is therefore this unconditional, precontractual, quasi-pristine trust among private individuals. Its condition is the above-mentioned agential capacity to recognize *ego*'s own interests and modulate them through the filter of a sense of affection for *alter*. Trust so defined is the only possible vehicle of cooperation among people outside of clearly defined, traditionally given, ascriptive roles. All too evidently its basis cannot be easily ascertained sociologically (cf. Seligman 1992: 44–5, 62). It remains little more than a moral imperative. We can start to understand how, if not a dream, as maintained by Mardin, civil society might be the outcome of a deceitful projection of the type of glue of the social bond that the Scottish moralists saw endangered by the rash transformations that led to the rise of commercial and industrial society—a process whose major epicenter was initially located in Scottish cities (primarily Glasgow) rather than in English ones.

Seligman has convincingly shown how this fragile view of civil society and its fundaments was the outcome of a gradual intervention on the ancient, medieval, and early modern natural law tradition. This tradition renewed itself over the centuries and within shifting socio-political conditions by placing an increasing stress on the rational basis of individual commitments to the contractually regulated social bonds. The rational, regulative framework becomes an even more highly integrative one when individuals—as in the modern societies increasingly characterized by commercial ties and a social division of labor—are ever more self-regulated automatons or scattered atoms. The transformation was premised on the alteration of the natural law tradition. To be natural now consists no longer in abiding by the law of human sociability, which postulates the spontaneous development of intersubjective cooperation and understanding between *ego* and *alter*. Rather, natural law is now a law of human attachment, sympathy, and affection activated by a principled, absolute, and autonomous agency of the subject as a fully autonomous *ego*-actor. This idea became a key condition for the modern concept of civil society to develop and enliven subsequent waves of social theory throughout the 19th and 20th centuries.

The doubt, however, is about the extent to which this *ego*-centered agency is entirely a natural endowment, as maintained by the Scottish moralists, or rather the outcome of a process of education, if not dis- ciplining, of the citizen to actively seek a cooperation with the fellow citizen (Foucault 1979). Within modern European conditions, the state was certainly active in inculcating such a cooperative attitude, which at the stage of the Scottish Enlightenment was still considered—in a yet (but lopsided) Aristotelian way—as a moral capacity. On the other hand, cooperation so defined was still short of circumscribing a full-fledged, organic form of solidarity based on a rational social division of labor, as sociological theory will claim, particularly with Durkheim.

This theorization of a trust-based social bond as the kernel of civil society replaced a more traditional notion of the social space as a partnership of faith in God among individuals. This traditional view was the result of a reformulation of the Aristotelian approach filtered through the prism of the Roman Catholic natural law tradition, whose champion was Thomas Aquinas (1225–1274). The alternate, emerging vision of the Enlightenment (Scottish or otherwise) preferred to stress rather new factors of cohesion in society, whose sociological moorings remained however suspended. What clearly emerged was a theological revision, or minimization, resulting from the new vision: the bond of trust now linked individuals without any divine mediation, mostly under the purview of a benevolent yet distant God. Yet as just highlighted, and not too surprisingly—given the Protestant and more particularly Calvinist background of such transformations, in Scotland as elsewhere—such an investment in trust de facto signified a highly irrational magnification of pure faith, which Aquinas had earlier yoked to Christian reason and virtues (faith being one of them).

This abridged and essentialized type of trust among individuals within civil society became the key to redefining a social bond increasingly exposed to the impersonality of factory work and of contract-based labor relationships within capitalist economies, and regulated by the faceless yet rational (at least in a Weberian sense) bureaucracies that during the 19th century replaced the arbitrary rule of absolutist autocrats. Civil society was considered in principle distinct from the modern state for resting on a pristine agency and trust, yet it fed into the latter's functioning almost via a symbiotic relationship. Optimally, civil society expresses legitimate interests and produces ties of solidarity, while the state guarantees the rules that protect those interests and provides a legal framework for warranting social order. Civil society is indeed the site of formation of largely autonomous citizens' associations, also including juries and militias (a type of association culminating in the modern 'police'), but these are then directly or indirectly reabsorbed under the domain of the state, via regulation if not incorporation.

Civil Society as a Site of Production of Modern Power

It would be far-fetched and anachronistic to impute this modern civilizing process entirely to a capillary intervention of the state (we will look more deeply at the specific dimension of state agency and the law in the next volume). Not by chance some 20th-century social thinkers, including Hannah Arendt (1906–1975), have spoken of the invention of the social and society as a newly determined space within Western modernity, producing interdependent, disciplined subjects. These are linked to each other through a socially functional division of labor, which favors cohesion in the context of the potentially unrestrained pursuit of interests that is typical of commercial and industrial societies (Arendt 1958). Foucault himself observed that in the 18th century's theorization of civil society, the first key innovation resided in the purported autonomy of society itself. This autonomy is located in the working of a third, intermediate socio-political space that mediates between the needs of governance, a prerogative of the state, and the aspirations and interests of the private citizens (Foucault 1979).

We see here more clearly how civil society was born in the 18th century as a crucial space for the production of modern power, situated at the confluence of public and private law, and which the state decisively shaped, without controlling it entirely. The notion of civil society certainly presupposed a work of deconstruction of Aristotle's social theory performed by such authors as Thomas Hobbes (1588–1679) and John Locke (1632–1704), who had earlier worked to discard the traditional natural law tradition. Yet the shaping of the new notion represented a leap forward from the work of these two key thinkers. They had still argued in terms of the state's prerogatives and individual liberties without the need to refer to an intermediate space. The trajectory itself of the Scottish moralists both culminated with and was overcome by Adam Smith (1723–1790), author of *The Theory of Moral Sentiments* (1853 [1759]). It is particularly revealing to see how a fundamental author of Western social and economic theory like Smith both assimilated and undermined the idea of civil society shaped by his predecessors. He did so by closely building on the last champion of the Scottish moralists, namely Adam Ferguson (1723–1816), while prefiguring key elements of 19th- and even 20th-century social thought. Smith's intervention is symptomatic of the instability of an idea of a civil society relying on a moral sense of social actors. Just a few decades after its elaboration, the concept started to be eroded from within by an emerging logic of social interaction that the idea of civil society had initially attempted to integrate and neutralize in order to conceal and attenuate, as much as possible, the mutating notion of power underlying the interactive logic itself.

Competition of interests and wills and the social game aimed at buttressing individual reputation had been increasingly acknowledged, in the second half of the 18th century, as formative of social interactions. This game was ultimately recognized as essentially constructive of the social bond by pointing out a factor, like the 'moral sense,' which manifested attraction and sympathy, and ultimately produced trust, between *ego* and *alter*, in spite of their potentially clashing interests. Apart from manifesting the benevolent orientation to other, and in this sense the altruistic component of social agency, the emerging trust was seen as essential and almost providential in facilitating contractual exchange among private individuals and so providing the necessary stability to social relationships spurned by the commercial and industrial revolutions. Thus even before Smith a sort of providential factor was seen to be at work in the process of production of society and in what makes it civil, cohesive, and disciplined.

The outcome, in social terms, of Adam Smith's interventions is a sociologically subtle redefinition of the primacy of the private sphere over both civil society and ultimately the public sphere as well (Salvatore 2007: 219–34). The prelegal engine of the process lies in the fact that a civilized, largely self-regulated formulation of individual interests is preventively channeled by socially interactive factors that can work both to moderate and to exalt those interests. This mechanism lies firstly in the plain anthropological fact that *ego* has to cope with *alter*, and secondly in the sociological constraint that the subject's interests would not subsist without the continuing existence (and, to some extent, wellbeing) of the other. Far from being just an occasional contract partner, the other provides a permanent screen to the self's projection of individual interests and identity. As stressed by Seligman, crucial in the process is not just the emergence of the autonomy of correctly modulated self-interest but also and even more the integrity of the self as such. The subject is now autonomous even from the virtuous dispositions and the orientation to a higher good that had characterized the traditional, Aristotelian conception of the social agent (Seligman 1992: 25–44). While such a traditional conception was still strong in Hutcheson, with Shaftesbury, and even more with Ferguson, the social mechanisms that single out the self in her entanglement with the other beyond sheer self-interest come to the fore with increasing vigor. These mechanisms culminate with Adam Smith in a coherent vision of the inner civilizing engine represented by the "moral sentiments," which now acquire a stronger socio-anthropological plasticity and plausibility than the prior vague "moral sense."

The engine of Smith's moral psychology, now turned into a challenging proto-sociology, is the cumulative power of the other's gaze. The hidden, yet necessary, membrane of the moral sense appears now as nothing less than a highly sophisticated version of the Panopticon (as infamously theorized by Jeremy Bentham in the late 18th century). Here each member of society, by becoming an impartial spectator, is both under surveillance and occupies the watchtower (Santoro 2003 [1999]: 164–5). Supported by an increasingly discrete though still all-powerful sovereign (Hobbes' Leviathan), this kind of society helps make every comrade an attentive, meticulous—and increasingly democratic—observer/supervisor. The result is that "in social interaction the individual replaces God as the regulator of her and others' behavior" (Santoro 2003 [1999]: 165; cf. also the interpretation of civil society in Foucault 1979; 1991; Burchell 1991). The civility of society is therefore part and parcel of a package deal where agency and freedom are matched by self-regulation via a network of mutual supervisions and organic surveillance.

We see here how the turning of the moral sense into a much tighter social mechanism acquired a sinisterly Foucaultian spin, which in turn revealed how surveillance lurks behind trust. The initial push in this direction was a recognition that agency is inherently complex for being based on a combination of the principled freedom of the *egos* and their dependence on the appreciation of others via the sentiment of vanity. Being too vague a construct, the moral sense (as the root of more discrete sentiments) needed to be turned, with Adam Smith, into the principle of the impartial observer, activated precisely by a vanity-dependent type of agency. The outcome was the postulation of a powerful, providential, yet potentially concentrated, source of social power: rather the obverse of trust, namely surveillance. This was the outcome of a sustained, modern Western breakthrough marked by the overcoming of the Aristotelian legacy of the citizen's virtue and the emerging primacy of a notion of disciplined, and in this sense 'civilized,' type of agency increasingly functional to capitalist development and new labor relations. The civil character of this type or dimension of society is ensured by the public exposure of the moral self. This exposure secures a degree of mutual involvement (but also scrutiny) among individuals that transcends commercial interests and contractual relations. It contributes to cement the moral roots of a new type of self, based on self-esteem and even self-love (which was yet a diabolic manifestation in traditional views of the virtues).

Adam Seligman has shown how the genuine thrust to transcend mere interests and sheer contractual obligations captures the necessity to postulate a dimension of solidarity irreducible to self-interest and self-respect. Yet at the same time, this *ego*-transcending impulse mystifies the capacity of the social system to preserve and nurture the postulated moral sense without recourse to an overarching technology of control. With Adam Smith, unlike his predecessors of the Scottish Enlightenment, moral sentiments appear as the facilitators of the providential glue of civil society, yet not as their ultimate foundation. This lies in a rather amoral, yet densely social, network of surveillance that draws from, yet also constitutes the strengths and weaknesses of, a new modern subjectivity. This tempting, rather extreme rationalization of the glue of civility as the outcome of the Western Enlightenment induced Ernest Gellner to provocatively describe the Western ideal of civil society as a kind of "failed *umma*":

> the would-be secular *Umma* of the immanentist, formally materialist socio-historical religion … signally failed as an *Umma* but has not yet demonstrated its capacity to produce a civil society either. All that the latter has achieved is to generate, at least amongst a significant portion of its citizens, an evidently sincere and ardent *desire* for civil society.
>
> (Gellner 1995: 39)

With this verdict, which largely matches Mardin's idea of civil society as a Western aspiration or a dream, Gellner also intended to stress that excessive expectations about a morally supported mutual trust as the real, effective glue of civil society (supposedly replacing without significant residues a communal bond of faith) risk neglecting its necessarily "modular" articulation. More than a moral sense, it is a modular sensibleness that allows agents to perpetually weave together contingent bits and pieces of a civil bond. However, modularity can never be fully pragmatic, since in spite of being upheld by the ever resurfacing desire for civil society like the one that resulted from the epochal failure, in parts of Europe, of "the would-be secular Umma of the immanentist, formally materialist socio-historical religion," it tends to fall back onto some non-liberal and premodern idea of social cohesion, which Gellner liked to exemplify in terms of the Islamic *umma*. Ultimately, according to Gellner, civil society, if we want to extrapolate its modern sociological significance and difference from any traditional idea of community, can only rest on the inherent fragility of such a modular sensibleness.

Modularity is unlike the principle of full inclusion (or exclusion) from a rather closed community or citizenry. It manifests rather the possibility (or indeed necessity) of simultaneous and multiple memberships in intermediate yet instrumental social groups. The modularity of the self that can selectively and intermittently join multiple groups unfolds without blood rituals of sort sanctifying any of those groups. "The importance of being modular," according to Gellner, reflects a basic freedom of the agent from ascriptive ties of real, ritual, or contractual consanguinity (Gellner 1995: 40–43). The problematic, tautological character of this modular civility is due to the fact that a basic freedom is both the outcome of the process and is presupposed by it. There are no in-built mechanisms that guarantee that agential freedom is matched by an open access to the differentiated social fields. This is due to the plain social fact that these fields are in reality social networks that modulate access based on the interests of their dominant actors, and are therefore potentially (and often actually) exclusive. The liberal, modular notion of civil society theorized by Gellner remains sociologically no less evanescent than the moral sense of the Scottish Enlightenment.

What is interesting, in Gellner's reformulation of civil society hinging on the cliff of a failed *umma*, is rather a lingering nostalgia of bygone faith, which we saw reflected by the Aristotelian residues that are latent within the arguments of the theorists of the Scottish Enlightenment, but also within the vision of the Marxist proponents of a radical secular society targeted by Gellner. This symptomatic ambivalence of civil society is even more evident when paired with the fact that the primacy of modern modularity vis-à-vis traditional, authoritative mediation seems to discount an excess of investment in the will and capacity of the agents to formulate (and circumscribe) their commitments in modular terms. It is indeed only this theoretical overinvestment that can ground the resulting autonomy of civil society as a largely self-regulated, intermediate social space, distinct from both the state and its bureaucracy and regulations, on the one hand, and from the capitalist economy and its emergent market rules, on the other.

This problem of an excessive investment into the modern novelty of civil society was keenly recognized by such a leading Western thinker as G.W.F. Hegel (1770–1831). He argued that the condition for the formation of a civil society (*bürgerliche Gesellschaft*) was a cluster of traditionally rooted intermediary institutions that incarnate an ethical idiom irreducible to trust and trust-based contractualism. This institutional cluster cannot simply result from projecting an evanescent moral sense. Such an intermediary space indeed needs an ethical foundation. This ethic is provided by the extent to which civil society facilitates and, as it were, encompasses the agency of individuals in the context of their institutionalized relations. For Hegel such relations and their ethical fundament are still imperfect, yet they do play a constitutive and stabilizing role in the social bond. Agency within civil society is therefore neither fully autonomous nor organically linked to a nakedly modular, civic bond of convenience.

This inherent vulnerability of historic Western notions of civil society and their ambivalent dependence on traditional notions of the social bond prompts us to walk a path that recalibrates civility by avoiding the Eurocentrism of civil society. This path shuns civil society's indigestible combination of tautology of attributes (by collapsing being moral into being civil and social) and overinvestment in agency (by presupposing a quite implausible type of diffuse, modular agency). Civility should be initially conceived, more modestly and realistically, as a slippery dimension of social action and of the social bond more than as the integrative code of an autonomous social space. Realizing this facilitates a shift from the specific ideal of civil society toward a wider, yet also potentially sharper, view of civility that is transversal to traditional and modern practices. This move can provide a more suitable terrain for building a transcultural view of civility emancipated from an excessive orientation to Western prototypes and stereotypes and to their burdensome (and largely unrealistic) expectations, which are often nourished by unaudited nostalgias for a holistic type of sociality. Civility should also help us to overcome the socio-centric bias of agency and cooperation conceived mainly as internal to a given society. Last, civility, by transcending the limitations of a civil society bound to the design of a nation-state, has the advantage of more realistically reflecting the modalities of relations innervating Western hegemony over an increasingly global society (and the earlier, premodern one similarly characterizing the Islamic ecumene). Such relations are not restricted to questions of citizenship or membership within a given, national society intent on maximizing its commercial and industrial comparative advantages.

In what follows, I will attempt to show a welcome collateral effect, for the sociology of Islam, of this shift away from civil society and toward a reconstructed, transversal concept of civility. This effect consists in deflating most if not all trivialities and negativities that resulted from applying an uncritically accepted, package-like notion of civil society to Islam and the Muslim-majority world. This shift is also necessary in order to minimize the collateral damages generated by the defective universalism of civil society and the toll taken on Western social sciences in general and sociology in particular as a result of this deficit. As put by Bryan Turner, one of the pioneers of the sociology of Islam, the lopsided ambition of the concept of civil society has resulted in the untenable, highly un-sociological, and deeply orientalist view according to which

Muslim society lacked independent cities, an autonomous bourgeois class, rational bureaucracy, personal property and that cluster of rights which embody bourgeois legal culture. Without these institutional and cultural elements, there was nothing in Islamic civilisation to challenge the dead-end of pre-capitalist tradition.

(Turner 1984: 23)

The road to a more sober, transversal view of civility requires a preliminary step. This consists in an effort to make visible the idea of civility that we can recuperate from scraping away the delusional incrustations overburdening the modern Western idea of civil society. While one obvious problem of civil society is its Eurocentric character, the other, and less obvious, major shortcoming is that it does not reveal the full extent of the global impact of Eurocentrism and the way it rested on (and altered) earlier hegemonic forms of global connectedness. Once we accomplish the preliminary step, we can start to see civility as the outcome not only of the specific modern history of the West (or of some parts thereof) but also of its relations with the (colonial and postcolonial, but also to a large extent precolonial) 'rest', first and foremost the Muslim-majority world, or the Islamic ecumene.

In other words, the transversality of civility vs. the ill-concealed exclusiveness of civil society resides in acknowledging the historical, process-like character of the former as the outcome of an ongoing, inherently global civilizing process that has been subjected to frequent, sudden turns, transformations and even reversals in the course of human history. This insight also entails that with the rise of Western modernity and with its subsequent mutation into diversified—both global and more localized—forms of modernity, civility could no longer be just the outcome of a civilizing process but became dependent on the West's colonial construction of itself (its hegemony) through a leap out of its purported 'metropolitan' cultural identity into the depths of its colonial Other. Far from us, then, to wish to construct civility as the unproblematically authentic (and thus genuinely universal) core of civil society. To paraphrase Gellner, the West's encounter with the long-term civilizing process of the Islamic ecumene created the delusion of a new, potentially global, cohesive Western *umma*.

Folding Civil Society into a Transversal Notion of Civility

In order to be able to look beyond the delusional dimension of civil society and into the sociological underpinnings of civility, we need to factor in both the dislocating trajectory and the contestation of the West's increasingly global hegemony that was construed, particularly in the heydays of colonialism, as a 'civilizing mission.' Yet while process trumps origin, one should be aware that the modern Western genealogy of civility is in the first instance the outcome of specific developments within North-Western Europe. It coincides with the basically simultaneous, early modern, rise of the European Westphalian state and of capitalist enterprise. While the Westphalian system of modern sovereign states has a certain primacy in kicking off the historical process, we have seen how—particularly with the formation of commercial and industrial societies, specifically in Scotland and England— reflections on the idea of what it meant to be civil sharply transcended the earlier, classic emphasis on natural law and ideas of good government and focused on the challenges of a new world of capitalist enterprise. It is important to keep in mind that such reflections occurred from within locations belonging to the fastest developing parts of Europe that were increasingly committed to ever widening colonial ventures. It might have been the unprecedented pace of transformations, and the attention paid to the role of entrepreneurial characters, that created a reductionist view of the civil dimension of the social bond as centered on individual agency. The rather unrealistic idea of the autonomy of trust and the attached moral sense was particularly reductionist, as if only responding to the push of interests and the pull of affections determining the prism of an enterprising self.

The Scottish idea of civil society, while keeping a tenuous symbolic continuity with the classic *societas civilis* of Aristotle, Cicero, and the Stoics, embraced a society that is civil and peaceful first of all because the institutionalization and internalization of the law of contract ensures a high degree of predictability of social relations. This reductive focus neglected the more unpredictable and unregulated mechanisms of construction of the social bond entailing protest and crowd behavior (the 'mob' as the antithesis of legal, contract-based action). This higher complexity of collective action was highlighted by the early 19th-century French thinker Alexis de Tocqueville (1805–1859). His attention not by chance went beyond the societies of North-Western Europe and was attracted by emerging, burgeoning non-European societies like those of the USA and Russia. This shift of attention reflected the need to look beyond those mechanisms of social integration that are framed within settled territorial polities (like those of old Europe) and which revealed an increasingly well-delineated, functional division of tasks between bureaucracies, enterprises, and associations. Additionally, Tocqueville paid attention to France's colonial occupation of

Algeria, which represented a watershed in the externally expansive and innerly integrative capacity of European colonial modernity, supported by the framing of a European civilizing mission (de Tocqueville 2001). Civility starts then to appear as integral to a web of colonial, imperial, and global relations that cannot be reduced to enterprise. Its genealogy cuts across all conventional inner and outer borders of Europe or the West but also complicates conventional wisdom (including the one reflected by the Scottish moralists) on the relation between tradition and modernity. Not least, the genealogy encompasses, in conflicted and hardly linear ways, the plural yet also fractured heritage of the Islamic ecumene, via the colonial process that put an end to the previous, long-term centrality of Islam in the Afro-Eurasian civilizational realm.

Tocqueville's integrative shift was not a particularly subversive move but had the merit of highlighting the complexity of the nexus between pre-colonial and colonial practices and notions of civility. It is hardly contested that the conceptual origins of the ideas of a civic realm of interaction and subjectivity-formation can be traced back to classical Greece, specifically to the experience of Athens. They reflect a collective dynamics of cohesion, contention, and governance that cannot be entirely captured by the modern liberal notion of civil society. The classic idea, and the related practices, were integral to the reflections and systematizations of philosophers like Plato and Aristotle. Yet these traditions influenced a particularly thriving knowledge field within Islamic civilization (not restricted to philosophy) which in turn affected processes of state formation within the Islamic ecumene in the early modern era (see Chapter 5). By retrieving this longer trajectory, one can embrace a more diversified fabric of reflections on civility which cuts across what became the colonial divide between the West and the Muslim-majority world, precedes the packaging of the modern Western idea of civil society, and has haunted the latter like a shadow in the course of the West's run-up to colonial hegemony and the subsequent process of decolonization.

As a result of such complex processes, civility is located not at the peak of a linear and mono-dimensional development transcending traditional social arrangements and roles but rather delimits a gray zone where the social gravity of familiarity and consanguinity ("the tyranny of cousins" according to Gellner) is pulled into new forms of cooperation. Accordingly, *ego*'s mirroring in the perception and consideration of *alter*—often (though not necessarily) through the mediation of a big Other represented by a transcendent God—has the capacity to dilute (or at least bracket out) the weight of both modern class cleavages and traditional status inequalities. Civility is then neither anchored within traditional modes nor quintessentially modern; it is the outcome of complex and often contradictory civilizing processes, involving both tension and conflict and the intermittent downplaying of inequalities and differences for the sake of the coordination of social action. Since the following chapters will distill civility and its trajectory within the Islamic ecumene out of a complex and entangled heritage, it would be far-fetched to postulate that civility possesses an intrinsically religious or moral kernel, or, alternately, an outright secular engine in the form of fully secularized civic morals, e.g. as in a Durkheimian view of organic solidarity. The formulas of civility should be more soberly identified in a mode of managing *ego*'s relations to *alter* with a modicum of recourse to symbolic and material violence and by implementing in its stead a connective modus between interactants. This modus cannot be reduced to a mild sentiment of sympathy. It reflects a type of connectedness that can only hold if based on some degree of shared social knowledge of the needs and trustworthiness of the members of a group. No doubt, within a wide variety of forms of civility supported by solidarity, some might be potentially conducive to major upheavals, whereby the religious heritage and articulation of modes of connectedness can certainly play a role. Yet as adumbrated by civilizational analysis (see Introduction), it is not religion or tradition per se (or, as it were, fundamentalism) at work in such cases. The inherent fragility of civic patterns can be rather subject to challenges when the unsettling of the ideals of fairness on a large scale tips the balance toward a radical reinterpretation of religiously grounded obligations and related ideas of justice.

What we need is to reset the stage and so relativize the prestige of the peculiarly Western dream of civil society. While acknowledging that in spite of a certain erosion of appeal, especially since 9/11, civil society still represents a major banner of Western conceptual and civilizational hegemony, civility could be well on its way to be able to supplant it in defining the grammar of a social idiom suitable for recognizing not just the needs, capabilities, and trustworthiness of actors but also and especially the alchemy of their conflicts and cooperations. This grammar can also provide the coordinates for a cooperative enterprise on behalf of the 'common good.' This is a rather traditional concept that is perhaps not by chance being revived on the contemporary stage, in parallel with the loss of prestige of civil society and alongside the increasingly global struggles for the safeguarding of the 'commons' of humankind. These are the ensemble of all resources and wealth (not just natural but also cultural, particularly with regard to knowledge acquisition and distribution) that should not be held privately. It is interesting that these struggles are also leading to a redefinition of the traditional notion of the 'commoners' (*al-'amma* in Islamic parlance: see Chapter 3): no longer to designate a member of the non-elite (i.e. neither noble nor notable), but whoever has a right on the commons. It is also important to clarify that the commons can include, but should not be limited to, the 'public goods', which are studied and defined by a variety of disciplines concerned with public policies.

Yet again, it would be risky to draw too sharp a line between traditional and modern views of the commons and commoners, and of their relations to changing patterns of civility. This can be shown by the historic Islamic case covered by the flexible institutional matrix represented by the pious/charitable foundation, the *waqf* (see Chapters 2 and 3). While it would be tempting to say that modern notions of the commons and of civility specifically revolve around the concept of rights, it could be argued that the case of the *waqf* shows that this concept was always at work. It would show that the modern turn was rather characterized by singling out from traditional injunctions of doing good to others an idea of functional, governmental charity. This has been finalized to address the (also modern) category of the (especially urban) poor, an idea that could then be extended to whichever 'target group' is in question. This approach to charity is much more disciplinary—in the above-mentioned Benthamian and Foucaultian sense—than it is oriented to rights, which actually tend to be suspended within modern disciplinary regimes (see Chapter 6). It would be interesting to verify whether the worldwide adoption of a technical vocabulary (rather than a grammar) of rights by certified international NGOs has fed into the genuinely modern, disciplinary approach to charity.

If we revisit the debates and investigations conducted since the 1990s on the empowerment and activism of civic groups and associations—including a vast range of case studies concerning Muslim-majority societies and Muslim communities with minority status—we see that there is often—explicitly or implicitly—something more at work than the liberal idea of civil society inherited from the commercial and industrial revolutions and the Enlightenment. Crucial are the processes through which ties of interest, affection, and solidarity reflect and renew the civic patterns of reciprocity and the quest for dignity inherent in traditional arrangements and institutions. This is the case irrespective of whether such traditional arrangements subsist intact (a rare case) or (most often) have been subject to disruption or reconstruction through the global push of the Western 'civilizing mission' and hegemony, which have also manifested a global impact through the basically universal adoption of civil codes.

In the Islamic case the Sufi brotherhood (*tariqa*) is an important traditional matrix of the associational bond that facilitates cooperation and a channel for its implementation via the acquisition of knowledge, spiritual elevation, and cohesive social networking. We will start examining the *tariqa* as a meta-institutional matrix in historical and comparative perspectives from the next chapter onward. In the Introduction we suggested how the meta-institutional foundation of the Islamic process of institution-building, as well as of the articulation of flexible ways to formalize the underlying social bond, primarily relies on the textual corpus of *hadith* (the transmitted and authenticated sayings and deeds of the prophet Muhammad: see Brown 2009). This was intended as an exemplary and normative narration inspiring both jurisprudence (and its main institutional infrastructure, namely the *waqf*) and the Sufi way, more than any compactly legal edifice mistakenly identified as a *shari'a*-centered body of law. A specific tradition of normative narrations and the complexly selective scholarly networks authenticating such narrations (Sentürk 2005) are what ultimately enacts and legitimizes, over several generations, a specific and highly malleable model of Islamic civility originating from the *hadith* corpus. While the process of formation of the matrix of brotherhood is mainly associated with Sufism and its organizational unit, the *tariqa*, it should not be reduced to it. We will also explore how the historic European counterpart to the Sufi *tariqa* shows elements of both similarity and difference (see Chapter 4). From the analysis it will be possible to derive not a scholastic comparison but a better understanding of the way Western and Islamic articulations of the knowledge–power equation relate to each other historically and not just in an abstract, rigged game of establishing norms and exceptions.

What comes to the fore here is precisely the crucial, further layer going one full step beyond the notion of civil society as the locus of sheer cooperation among self-interested individuals. This layer also transcends civil society's purported fundaments, identified with the type and level of trust that facilitates entering and implementing contracts between individuals or companies. It is the dimension of cooperative action whose bottom line is mutual help, but that is ultimately supported by culturally shared expectations of all consequences (including those potentially going beyond the individual life span) of one's behavior. This engine of civility does not need the mediation of the stimulus of self-recognition and aggrandizement, as theorized by Ferguson and Smith. The shared expectations underlying such ties of civility rather presuppose common narrations with a widely consensual normative impact, including salvational narratives. The consensus is provided by integrated networks where knowledge is produced. This means that networks count not just as the facilitators and beneficiaries of the mere sharing of interests but as the knowledge machines themselves that create and authorize the mechanism of sharing. It would be difficult to conceive of forms of civility that are produced outside such sociologically refined dynamics, which we can consider the hub of civilizing processes. Such longer-term matrices continue to represent a hard kernel of civility even when the later focus on the individual happens to be legitimized by modern transformations in state-led, law-inspired, and outwardly powerful disciplinary mechanisms of the type instantiated by Norbert Elias (Elias 2000 [1939; 1968]; 1983 [1969]).

Often wrapped in a web of formal rules of tact and manners, civility thus conceived reflects the realization that there is a more profound communicative substratum that facilitates cooperative social action and sociability, which is often as ethical as it responds to canons of beauty (see Ikegami 2005). Civility is accordingly network based, being often activated and maintained by a variety of individuals across ties of kin and neighborhood through an iterative, shared, or at least overlapping invocation of some higher goods (often but not necessarily warranted or exacted by a transcendent reference). What counts here is the working of a shared habitus that induces people to bracket out localized interest and pursue overlapping goals either by reference to a 'common good' or at least to discrete goods, which might be social and cooperative or more broadly cultural, or artistic. The resulting patterns of interaction do not merely serve the need of self-interested cooperation or secure an immediate, tangible gain to the interactants. This difference marks a crucial divergence from the civil society model. Of course this higher autonomy of the goods of civility does not prevent it from frequently serving the needs of commercial networks and markets, which depend on the solidity of interconnections and their careful maintenance by reference to those higher goods that are shared or overlapping.

This type of civility, grounded on classic models and traditional practices but also continually transcending and complexifying them, goes beyond not just ties of good neighborhood and codes of courtesy. It also transcends ideas of interest narrowly conceived on the basis of the modern idea of contract between individuals assumed to be in full control of their willed agency, and in this sense, technically free in contractual terms. On the other hand, as we will see in the specific case of the Islamic ecumene, civility does cover an idea of contract and underlying patterns of a rather systemic contractualism imbued with a common idiom of connectedness. The system and the idiom facilitate the search for joint interest and the summoning of a common good not in merely abstract terms, but based on recognized methods for pondering, valuing, and ordering the plurality of goods and intentions entering a given interaction. This type of civility, in the preliberal West as much as in precolonial Islam, is directly or indirectly tied to Aristotelian categories, while it does not eschew per se a contractual logic and an orientation to the market.

It is therefore important not to reduce civility so defined to the moral work of building virtuous dispositions. While ideas of discernment and recognition of the goods and attendant practices are an important engine of civility, civility is relevant sociologically also, if not especially, for its habitualized, outer dimension reflected in self-composure, modulated exposure, porousness to communication and understanding, and, as a cumulative result, its capacity to build connectedness. If this were not the case, we would get stuck in a dichotomy between a basically normal and normative, Aristotelian view of civility, on the one hand, and altered versions thereof— including modern liberal ones—merely reproducing a technical vocabulary of contract and rights, on the other. We should overcome the temptation of adopting such an alternate, Aristotelian Western-centrism and rather conceive of patterns of civility as intrinsically plural and prone to circulation, transgression, and metamorphosis.

There is no possibility of postulating a common, normal, and/or universal ethical basis to civility. Such an axiom would make civility sociologically implausible. Yet by recognizing such an impossibility, one should also acknowledge that within the longer and diverse trajectory of Islamic history it was not just more difficult, but less necessary, to build up a modern state exactly like the one that emerged in Westphalian Europe. This is the type of state that became the ultimate guarantor of the specifically liberal type of civility underlying the civil society model. This civility could only be implemented through holding a monopoly on violence as the ultimate way to guarantee a centralized enforcement of contracts. Undoubtedly in various societies and regions of North-Western Europe this modern liberal type of civility also relied on varying degrees of intervention of intermediate bodies, as stressed by Hegel's recalibration of the Scottish notion of civil society. Through this move, civil society retrieved a foundation within traditional patterns of civility.

Yet once the model of civil society was concretely forged (not least, in continental Europe, in the shape of codes of civil law throughout the 19th century) and further refined via the elaboration of a variety of theorists, a key difference between the modern, mainly liberal, West and the colonized rest, including the Islamic ecumene, happened to be inscribed in social theory. This is the modernity gap, as it were, according to which the wider West owned the source code of modernity and the rest could at best be on its receiving side, often by hacking into it as if from the margins of the new global civilization called modernity. This idea of an essential gap disguises the much more intricate, though certainly unequal, relations unfolding within the workings of an increasingly global civilizing process. Particularly in a postcolonial context, it became easier to elaborate non-Western responses to the implicit but powerful assertion of a civilizational gap. The responses to Western colonialism and imperialism by a vast array of non-Western reformers, intellectuals, and agitators revealed the diversity and complexity of civilization as an ongoing and largely unpredictable process and of civility as a set of mobile and often vulnerable patterns. It is probably true that the hypothesis of multiple modernities, briefly illustrated at the end of the Introduction and intended to include and almost coopt alternative, non-Western modernities, does not redeem the weight of the Western primogeniture over the modern world. The remedy to this shortcoming can be an emphasis on a dislocated global civility that is nurtured by partly converging, often conflicting, civilizing processes. This idea accounts for both the contestability of modern Western hegemony and the relative originality of non-Western responses and reconstructions.

This is the level of analysis where we can reintroduce the doublet of knowledge and power as the key variables leading up to civility, as preliminarily discussed in the Introduction. The triadic field of knowledge, power, and civility, which provides the main focus of this volume, replaces the slightly mystifying, almost idyllic vision of a civil society based on a moral sense merging affectionate sympathy with sober interest. Knowledge and power appear as the twin basic factors of the equation that produces a social and cultural force, namely civility, which covers simultaneously both the intersubjective nexus among agents and a mode of subjectivity and agency. The modern European Westphalian state effectively redefined politics as an autonomous sphere by occupying the center of the political realm. This has occurred both through the monopolistic exercise of real power and through the cultural orchestration of symbolic power. In this Westphalian context civil society needs to fit into the politics, or, to be more precise, the political publicness, of the modern state.

Civility is instead conceived in broader terms than within the historic cage of the modern Western Westphalian state. It delimits a relatively autonomous yet mostly inertial dimension of construction and maintenance of the social bond. This process can impinge in a variety of ways upon politics as the most specific field of power, embracing the contestation and adjudication of values and resources tied to the institutional and regulative machinery of the modern state. However, civility does not fit into the modern state as a hand in a glove. It is not caged in the Westphalian state as civil society is, but it is not isolated from it either. The extension of the Westphalian form of the state worldwide via Western colonialism did integrate the global civilizing process in the international, i.e. the interstate order originating from the peace of Westphalia, but not to the point of making the civilizing process fully subordinate to the Westphalian logic. Responses to this logic varied according to time, locale, and the civilizational resources available in each case. Surely we would need a deeper treatment of the question of the modern state as a unique integrator of the knowledge–power dynamics in order to profitably extend this historical and theoretical argument, but we need to postpone this deepening of the argument to a future volume on the sociology of Islam.

We should here remain focused on the overlapping, rather transcultural, conceptualization of civility as often promoted by alternate views to the mainstream hegemonic theorization of civil society that took form within the core of the West itself, in a tight symbiosis with its commercial and industrial revolutions and global colonial expansion. Such alternate views might resonate particularly well with non-Western, and, as we will see, specifically Islamic, conceptions and practices. The contestation of the hegemony of one-sided, overly streamlined notions of civil society, which are quite neatly aligned with Western-centered modern state formation and capitalist development, basically overlapped with the latest phase of Western colonial domination. In this sense, Islamic critiques of civil society and Islamic reconstructions of civility are not instances of an anti-Western Islamic exceptionalism. They rather reflect the combination of civilizational originality with the postcolonial predicament of contemporary Muslim-majority societies, which often encourages a critique of Western Eurocentrism. Yet it is also important to consider that this critique has been directly or, more often, indirectly, influenced by earlier Western voices not aligned with the hegemonic trajectory of first Anglo-Scottish and later Anglo-American articulations of civility.

We see in the process a conceptual bifurcation between a notion of civility rather functional to bourgeois society (in the guise of 'civil society') and a more connective notion, which can better reflect other types of social arrangements or hegemonies. This latter conceptualization is never the outcome of a deterministic reaction to Western hegemonic experiences but has been largely stimulated by self-critical reflections, within the West itself, on one-sided (and often ideologically self-congratulatory) views of Western modernity. We should therefore recognize that there is no single uncontested idea of civility, not even in the hegemonic trajectory of the modern West. Civility is not just continually subject to variations, contestations, and new entanglements but also circumscribes, by reflex, a global arena of, as it were, cultural wars. It is nonetheless possible and even necessary to distinguish between a more genuinely sociological dimension of civility constituted by patterns of habitualization of social behavior and the cultural discourse that originates from reflecting on the importance of such processes. This latter dimension of reflection is subject to frequent oscillations between holding onto a claim of absolute originality of specific (and mostly Western) experiences and the recognition of inevitable patterns of mutual dependence among various experiences, both between the West and the non-West and within the West itself. Clearly the sociological reconstruction of the concept of civility benefits from the discourse which, by emphasizing the non-normativity of powerful Western models and the diversity of historic patterns of civility, also stimulates investigations into how such diverse patterns have been shaped in history and are being shaped in the present.

One early, major instance of alternate Western views of civility can be identified in the social thought of the early 18th-century Neapolitan thinker Giambattista Vico (1688–1744). Vico's work roughly coincided with the beginnings of the Scottish Enlightenment, but was directly or indirectly influential on many thinkers who wrestled with civil society well into the 20th century, the most famous of them probably being Antonio Gramsci (1891–1937). Particularly in his *magnum opus*, entitled *The New Science* (Vico 1999 [1744]), Vico produced a lucid analysis of how civility copes with modern power constellations without mystifying its traditional underpinnings often associated with the weight of religious institutions. Even if he could not directly engage with the slightly later Scottish notion of civil society and even if he articulated civility as an attribute more than as a noun (and therefore as an autonomous social force), his acerb theorizing on civility provides unique insights into the process-like character of the force at stake, particularly in its self-transformative potential. Rather than simply reproducing a dichotomy between a traditional model based on virtue and a modern one based on a moral sense (MacIntyre 1984 [1981]); 1988), Vico delineates a continuous process of transformation that approximates a civilizing process determined by complex sociological much more than by sheer ethical factors.

The merit of Vico's argument on civility ultimately consists in how it spelt out much more transparently than those of his Scottish counterparts how the reshaping of the civic realm is a process through which the ethos of the premodern, 'heroic' ages is diluted into the more relaxed, civic mores of the members of an increasingly complex society. According to Vico, the civilizing process, far from marking a linear evolution, is subject to depletion and exhaustion through cyclical, spiral motions (Stark 1976). Centuries before other authors, like Michael Walzer, articulated a similar view (see Volpi 2011), Vico clearly showed the intrinsically 'post-heroic' character of modern civility. In this sense, the lopsided view of the moral sense as articulated by the Scottish Enlightenment can be more sharply seen not as an essential, atemporal cement of the social bond but as the outcome of an increasing relaxation of heroic virtues: a depotentiation of the social bond once supported by a shared, virtuous orientation to the common good. Going one step further, and adopting a somewhat Nietzschean reading of Vico's view of civil virtues as a codified emasculation of heroic virtues, one could even hypothesize that Aristotelian ethical references to a hierarchy of goods and to the highest, common good were themselves early symptoms of civilizational impoverishment and relaxation of mores. The axial Aristotle neutralizes the preaxial Homer, who is the main reference of Vico on the matter. The pursuit of heroic, preaxial codes of honor cannot afford ordering and ranking goods and their matching virtues once for all in a pragmatic and almost calculative way. Nonetheless, the acceleration and unpredictability of civilizing processes and cycles are to a large extent favored by the ethical and cognitive prestige acquired by this Aristotelian scheme both within the West and in the Islamic ecumene. This process is also signaled by the fact that, from the Scottish Enlightenment onward, as we have argued, liberal conceptions of civility fall back on Aristotelian ethical grammars whenever they meet obstacles or reach stalemates.

Vico's view was also reliant on a deeper anthropological awareness of the coordinates of the social bond and its developmental potential, including the symbolic underpinnings of diffuse authority, which not even the densely commercial, Scottish type of civil society could completely dispense with. In this sense, he also showed that patriarchal authority, what Gellner called "the tyranny of cousins," is diluted but not necessarily erased by modern liberal civility (Salvatore 2007: 186–209). Particularly, Vico tackled head-on an issue that is often kept latent in discussions of the conceptual cluster coagulating into civility: the question of how, at the conclusion of the transition from heroic to civil modes of taming violence, the associational bond based on collective violence-control and individual self-restraint is institutionalized. Only by addressing this issue was he able to suggest how institutionalization on a large scale, like the one corresponding to the rise of modern states, i.e. nation-states (and which in Weberian parlance amounts to a routinization of charisma: see Chapter 2), is also premised on a depletion of the ethical substance of Aristotelian civility.

This Vichian view raises questions that are unsolvable through the Anglo-Scottish paradigm of civility: Is 'contract' per se enough of a condition to operate such a 'prosaic' transition from heroic to civil modes of social interaction? Are there cultural variables and communicative factors that under normal conditions determine the key threshold of the transition? Could such factors, in times of crisis, even surrogate the institutional ties themselves? Due to his contribution in helping us formulate such crucial questions, Vico acquires a unique importance as representing the alternate modern (yet Western) theorist of a type of civility not intimately married to the disciplinary power of the modern Westphalian state-society complex and to its normatively liberal articulations. This is why I am electing Vico as the best possible guide to help us transition from Western-bound to Islamic articulations of civility, to which the rest of this book is dedicated.

References

Arendt, Hannah. 1958. *The Human Condition*. Chicago: University of Chicago Press.

Brown, Jonathan A.C. 2009. *Hadith: Muhammad's Legacy in the Medieval and Modern World*. London: Oneworld.

Burchell, Graham. 1991. "Peculiar Interests: Civil Society and Governing 'the System of Natural Liberty'." In *The Foucault Effect: Studies in Governmentality*, edited by Graham Burchell, Colin Gordon, and Peter Miller, 119–50. Chicago: University of Chicago Press.

Challand, Benoit. 2011. "The Counter Power of Civil Society and the Emergence of a New Political Imaginary in the Arab World." *Constellations. An International Journal of Critical and Democratic Theory*, 18/3: 271–83.

Cohen, Jean and Andrew Arato. 1992. *Civil Society and Political Theory*. Cambridge, MA: MIT Press.

Elias, Norbert. 1983 [1969]. *The Court Society*, translated by Edmund Jephcott. Oxford: Blackwell.

Elias, Norbert. 2000 [1939; 1968]. *The Civilizing Process*. Oxford: Blackwell.

Foucault, Michel. 1979. *'Civil Society' and 'Interest.'* Lecture, Collège de France, April 4 (English transcript).

Foucault, Michel. 1991. "Governmentality." In *The Foucault Effect: Studies in Governmentality*, edited by Graham Burchell, Colin Gordon, and Peter Miller, 87–104. Chicago: University of Chicago Press.

Gellner, Ernest. 1995. "The Importance of Being Modular." In *Civil Society: Theory, History, Comparison*, edited by John Hall, 32–55. Boston: Polity Press.

Gervasio, Gennaro. 2014. "When Informal Powers Surface. Civic Activism and the 2011 'Egyptian Revolution.'" In *Informal Power in the Greater Middle East: Hidden Geographies*, edited by Luca Anceschi, Gennaro Gervasio, and Andrea Teti, 55–70. London: Routledge.

Hefner, Robert W. 2000. *Civil Islam: Muslims and Democratization in Indonesia*. Princeton, NJ: Princeton University Press.

Ikegami, Eiko. 2005. *Bonds of Civility: Aesthetic Networks and the Political Origins of Japanese Culture*. Cambridge: Cambridge University Press.

MacIntyre, Alasdair. 1984 [1981]. *After Virtue: A Study in Moral Theory*. Notre Dame, IN: University of Notre Dame Press.

MacIntyre, Alasdair. 1988. *Whose Justice? Which Rationality?* London: Duckworth.

Mardin, Şerif. 1995. "Civil Society and Islam." In *Civil Society: Theory, History, Comparison*, edited by John Hall, 278–300. Boston: Polity Press.

Norton, Augustus Richard, ed. 1995. "Introduction." In *Civil Society in the Middle East*, I, edited by Augustus Richard Norton. Leiden: Brill.

Salvatore, Armando. 2007. *The Public Sphere: Liberal Modernity, Catholicism, and Islam*. New York: Palgrave Macmillan.

Salvatore, Armando. 2011. "Civility: Between Disciplined Interaction and Local/Translocal Connectedness." *Third World Quarterly*, 32/5: 807–25.

Santoro, Emilio. 2003 [1999]. *Autonomy, Freedom and Rights: A Critique of Liberal Subjectivity*. Dordrecht: Kluwer.

Seligman, Adam B. 1992. *The Idea of Civil Society*. New York: The Free Press.

Seligman, Adam B. 2002. "Civil Society as Idea and Ideal." In *Alternative Conceptions of Civil Society*, edited by Simone Chambers and Will Kymlicka, 13–33. Princeton, NJ: Princeton University Press.

Şentürk, Recep. 2005. *Narrative Social Structure: Anatomy of the Hadith Transmission Network*, 610–1505. Stanford, CA: Stanford University Press.

Silver, Allan. 1997. "Two Different Sorts of Commerce: Friendship and Strangership in Civil Society." In *Public and Private in Thought and Practice*, edited by Jeff Weintraub and Krishan Kumar, 43–76. Chicago: University of Chicago Press.

Smith, Adam. 1853 [1759]. *The Theory of Moral Sentiments*. London: Henry G. Bohn.

Stark, Werner. 1976. "The Theoretical and Practical Relevance of Vico's Sociology for Today." *Social Research*, 43: 815–25.

Tocqueville, Alexis de. 2001. *Writings on Empire and Slavery*, edited and translated by Jennifer Pitts. Baltimore and London: The Johns Hopkins University Press.

Turner, Bryan S. 1984. "Orientalism and the Problem of Civil Society in Islam." In *Orientalism, Islam and Islamists*, edited by Asaf Hussain, Robert Olson, and Jamil Qureshi, 23–42. Brattelboro, VT: Amana Books.

Vico, Giambattista. 1999 [1744]. *New Science: Principles of the New Science Concerning the Common Nature of the Nations*, 3rd ed., translated by David Marsh. London: Penguin.

Volpi, Frederick. 2011. "Framing Civility in the Middle East: Alternative Perspectives on the State and Civil Society." *Third World Quarterly*, 32/5: 827–43.

2

Brotherhood as a Matrix of Civility
The Islamic Ecumene and Beyond

Between Networking, 'Charisma,' and Social Autonomy: The Contours of 'Spiritual' Brotherhoods

From the viewpoint of the conventional self-understanding of European modernity, especially in the way it is reflected upon by sociologists, talking about Islamic articulations of civility might sound as almost an oxymoron. The reasons why Islam has often represented a civilizational model neatly contrasting with the European historical trajectory of transformation of religion and its relations to societal and political power cannot be reduced to cultural asymmetries or to a divergence of values and sensibilities. It cannot be explained either by an alleged deficit of Islamic traditions to turn the tension inherent in the God–man relation into a socially fruitful and polit-ically effective differentiation of societal spheres. The Western tendency to single out Islam as a convenient Other within easy grasp depends rather, and paradoxically, on the historic closeness and density of the West's interaction and competition with the Islamic ecumene and its political centers, more than on any purported cultural distance and civilizational alterity.

The Western derogatory view and the ensuing diminishment of Islam's dynamism and complexity with regard to the relations among religion and society as well as religion and politics have often been dubbed as manifestations of a cultural and cognitive 'essentialism.' Its roots have been situated within the power-knowledge coordinates of what has been defined (rather wholesale), in the wake of Edward Said's powerful, critical intervention (Said 1978), as the academic discourse of Western Orien-talism. It is within the normative perimeter of this discourse that the

The Sociology of Islam: Knowledge, Power and Civility, First Edition. Armando Salvatore.
© 2016 John Wiley & Sons, Ltd. Published 2016 by John Wiley & Sons, Ltd.

purported absence of civil society in the Muslim-majority world (Turner 1984: 20–31) has strengthened by reflex the West's self-understanding as the unique repository of civility. Further, what Weber called the 'Occident' has legitimized its uniqueness—as well as its self-positioning at the cusp of human development—by propagating a special civilizational mission (often coupled with concrete, i.e. confessionally oriented, religious missions). This sense of mission not surprisingly originated in the presumption of holding the power to bring civility to the entire world, including the area of once flourishing but, by colonial times, allegedly decayed civilizations.

We have seen in the Introduction that the sociology of religion of European origin is intimately connected with the sociology of modernity and modern societies. Modernity, in turn, has been primarily understood as a distinctive product of European civilization. Ergo, from the perspective of the West the trajectory of European Christianity must be representative of a civilizational culmination: as stated by Marcel Gauchet (1997 [1985]), in its European venture Christianity becomes the religion of exit from all religions. From this Western perspective, Islam constituted an ensemble of social and cultural potentialities that were never adequate to European benchmarks of self-transformation, and so never became truly modern. Precisely by being perceived as such, Islam has posed a permanent challenge to European modernity.

This challenge unfolded through the development of what across several epochs (indeed, well into the modern era) has been perceived in Europe as a lively and powerful counter-model of civilizational flowering and expansion. This civilizational tension was made even more effective through the original, non-replicable ways through which the Islamic ecumene was able to extend its influence across Afro-Eurasia through the building of overlapping patterns of translocal connectedness. Yet as much as it affirms a teleology of divergent civilizational trajectories and underplays civilizational interaction, Western essentialism is very much the product of the intense exchange with Islam/Islamdom and of the resulting, often tense, and at times traumatic transcivilizational entanglements. This essentialism is therefore the outcome of a climax of combined and in principle contrasting sentiments: the Western fear of being overwhelmed by the expanding Islamic ecumene and the trust to be able to become ever more superior to it and to reverse and extinguish the Islamic 'tide.' This was long perceived as a threat incarnated in the civilization against which European benchmarks of civilizational power were built and nourished. In the course of history the Islamic trajectory has indeed become ever more enmeshed with the fate of the emerging European, hegemonic model of modernity. In this sense, and in spite of the resilience of the self-limiting essentialism of a European perspective, Islam should be realistically seen as both internal and external to the rise of European modernity and therefore as not entirely innocent of the former's essentialism.

This is why essentialism should be considered as the cognitive outcome of a Western overreaction to dense vicinity and tense interaction with Islam, more than as an outright bias or a facile instrument of otherization turned against an inscrutable and distant rival (Salvatore 1997). If we relate essentialism, as Edward Said (1978) famously did, to the knowledge–power equation, one should take the knowledge variable seriously in its own right and, most importantly, relate it explicitly to the founding paradigms of sociology (Stauth 1993; Salvatore 1997). Nonetheless, it cannot be denied that essentialism, by cognitively privileging airtight formations (civilizations, nations, municipalities), diminishes the capacity of Western social sciences to grasp patterns of translocal connectedness. These are precisely the circulatory dynamics that ensured the large socio-political success of Islam going into the Middle Periods and after. Some of these patterns seem to resurface piecemeal in the contemporary world, though in often lopsided forms, under the ambivalent banner of Islamic transnationalism that will deserve a separate, dedicated analysis in a future volume.

Hodgson was not the first nor has he been the last among the historians of Islam who particularly emphasized the seminal role that Sufi movements played especially in the Middle Periods, during the centuries that preceded the advent of the modern era. These groups, mostly organized in the form of large, translocally operating brotherhoods, played a particularly crucial role in articulating Islam's capacity to weave dense long-distance ties and turn them into a versatile source of civility. The state authority prevailing within the Islamic ecumene prior to the Middle Periods was characterized by an oscillation between convenient configurations of the charisma of succession to the prophet Muhammad (mainly via the institution of the Caliphate) and the more autonomous charisma of statesmanship and cultured administration. However, during the entire Middle Periods the Islamic ecumene relied on largely self-steered local, regional, and long-distance networks. This type of rather horizontal cohesion overtook top-down regulations promulgated by rulers and administrators seeking to impose a stable governance over populations and territories.

The earlier state culture had as its carriers the pre-Islamic Persianate courtiers and literati and the agrarian aristocracies connected to them. It was later absorbed by different types of Islamicate courts of suzerain entities responding to the central caliphal authority. Through the crisis of the caliphal model in the 10th century (and the end of the period that Hodgson called the "High Caliphate"), the increased florescence of translocal connectedness that prevailed during the Middle Periods exalted the egalitarian dimension that Islam had inherited from the broader, earlier Irano-Semitic civilizational developments going back to the Axial Age. Such developments had traditionally favored a widespread suspicion, if not hostility, toward court culture, particularly among urban craftsmen and traders. The demise of the cohesive power of the Caliphate around the middle of the 10th century weakened politically centralized governments and often ignited transformations characterized by potential or actual anarchy or self-rule. This relative anarchy not surprisingly favored both collective self-organization and individual social mobility. Often, if not always, the involved populations seemed willing to pay the price of a diffuse sense of longer-term precariousness in order to keep those advantages. As remarked by Hodgson, "Islam became a badge, not of a ruling class, but of a cosmopolitan, urban oriented mass; it became a symbol of the newly intensified social mobility" (Hodgson 1974, I: 305). In this chapter I will provide examples of such patterns particularly through the matrix of the brotherhood, though they were also nourished by other mildly institutionalized mechanisms of governance of the social bond which we will explore in subsequent chapters.

Clearly, the balance sheet was mixed. In this sense, it is important to observe that Hodgson never intended to celebrate the Middle Periods (and even less its last phase that he called the Later Middle Period, which followed the Mongol conquests) as a stable or ideal model of governance transcending the tyrannical and exploitative dimension of state authority. This instability was the obverse of Islam's expansive capacity and surely represented a heightened vulnerability, which became most acute during the Mongol expansion that sealed the Earlier Middle Period. Hodgson rather argued that some of the most typically Islamic articulations, in institutional terms, of the knowledge–power equation matured and prospered, and not by chance, during the Middle Periods. Undoubtedly he saw these forms as being close to the aspirations to social autonomy of particularly the (more or less) pious urban strata. It is however important to locate patterns of piety, as I will try to do, in their proper socio-political context. One recurrent fallacy put forward by contemporary sociologists is to read such patterns against the background of modern Western forms of pietism and puritanism (or, correspondingly, of Islamic Wahhabism: see Chapter 5) and attendant notions of 'morality' (Zubaida 1995). Following Hodgson, piety should rather be read almost in the opposite way, namely for its contribution to building wider, not strictly religious, patterns of the social bond: i.e. for its contributions to Islamdom as a social nexus.

This investment of autonomy into the social bond (be it driven by forms of piety or by transgressive, 'heterodox' teachings and practices) was possible since the looming anarchy did not necessarily translate into a contagious anomy. The dynamics rather led to a strengthening of the consensual basis of common norms. The result of this shift toward translocal, quite horizontal governance in the postcaliphal era was that the expansion of Islam solidified the predictability of transactions and patterns of mutuality over long distances. This development obviated the need for enduring centralized state authorities who rather tended to curb and overtax the socio-economic process, as it was carried by largely autonomous social forces. This is how the Islamic ecumene was able to thrive not just in spite of, but largely thanks to, the virtual absence of stable patterns of governance, particularly if we understand governance (as we often, anachronistically do) in the sense acquired by the term in modern Western Europe, notably under Leviathan's shadow.

As we earlier saw, the socio-political order within modern Western formations depended on an ultimate provider and exclusive warrant of societal convergences of interest and cohesive patterns of solidarity in the form of a sovereign and fully legitimized state. From this perspective, the Islamic socio-political order during the Middle Periods, even before the Mongol conquests, might appear as inevitably threatening societal flourishing and collective welfare (Bamyeh 2000: 39–40). Yet almost the opposite was true, based on Hodgson's analysis. Not only did Islam expand thrice, territorially, during the Middle Periods, but the epoch also witnessed the zenith of the social power of the *'ulama'* and of their autonomous and flexible institutions of learning and adjudication. The multiple social nexus of the *'ulama'* provided a largely coherent grammar and practical coordination to intricate, yet quite well-ordered, social arrangements. What we call society was kept together by an articulate yet shared Islamic idiom that included both a moral and legal dimension. Both dimensions pivoted upon Muhammad's exemplary conduct (*sunna*) teased out of the previously mentioned *hadith* corpus, and which regulated individual life as well as social transactions. But Hodgson importantly stressed that the Middle Periods were also, most typically, the era when Sufi brotherhoods unfolded their full potential, both organizationally and charismatically.

Several Western scholars have attempted since the 19th century to reduce Sufism to an odd component within Islam, often even surmising, without providing cumulative evidence, that it originated from extra-Islamic sources (Masuzawa 2005: 197–206). Yet a quite solid scholarly consensus now maintains that Sufism's remote roots are as old as the translation of Muhammad's message into pious practice by his companions. This occurred particularly on the basis of the Qur'anic notion of faithful trust in God (*tawakkul*) and of love for the Creator. This practice did not directly conflict with the regulation mechanisms of the proto-state in Medina, nourished by the charisma of Muhammad, but neither was such a pious practice perfectly absorbed into them. Yet, this model of piety-based community life contributed to form the early visions of the Islamic *umma* and facilitated successive adaptations of the socio-political coordinates of the Islamic ecumene (Abun-Nasr 2007).

The gradually emerging Sufi piety first thrived during Hodgson's High Caliphate (stretching up to the middle of the 10th century). It manifested the widespread sentiment that the process of canonization of the law led by the jurists over several generations—also via the institutionalization and drastic consolidation of the number of their schools—reflected a specifically practical dimension of Islam, as inherent in jurisprudence (*fiqh*). This discipline was based on a notion of human reason that can be best explained by reference to the classic, axial, Hellenic virtue of *phronesis*, consisting in finding the best means to a given end or *telos* (Salvatore 2007). The fact that *fiqh* reflects a notion of practical rationality before feeding into the production of legal rulings is quite crucial. It illustrates that Islamic jurisprudence developed as a much more sophisticated field than just as the institutional machine for the production of rulings covering the outward dimension of cult and transactions.

Fiqh embraced the art of governing common practice by the social actors themselves and so instituted a crucial feature of social autonomy. It was built on a principle that we would define as subsidiarity. Accordingly, social actors invoke the knowledge and authority of jurists only to the extent that they are not able to find a rule in a given context, be it an issue of worship (e.g. concerning how to pray) or of transactions (e.g. on a matter of inheritance). Yet the art of practice enshrined in *fiqh* was not exhaustive of the complexities entailed by the pursuit of a righteous individual life conduct and of the enactment of harmonious social bonds. This is where the inner truth of Islam, the *haqiqa*, intervenes and finds a place that is far from just spiritual or 'mystical.' The search for the *haqiqa* innervated a parallel tradition of pious practice that needed to be kept as far as possible immune to the formalistic fixings and the pragmatist moorings within which jurisprudence, after having entered the precinct of specialists (the practitioners of *fiqh*, the *fuqaha'*), became inevitably entangled (Rahman 1979 [1966]: 130). Sufism affirmed itself as the ensemble of disciplines (and attendant organizational forms) facilitating this search for the *haqiqa*.

The first manifestations of a piety oriented to the inner truth, which we can identify with Sufism as we know it, crystallized between the end of the 8th and the beginning of the 10th centuries, most notably in Abbasid Baghdad. Here several strands of pietism came to represent a quite unitary and identifiable movement that happened to be labeled *sufiyya*, and later *tasawwuf*. To be sought within Sufism was particularly the inner meaning of the Qur'an and the *sunna* (Karamustafa 2007: 1–7). Yet a variety of styles of piety soon appeared to characterize Sufism during this formative phase, when renunciation (*zuhd*) played an important role, but not necessarily an overwhelming one. It would be nonetheless a misrepresentation to drastically separate Sufi practices from the normativity propagated by jurists and theologians and normally associated with the notion of *shari'a*. Based on a Qur'anic keyword meaning the "straight path," the *shari'a* was first elaborated by Muslim scholars as a philosophical and theological rather than as a strictly legal concept (W.C. Smith 1962).

Yet over time and by virtue of the force represented by the rising importance of Sufism as a discipline stressing the inner truth, the *shari'a*, as much as it was seen as the manifestation of divine Will (*shar'*), also came to represent the outer dimensions of the ethico-religious code of Islam. The *shari'a* happened to be identified with the more systematic dimension of Islamic normativity, the one that could be formulated in terms of legal norms which, in turn, would be liable—to a not yet exclusive extent—to be enforced. Apart from this technically legal dimension, the *shari'a* covered a comprehensive concept of norm, which included ritual and dietary rules, as well as rules about family, commerce, and social relations more in general. However, this normative idiom, reflecting basic values of humanity, justice, and equality, never became a code in the sense of a closed (and univocally 'searchable') text. It rather preserved an inherent, inner pluralism and contestability in the form of a cumulative tradition articulated in translocal schools and local, contextualized sets of practices variably drawing from mostly pre-Islamic customs.

This is why the understandings of *shari'a* and related practices have been historically dependent on the types of knowledge and the varieties of culture prevalent on a local scale, as well as on the degree of social contention and reconstruction that they authorized. The convergence between concretely practiced Islamic jurisprudence and the idea of *shari'a* was therefore a diversified, gradual, and (at least till the colonial era) never fully accomplished process. It is unlikely that a substantial degree of convergence of diverse views on what is *shari'a* occurred before the Earlier Middle Period. Only in modern, colonial contexts was the notion of *shari'a* subject to an intense process of reification and systematization, both discursive and legal (see Chapter 6; this theme should be ideally deepened in a future volume). Such modern attempts to systematize and implement *shari'a*, whether associated with 'liberal' and 'reformist' or with 'fundamentalist' and 'puritan' interpretations (all labels that, originating in Western history, should be taken with a pinch of salt), have been hardly able to extinguish its historic dynamism. Yet they certainly contributed to obfuscate the consciousness of this dynamism among a mass public, which in the colonial and postcolonial eras has been more prone to appreciate its newly rigidified contours (Salvatore 2004).

It is however important to recognize that the 'inward turn' promoted by Sufis around the notion of *haqiqa* as the inner match to *shari'a* was integral to the wider and longer-term process through which *shari'a* emerged as a key Islamic notion. Therefore Sufism should not be equated with an escape from the type of mainstream social normativity and cultural idiom which only gradually—and not quite linearly—happened to be covered by the conceptual and doctrinal umbrella of *shari'a*. Sufism rather contributed to *shari'a*'s formation and diversified appreciation. It did so mainly by supporting the ethical and spiritual kernel of a code of life conduct that became increasingly ingrained into the more public, rather externalized views of Islamic normativity. Therefore we should consider Sufism as a parallel but largely convergent and increasingly central Islamic tradition, which was never confined to a purely spiritual level or to a mere private sphere. Through its elastic yet formative relation to Islamic normativity, Sufism became a major—if not the principal—arrow of Islamic civility. Therefore it would be reductive to state that Sufism represented the biggest challenge to the hegemony of the jurists (*fuqaha'*). There were neither winners nor losers, for the simple reason that several jurists (including *qadis*/judges) were also Sufis and several Sufi masters were also practicing *fuqaha'*.

Nonetheless, it was only during the Middle Periods that Sufism entered the mainstream of Muslim practices in full. During this epoch the Sufi way became ubiquitous in the Islamic ecumene thanks to a fresh wave of diffusion and institutionalization of its semi-formal matrix of organization, the brotherhood (*tariqa*). It was in this period that the competition, yet also complementarity, between Sufism and jurisprudence helped to redefine the place of *shari'a* within the Sunni consensus. This dynamic relation between the two core components of Islamic traditions also highlighted the productive tension (and to some extent even mutual complicity) between the spiritual dimension of thought, on the one hand, and its practical and juridical implications, on the other. However, it would be a mistake to identify Islam's spiritual dimension entirely with Sufism and its normative aspect with the *shari'a*. The productive tension between the two dimensions was largely internal to both fields of practice and their respective institutional crystallizations.

The formula that legitimized the increasing role of Sufism not just as a key component of Islam but also as an institutional generator of the social nexus that we have dubbed, with Hodgson, Islamdom, was the opportunity provided to individual Muslims belonging to a variety of social layers and groups to embrace the *sunna* of the Prophet via an active membership in an organized brotherhood, the *tariqa*. At its core was a training under the guidance of a master, whose uninterrupted *silsila* (chain) of initiations and corresponding transmission of charisma usually went back to Muhammad himself. The end goal of the training was to gain access to the essential truth, the *haqiqa*. This inner truth could only be conquered through establishing a close relationship with the human being who is particularly close to God, the prophet Muhammad, and with the "friends" (*awliya'*) of God, the new Sufi saints.

During the Middle Periods *tariqa*-based Sufism flourished across vast regions of the Islamic ecumene well into South and later Southeast Asia. Here Sufism acted as the main vector of Islamization along with trade, thus magnifying a synergic trend already well at play within and in closer vicinity to the Irano-Semitic realm before the advent of Islam and during its early stages. No doubt institutionalized Sufism was often perceived as an alternate authority by the hierarchies that presided over the production and dissemination of normative and legal knowledge that was mainly based on college learning. These were the authorities and institutions that provided for the acquisition and transmission of *'ilm*. This term embraces the different branches of knowledge that were mainly though not exclusively centered on theology and jurisprudence and which prior to the Middle Periods were cultivated, learned, and taught largely within mosques but not under homogeneous curricula. This educational field underwent a gradual homogenization, was administered by the '*ulama*', and happened to be centered, quite in parallel with the rise of the *tariqa*, on the college or *madrasa*.

A largely constructive sense of competition between the *madrasa*-based '*ilm* and the *tariqa*-based *tasawwuf* was nurtured by the extent to which Sufism itself played a quite crucial role within the field of production and dissemination of socially implementable knowledge. This knowledge was authorized by the prestige of lineages of teachings associated with the Sufi masters. A crucial component of Sufi teachings and practices was the work on the practitioners' bodies and the emphasis laid on collective sessions. The prototypical case of collective bodily practice in Islam is the Friday prayer that gathers the faithful to a communal event, where the individual bodies, while being the specific loci of channeling prayer and pious intention, cohere into one collective body. However, Sufi practices introduced a greater variety of specifications and sophistications on this model by focusing on the practice of collective remembering (*dhikr*) of the Creator and His names. This type of practice required deploying a variety of bodily techniques, most prominently with regard to breathing, but often also chanting and dancing, from the most transgressive and ecstatic to the most sober and bent on bodily composure. In developing such practices Sufism invested into the core dimension of Islam called *ihsan*, meaning "doing what is beautiful," through transforming the basic act of surrendering (*islam*) to God into a correct modulation of the intention to act. This endeavor, presupposing intense cultivation, educates the faithful subject to tune her inner self into the harmonious beauty of the creation and the Creator (Murata and Chittick 1994: 265–317).

In this sense, Sufism cannot be reduced to a mere 'mystical path' as it has often been by Western Orientalists. Sufis appropriated and sedated the tension between the spiritual and the practical levels of faith commitments through the construction of suitable associational forms in the form of brotherhoods. Also via the type of practices just sketched, the Sufi *turuq* (plural of *tariqa*) accomplished a variety of psychological, social, and, particularly but not exclusively in urban contexts, civic functions. In this sense Sufis constituted the flipside of the authority of the jurists (the *fuqaha*'), to the extent that they worked to provide a permanent form of trust among brothers in faith that the juridical discourse and practice were not able to capture on their own. The only imbalance in the relationship was largely due to the higher formalization and public exposure of the authority and social function of the *fuqaha*'. Competition did not exclude a potentially large level of complementarity in the interaction between the two institutionalized traditions.

The Sufi capacities to build and project social power reached a peak in the crucial phase of the Middle Periods, during the 12th and 13th centuries, when the Sufi brotherhoods played a key role in Islam's global expansion across the Afro-Eurasian depths, into the Indian Subcontinent, Southeast Asia, and Sub-Saharan Africa. Their flexible and semi-formal model of internal organization and long-distance connectedness with fellow groups, along with their capacity to balance competition, cooperation, and hierarchy in their inner ranks as well as in their mutual relations, appeared particularly well suited to the characteristics of the epoch. Representing variations on a common theme of spiritually oriented practice, Sufi brotherhoods were able to reach out to a variety of constituencies, like traders, townspeople, peasants, and tribesmen, as well as to individuals belonging to diverse social classes, regions, and economic conditions.

Sufism also expressed new intellectual voices engaging in a fresh wave of reflection on the necessity to integrate various dimensions of Islam: juridical as well as philosophical, exoteric as well as esoteric. In many ways, the Sufis filled the legitimacy gap left by the collapse of caliphal author-ity through their construction of grids of relations that balanced vertical authority (the role of charismatic masters and living saints) with horizontal cohesiveness (the brotherhood pattern). The brotherhoods could expand over long distances through dense, translocally replicable webs of relations between masters and disciples. Their 'globalization' across the hemisphere proved more capillary and thus successful than the diffusion of the model of the *madrasa* (college), which enjoyed a golden age during the Earlier Middle Period within the Saljuq realm roughly corresponding to the Irano-Semitic core of Islamdom and was integrated into a larger "educational-charitable complex" in the Later Middle Period (Arjomand 1999). The translocal expansion of Sufi brotherhoods was particularly continuous and consistent and embraced vast regions during the entire Middle Periods. Yet it did not shield the brotherhoods from a high dependence on local patterns of political power and patronage, due to their lower degree of institutional autonomy if compared with the *madrasa* model of knowledge transmission (Arjomand 1998).

Sufi *turuq* epitomized this networking momentum and the underlying, inertial force of social self-organization well served by locally adapted *shari'a* practices. Their leaders and members mostly acted in ways that were particularly congenial to the constellations of social power of the Middle

Periods. The process helped create lasting patterns of group practice and intergroup connectedness which endured over time and can be still found in the contemporary world. This long-term momentum of the Sufi way comes close to representing the quintessentially social characteristics of the self-sustained expansiveness and resilience of patterns of largely self-enacted life conduct inspired by Islam's combination of moral idiom, spirituality, and sociability. On the one hand, Muslim traders were successful in imposing their control on the commercially strategic Silk Road by the Middle Periods and encouraged conversion to Islam among fellow urban-based businessmen they met on the road and who wished to share in the benefits of commercial partnerships beyond partaking a common moral idiom. On the other, Sufis were particularly effective in reaching out to remote, non-urban areas, most notably among nomads and pastoralists (Foltz 2010: 92–3). Thus in overall organizational terms, the Sufi activities impacted the socio-political configuration of forces in all three sectors, the urban, the nomadic and the rural. They therefore provided the most effective glue of intercivility. As we will see, the result was the prevention of an urban monopolization of civility of the kind that prevailed in other civilizational realms, most notably within Western Christendom.

Most crucially, Sufi lodges and shrines often constituted the nodes for long-distance networks, by simultaneously comprising the channels of communications and the loci of stability needed by travelers. They could thus help balance the precarious character of sultanic rule in the highly fragmented political environment of the Middle Periods. Sufi leaders often played the role of conciliators and umpires within civic disputes, while saints' shrines provided symbolic orientation and sacred steadiness to the life of Muslims exposed both to the vulnerability of the countryside and to the volatility of urban life (Fromherz 2010: 8). It was not uncommon for the houses of Sufi masters, often attached to shrines, to be considered as sanctuaries in their own right. At times they even provided extraterritorial sites for negotiations, arbitrations, and adjudications among conflicting interests of various kinds, and therefore safe havens from factional violence (Levtzion 2002: 110). It is also noteworthy that Sufi masters were particularly eager, unlike their *fuqaha'* counterparts, to set aside the use of scholastic Arabic to the advantage of the vernacular languages of the regions where they operated and traveled (such as Turkic languages, Hindustani, Javanese, and Malay). This readiness was of great help in promoting the rapid and capillary expansion of *tariqa* Sufism well beyond the Irano-Semitic civilizational core of Islam.

One consequence of this cumulative success was that ruling elites were sometimes suspicious of the Sufi orders because of their capacity for autonomous organization and for keeping connections with much wider spheres of communication and influence than the rulers themselves were able to entertain. However, and for exactly the same reasons, rulers often sought links with, and advice from, successful Sufi masters and reciprocated the support by funding their activities via pious endowments (*awqaf*, sing. *waqf*). Even when deprived of such ties of recognition and cooperation with political authorities, Sufis often wielded a degree of social power and prestige allowing them to act as bulwarks against the arbitrary rule of sultans and emirs and as potential sources of popular unrest (see Heck 2007). Yet the ideal situation consisted in mutually beneficial relations between rulers and Sufis, whereby charismatic Sufi leaders bestowed their blessing (*baraka*) upon the rulers, under the condition that they would rule justly over the masses and lend their patronage to Sufi lodges and complexes (Safi 2006: 128). *Baraka* was a scarce resource associated not just with good fortune but also with healing powers (Green 2012: 96). The making of saintliness itself became strictly associated with the display of 'wonders' inherent in the acquisition of concrete merits, which could often feed into the development of autonomous civic powers and even wealth. Omid Safi relates how a famous Sufi master of the Saljuq era, during the Earlier Middle Period, asserted that

> [a real saintly] man is he who sits and rises in the midst of people, eats and sleeps, conducts trade with people in the bazaar, and mixes with the people— and yet for one moment does not become neglectful of God in his heart.
>
> (Safi 2006: 127)

Beyond Sufism: The Unfolding of the Brotherhood

The most important associations that interacted and even overlapped with the Sufi brotherhoods were the craftsmen guilds (see Faroqhi 2009). They operated on the basis of customary law, which in turn found recognition in the *shari'a* (Arjomand 2004: 219). The famous Sufi master 'Umar al-Suhravardi (1145–1234) supported with two tracts the firm integration of civic associations, primarily of the professional guilds, within the galaxy of organized Sufism (Arjomand 2004: 227–8). Among the other social groups that were involved in the process, one can even count military or paramilitary organizations entering intense interactions with Sufi brotherhoods.

This was also the case, during the Ottoman advances in the Anatolian peninsula in the course of the 13th century, of units of warriors organized on the basis of a combination of the ethos of frontier chieftaincy (whose *ghazi* spirit, inspiring the 'faith warrior', has a clearly Islamic legitimacy) and the intricacies and balances of tribal confederations, resulting in a kind of Sufi-influenced knightly culture. This civil-military nexus promoted by Sufism was further developed with the flourishing of the Ottoman dynasty from the end of the 14th century. It involved the building of a special corps known as the Janissaries, a military elite of slave origin that absorbed and replaced the more complex and fluid, early Ottoman, Sufi-knightly nexus, and which entertained very close relations with popular Sufi milieus (Rahimi 2004: 68).

Most typically and effectively, however, the type of organization that in some locales and epochs reached a close symbiosis with Sufi orders was that of the so-called *futuwwa*. This consisted of urban youth groups (or gangs) guided by a kind of chivalry code and committed to the protection of communal values. It appeared as a brotherhood-based organizational form suitable to sublimate lower-class violence into charismatic, collective power (Green 2012: 56). The groups were also (if not mainly) intent on providing order and security within urban contexts in exchange for prestige and also wealth. Sufi brotherhoods and *futuwwa* associations, often densely overlapping with each other (as well as with the authorities of city neighborhoods), became at times and in various locales even more tightly wedded in organizational terms. This became strikingly evident in the brief revival of caliphal power under the rule of al-Nasir toward the end of the Earlier Middle Period (1180–1225). He used the brotherhood pattern, common to *tariqa* and *futuwwa*, in order to provide glue to the members of his court (Arjomand 2004: 224). As remarked by Babak Rahimi (2004: 89): "Ties of blood and kinship affiliations were less important than competition for the sacred status of leadership."

The illustrated case of a symbiosis between *tariqa* and *futuwwa* situated at the symbolic core of an otherwise waning caliphal power at that particular juncture (well into the Middle Periods) presented the single strongest case of a bottom-up civilizing process. This is one through which patterns of civility, instead of trickling down from the court to lower social classes as in the Eliasian model, traveled upward and met half-way the determinations of court administrators. Symptomatically, however, the process was intentionally manipulated into a typical top-down model by al-Nasir. Nonetheless, in its reliance on the teaching of the above-mentioned Sufi author Suhravardi, the model remained quite balanced. It was based on the assumption that the only hope of reviving the Caliphate was precisely through making it fit into the decentralized mode of power-building and distribution that was typical of the Middle Periods in general, and of the Earlier Middle Period in particular. This program required making the Caliphate not just the hub of the *shari'a* but also, and even more strongly and explicitly, the pinnacle of the Sufi way (Hodgson 1974, II: 282)

The Islamic philosophers, i.e. the practitioners of *falsafa*, were heirs to and developers of the Hellenic philosophical tradition. Some of them, such as al-Farabi (c. 872–950), could even reclaim a continuous chain of transmission of knowledge going back to no-one less than Aristotle (not unlike the Sufi way of tracing genealogies of charisma). Since the latest stage of the High Caliphate, philosophers were raised to an important status, not just in the hierarchy of knowledge but often also in terms of the power and prestige they retained within court milieus. The Sufis did not just respond to this initial success by claiming that the philosophers were wrong in their intellectual approach to ultimate issues of knowledge on the grounds that they evaded the attainment of a higher wisdom. They rather recognized in the *falsafa* a potential challenge to *tasawwuf* in the articulation of the knowledge–power equation. Thus quite often Sufis, unlike many among the *'ulama'*, unsurprisingly argued that philosophical theories were not wrong per se but too intellectualized and divorced from practice, and therefore rather wrongly targeted.

Yet in their competitive stance toward philosophers, Sufis did not oppose to the purer rational search of knowledge represented by *falsafa* a stance merely resting on a spiritual dimension. Thanks also to the broadening competition among Sufi *turuq*, in the course of the Middle Periods philosophy was put on the sidelines of the socio-cultural scene due to its limited capacity (and, arguably, interest) to capture the imagination and consensus of the masses in ways like those successfully practiced by the Sufi masters. Ibn Khaldun himself, who was active in the late 14th century— the most politically fractured yet equally formative part of the Later Middle Period (Fromherz 2010: 9)—decried that philosophy was far from innocent of the civilizational, urban syndrome that led the scholars as a whole to misconceive their knowledge as able to grasp and control reality without residues: an attitude (which later Vico described as the "conceit of the scholars": see Salvatore 2007: 187) that in fact contributed to curtailing the otherwise quite open character of the Islamic civilizational expansion of the era (Arnason and Stauth 2004: 38). As against this self-disruptive dimension of urban and elite-based Islamic cultures, Sufism successfully claimed to stand solidly on the constructive side of the civility equation by catering to the practical and spiritual needs of diverse social layers.

The overlapping balance that resulted from the coexistence of distinctive roles and the combination of approaches favored the crystallization of weakly institutionalized, broadly consensual models of civility in the shaping and governance of the social bond. The advantage of the orientation to piety of organized Sufism, compared to the systematic and to a large extent certified scholarship of jurists, theologians, and philosophers, consisted in the fact that Sufi forms of organization anchored spiritual claims within ritualized collective practices. These in turn facilitated building intersubjective connectedness and therefore also accommodating mutual interests, be they in a vertical and dyadic (master–disciple) or more horizontal and transversal manner (brother to brother). The elaborate pattern consisted in integrating the triadic matrix of the social bond through which *ego* relates to *alter* via *Alter*, the Big Other, i.e. the Godhead, into cohesive groups. This solution shunned both a dogmatist impasse and an elitist backlash (for the simultaneously anthropological and theological root of this triadic type, which, far from being exceptional is quintessentially 'axial' in the sense delineated in the Introduction, see Salvatore 2007: 54–8). Moreover, the organized Sufism of the *turuq* responded to the resurfacing need for charismatic mediation. The absence of priesthood in Islam had first contributed to make this mediation obsolete in principle, but the teaching and legal professions reinstituted the need for cultured leadership in the footsteps of Muhammad, without being able to absorb the resurfacing need. One might even dare to state that the type of knowledge that Sufism invested into flexible and replicable organizational forms reconstituted a charismatic kernel also for the benefit of more formalized institutions, like the court of law and the college. Role diversification was matched by a certain transversality of cultured personnel across the entire Islamic institutional spectrum: at the cost of some simplification, we can identify all of them as the '*ulama*', a highly stratified social role also comprising most Sufi masters, more than a corps or a cohesive social group.

We have seen that the Sufi organizational unit, the *tariqa* (meaning primarily the "way" or "path," though the term is mostly translated as "order"), should be usefully identified as a brotherhood (sometimes an alternate rendering of *tariqa*). I stick to the latter definition since it fits a comparative view (see Chapter 4). Moreover, it stimulates some theoretical reflections on the social nature of the bond innervating Sufism and the already mentioned, related cooperative hubs (like craft guilds, urban quarters, and youth groupings: see Zubaida 1995: 165). These, like the *tariqa*, were characterized by similarly flexible and equally consistent organizational modes. There is nothing inherently 'primordial' in the nexus of brotherhood, if we understand it—as we should do sociologically—as an increasingly successful form of organization of the social bond and of related forms of civility, as they took a solid shape and peaked in the crucial phase of Islamic history that we have identified as the Middle Periods. Let us consider as primordial articulations of the social bond all those groups, from family through clan to tribe, whose roots are forms of real or mildly altered consanguinity which are often turned into generators of increasingly imagined and symbolic affinity. Within this pattern, the brotherhood is a key intermediate mold facilitating the passage from the primordial (kin-based) to the civil (kin-independent) level of social organization. But, aside from facile evolutionary views, brotherhood can and should be even considered as the fundamental matrix—both organizationally and at the imaginary level—of civility as such, even if (or probably even more if) propped up by a chivalric ethos or by ecstatic drives.

It was Weber himself who saw the potential root of the type of civility that ultimately supports modern polities in the idea and organizational matrix of the brotherhood (*Verbrüderung*), more than in the often-invoked Aristotelian constructions of the *polis* (Weber 1980 [1921–22]: 425–37). A brotherhood is intended as a dynamic mode of instituting social connectedness: "a community based on artificially created and freely willed mutual ties, not on consanguinity" (Nippel 2002). Far from being either a residue of the non-modernized part of the non-West or, inversely, an evolutionary stage in the unique modernizing trajectory of Western Europe, in Weber's approach, the confraternal bond characterizes the overall civilizational development of Western Eurasia. It therefore includes Islamic civilization, as opposed to what he saw as the "East" or "Asia" represented by India and China. According to the interpretation of Wilfried Nippel, in Weber's view

> the rigid caste system established in India after the victory of Brahmanism prevented (particularly through its exclusion of any kind of commensality between members of different castes) the emergence of any confraternal structure. In the Chinese case it was the ancestor cult that had the corresponding effect, since it bound the city-dwellers to their respective sibs, or clans, and villages of origin.
>
> (Nippel 2002: 132)

Indeed this inclusion of Islam in the wider 'Western' (though not in the stricter 'Occidental') constitution of the type of social bond and organiza- tion identified as brotherhood confirms a tendency by Weber to orientalize China (here evident in the excessive stress laid on the Sinitic "tyranny of cousins," to use Gellner's words) and to (in principle) deorientalize Islam by seeing in it a defective manifestation of a typically Western socio-religious ethos. This assessment mainly results from the fact that he focused on the appropriation of Islam's purportedly original, 'Meccan' salvational ethos by a class of warriors bent on conquest. It was as if he reproached Islam for orientalizing itself in spite of its primary 'Western' root and potential (yet failed) 'Occidental' destiny. This is a further twist to the more typical mode of orientalist construction of Islam as a bundle of deficits rooted in an allegedly closed 'Semitism', and confronted with the supposedly open Western, Christian, Indo-Germanic model, which is indeed at the root of Western anti-Semitism (see Masuzawa 2005: 156–78). In operating this twist, which rehabilitated Islam's origin just to decry its defective develop- ment, Weber was probably influenced by the leading Protestant theologian Ernst Troeltsch, no less than by the Islamic Studies scholar C.H. Becker (Salvatore 1997: 121–2).

In this sense, and though he never explicitly stated so, the problem with Weber's interpretation might consist in his overlooking Islam's capac- ity to exalt the brotherhood patterns to a successful model of institu- tional malleability and to a potential vector both of local cohesion and of long-distance, translocal connectedness. The Heidelberg sociologist rather opined that Islam did not evolve significantly beyond a 'Western' model of brotherhood purportedly rooted in the ancient Greco-Roman world, due to factors of self-limitation inherent in the warrior ethos on which Islam's expansion supposedly depended (Weber 1980 [1921–1922]: 289). Inciden- tally, we should observe that Weber could only deliver such a lopsided judgment by entirely neglecting that Islam's most spectacular expansion occurred not during its early stage but during the Middle Periods—largely thanks to the brotherhood pattern.

However, what is interesting here is the sociologically constructive side, on potentially comparative terms, of Weber's concept of *Verbrüderung*, which actually denotes the act and the process of building a brotherhood, of becoming brothers more than the static matrix of the brotherhood. This notion can provide the premodern platform for all subsequent organized forms of acting in common, mutual solidarity, and participation in local and translocal social life, including those unfolding in a city or neighborhood.

Such capacities are obviously bound by a type of authority that, as Vico recognized, is intrinsically inseparable from some form and degree of violence, be it material, symbolic, or both, and, as Weber saw, is ultimately dependent on obedience. To the extent that one can detect in the brotherhood—both in its collective body and in its leadership through the masters and saints— a sacral aura or charisma that legitimizes the bond, charisma circulates through the grids of mutuality and hierarchy and is both educational and fraternal. In this sense charisma is concretely, i.e. contractually, based on explicit and implicit understandings among the 'brothers' and is as such the source of enforceable authority. We will come back to the contractual dimension of the social bond that is related to the Islamic articulation of brotherhood as a key matrix of civility. For now, let us emphasize that within a brotherhood, authority is kept flexible, i.e. not fully institutionalized, while it is also structured through recognized chains of command. It is distributed along the overlapping layers of dual relations among imagined 'brothers.'

Yet the deepest layer of Weber's argument on *Verbrüderung* denoting the dynamic process of 'becoming brothers' and what makes out the West as 'Occident' (and therefore excludes Islam) is that the flipside of the Western-European investment into processes of rationalization of the associational bond that are able to transcend the confraternal patterns, and most notably their late-medieval developments within burgeoning city life (see Chapter 4), was helped by the rise of the idea of *Anstalt* (basically signifying "institution" as opposed to *Verein*, meaning "association"). This metamorphosis of the confraternal bond required some sort of sacralization of the bond itself, consisting in making 'one' out of 'many,' as in the constitution of a unitary juridical personality out of a multitude of associates. It did not escape Weber's attention that such a corporate personality can only be the outcome of a mutation of the dynamic model of the brotherhood which in itself, though reflecting traditional or charismatic forms of authority, stays clear of such a full-fledged sacralization and rather relies on codes of honor based on appropriate grids of mutual respect and reverence toward the older 'brothers.' The confraternal pattern is therefore much less 'collectivized' than in the case of a formal incorporation of the associational bond into a unitary juridical personality. This result was uniquely achieved through the kind of legal, institutional, and political developments within Western Christendom, particularly during the Late Middle Ages, which have been emphasized by Weber as leading up to the shaping of the unique notion of *Anstalt*. Through this Weberian conceptual grammar we understand that the idea itself of a full-fledged "institution" reveals a considerable investment into a "sacramental" homogenization of the collective bond in the form of a "corporation." In some crucial yet infrequently heeded passages of Weber's *Economy and Society* the discussion of *Anstalt* densely intersects the one on *Verbrüderung*. The threshold of the passage from a "brotherhood" to an "institution" is given by the sacramental institutionalization of the former. This appears as a quite delicate, albeit decisive, passage or transformation (Weber 1980 [1921–1922]: 425–36). We can therefore argue that what characterizes the Islamic articulation of brotherhood vs. its trajectory in Europe is precisely an attention not to cross that threshold determined by a sacramental institutionalization of the confraternal bond. In the Islamic matrix, the brotherhood remains a clearly 'lay' type of bond.

Rewriting Charisma into Brotherhood

Some basic comments are needed here regarding 'charisma,' since it is a concept that can generate misunderstandings if consigned to its intuitive meaning. These comments will also facilitate the discussion of the delicate threshold of institutionalization. The notion of charisma remains a controversial Weberian idea. It inhabits Weber's *Economy and Society* from the beginning to the end. While this is not the place to revisit the concept in encompassing theoretical terms, some observations are useful as they may have strategic importance in redirecting the program of the sociology of Islam. Let us start by observing that Weber needed the idea of charisma in order to explain social change, down to modern transformations, through processes other than the formal rationalization of the management of material factors and resources (see Introduction). According to Weber, formal rationalization reflects a type of modern rationality that he identifies as the default vector of socio-political transformations. Yet he also realized that although the rationalization of the law, the economy, and the state bureaucracy is the main engine of socio-political change, transformations need in turn to be explained by more singular factors, ones that have a basically immaterial, cultural, or religious nature. As such, these latter factors defy the iron logic of modern 'structural' determination of the social powers. Charisma is then for Weber a kind of golden distillate of the role of the 'irrational' in human society and history. It is incarnate in the personal aura of exceptional leaders who are able to build constituencies that significantly alter the given knowledge–power equations in a specific social context, even when material and structural factors are not necessarily working in their favor and would have by themselves prevented their rise and success.

Weber reconstructed his own notion of charisma primarily from contemporary theological discussions related to the bestowal of the gift of grace through the ministering of sacraments by the Church. Paradoxically for the author of the famous (or, according to alternate judgments, infamous) essay on *The Protestant Ethic and the Spirit of Capitalism* (Weber 1986 [1920]: 17–206), the notion of charisma in Weber derived from a quite oblique borrowing from the institution of the sacraments in the Catholic Church (D.N. Smith 1998). Only after this basic step did Weber make the concept less theologically impregnated and more sociologically plastic. He did so by discussing the military hero and the charismatic magician through further borrowings, this time from anthropology and mythology. Both anthropology and mythology tend to localize charisma in specific personality types, away from the institutional underpinnings of the sacramental concept. Yet from what we have seen it is evident that rather than proceeding from anthropology to theology, Weber took the opposite road, or better, shortcut. In its kernel, Weber's concept is still strongly sacramental (Joas 2012: 17–20). He tried to remedy that by implying that sacraments are just a genre of magic and that after all, as we just saw, the making itself of *Anstalt* entails a quasi-magic turning of a multiplicity of subjectivities and interests into the unitary body of a corporate institution.

It remains, however, that Weber's exhumation of the quite unsociological, originally theological notion of charisma was intimately related to his urgency to explain the exceptionalism of the West vis-à-vis the rest of the world, something that purely rational explanations and structural factors could not entirely perform. This move reflects his conviction that the modern Western trajectory and ensuing global hegemony must ultimately be rooted in some immaterial singularities directly or indirectly related to the evolution of Latin Christianity/Christendom, i.e. Europe, while being also derivable from a more general typology that can be universally applied. The invocation of charisma by Weber appears in this context as a rather weak solution to a specifically Western problem addressed with peculiarly Western (mostly Christian or post-Christian) theological or theologized ideas. Not surprisingly the idea of charisma, although it has become massively popular and even a notion of common knowledge and discourse in several languages also (if not primarily) thanks to Weber's elaboration of it, has proven to be rather inadequate to deal with the sociological problem it intended to solve. The concept was called to explain how extraordinary forms of leadership in religion and/or politics can trigger, thanks to immaterial factors, collective movements and transformations that defy the rationality of formalized, institutionalized power—only to recede into routinized institutional patterns in their turn after they are met with success and the original charisma is eroded. Weber's idea was that what gets routinized and innervates a new institution is nothing less than the original, exceptional charisma of the leader, which however after the success of a socio-political or socio-religious movement (or a revolution) is subject to stabilization and crystallization into a determining structure or institution (see S. Turner 2003).

In other words there is a double bias lurking behind the curtain of Weber's charisma: the idea of the extraordinary character of the 'original,' pristine charisma of exceptional personalities (and/or the movements and groups they lead), and the notion of a narrowly 'institutional,' formalized outcome of its long-term social working. Early Christianity and the building of the Church are themselves a primary example of the duality of charisma. Had Weber not conceived of such polar opposites (the pristine vs. the institutional, or the prophetic vs. the priestly), he would not have needed to deliver such a lopsided notion of charisma. It is well known that the notion of the 'original' (when not 'originary') was foundational to several scholarly disciplines (from linguistics through archaeology to comparative religion) institutionalizing themselves into the academic landscape of Western learned and educational institutions in the course of the 19th century, in parallel with ever more spectacular colonial enterprises (Turner 2001). As a founding father of sociology, Weber has to be singled out for reiterating rather than challenging this foundational Western, modern, and colonial epistemic bias.

An influential and quite outspoken critique (though certainly a sympathetic one) of Weber's view of charisma was put forward by Shmuel Eisenstadt (1968). In spite of being framed in a strongly Weberian vocabulary (like all subsequent contributions of Eisenstadt, including his comparative civilizational analysis and his approach to multiple modernities: see Introduction and Conclusion), the Jerusalem sociologist proposed to overcome Weber's double bias concerning the allegedly pure and the routinized charisma as separate and to focus instead on their inherent combination. Eisenstadt clearly stated that initiative and leadership can only exist in an already given institutional environment (Eisenstadt 1968: xviii). We should understand that charisma is nothing other than a collective capacity to reshape already existing forms of leadership, and so to remold the prevailing institutional environment, whether mildly or deeply (from here the metaphors of 'reform' vs. 'revolution' come into common use). The fact is that this capacity is basically a collective one and does not exclude, but indeed requires, a leadership or elite in its production and management. Above all, this capacity rather resides on the knowledge side of the knowledge–power equation. Ultimately Weber's lopsided definition of charisma expresses a real sociological need, namely to have a counterpart to sheer power, which we express (imperfectly, as ever, due to the inherent limitations of any disciplinary vocabulary, including the sociological one) as 'knowledge.' This never amounts to a 'gnostic' option of sorts, as knowledge and power, as stressed in the Introduction, are by necessity mutually implied.

The salience of this 'x-factor' weakly covered by the term 'charisma' is due precisely to how it empowers and equips a group or movement to challenge the established political powers by pooling anew the social powers available in a given social setting, and thus to generate new sources of social mobilization and cohesion. Not by chance did Weber refer charisma primarily to prophecy, and one could even speculate that Muhammad fits Weber's notion of prophetic charisma even better than any biblical prophet (Weber 1980 [1921–1922]: 268–71). This is not entirely surprising since Muhammad sums up and synthesizes the characters of several such prophets. To the extent that this is plausible, we should recognize that the specific power of charisma originates from the knowledge of forms and the capacity to reshape them. In Muhammad's case this re-forming capacity concerns the images and symbols of cosmic and social order that were widespread within the Irano-Semitic civilizational area. They underwent a particularly lively process of recombination and reconstruction on the semi-periphery of the two big empires (the Byzantine and the Sasanian) that encompassed various brands of Judaism, Christianity, and Zoroastrianism, including several heterodox versions and challenges, some of which recombined the heritage of those religious traditions. In the context where the final (yet almost prototypical) prophet Muhammad operated, such ideas were not just up for grabs and free-floating but already to a significant extent integrated in established or fluid institutional frameworks. To rework forms out of existing frameworks might then be of the essence of 'charisma': only that, once clarified in this way, we can take a step back from Weber's rather mysterious and overly personalized notion and rather focus on the process itself.

To recapitulate, in Weberian parlance charisma might appear as the exception to the hard rules of economics, politics, and the law: an exception manifested through the 'charismatic' power consisting in evoking and imposing a higher order on a larger group or community, a power able to transcend sheer particular interests. This process occurs through the mobilization of various social segments of a given community (as Muhammad did in Mecca) but also through arbitration and reconciliation among conflicting parties transcending the original community (as Muhammad did in Medina). This type of power might at first sight appear as based on the primacy of personal ties of persuasion over formal regulations. Yet more attentive scrutiny reveals it as a sociologically 'normal' component of the construction of the social bond everywhere, in the sense that its regulative dimension does imply the social preexistence of forms and their continual re-forming. The notion of 'reform' (more than the idea of Reformation that evokes Luther and Protestantism) in Islamic history has even been elevated to an alternate typology of collective action particularly fitting the competition for acquiring credentials for the implementation of the 'charismatic' knowledge and leadership of Muhammad (see Nafissi 2006). The above-mentioned competition, as well as the overlapping of roles, between *'ulama'* and Sufi masters, between *madrasa* and *tariqa*, is an exemplification of the process of 'charismatic' appropriation.

In order to complete this work of reinterpretation and deflation of Weber's charisma, we would need a deeper reading of often understudied key Weberian passages which, like many in the parts of *Economy and Society* that I have quoted, frequently take the form of scattered, though brilliant, notes, often dislocated through a somewhat artificial divide between the parts on the sociology of religion and those on the sociology of law and domination. Pending such a work (one which might fit into the plan for the next volume of the sociology of Islam trilogy), a notion of 'charismatic' power provisionally purified from its obscure Weberian encrustations can still be suitable for delineating the terms and patterns of authority which are part and parcel of the cultural dominance of socio-political elites and of their struggles to gain legitimacy. This can be done without the need to invoke any 'aural' factors of extraordinary powers able to induce major changes, like those covered by Weber's charisma. We have seen in the Introduction how Eisenstadt, building on a constructive criticism of Weber's idea of culture, was able to describe an ambivalent dynamics of social conservation and challenge by focusing on the recurrent clashes of elites and counter-elites. This is indeed a trajectory of enquiry that might ultimately even push us to give up on any sociologically hardened idea of charisma. Within the Weberian framework and Eisenstadt's reformulation thereof it might be suitable to retain the idea of knowledge attributes or prerogatives concerning the capacity to reshape existing forms of the social bond and governance. Knowledge thus defined is as potentially conducive to major transformations as it might be integral to the everyday maintenance of the social bond through patterns of civility. Historical developments in the Islamic ecumene, like those exemplified and discussed in these books, would then be ideally suited to such sociological explorations and conceptual reformulations.

Unlike the foggy notion of charisma, the Weberian idea of brotherhood, if purified of its spuriously theological accretions, can be used profitably for working on an open, not too formalized, notion of civility, which needs to be at the center of the sociology of Islam. Such a notion could be profitably oriented to the Eliasian vision of a civilizing process. Elias himself felt motivated to cope seriously with the Weberian lesson while trying to transcend some of the biases and strictures characterizing Weber's theoretical apparatus. Therefore, I propose that we retain and rework Weber's dynamic idea of brotherhood (*Verbrüderung*) in order to explain civility and its transformation in the Islamic case, without the need to adopt (or reject) *in toto* the Weberian notion of charisma. The resulting view allows us to consider the analysis of formal vs. informal social relations and patterns of civility in a manner that avoids either a Western or an Islamic exceptionalist bias.

While the need to escape such an exceptionalist bias is entailed by the previous criticism of Weber's urgencies in building up his typologies and comparisons, there is no need for an inverted Islamic exceptionalism either, such as the one that is reflected in its constitution as the counter-model to the West. This would be expressed by an excess of informality of social relations which shuns the rationality of formal law and formalized, chartered institutions in a Weberian sense. Indeed, rather than being a problem of rationalization of the social bond, the issue at its root concerns first of all whether the bond of brotherhood remains contained within a distribution of knowledge–power inside of the network of both vertical and horizontal, dual and brotherly bonds. Alternately, the bond of brotherhood could be interpreted (and normalized through the crypto-theological subtext of Weber's sociology) as being sacralized as an outright collective bond. A sacralization would occur, for example, through enthroning ritual as a privileged way to constitute and legitimize singular forms of authority. This solution to the problem of how to understand the glue of brotherhood would probably tilt toward the Durkheimian side of classic sociology. Admittedly, the unacknowledged theological roots of Durkheimian sociology are different from those we detect in Weber (Milbank 1990: 51–73). What's more, their discussion would be less interesting here since other than in

Weber the sacralization of the collective bond is rather taken for granted by Durkheim.

This is why it is better to keep the discussion of the threshold separating brotherhood and institution (and marking the incorporation of the brotherly bond) anchored on the Weberian side of sociology. Accordingly, if not a full-fledged ritual sacralizing of the brotherhood in the form of a collective body, one would require at least an oath, as in Weber's notion of *schwurgemeinschaftliche Verbrüderung* (Weber 1980 [1921–1922]: 748). It is not so easy to translate this term in English with enough precision. It signifies a type of brotherhood that is communally consecrated via an oath. Actually and not by chance the discussion of this type of brotherhood occurs in the context of Weber's exploration of the exceptional character of the late-medieval European city, so it is at the core itself of Weber's theory, with its Occidental bias and orientalist fallouts. The oath is precisely what quasi-magically facilitates the incorporation of the bond of brotherhood into a type of collective agency that can be recognized institutionally, since it clearly goes beyond the scattered, crisscrossing ties among a bunch of 'brothers.' Initiation rituals, which were far from extraneous to Sufi brotherhoods and to the other mentioned organizational forms partly overlapping with them (like craftsmen guilds and *futuwwa*), can be considered as elaborations on an oath. Weber's notion denotes namely a brotherhood formalized through swearing in or initiating its members: a type of ritual usually finalized to pinpoint loyalty and, frequently, strengthen secrecy.

Weber's model was represented by the confraternities that provided the living cells of reciprocity and membership to the urban citizenship emerging in the European late-medieval municipalities. It would not be appropriate to assimilate the Islamic brotherhoods to them, also for the reasons that we will examine in Chapter 4. While clearly Weber's bias is bent toward demonstrating the uniqueness of such developments as a European exception, the Sufi brotherhoods distinguished themselves precisely for being able not to cross the boundary of quasi-magical sacralization in their ritual settings and to keep their group as a brotherly but essentially lay gathering of the faithful. Sufi orders rather relied on supple ritual forms, even if they may have sometimes lingered on the borders of the magic that, according to Weber, is implicit in an oath. On the other hand, the *futuwwa* might have probed more intensely the border between the pragmatic and the magic or sacral constitution of the brotherly bond. Such a sacralization of the collective glue of a group is understood by Weber to be the necessary price to be paid for developing civility in its modern—both strongly formalized and internalized—Western sense. Crossing the border to the sacralization of the collective body into a full incorporation of the bond is considered necessary to constitute a collective personality and thus inscribe charisma into institutional charters, like those regulating and legitimizing urban municipal powers, city autonomies, and the rising citizens' rights. This was a wider phenomenon that embraced a variety of organizational forms well beyond those enlivening the type of late-medieval European municipality according to Weber: from the Church itself through the *universitas* (the antecedent to the modern university) to the rising states, and, not least, the business companies or corporations (for the tightest, densely technical passages in *Economy and Society* reconstructing this process through the terminology of his sociology of law, see Weber 1980 [1921–1922]: 425–46).

Therefore we can say (and here I might look more Weberian than I have so far) that if a sacralization of the collective bond is the price to be paid for magically turning the many into the one, i.e. for transforming a scattered bunch of individual commitments into collective accountability and corporate personality, then it might be rational *not* to be willing to pay this price. It might be rational to opt to retain a principled sense of autonomy of the individual. In this case the Islamic difference (rather than exception) merely consists in the pragmatic and thoroughly reasonable option for a type of civility shorn of outright sacralization. This type of rationality might not even be confined to Weber's typology of what is rational in terms of values. It might spill over into what he intended by the purposive rationality that facilitates a maximization of power. It is in the Islamic case the power of the connective bond and its agential capacity over long distances, which characterized Islamic civility, rather than the power of the collective body within the city walls, as in its European counterpart.

The civility embodied in a type of brotherhood not depending on sacralization has the advantage of keeping the boundaries of the organizational bond at a safe distance from the exclusivity of a corporate personality and more porous to the informal interferences and inputs from the external social world. This type of civility keeps the brotherhood ultimately rooted in a reversible assent of its members. The almost kaleidoscopic proliferation of local and translocal branches and sub-branches of the Sufi brotherhoods, depending on the vagaries of the recognition and misrecognition of the charismatic claims of masters and their lineages by the adepts (and among the masters themselves), is a testament to this different, non-sacralized, permeable, and dynamic model of Islamic brotherhood. This type of civility is conducive not just to a coexistence of different loyalties but also to a patterned overlapping of belongings. These can then also be deployed over long distances and across borders without the need to stick to a formal template of institutionalization. How a flexible approach to institutionalization became key to the expansiveness of Islamic civility is the topic of the next chapter.

References

Abun-Nasr, Jamil M. 2007. *Muslim Communities of Grace: The Sufi Brotherhoods in Islamic Religious Life*. London: Hurst and Co.

Arjomand, Said Amir. 1998. "Philanthropy, the Law, and Public Policy in the Islamic World before the Modern Era." In *Philanthropy in the World's Traditions*, edited by Warren F. Ilchman, Stanley N. Katz, and Edward L. Queen II, 109–32. Bloomington and Indianapolis: Indiana University Press.

Arjomand, Said Amir. 1999. "The Law, Agency and Policy in Medieval Islamic Society: Development of the Institutions of Learning from the Tenth to the Fifteenth Century." *Comparative Studies in Society and History*, 41/2: 263–93.

Arjomand, Said Amir. 2004. "Transformation of the Islamicate Civilization: A Turning Point in the Thirteenth Century?" In *Eurasian Transformations, 10th to 13th Centuries: Crystallizations, Divergences, Renaissances*, edited by Johann P. Arnason and Björn Wittrock, 213–45. Leiden: Brill.

Arnason, Johann P. and Georg Stauth. 2004. "Civilization and State Formation in the Islamic Context: Re-reading Ibn Khaldun." *Thesis Eleven*, 76: 29–47.

Bamyeh, Mohammed A. 2000. *The Ends of Globalization*. University of Minnesota Press.

Eisenstadt, Shmuel N. 1968. "Introduction: Charisma and Institution Building: Max Weber and Modern Sociology." In *Weber on Charisma and Institution Building*, edited and with an Introduction by Shmuel N. Eisenstadt, ix–lvi. Chicago and London: University of Chicago Press.

Faroqhi, Suraiya. 2009. *Artisans of Empire: Crafts and Craftspeople under the Ottomans*. London: I.B. Tauris.

Foltz, Richard. 2010. *Religions of the Silk Road: Premodern Patterns of Globalization*. New York: Palgrave Macmillan.

Fromherz, Allen James. 2010. *Ibn Khaldun: Life and Times*. Edinburgh: Edinburgh University Press.

Gauchet, Marcel. 1997 [1985]. *The Disenchantment of the World: A Political History of Religion*, translated by Oscar Burge. Princeton, NJ: Princeton University Press.

Green, Nile. 2012. *Sufism: A Global History*. Oxford: Wiley Blackwell.

Heck, Paul L., ed. 2007. *Sufism and Politics: The Power of Spirituality*. Princeton, NJ: Markus Wiener.

Hodgson, Marshall G.S. 1974. *The Venture of Islam: Conscience and History in a World Civilization*, I–III. Chicago and London: University of Chicago Press.

Joas, Hans. 2012. 'The Axial Age Debate as Religious Discourse.' In *The Axial Age and its Consequences*, edited by Robert Bellah and Hans Joas, 9–27. Cambridge, MA: Harvard University Press.

Karamustafa, Ahmet T. 2007. *Sufism: The Formative Period*. Edinburgh: Edinburgh University Press.

Levtzion, Nehemia. 2002. "The Dynamics of Sufi Brotherhoods." In *The Public Sphere in Muslim Societies*, edited by Miriam Hoexter, Shmuel N. Eisenstadt, and Nehemia Levtzion, 109–18. Albany, NY: SUNY Press.

Masuzawa, Tomoko. 2005. *The Invention of World Religions: Or How European Universalism Was Preserved in the Language Pluralism*. Chicago: University of Chicago Press.

Milbank, John. 1990. *Theology and Social Theory: Beyond Secular Reason*. Oxford: Blackwell.

Murata, Sachiko and William C. Chittick. 1994. *The Vision of Islam*. New York: Paragon.

Nafissi, Mohammad. 2006. "Reformation as a General Ideal Type: A Comparative Outline." *Max Weber Studies*, 6/1: 69–110.

Nippel, Wilfried. 2002. "Homo Economicus and Homo Politicus. In *The Idea of Europe: From Antiquity to the European Union*, edited by Anthony Pagden, 129–38. Cambridge: Cambridge University Press.

Rahimi, Babak. 2004. "Between Chieftaincy and Knighthood: A Comparative Study of Ottoman and Safavid Origins." *Thesis Eleven*, 76: 85–102.

Rahman, Fazlur. 1979 [1966]. *Islam*. Chicago and London: University of Chicago Press.

Safi, Omid. 2006. *The Politics of Knowledge in Premodern Islam: Negotiating Ideology and Religious Inquiry*. Chapel Hill: University of North Carolina Press.

Said, Edward W. 1978. *Orientalism*. New York: Pantheon.

Salvatore, Armando. 1997. *Islam and the Political Discourse of Modernity*. Reading: Ithaca Press.

Salvatore, Armando. 2004. "The Implosion of *Sharia* within the Emergence of Public Normativity: The Impact on Personal Responsibility and the Impersonality of Law." In *Standing Trial: Laws and the Person in the Modern Middle East*, edited by Baudouin Dupret, 116–39. London and New York: I.B. Tauris.

Salvatore, Armando. 2007. *The Public Sphere: Liberal Modernity, Catholicism, and Islam*. New York: Palgrave Macmillan.

Smith, David Norman. 1998. "Faith, Reason, and Charisma: Rudolf Sohm, Max Weber, and the Theology of Grace." *Sociological Inquiry*, 68/1: 32–60.

Smith, Wilfred Cantwell. 1962. "The Historical Development in Islam of the Concept of Islam as an Historical Development." In *Historians of the Middle East*, edited by Bernard Lewis and P.M. Holt, 484–502. London: Oxford University Press.

Stauth, Georg. 1993. *Islam und Westlicher Rationalismus: Der Beitrag des Orientalismus zur Entstehung der Soziologie*. Frankfurt und New York: Campus.

Turner, Bryan S. 1974. *Weber and Islam: A Critical Study*. London and Boston: Routledge & Kegan Paul.

Turner, Bryan S. 1984. "Orientalism and the Problem of Civil Society in Islam." In *Orientalism, Islam and Islamists*, edited by Asaf Hussain, Robert Olson, and Jamil Qureshi, 23–42. Brattelboro, VT: Amana Books.

Turner, Bryan S. 2001. "On the Concept of Axial Space: Orientalism and the Originary." *Journal of Social Archaeology*, 1/1: 62–74.

Turner, Stephen. 2003. "Charisma Reconsidered." *Journal of Classical Sociology*, 3/1: 5–26.

Weber, Max. 1980 [1921–1922]. *Wirtschaft und Gesellschaft: Grundriß der verstehenden Soziologie*, edited by Johannes Winckelmann, 5th ed. Tübingen: J.C.B. Mohr (Paul Siebeck).

Weber, Max. 1986 [1920]. *Gesammelte Aufsätze zur Religionssoziologie*, I. Tübingen: J.C.B. Mohr (Paul Siebeck).

Zubaida, Sami. 1995. "Is there a Muslim Society? Ernest Gellner's Sociology of Islam." *Economy and Society*, 24/2: 151–88.

PART II

ISLAMIC CIVILITY IN HISTORICAL AND COMPARATIVE PERSPECTIVE

3

FLEXIBLE INSTITUTIONALIZATION AND THE EXPANSIVE CIVILITY OF THE ISLAMIC ECUMENE

The Steady Expansion of Islamic Patterns of Translocal Civility

The importance of the theoretical reflections of the last chapter becomes apparent the moment we take into account the following development. While Islam originated out of the older dynamics of the Irano-Semitic civilizational area, in the wider Afro-Eurasian semi-arid zone even before the advent of Islam and, increasingly, with its expansion, the pressures toward a cosmopolitan dissolution of local, especially agrarian-based, legitimations of power was particularly strong. As a consequence, institutions in this wider zone tended to be less tightly structured and highly flexible. This is a broad, hemisphere-wide background that explains the success of the Islamic brotherhood as an organizational form during the Middle Periods. Yet the wider articulations of the knowledge–power equation in the Islamic ecumene within which the brotherhoods thrived was largely one that left the individual, more than elsewhere in the Eastern hemisphere (with the possible exception of the Tibetan plateau), in a particularly forceful (and potentially threatening) free-floating state within the wider networks of social connections. In a quite powerful sociological sense, the full-fledged, non-sacralized, Islamic model of brotherhood we have discussed in the previous chapter as the main matrix of civility can be understood as a powerful response to precisely this 'structural' type of individual exposure.

In many ways, it was precisely the individual exposure to an almost face-to-face relation with Allah, without a guarantee of solid and secure intercessors (Bellah 1970: 146–67), which found its sociological correspondence

The Sociology of Islam: Knowledge, Power and Civility, First Edition. Armando Salvatore.
© 2016 John Wiley & Sons, Ltd. Published 2016 by John Wiley & Sons, Ltd.

in the social actor's need to approach any potential brother in a rather 'contractual' way, as an (in principle) equal and free human being (Hodgson 1974, II: 63). Of course, as Hodgson insistently stressed, the uniquely egalitarian predicament and cosmopolitan opening of Islam/Islamdom never completely offset the hemisphere-wide primacy of status crystallizations tied to the hegemony of the agrarian aristocracy, not even during the Middle Periods. Yet the mercantile counter-hegemony of the urban bourgeoisie was particularly strong. This strength was largely due precisely to the impossibility of setting up politically independent city–states. Such a predicament forced the urban businessmen to seek connections and income in their wider region and across transregional spaces. Cities were important, but as nodes within wider circulatory nexuses rather than as progressively self-centering entities controlling and exploiting the countryside and constituting themselves as corporate powers. In parallel, long-distance trade, which was never a pure business enterprise, became robustly bound up with wider knowledge–power networks carried by the brotherhoods, and particularly by Sufism. Overall the urban bourgeoisie could take advantage of being a largely rootless class, which could exploit its tight links to the *'ulama'* and so represent the ethos of a market morality and of an egalitarian cosmopolitanism selectively open to other civilizational inputs. At the same time, their socio-cultural milieus could express and perpetuate their hostility to the nature-bound cults inherently associated with the landowning gentries and so understand themselves as the most legitimate carriers of the Islamic 'contractualist' and connective ethos (Hodgson 1993: 111–12).

More deeply than that, one can dare to say that the Islam of the Middle Periods configured an anthropological culmination of the dilemma of connectedness intrinsic to the axial triadic nexus *ego-alter-Alter*. This microsociological type of connectedness was translated into a macro-sociological force picking up a longer-term historical momentum during the Middle Periods in general and the Later Middle Period in particular. It showed a capacity to expand into the depths of a hemisphere-wide—and within the framework of the age, global—ecumene. This process facilitated the absorption of patterns of civility from other Afro-Eurasian civilizational realms, and was particularly the case with regard to the Central and Inner Asian constellations that provided the springboard to the political-military dominance of the nomadic component of translocal connectedness that triumphed in the Later Middle Period with the Mongols. This development culminated in the establishment of the Yuan dynasty by Kublai Khan in China and in the renewed unifying attempts performed by the ruthless campaigns of Timur across the Islamic ecumene.

At this crucial stage of Islamic history, and particularly during the Earlier Middle Period, the Islamic ecumene appeared to be a society of networks, fed by concentric and/or overlapping circles of connectedness, more than consisting of states or empires. It was an era characterized by minimal bureaucracies and by the maximal role of social organizations, especially those with a flexible degree of formalization. At the same time, the idea of a civility to be legitimized in Islamic terms was collapsed into more fundamental speculations about issues of general order, particularly through the original combination of teaching and practice emanating from Sufi environments. This orientation often contributed to a view of human life as characterized by an extraordinary (and astonishingly optimistic) opening to human potentialities of beauty, love, and knowledge (both of love-as-knowledge and of knowledge-as-love). This development reversed the rather pessimistic twist that gnostic doctrines had experienced (and instilled into the social bond) within both the Irano-Semitic and the Hellenic environments in Late Antiquity. The bottom line in sociological terms of this wider process was that civility and the underlying need for predictability of transactions happened to be seen as largely divorced from state power. Civility became variably related to the manifold dimensions opened by Islam's steady growth: territorial, social, intellectual, and even 'spiritual.'

Military conquest played a significant role particularly in the Later Middle Period through the ongoing Mongol expansion and consolidation. It was also propelled by the wish to control trade centers along with their lucrative activities across the networks that we label the Silk Road. But it is also remarkable that Turkic and Mongol nomadic formations with an interest in sharing in the benefits of trade increasingly joined the Islamic ecumene. This long-drawn-out process matching participation in trade networks with state-building activities and the adoption of Islam not just as a faith commitment but also, if not mainly, as a transregional normative idiom was not exhausted before the 17th century. In the process, being Muslim became synonymous with being global, in the sense of enjoying full recognition as a partner in the hemisphere-wide circulation of goods, people, ideas, and healing practices along the Silk Road, across the Sahara desert region into the Sudanic lands of Africa, and even more along the commercial sea routes of the Indian Ocean linking East Africa to India and ultimately to the Malay archipelago. Nonetheless, while the process was ongoing Islam was never unchallenged: it competed with Christianity (mostly Nestorian but also Roman Catholic, through missions that were effective until the 14th century and were only discontinued by the great plague of that century), Manicheism, Zoroastrianism, and especially Buddhism.

Such varied religious traditions retained an enduring legitimacy within the circulatory system associated with the Silk Road, whose Eastern ends were located within the purview of the Chinese empire, within which Islam made a dent only in relatively isolated pockets and particularly on its North-Eastern fringes in the vast region known today as Xinjiang. In spite of this limitation, Muslim scholars and Sufis were usually present at the central Chinese courts under various dynasties, most strongly under the Yuan, who were strictly connected to the other Mongol potentates of the Later Middle Period. In various Central and East Asian courts Muslims wrestled for long periods with other religious groups to attract the rulers' favor, until Islam achieved an enduring breakthrough under Timur and his successors in the 14th and 15th centuries. The misplaced prejudicial idea that conversions to Islam occurred through the sword is particularly well dispelled with regard to the commitments of rulers of Mongol origin who were exposed to the teaching of Sufi masters. Several tales suggest how most enduringly effective the work of Sufi missionaries was in converting not just important rulers but large masses, thanks to the complex pattern of leadership we redefined in the last chapter under the umbrella of a revised notion of charisma, and which excludes a substantial recourse to brute force. Some of these mechanisms were of a quintessentially communicative nature, as when wondrous tales actually preceded the arrival of the holy men. Substantially and in the long term, therefore, the expansion of Islam across the Afro-Eurasian depths was not decisively facilitated by military might but by a mixture of appeal, convenience, and patronage, which often combined smoothly through the effectiveness of embracing Islam as a spectacularly transregional (and largely transcivilizational) social and moral idiom.

The strong impulse of various Muslim groups to impregnate culturally and integrate civilly—rather than just conquer militarily—ever vaster areas within the Afro-Eurasian macro-civilizational block was hardly impaired by the unfolding of the heterodox challenges of Shi'i groups and formations directed against the Sunni orthodoxy. During the Earlier Middle Period Sunni orthodoxy reigned particularly vigorously in the vast territories controlled by the Turkic Saljuq dynasts who, after starting their conquests in Transoxiana and Khorasan, happened to be centered in Baghdad, the Abbasid caliphal seat, during the second half of the 11th century. This was the first instance of a Central Asian nomadic potentate absorbing the ethos of the Irano-Semitic realm and occupying its very center, from which the Saljuqs ruled by projecting a strong sense of commitment to Sunni norms. They succeeded to the Persianized Ghaznavid military slave elites of Turkic origin which had effectively weakened Abbasid rule and thus marked the end of Hodgson's High Caliphate. During this epoch, the Islamic ecumene effectively integrated the Turkic (and, later, Turko-Mongol) nomadic civilizational components most effectively via the mediation of Persianate culture. The latter should not be reduced to mere court refinement and the art of statesmanship, since it also carried over a strong element of popular messianism. Such a fusion was determinant in ensuring that the already mentioned *futuwwa* (and the similarly organized Anatolian *akhi*s, whose Turkish etymological root does not mean brother but rather "knightly-noble") could provide a key matrix of civility developing and competing alongside the Sufi brotherhoods.

The subsequent merging of the two types of brotherhood, as in the case of *al-akhiyat al-fityan* succinctly captured by Ibn Battuta (1304–1369), represented a powerful new synergy between the horseback warrior ethos of Central and Inner Asia and the messianic impetus of the Irano-Semitic traditions. It strove to bring to a higher synthesis the heroism prized by life in the steppe and the ethical egalitarianism preached by the Qur'an, which deepened earlier key motives of the Irano-Semitic, urban ethos (Rahimi 2004: 67). The result was the formation of a kind of veritable "transcultural hybridity," as between Sufism, shamanism, Zoroastrian Gnosticism, Tibetan Buddhism, and Eastern Christianity, which contributed to new original crystallizations of modes of knowledge and related practices (Rahimi 2006: 48–52). Through an entropic whirlpool of crossborder relations and hybridizations, "the high degree of decentralization in every social institution seems to have favored a ready expansion of these institutions wherever an opportunity presented, whatever the apparent political situation" (Hodgson 1973, II: 271). Islamdom becomes here the hub of a hemisphere-wide transcivilizational spin also affecting neighboring regions and civilizations. It would be unwise to consider the recession of central bureaucratic steering of the state, in the old-fashioned orientalist way, as a symptom of decay and deviance from the golden, original model of the 'classic' age of the High Caliphate. According to Hodgson, quite the opposite might have been the case:

> In a long-run perspective, one may almost regard the High Caliphal state as an interlude, a means of transition from the aristocratic agrarian monarchy of Sasanian times to a social order at once more urbanized and more decentralized, which was emerging in the region as a result of millennial forces in the hemisphere at large.
>
> (Hodgson 1973, II: 69)

Ibn Khaldun (1332–1406), whom we consider a sort of proto-sociologist much like Vico (see Chapter 1), is the scholar who best reflects—both in his work and life—the dynamics of the age as just summarized, matching dynamism with instability. He has become particularly famous for formulating the intrinsic laws of power and cohesion in the cycle of alliances and fragmentation linking nomadic groups and urban elites in his epoch. The cycle consisted of a build-up of mobilization and state formation followed by a dynamics of decay and dissipation (for the most recent account of Ibn Khaldun's comprehensive theory, see Alatas 2011; 2013). The fact that he was most immediately enmeshed in the historical and contemporary socio-political realities of North Africa, within which he also played the role of a major political stakeholder on behalf of rulers and tribal confederations, fed into his extraordinary capacity to produce precious elements for what we might call a general theory of Muslim society. This was due to the very complexity of the reality on the ground with which he coped on a daily basis, and which reflected a crystallization of social institutions and a diversification of culture that also favored social autonomy (Fromherz 2010: 6–11).

Ibn Khaldun crucially suggested that civility, which is primarily urban based, and which he called *'umran*, has an inherently dual dimension that cuts through all cycles, being as much their underlying cause as it is their outcome. Civility as defined by Ibn Khaldun amounts to a life form based on refinement, culturedness, and etiquette. It is built on the overcoming of primordial, heroic virtue. Therefore it is based on a delicate trade-off between gains in sophisticated knowledge and losses in raw power. Probably in no other notion of civility is the knowledge–power equation so vividly laid bare as in Ibn Khaldun's plastic and comprehensive notion of *'umran*. This is particularly interesting for the sociology of Islam, irrespective of any evaluation we might provide concerning the broader civilizational cycle depicted by Ibn Khaldun. Essentially, the Maghrebi scholar saw in tribal solidarity, *'asabiyya*, the primary factor of social cohesion and political strength which becomes particularly effective as a factor of change in non-routine periods of transformations. These occur typically when a polity's integrity is challenged internally, externally (or both), but also inversely, when innovative movements are supported by a reform-oriented zeal of a religious nature (if not by prophecy itself). Such situations and movements attracted the attention of Ibn Khaldun for their capacity to magnify the activist dimension of group solidarity in ways that reactualized—albeit on a reduced scale—the advent itself of Islam via Muhammad's preaching and leadership (Arnason and Stauth 2004: 34, 36).

'*Asabiyya* is here not just the primary engine of the cycle (and the remote factor of civility) but also a sociologically plausible substitute for charisma, especially to the extent that it is not isolated from, but actually requires, the virtue of exercising leadership over larger groups, a virtue rooted in 'spiritual' power. Ibn Khaldun's analysis reveals no prior and unexamined differentiation between religion and politics while he observes and detects this primary force of social cohesion and transformation. At the same time, '*asabiyya* exposes the fragility of the conception of civil society illustrated in Chapter 1 which rests on a combination of interest and affection in the form of a mild human sympathy. It restitutes the ineliminable element of force and organized violence (which is first deployed and then tamed) to the formation of ties of civility. The strong historical background to this theory was the building of Almoravid and especially Almohad potentates in North Africa some generations prior to Ibn Khaldun, during the Earlier Middle Period. Their success stories owed decisively to the cohesive impetus of some Berber tribes initiated by the spiritual leadership of Ibn Tumart (1080–1130). This leadership was impregnated with a Sufi sense of saintliness and was brought to a formidable level of expansive strength in the subsequent generations (roughly from 1147 to 1230).

Although Ibn Khaldun's theory was most directly based on his life experience at the service of various potentates in North Africa and as a mobilizer, on their behalf, of tribal solidarity, his ideas, if duly interpreted, may also apply, and particularly well, to developments across the Eurasian depths. He was himself conscious of their potential relevance to the Mongol conquests across vast territories. This view well reflected what most Muslim actors of the Middle Periods keenly perceived, namely that the political contingencies, military conflicts, and power contests of the epoch, even those associated with the often brutal campaigns of the Mongols, did not preclude a longer-term unfolding of patterns of transborder mobility and connectedness but were actually part and parcel of them. The Islamic *umma* (whether we intend it as the ensemble of social actors sharing a moral idiom or as the aristocracy of the faithful) nested in such a worldwide web of long-distance routes and connections, but was also able to transcend its porous borders. Nonetheless, this was not just a fluid dynamics but one structured by the constraints and parameters of the knowledge–power equation. Local and translocal connectedness, in order not to prove evanescent (e.g. in the expansive impetus of a given Sufi order, or in the solidity of trader networks) could not just be based on mere sharing (e.g. of profits, or of spiritual accomplishments) but had to comply with choosing the most viable combination (or trade-off), in a given constellation, between solidarity and civility. These two factors might have weighed on the two opposite sides of the scale in specific, highly conflicted, constellations, which were far from uncommon during the Middle Periods.

Paradoxically, *pax mongolica* itself, the stabilizing outcome of the devastating wars and destructions wrought upon a large part of the Islamic ecumene by the conquering armies of Genghis Khan (d. 1227) and his successors, contributed to retrieve the importance of long-distance connectedness. As aptly formulated by Mohammed Bamyeh:

> [t]he model highlighted action and potential over nature and essence: People oriented toward the road experience solidarity as expansive rather than tied irretrievably to self-enclosed and nonnegotiable local systems of reference.
>
> (Bamyeh 2000: 104)

The North-African model that constituted the most immediate system of reference for Ibn Khaldun bears some partial, yet significant, analogies with the patterns of fragmentation and usurpation of authority that provided the background to the imperial advances of Timur (1336–1405) in the East. Timur was the leader who gathered the inheritance of Mongol rule in the Later Middle Period and unleashed a further wave of conquests. This tide stopped, westward, close to annihilating the two other major power formations of the Middle Periods, namely the Ottomans in Anatolia and the Mamluks in Egypt and Syria. In both cases, there is ample evidence of an involvement of overlapping urban groupings like those earlier mentioned and of the crucial role of craftsmen (regularly deported by Timur who saw in them an economic resource and a potential challenge) in representing urban interests and a capacity of self-organization throughout this cycle of violence (Arjomand 2004: 231).

Not entirely by chance, perhaps, late in his life Ibn Khaldun met Timur. Apart from the more anecdotal details of the encounter, the Maghrebi scholar probably saw in the Mongol conqueror the actual epitome and the potential crowning of an otherwise inconclusive civilizational dynamics. This had left Ibn Khaldun, toward the end of his diversified career (after his long experience as a minister, negotiator, and judge in the Maghreb and Egypt), in the grip of the suspicion that socio-political cycles and the rules governing them would ultimately favor corruption and intrigues. He might have become resigned to the prevalence of such dynamics over the type of cohesive and charismatic power formations like those that, on the North-African stage, were yet vividly remembered by his generation, with particular regard to the Almohad paradigm of the Earlier Middle Period. Interestingly, Ibn Khaldun did not consider real the possibility that the denouement of the cycle could be achieved through a form of highly stable charismatic power comparable to the High Caliphate of the first centuries of Islamic history, prior to the Middle Periods (Arnason and Stauth 2004: 39). This inclination supports our consideration of the Middle Periods as the sociological benchmark of the long-term development of the Islamic ecumene. This assessment works against all orientalist and classicist biases that tend to consider the 'golden age' of the High Caliphate as a paradigm of Islamic excellence, yet also normality: a narrative that sees the Middle Periods as just the beginning of a long, ineluctable decadence allegedly lasting until the onset of the modern colonial era.

As we will see in the following chapters, the heritage of the Mongol conquests did affect, and quite deeply, the reconfiguration of powers of the early modern era that followed the end of the Middle Periods. Yet Timur's subduing of wide Eurasian regions did not completely sedate the Khaldunian civilizational cycle of flourishing and dissipation. Deviations from the cycle are not evidence of an insufficiency within the theory but signal the need to make the theory slightly more complex by moving beyond the cover-all notion of *'asabiyya*. Such a complexification, which cannot be undertaken here, could provide us with the opportunity to better capture the rather open dialectic of knowledge and power. This would be facilitated by fully including in the process the never-extinguished messianic component that magnified the spiritual dimension of power and was due to play a key role in vital political developments during the subsequent, early modern era. One of the most interesting cases in this regard during the Middle Periods reflects the ongoing tension between city commoners and urban aristocracies. It is the case of the Sarbadar republic in Sabzavar, in the crucial region of Khorasan, during the 14th century. Though short-lived and finally overwhelmed by Timur, the republic marked an important attempt to establish a ruling power on the basis of a translocal Mahdist (messianic) movement rooted within popular Sufism and promoting full-scale self-government (Arjomand 2004: 238). More generally, even Maghrebi cases unfolding under the very eyes of Ibn Khaldun showed that urban craftsmen and commoners were far from just being the passive spectators of a political game involving tribal leaders and the urban elites comprising rich merchants and high-ranking *'ulama'*. Such instances help highlight how a reading of civility through the lenses of Ibn Khaldun's theory does not just point out that civility is not exclusively city based, for being the outcome of the tension between urban and nomadic life. It also shows that the significance itself (which can hardly be denied on the basis of orientalist and Weberian stereotypes) of the cycles of urban autonomous mobilization and dissipation in the Islamic ecumene affects the way we should conceive of the civic role of brotherhoods as well as of their translocal ramifications.

Authority, Autonomy, and Power Networks: A Grid of Flexible Institutions

In developing the specifically axial potential of the wider Irano-Semitic civilizational realm, the dynamics of formation and transformation of Islamdom produced an unusually flexible social order allowing any Muslim a degree of upward mobility to an extent unknown to other civilizations in the premodern eras (Hodgson 1974, II: 6). Remarkably, members of the Islamic ecumene possessed rights by virtue of belonging to the wider realm where Islamic law in all its facets (from moral to commercial) was either already hegemonic (within *dar al-islam*, "the abode of Islam") or on the way to establishing itself as such (within *dar al-hijra*, the "realm of migration," yet also, sometimes significantly, denoting the mobility and unpredictability of city life per se, with all its translocal ties and extensions). Therefore Muslims enjoyed rights not as members of a specific municipality or commune, as in Europe, where differential rights and statuses prevailed, but simply as Muslims (Hodgson 1974, II: 108). As succinctly put by Hodgson:

> The very urbanization of society militated against an autonomy for the towns as such: the ruling element of the land was so closely related to the towns that the countryside was largely assimilated into the political processes of urban society, so that city and countryside shared a common political fate ... Yet in their own ways the towns did build mechanisms of maintaining social norms and of achieving social goals: of mediating between the individual and a vast impersonal social environment.
>
> (Hodgson 1974, II: 106)

The weak character of institutional intermediaries in the Islamic ecumene, which contrasts with the strength of their counterparts in Western Europe, reinforced the capability of the individual to pool his own power with the power of other individuals. These were potentially to be seen as 'brothers': primarily for sharing in the general membership of the Islamic ecumene but secondarily and concretely through shared memberships of one or several brotherhoods, which were far from exclusive. Ibn Khaldun's notion of *'asabiyya* as group cohesion should be then reinterpreted, going beyond his own approach, as also potentially transcending the 'tribal' coveting of the power and riches of political centers. It should be seen as reflecting the open-ended yet well-channeled dimension of the social bond through the prism of brotherhood. This prism is based on the notion and practice of a symbolic consanguinity. As such, it is a bond that can be relaxed or tightened according to circumstances, including in cases of cyclical renewals of the stratum of power holders. Accordingly, group cohesion based on symbolic consanguinity (ranging from tribal *'asabiyya* proper to the *'asabiyya* of the brotherhoods) can provide the vital collective power needed to support the leaders, challengers, or upstarts who reclaim the power centers during situations of instability and/or on the cusp of innovative, 'charismatic' movements.

This sociological snapshot is not contradicted but made more plausible by the observation that during the Middle Periods the strictly conceived political realm was ever more monopolized by professional warriors. Yet also thanks to this quasi-monopoly, the social process was remarkably autonomous. Certainly this autonomy was not spontaneous or inertial, since the elites of knowledge and the guardians of normativity attempted to steer and protect it by formulating and implementing the common good on behalf of smaller or larger groups or loose social coalitions. Social autonomy relied on largely shared social power reflected at the cultural level by perfecting a mechanism that had characterized the Irano-Semitic civilization even before the advent of Islam. Accordingly, urban strata (but also, albeit selectively, rural commoners) were habilitated to counter the Eurasian-wide cultural hegemony of the agrarian gentry through reliance on a stratum of specialists (or virtuosos) of the norm. Though internally differentiated in terms of professional tasks and depending on the specificities of region and epoch, the overlapping socio-political power of the *'ulama'* fulfilled such requirements not just by watching over individual probity but also and especially by promoting fair interaction and the quality and cohesiveness of the social bond. The role of the *'ulama'* as administrators of the knowledge side of the knowledge–power equation largely consisted in producing and disseminating acceptable and effective norms based on such principles.

According to Ibn Khaldun's approach, the *'ulama'* were a transversal social group that neither possessed a cohesion of their own nor provided one to larger groups or classes. They were a *sui generis* socio-cultural layer of specialists of the norm and administrators of the knowledge side of civility. On the other hand, a specific group's *'asabiyya* was according to the Maghrebi scholar inconceivable without a key contribution of leaders who were able to mobilize a know-how usually commanded by the people of learning, i.e. the specialists of the norm. The already mentioned Ibn Tumart, leader of the Almohads, provides in this context a prototypical example (which certainly impressed Ibn Khaldun) of how a powerful tribal confederation could only acquire state-building capacities thanks to the leadership of a 'charismatic' scholar. Given such combined social and cultural premises, it should not be too surprising that what we might call the 'power of knowledge' reached its zenith during the Middle Periods, the epoch that saw the eclipse of the legitimacy of political rule in strictly Islamic terms (based on various conceptions and practices of the Caliphate), which not even the pre-Islamic Persianate court culture could protect from erosion. If the Islamic High Caliphate represented the culmination and decline of the tradition of Persian imperial statesmanship, the Middle Periods inaugurated the era of the rising social power of the *'ulama'*. This power relied on the autonomous culture of the *'ulama'* consisting in investing knowledge into the administration of the social bond at various levels (from moral through service-oriented to commercial), thus providing an articulate coherence (if not a blunt cohesion) to intricate yet well-ordered social arrangements.

We can even detect some deep historical memory of this period among the *'ulama'* of the modern age, to the extent that they have tried as much as possible to accommodate the rising powers of the modern state (precolonial, colonial, and postcolonial) on a pragmatic level. They have, however, conceded relatively little in principle at their end of the knowledge–power equation, by retaining large prerogatives as guardians of the moral and social language of the ecumene (Zaman 2002). This control pattern has been kept together by their mastering of an articulate Islamic idiom combining formal legal pronouncements with a flexible degree of informality and adaptability to local customs. The complexities of the idiom are bound together by the outward adherence to the same moral norms—what resulted in a rather decentralized and self-regulated, 'contractual' approach to shaping civil life. These patterns differed sensibly from the model that prevailed in Europe through the symbiosis of modern commercial society with an increasingly centralized state (ever more so through the transition from absolutist to liberal constitutional models). It is true that the matrix of brotherhood configured a source of power in principle alternative to the one that the guardians of the law enshrined in the relatively high degree of formalization of legal regulations through the administration of the *waqf*, the statutes of the colleges (*madrasas*), and the manuals of jurisprudence (*fiqh*). Yet even the informal patterns associated with brotherhoods ultimately fed into the social centrality of the '*ulama*', to the extent that brotherhood itself depended on the same moral idiom managed by them. Not by chance many '*ulama*' (even among the most rigorist in legal terms) were also, and not too surprisingly, practicing Sufis.

It is important to delineate a profile of the social skills and institutional articulations associated with the '*ulama*' in order to understand how the Islamic social fabric was staffed at both a micro- and a macro-level of organization. The category of the '*ulama*' becomes here broader than the rank of the *fuqaha*' or specialists of *fiqh*, and ends up overlapping with Sufi leaders as well. The diversity of opinion among '*ulama*' on various issues of both practical import and conceptual interest and the ensuing, often publicly manifested, disagreements encouraged them to seek the support of the restricted public of their peers (*al-khassa*) on the more theoretical and specialized questions, and of a wider, common public (*al-'amma*) on issues of public interest (Rahman 1979 [1966]: 261–2). Their multiple functions— as teachers, jurists, notaries, judges, guardians of orphans, preachers, *waqf* administrators and, not least, Sufi masters—brought them into daily contact with all sectors of the population. As de facto representatives and inter- preters of a variety of interests, they shaped civic spaces and channeled public opinion. There is no doubt that the emergence of the commoners during the Middle Periods created a pressure on the '*ulama*' to shift the border between *al-khassa* and *al-'amma* and to adjust related strategies of production and dissemination of knowledge. Both the access to literacy of an increasing number of commoners and the influence among them of preachers and storytellers further complexified the knowledge–power equa- tion, by strengthening the exposure and potential accountability of the '*ulama*' as a whole (Berkey 2001; Herzog 2013).

The wider code of service of the '*ulama*' consisted in providing guidance on life conduct and social intercourse, from a broadly social and economic to a specifically religious or moral level. Obviously this role did not pre- vent them from seeking and protecting their autonomous interests. They capitalized on the power inherent in their knowledge and skills, as well as in their social standing. More than that, they frequently entertained symbiotic relations with the merchant class, the most direct supporter and beneficiary of a contractual ethic of social relations favoring equality of chances and cosmopolitan opening. No doubt phenomena of corruption concerning the multiple roles of the '*ulama*' were far from rare. Situations of disagreement among them could furthermore degenerate into defamation and intrigue. These were also tokens of a heightened competition within their field, since their knowledge could translate into stable power only via a careful management of individual reputation. Yet in order to appreciate the complexity of the picture and its nuances, one has to be aware of both the wide social impact of the norms they managed and of the related social expectations. What is remarkable is the relative constancy and consistency of such norms and expectations over distant regions and through a variety of epochs in spite of the absence of a centralized, Church-like organization. Both expectations and abuses could doubtless be fueled by the mobility and fluidity that characterized the Middle Periods.

The Permutable Combinations of Normativity and Civility

We can now provide a broader snapshot of the outcome of the overall dynamics through which the Islamic ecumene entered its most representative period of thriving and expansion after the eclipse of the High Caliphate. We can point out an assortment of variably institutionalized loci of education, cultivation, cooperation, and solidarity: a variable geography of legal schools (several hundreds in the early centuries, then consolidating into a dozen, and with just a few emerging as 'canonical schools' at the beginning of the Middle Periods), as well as craftsmen guilds, brotherhoods, neighborhoods (whose leaders where often the masters of local branches of a leading translocal *tariqa*), and a variety of communities of what we would nowadays define (somewhat anachronistically if referred to the Middle Periods of Islamic history) as of 'ethnic' or mixed ethnic and confessional-sectarian kinds. The low degree of formalization of social power indeed favored an interpenetration among the multiple social localizations of groups and communities: as between the Sufi lodge, the college of teaching governed by the 'ulama', the craftsmen association, and the *futuwwa*, but also between inns, baths, and markets. These were all loci of civic encounters and social transactions.

This variegated social map found a transversal glue in how services were funded: not by non-existing municipalities but by a variety of discrete pious endowments, originating from the meta-institutional matrix of the *waqf*. Originally devised to protect family property from a type of state intervention that would favor the formation of a feudal system, the *waqf* became the source of funding for a variety of social, educational, and 'charitable' activities and spaces. The *waqf* facilitated flexible and often inclusive Islamic understandings of the civil realm, within a variety of instances of goods and enterprises, like schools, fountains, hospitals, and burial societies, as well as various configurations of urban spaces, like markets, large mosques, and public squares. Yet the *waqf* also became the source of funding for bundles of services, which became institutions in their own right, like those of the *madrasas* (the teaching colleges). The way the *waqf* worked as such a flexible matrix was via endowments made with pious intentions by anybody who could afford them. Endowers were mainly the rulers and the political, bureaucratic, and economic elites. As a result, the *waqf* happened to cover the provision of health, the funding of educational and infrastructural services, and the administration and management of institutional ties to strong family interests (including those of the warrior class up to the emirs, the local power holders, and the sultans, the centralized rulers). The *waqf* as a meta-institutional matrix was based on a quite clear-cut, civil type of law which regulated the way the endowments supported the various localized institutions. Yet the civil law of the *waqf* fell short of matching the Western idea of incorporation for the reasons explained in the previous chapter (Hennigan 2004). The establishment of charitable endowments benefited the elites in that it fostered bonds of loyalty with the lower classes with the mediation of the authority and trust generated by the *'ulama'*, and so partly compensated for the inherently fragile legitimacy of those in a privileged position within society. On the other hand, it is not surprising that among all such services the rulers were particularly eager to institute and fund the colleges, in order to employ *'ulama'* and attract their benevolence.

As the main (if not only) full-fledged (though not fully incorporated) general or meta-institution of Muslim society, the *waqf* was imbued with the sense of piety (or, more plastically and concretely, of 'doing good' to others) that supported the moral law. Neither private nor public, the *waqf* cut across both spheres and reached into the realm pertaining in principle to the Other, the ultimate mediator of human affairs, God (Barnes 1986: 5). The *waqf* thus represented nothing less than the infrastructural hub of Islamic traditions and their institutional route into building the social nexus of Islamdom. It institutionalized in mild and flexible, yet legally certain, forms the religious imperative of creating connectedness between self and other particularly by targeting the needs of wider collectivities or of particularly disfavored members of the community. The *waqf* therefore became the main historical infrastructure of a translocal, free-floating, rather cosmopolitan type of civility (Eisenstadt 2002).

Yet it would also be misleading to celebrate the flexible character of the *waqf* without reservations or specifications. Abuses in the institutional, civic, service-oriented role of the *waqf* were not only widespread but often at the very source of their foundation. That the *waqf* throve nonetheless is a strong sociological proof of its viability as the leading institutional infrastructure of Islamic civility. More than furthering the prevalence of outright informal ties in the relationships among scholars and between scholars, commoners, and rulers, we see in the overall picture of Islamic civility and in the specific function of the *waqf* therein the success of an approach to organization of a more scalable kind than in its European counterparts. The difference is palpable in terms of the degree (and reversibility) of institutional formalization, irrespective of the sincerity of the moral intent of the initiators and administrators of the foundations.

We have seen that *shari'a*-oriented jurisprudence provided the mainstream normative coordinates to Muslim society, while Sufi orders lent it a pervasive moral leadership. With regard to both, the *waqf* represented the social platform and fiscal infrastructure that secured the common good and public weal as formulated through Islamic norms, by balancing the inner faith and the externalized regulations and provisions. The *waqf* was a clearly formalized type of general institution based on a specific law, unlike the semi-chartered colleges and the unchartered Sufi brotherhoods. As such it retained and over time optimized the scalability of formalization of rules and the flexibility in the use of resources for the pursuit of its institutional ends. These were oriented to local demands but also responded to the power of extended networks and to the influential interests of families and clans. For sure, this flexibility did not protect it from becoming the object of abuses and diversion of resources from its institutionalized objectives.

Not untypically, and not unlike a college, a Sufi lodge could also be established as a *waqf* by the ruler. Such an act was, however, hardly perceived as a particularistic, preferential treatment of a specific group, precisely due to the original idea of instituting a *waqf* as a gesture of pious commitment to the common good warranted by God's mediating 'thirdness' toward all kinds of dyadic, self–other relations. Sufi brotherhoods (*turuq*) fulfilled this role in full and competed with each other for support and funding in exchange for the capacity to relay their power as brotherhoods to the goals of the power holders. Yet more in general, for the commoners to be entitled to care dispensed by means of a *waqf*, one did not need to be a member of the specific Sufi order that benefited from the foundation. The pious orientation to 'doing good' facilitated by the civil law of the *waqf* and the underlying principle of the 'common good' (*maslaha*: see Chapter 4) that often supported its use as a social service were frequently subjected to a continuous interpretation, negotiation, and weighing of a variety of legitimate interests at stake in a given context first determined by the donor's intentions. A balanced solution could be approximated through an appropriate blending of equity and reflexivity, through weighing up plural interests and bringing them to an acceptable common denominator. Such a condition for a social, i.e. not purely scholarly, consensus on the living goals of the *waqf* was a fair inclusion of commoners in the practices and discourses of doing good to others: not just as beneficiaries but also as at least intermittent participants in expressing interests and manifesting acceptance or dissent (see Ghazaleh 2011; Isin and Lefebvre 2005).

The institutionally unmarked character of the *umma*, the community of believers, made the *waqf* a terrain of competition for community leadership among elites. This competition was measured by their capacity to mobilize resources dedicated to the care of significant groups of commoners (whether identified by social conditions, like the poor or orphans, or as the inhabitants of a certain neighborhood), or at least to gain the respect deriving from publicly displaying such a care. This was possible since while rulers were responsible for the public order, they were not per se, as rulers, deputed to secure civic cohesion and the public weal. They needed to compete on the terrain of the provision for the public weal as community leaders among others who acted as endowers of *waqf*, by redistributing wealth and displaying pious intentions (Hoexter 2002: 123). Additionally, as rulers they were expected to create the practical conditions for fair competition in the field of *waqf* among potential endowers and prevent or at least limit its abuse. This process culminated during Timur's time in the Later Middle Period with Muslim princes granting *awqaf* (plural of *waqf*) to *'ulama'* and Sufis and so establishing their families as socio-cultural elites over generations. This *waqf* business inserted itself powerfully within the Silk Road exchange economy, especially in such nodes as Samarkand and Bukhara. The argument frequently invoked that the *waqf* prevented the rise of capitalism by inhibiting the market circulation of potential investment capital (Kuran 2001; 2011) does not take into account that the *waqf* favored the formation of nodes within circulatory networks that had a crucial function in furthering long-distance trade, which was the *sine qua non* of all hemisphere-wide capital accumulation. Due to the high risk of investing into such nodes (where markets often overlapped with saints' shrines and learning centers), without the *waqf* these nodes would have likely been either underfunded or not funded at all. Long-distance commerce survived and thrived also if not mainly thanks to the *waqf* economy.

It is remarkable that what best reflected Islamic notions of duties, rights, and responsibilities underlying collective welfare and its public management was less the formal conception than the concrete management of *waqf* conglomerations. Indeed the *'ulama'* retained a central role not only in the formulation of the common good but also in its daily and concrete management via their staffing of *waqf* institutions. This task required a considerable administrative and especially legal competence in accommodating the composite and mobile interests that the *waqf* was called to satisfy. One could dare a sociological definition of the *'ulama'* as those professionals selected to lead the community based on their knowledge (*'ilm*) and so legitimized to shape civic space by employing their legal reasoning in a variety of settings, but most crucially in running *waqf* institutions. Of course in concrete circumstances it is often the control itself of resources to distribute that retroactively, so to speak, bestows upon a community leader the required credentials as a knowledgeable and reputable personality. This function legitimized the *'ulama'* as intermediaries between rulers and commoners even more than their possession of knowledge per se, or their role as scholars, teachers, and preachers. Of course a sociological definition of the group can only be complete by including the ways their interests were intertwined with those of other groups belonging to the middle and upper classes, most crucially traders and craftsmen, in a given locale.

The existence and thriving of the *waqf* weakens the orientalist argument on the "Islamic city" as being almost the antithesis of the European city, most notably as typified by Weber, to the extent that the former allegedly lacked civic autonomy and particularly those crucial intermediate associational structures situated between the individual and the community, in this case the *umma* (Eickelman 1974; 1994; J. Abu-Lughod 1987; Zubaida 2006). The civil law of the *waqf* was not derived from any purportedly original Islamic doctrine but rather constituted the contingent outcome of Islam's development and expansion over vast civilizational areas also outside the Irano-Semitic region. This legal framework supported and regulated the above-mentioned array of activities and accorded to the urban officials and community leaders an instrument for promoting civic cohesion. It might not have exposed the work of the *'ulama'* as if to a formal control comparable to the emergent representative institutions of late-medieval European cities. Yet it constrained them to prove their ability to strike a balance between a variety of stakes on the ground transcending the vested interests of a restricted political-military and aristocratic elite. Here as elsewhere, as felicitously formulated by John Hall, "Islam was so advanced as to disallow some of the social institutions involved in the European dynamic" (Hall 1985: 99). Extensive civil monitoring (no doubt dependent on the personal honesty of the *'ulama'* who administered the *waqf*) replaces here a tight formal control based on legal accountability—or rather makes the latter unnecessarily cumbersome. Yet this monitoring could not be achieved without the protective umbrella of a formalizable normative network providing a basis not only to the abstract legitimacy of the institution of *waqf* but also to its daily management, based on legally rational, i.e. non-arbitrary, rulings. Arjomand argues in favor of the Iranian origin of the civil law of *waqf*, a hypothesis that is perfectly aligned with the social trajectory of development and crystallization of the Islam/Islamdom civilizational complex that we have been reconstructing (Arjomand 2004: 218).

We should, however, take care not to reduce the essence of Islamic civility to the *waqf* per se as a meta-institutional matrix. Rulers' courts—whose sheer number increased during the Middle Periods due to political fragmentation—and their inner codes of interaction rested on a time-honored, indeed pre-Islamic, high culture and continued to figure prominently in the production of patterns of civility. Their culture was mostly associated with the notion of *adab* and related practices, which decisively determined the character (and even more the self-understanding) of the carriers of statecraft and administrative knowledge. *Adab* should be considered as a parallel knowledge tradition that the Islamicate civilization inherited from Persianate court culture. Therefore it should be fully distinguished, at least in principle, from the core Islamic traditions of the *'ulama'* gravitating around the *hadith* corpus, instituting specifically Islamic patterns of probity and fair interaction based on the living example of Muhammad.

The most general definition of *adab* would embrace the ensemble of the ethical and practical norms of virtuous and beautiful life ideally cultivated by a class of literati. These consisted not only of the cultural embellishments but also of the educational requirements, in communicative terms, associated with the tasks of courtiers and secretaries. Literature and poetry, and the modes of their cultivation, therefore figured prominently within *adab*. In this sense the *adab* tradition directly ingrained into the developing civility of Islamdom while also interacting with Islam proper, intended as a faith-centered religious tradition. *Adab* survived the eclipse of the High Caliphate and its intensely knowledge-centered court life and stood out as an elite-oriented, yet flexible, matrix of rules of good life, courteous exchange, and civic cohesion based on bundling together cultured life forms considered adequate to respond to Islam's core message.

Adab legitimately intersected Islam's dynamics and throve alongside the *shari'a* tradition and its norms based on Qur'an and, even more, *hadith*. The classic era of the Caliphate from the middle of the 7th to the middle of the 10th century CE, i.e. prior to the Middle Periods, was the epoch that first set the terms of the future continual dialectic (and, to a considerable extent, crossfertilization) between these two traditions. It is important to observe that unlike their Sasanian predecessors, in the Islamic ecumene merchants often had a share in this court culture. This participation of non-aristocratic strata in *adab* also facilitated an intense interfacing, if not exchange, between *adab* and *hadith*. Some Sufi trends also contributed to this blending of *adab* and *hadith* over the course of the centuries, particularly during the transition between the Middle Periods and the modern era (see Lapidus 1984 and Papas 2008). Ultimately even the virtuous jurist (*faqih*), intent on delivering legal advice in the form of *fatwa*s, and therefore acting as a *mufti*, had to respond to a model of *adab* tailor-made to this lofty task (Masud 1984). Therefore *adab* and *hadith* cannot be construed as mutually exclusive traditions since they were subjected—quite variably and according to epoch and locale—to a process of amalgamation as providers of exemplary models of life conduct, good life, and civic intercourse. The ongoing and overlapping patterns of Islamic civility remained to a large extent inscribed within the tension between these two major fields of knowledge and associated life forms. This dialectic was carried over into the modern era, where it was distorted and complicated by Western colonial encroachments and the attendant global civilizing process, as we will see in Chapter 6.

The culture of *adab* contributed from within the fold of Islam/Islamdom to an original, long-term type of civilizing process not radically different from the sense highlighted by Norbert Elias with regard to the European trajectory: i.e. radiating from a court but with the potential to trickle down and civilize entire populations, particularly through its reception by commercial bourgeoisies eager to appropriate noble and cultured life styles. *Adab* provided significant nexuses between general ideas of the body politic, patterns of intervention on society (essentially, the organization of violence and taxation), the self-understanding of emerging elites, and the violence-containing inward projection of the norms produced in the process. Far from being eclipsed with the collapse of the High Caliphate, which by and large represented an extension of Persianate rule, *adab* became particularly influential during the Middle Periods. It contributed to regulating the relations between a political elite of ever more markedly military origin led, in each potentate, by an emir (*amir*), and the urban notables (*a'yan*), including both leading *'ulama'* and traders.

Adab was therefore instrumental in solidifying what Hodgson called the *a'yan-amir* system of rule and consensus that characterized the Middle Periods (Hodgson 1974, II: 64–9). The key relationship here is between emirs as overlords stemming from the military classes on the one hand, and urban notables, be they 'patricians' or 'plebeians' in terms of their class origin and wealth, on the other. The relation was inscribed within a permanent search for localized and contingent balances between a politico-military type of power and knowledge-based, socio-cultural power. Within these dynamics the class of the *'ulama'* provides the knowledge-oriented core of the *a'yan* groups, i.e. of the wider stratum of urban notables. It therefore exhibits a socio-political competence to face the emirs through the specific yet broad skills originating from various branches of *'ilm*, which were ultimately secured under the umbrella of the administration of civic space and public services in the form of the *waqf*. *Adab* therefore complexifies (and to some extent civilizes) the supposedly military character of rule in the Middle Periods and provides glue to the social nexus of Islamdom.

This fundamentally urban dual structure of power governed by *adab* and *shari'a*, somewhat reflecting the knowledge–power doublet as a complex dynamics more than as a sheer dual tension, should be joined by the consideration of two other key groups vying for social power. The first of these was the agrarian gentry, whose power basis was the portion of landed property which was not absorbed into the *waqf* system (and which thereby ensured a permanent channel of access to political office at court). The second group was represented by the leaders of the nomadic sphere, often (and reductively) dubbed the 'tribal elders,' whose importance cannot be reduced to merely being the cyclical providers of ever new breeds of overlord elites. While wielding a considerable amount of informal power thanks to their command of sheer military might and inner cohesion (the kernel of Ibn Khaldun's *'asabiyya*), nomadic forces were not confined without residue to the military side of the dual structure of power. They also represented a social potential of resistance to the capacity of urban elites to shape their societies through concentrating force and organizing violence in a centralized system of court and government administration (most typically, the inertial side of this nomadic resistance to centralized power is the capacity to avoid taxation).

The complex picture of the ideal-typical Islamic society of the Middle Periods and of the sources of civility therein should be completed by adding the crucial role played by long-distance traders, often in association with pastoralists and craftsmen (the latter strongly tied to Sufi brother-hoods). Their role was decisive in the long-term integration of the Islamic ecumene, not just economically but in terms of translocal connectedness (Hodgson 1993: 106–7).The increasing importance of such traders during this epoch highlights the growing centrality of the Nile-to-Oxus cradle of Islamic civilization within its wider perimeter of expansion along the networked, long-distance routes mostly known as the Silk Road (which also included a maritime counterpart to the land, particularly across the Indian Ocean). It should also be observed that long-distance caravans included religious missionaries, often of a Sufi kind, alongside a broader range of scholars/*'ulama'*. The expansion of trade networks centered on Persian and Arab merchants entered a positive loop with the propagation of Islam as not just a religious-ethical idiom but also as a code regulating a wide range of relations and transactions, with commercial ties figuring prominently in it basically from Islam's inception. This was not a new phe-nomenon but the culmination of a process of marrying trade and mission across Eurasian depths previously carried over by Zoroastrian, Buddhist, Christian, and Manichean long-distance travelers, among which Iranic populations (including Central Asian Bactrians and Sogdians) played a leading role.

We have now gained the picture of a quite complex (and certainly unstable) social equilibrium where ever new local configurations of forces and regional arrangements were affected by the power balance of specific conjunctures and places. This inherent instability discouraged the search for too formal a level of institutionalization of the knowledge–power equation. Yet in no way did it inhibit the scholarly longing for understanding rules of a more general order, be they socio-political (as in the case of Ibn Khaldun) or cosmic and 'spiritual' (as with the several Sufi thinkers of the Middle Periods, the most prominent of all being Ibn al-'Arabi, who will be mentioned in the next chapter). In this wider process Sufism and its inner balances should never be confined to an asocial realm, as Ibn Khaldun also helped to illustrate. They should be considered as a key vector of the Islamic construction and maintenance of the social bond and attendant patterns of civility, which we are now going to compare with its counterparts from Latin Christendom.

References

Abu-Lughod, Janet. 1987. "The Islamic City – Historic Myth, Islamic Essence, and Contemporary Relevance." *International Journal of Middle East Studies*, 19/2: 155–76.

Alatas, Syed Farid. 2011. "Ibn Khaldūn." In *The Wiley-Blackwell Companion to Major Social Theorists: Classical Social Theorists*, I, 2nd ed., edited by George Ritzer and Jeffrey Stepinsky, 12–29. Chichester, West Sussex: John Wiley & Sons.

Alatas, Syed Farid. 2013. *Ibn Khaldun*. New Delhi: Oxford University Press.

Arjomand, Said Amir. 2004. "Transformation of the Islamicate Civilization: A Turning Point in the Thirteenth Century?" In *Eurasian Transformations, 10th to 13th Centuries: Crystallizations, Divergences, Renaissances*, edited by Johann P. Arnason and Björn Wittrock, 213–45. Leiden: Brill.

Arnason, Johann P. and Georg Stauth. 2004. "Civilization and State Formation in the Islamic Context: Re-reading Ibn Khaldun." *Thesis Eleven*, 76: 29–47.

Bamyeh, Mohammed A. 2000. *The Ends of Globalization*. University of Minnesota Press.

Barnes, John R. 1986. *An Introduction to Religious Foundations in the Ottoman Empire*. Leiden: Brill.

Bellah, Robert N. 1970. *Beyond Belief: Essays on Religion in a Post-Traditional World*. New York: Harper and Row.

Berkey, Jonathan. 2001. *Popular Preaching and Religious Authority in the Medieval Islamic Near East*. Seattle and London: University of Washington Press.

Eickelman, Dale F. 1974. "Is There an Islamic City? The Making of a Quarter in a Moroccan Town." *International Journal of Middle East Studies*, 5/3: 274–94.

Eickelman, Dale F. 1994. "The Comparative Studies of 'Islamic' City." In *Urbanism in Islam*, edited by Tadeshi Yukuwa, 309–19. Tokyo: The Middle Eastern Culture Center in Japan.

Eisenstadt, Shmuel N. 2002. "Concluding Remarks: Public Sphere, Civil Society, and Political Dynamics in Islamic Societies." In *The Public Sphere in Muslim Societies*, edited by Miriam Hoexter, Shmuel N. Eisenstadt, and Nehemia Levtzion, 139–61. Albany, NY: SUNY Press.

Fromherz, Allen James. 2010. *Ibn Khaldun: Life and Times*. Edinburgh: Edinburgh University Press.

Ghazaleh, Pascale. 2011. "Introduction. Pious Foundations: From Here to Eternity?" In *Held in Trust: Waqf in the Islamic World*, edited by Pascale Ghazaleh, 1–21. Cairo: American University in Cairo Press.

Hall, John A. 1985. *Powers and Liberties: The Causes and Consequences of the Rise of the West*. Oxford: Basil Blackwell.

Hennigan, Peter C. 2004. *The Birth of a Legal Institution: The Formation of the Waqf in Third-Century A.H. Hanafi Legal Discourse.* Leiden and Boston: Brill.

Herzog, Thomas. 2013. "Mamluk (Popular) Culture." In *Ubi sumus? Quo vademus? Mamluk Studies – State of the Art*, edited by Stefan Conermann, 131–58. Göttingen: Bonn University Press.

Hodgson, Marshall G.S. 1974. *The Venture of Islam: Conscience and History in a World Civilization*, I–III. Chicago and London: University of Chicago Press.

Hodgson, Marshall G.S. 1993. *Rethinking World History: Essays on Europe, Islam and World History*, edited, with Introduction and Conclusion, by Edmund Burke III. Cambridge: Cambridge University Press.

Hoexter, Miriam. 2002. "The Waqf and the Public Sphere." In *The Public Sphere in Muslim Societies*, edited by Miriam Hoexter, Shmuel N. Eisenstadt, and Nehemia Levtzion, 119–38. Albany, NY: SUNY Press.

Isin, Engin F. and Lefebvre, Alexandre. 2005. "The Gift of Law: Greek Euergetism and Ottoman *Waqf.*" *European Journal of Social Theory*, 8/1: 5–23.

Kuran, Timur. 2001. "The Provision of Public Goods under Islamic Law: Origins, Impact, and Limitations of the Waqf System." *Law and Society Review*, 35/4: 841–97.

Kuran, Timur. 2011. *The Long Divergence: How Islamic Law Held Back the Middle East.* Princeton, NJ: Princeton University Press.

Lapidus, Ira M. 1984. "Knowledge, Virtue, and Action: The Classical Muslim Conception of *Adab* and the Nature of Religious Fulfillment in Islam." In *Moral Conduct and Authority: The Place of Adab in South Asian Islam*, edited by Barbara Daly Metcalf, 38–61. Berkeley and Los Angeles: University of California Press.

Masud, M. Khalid. 1984. "Adab Al-Mufti: The Muslim Understanding of Values, Characteristics, and Role of a Mufti." In *Moral Conduct and Authority: The Place of Adab in South Asian Islam*, edited by Barbara Daly Metcalf, 124–5. Berkeley and Los Angeles: University of California Press.

Papas, Alexander. 2008. "No Sufism without Sufi Order: Rethinking Tarîqa and Adab with Ahmad Kâsânî Dahbidî (1461–1542)." *Kyoto Bulletin of Islamic Area Studies*, 2/1: 4–22.

Rahimi, Babak. 2004. "Between Chieftaincy and Knighthood: A Comparative Study of Ottoman and Safavid Origins." *Thesis Eleven*, 76: 85–102.

Rahimi, Babak. 2006. "The Middle Period: Islamic Axiality in the Age of Afro-Eurasian Transcultural Hybridity." In *Islam in Process: Historical and Civilizational Perspectives*, edited by Johann P. Arnason, Armando Salvatore, and Georg Stauth, 48–67. Bielefeld: Transcript; New Brunswick, NJ: Transaction (*Yearbook of the Sociology of Islam* VII).

Rahman, Fazlur. 1979 [1966]. *Islam*. Chicago and London: University of Chicago Press.

Zaman, Muhammad Qasim. 2002. *The Ulama in Contemporary Islam: Custodians of Change*. Princeton, NJ: Princeton University Press.

Zubaida, Sami. 2006. "Max Weber's *The City* and the Islamic City." *Max Weber Studies*, 6/1: 111–18.

4

SOCIAL AUTONOMY AND CIVIC CONNECTEDNESS
The Islamic Ecumene in Comparative Perspective

New Patterns of Civic Connectedness Centered on the 'Commoners'

Based on the previous chapters, what is most unsettling for familiar Eurocentric schemes is that the Islamic expansive trajectory during the Middle Periods displayed some factors of change that, particularly during the 12th and 13th centuries, were simultaneously at work in Western Europe, i.e. during the period conventionally identified as the European Late or High Middle Ages. While Middle Ages is a term that on the surface seems to exactly match Middle Periods, both its common and its scholarly understanding has in reality vastly different implications with regard to modernity. Although historiography has located in the Late or High Middle Ages the seeds of crucial factors of change that then manifested themselves in full with the onset of modernity, the adjective 'medieval' is outside of scholarly circles still quite often synonymous with traditional and premodern, if not backward. This understanding has contributed significantly to how Hodgson devised a matching term to be applied to Islam/Islamdom: he chose "Middle Periods" in order not to squeeze Islamic developments into European grids, which were characterized by a preventive downgrading of the dynamic character of the Middle Ages.

Hodgson intended to stress how, other than the Middle Ages in European history, the Middle Periods (and particularly the specific epoch that cuts the Middle Periods in two parts, the 12th and 13th centuries) have a crucial importance in helping us to grasp the long-term trajectory of what he aptly called *The Venture of Islam* (the title of his trilogy). Hodgson also

The Sociology of Islam: Knowledge, Power and Civility, First Edition. Armando Salvatore.
© 2016 John Wiley & Sons, Ltd. Published 2016 by John Wiley & Sons, Ltd.

stressed that this was "the first period during which a comparison of the Occident with Islamdom can be particularly fruitful" for the simple fact that "up to that time, the Occident had been, on the whole, too backward to compare with one of the major centers of civilizations" (Hodgson 1993: 126). In other words, it is exactly Europe's exit from the 'darkest' thick of the (Early or Low) Middle Ages during those centuries that allows for a fair and fruitful comparison. The apparent similarities between Islamic and European developments in the period that interests us here concerned in particular the emerging patterns of distinction and reconciliation between 'spiritual' drives and the construction of civic ties. The putative commonalities stand in tension with an accentuation of divergent rhythms and modes in the cultural reproduction of social power in the two cases, as will become evident by the end of this chapter.

Within Latin Christendom, new monastic movements and a resurgence of urban life occupied center stage from the 11th century onward and reached a climax in the 13th century. The rise of heretical movements and the almost simultaneous emergence of radical mendicant orders—in particular during the 12th and 13th centuries—highlighted the pressures on ecclesiastical institutions of the practical necessities and desires of renewal that spread among popular classes and the rising urban middle classes. Models of ascetic life conduct based on discipline and piety originating within monastic walls were transposed and adapted to the *civitas*, representing the urban world of an expanding laity.

The leading European theologian Thomas Aquinas (1225–1274) is mostly considered the intellectual champion of the epoch on the European side. His theological synthesis emphasized a renewed faith conjoined with reason and an underlying freedom of the will. His work is representative of the socio-political sensibility of the age and was at the center of a larger movement of mendicant orders like the Franciscans and the Dominicans. During the 13th century, these new monastic orders became not only a civic force but also an intellectual vanguard militating for a practical and institutional reconstruction of the *respublica christiana*. This notion reflected the conceptual, theological, and practical views facilitating the pursuit of the common good based on a harmonious articulation and implementation of Christian virtues. Simultaneously, Aquinas' work was also intended to meet the challenge of a more radical spiritual individualism, propagated by Francis of Assisi (1181–1226) earlier in the century and integral to the wider innovative movement represented by the mendicant orders. Aquinas emphasized *caritas* as the pillar of his entire anthropology. *Caritas* represented the queen of all virtues and consisted in doing good to others, on a par with *prudentia* as the vehicle of judgment incumbent on the individual. This theoretical option in favor of *caritas* (which thus cannot be reduced to the insulated function of 'charity' in a modern colonial setting: see Chapter 6) was intended to provide coherence and direction to the thriving urban worlds of the epoch, which saw the emergence of new bourgeois strata and corresponding civic autonomies.

Aquinas' approach both animated and reflected the spiritual ferment from which his own mendicant order, the Dominicans, alongside the more radical Franciscans, had sprouted. While both orders had to cope with the new challenges of a dynamic urban laity, the Franciscans stood out as a type of socio-religious movement that, unlike the Dominicans, rejected intellectualism and insisted on the intrinsic power of *caritas*. This virtue, especially if sustained by grace, could be seen as largely independent from any magisterial regime, as the virtue directly emanating from the commoner's good heart. This view also implied an impulse of renewal that, originating from the commoners, directly impacted the civic realm, whose autonomy and vigor the theoretically powerful synthesis of Aquinas was only partly capable of capturing. The more deeply radical character of the Franciscans lay primarily in a stronger evocation of the community of the politically free, which led them to develop a particularly versatile capacity to permeate social life and act as intermediaries in civic contentions (Voegelin 1997: 231; Santoro 2003 [1999]: 71–88).

The reform impetus of both movements unfolded during and after the unsettling of the fragile institutional balance of the *respublica christiana*, effected by various macro- and micro-institutional failures in the redefinition of the authority of the pope and the emperor, as well as of the pastoral role of bishops and priests. This is also why one cannot understand the impact of Aquinas' theory without looking at the monastic revolution of the mendicant orders as a whole, which aimed to overcome the self-enclosed, limitedly social character of the original Christian monastic model. The new monastic brotherhoods launched a program for capturing and domesticating the proliferation of popular drives toward heterodox life practices affecting the *respublica christiana* during the Late Middle Ages. They were able to incorporate these potentially transgressive drives into innovative forms that could be aligned both with the monastic tradition and with the doctrinal orthodoxy of the Church. Their tasks ranged from redesigning the imitation of Christ through a life of poverty, through healing the sick, up to performing a capillary work of preaching and conversion. In this way, the new orders became the true civic vanguards of the renewal and reform not only of the Church but of Latin Christendom and its society at large. Their discursive arsenal powered by this resystematization of the Christian virtues relied on the deployment of a highly mobile intellectual impetus directly functional to the refinement of the power of speech. This was geared toward promoting civic cohesion and cooperation, especially among crucial segments of urban populations (Friedrich Silber 1995: 140).

Concurrent with the erosion of the high politics of the Church, the Franciscan friars in particular contributed to building up notions and practices of the civic life in which they were embedded from the start of their movement. They did not have to go outside the monastery walls since they had understood themselves, from the beginning, as the purest commoners and townspeople. In spite of the radical dimension of the original message, they invested Franciscan authority into routine-like functions of reproduction of civic connections. For example, they became fiduciary persons in giving witness and executing testaments, guaranteeing a wide variety of agreements, and giving counsel to individuals and organized groups. In exceptional cases, i.e. when a city's factionalism heightened their authority as arbiters, some monks were even conferred direct ruling responsibilities. They also promoted new, largely autonomous associations combining monastic and civic ideals, like a vast assortment of lay brotherhoods and congregations. There the friars tutored lay citizens (especially those from the merchant and artisan classes) into practicing Christian virtues, while preparing them to take up tasks in community life, offices, and urban government. Moreover, they were able to infiltrate patronage networks, without necessarily disrupting them. In this way they often gained an ideal position for providing the intellectual know-how and the organizing backbone to a parallel social hierarchy pivoting on a religious-*cum*-civic type of virtue. The corresponding patterns of authority flourished within the urban laity and coexisted with the hard sociological hierarchy determined by wealth, prestige, and status (Salvatore 2007: 128–30).

In the final analysis, these movements facilitated the institution of an organic fit between the Christian practice of doing good and more purely social types of civic habitus. These were related to the requirements of socioeconomic life and reflected corresponding modes of entrepreneurship, solidarity, and patronage. In all these cases the role of the Franciscans as urban brokers upheld in quite explicit and immediate ways the ideas of the common good formulated and practiced on behalf of both commoners and wealthy townsmen. In their role as conscious intruders and mostly welcome outsiders—because free from specific, local, material interests—they were able to reflect on the civic conflicts they were confronted with, and to communicate to local communities the results of their reflection. They could finally translate these reflections into non-coercive templates of solutions to specific civic problems. The Franciscans were thus a living example of how a reflective process of stepping back from particularistic interests constitutes a condition for cohesion among the citizenry (Salvatore 2007: 130–1).

The main Islamic counterpart to the mendicant orders in Europe was represented by the simultaneous growth and consolidation of spiritually oriented movements and groups in the form of increasingly organized Sufi orders, whose importance we have highlighted in the previous chapters. Both in Europe and in the Islamic ecumene such Christian and Islamic movements were able to draw on the imagination and the needs of the commoners, including the city dwellers. They laid claim to grasping the essence of the transcendent truth while turning this search into a life-orientational path feeding into collective practices and disciplines. Such practices, increasingly ingraining into the civic sphere, were significantly more innovative than those of the earlier institutional subjects in the Church (including older monastic orders) and in the *umma* (including earlier forms of Sufism). Here spirituality denotes, sociologically, a dimension of direct access to the ultimate source of inner power with a modicum of specialized cultural mediation. It is a well of empowerment to orient and shape an exemplary life.

These movements, though battled by part of the orthodox powers, were mostly integrated into the mainstream of the practiced faith, while also being able to affect the shape of new forms of orthodoxy. They were able to significantly influence the institutional configurations of the knowledge–power equation both within Latin Christendom and Islam (both Sunni and Shi'i), with enduring consequences that remain today. They were equally significant, in both civilizational realms, in the work directed at enhancing the importance of the lower and middle strata, especially within urban environments, what we have termed 'commoners.' Particularly well addressed was the commoners' frequently manifested desire for a renewal of norms of life conduct within wider socio-economic waves of transformation spawned by thriving urban economies and crossregional trade. These were nurtured by cycles of prosperity but also threatened by an accentuating gulf between the rich and the poor (cf. Arjomand 2004 and Rahimi 2006).

There is a partial yet significant analogy between the success and expansion of the mendicant orders like the Dominican and the Franciscan friars, beyond the monastic walls and into the revived civic economies and cultures, and their Sufi counterparts. This is apparent through processes of practical and institutional reconfigurations of notions of human reason and agency related to new majestic systematizations of scenarios of transcendence and paths of salvation. Think not just of Aquinas' monumental theological work but also of Dante Alighieri's *Divina Commedia*, in which some commentators have seen the influence of key Muslim thinkers of the Middle Periods, and particularly of the greatest Sufi master Muhyiddin Ibn al-ʿArabi (Palacios 1919). Both Ibn al-ʿArabi (1165–1240) and Dante (1265–1331) asserted in poetically and conceptually sublime ways the centrality of a renewed commitment of the faithful to one's own city or community and, one layer deeper, to a mystically conceived universal citizenship.

Even more consistently than with the new monastic movements within Latin Christendom, the organizational consolidation of Sufism as a spiritual path during the Middle Periods was often indistinguishable from a civic movement of the commoners. *Nasab al-khirqa*, one of the last writings of Ibn al-ʿArabi, can be considered the testament to his practice-oriented (albeit conceptually sophisticated) spirituality. It delineated the relationship between the inner and the outer dimensions of the truth. The text provides an almost prototypical catalogue of axial compassion, calling to the observance of pious behavior to Other (Elmore 1999). The *khirqa*, i.e. the mantel of Sufi initiation, is called *malabis ahl al-taqwa*, i.e. the investiture of the God-fearing. *Taqwa* (corresponding to the Latin Christian *timor Dei*) spells out the core of the Islamic virtue calling the Muslim to operate wisely and interactively in a social and practical life of orientation to all forms of otherhood, the terrestrial and the heavenly. The transmission of the master's garment that symbolizes the initiation does not result in a personal attachment to a master's charisma but rather in the reception of the multiplicity of spiritual affiliations condensed in the master's life course, also thanks to his journeys. Therefore initiation serves multiple, diverse, and overlapping, far from exclusive, affiliations.

The focus is on a sequential plurality of highly individualized voyages (each of them called a *rihla* or *siyaha*) to acquire knowledge through the experience of various encounters, and potential corresponding initiations. The simultaneous emphasis is on movement and knowledge rather than on the sacralization of a locus and collective bond. Even in the context of initiation, with all its dense symbolism, the spiritual realm is not constructed as a separate domain but is solidly anchored in the human diversity of relations and practices. The higher the mobility, the more diverse became the grid of affiliations: the 18th-century Sufi Murtada al-Zabidi (1732–1791) could boast of belonging to more than a hundred, highly diverse brotherhoods, which in his autobiography he listed one by one, entailing relations and networks spanning the Islamic ecumene from Java to West Africa (Reichmuth 2010). This approach offers a stark contrast to the quasi-magical initiation oath highlighted by Weber with regard to urban brotherhoods within Latin Christendom, and that we examined in the last chapter. As eloquently summarized by William Chittick, "[w]hat stands out in Sufi esotericism is that it relates to the domain of Islam's faith and works, and it is contrasted with an exotericism that relates to the same domain" (Chittick 1992: 9).

Ibn al-ʿArabi was born and grew up in al-Andalus, in the Iberian peninsula, in the far West of the Islamic ecumene. He was influenced by earlier Sufi masters but also measured his own spiritual path against the background of the great philosophical teachers, among which, prominent in his age, we count Ibn Rushd (Averroes), whom he knew personally. At the age of 35 Ibn al-ʿArabi started disseminating, in a continual development, his teachings toward the East, through North Africa, toward Mecca and Damascus, i.e. ever closer to the core of the Irano-Semitic civilizational area. At that stage, the Sufi path appeared as highly innovative in that it formulated a solution to the problem of the relationship between rational speculation on the one hand and the impact of models of prophetic piety on the dispositions of practitioners on the other. This development was emblematic of how the pristine Islamic emphasis on egalitarian consensus became in the Middle Periods strongly reflected in forms of social organization which balanced vertical obedience to masters with solidarity among brothers. The Sufi way compares well here with its European counterpart represented by how the mendicant orders coped with the embryonic formation of an urban bourgeoisie in the Late Middle Ages.

However, in comparison, the rise of the commoners within the Islamic ecumene was more vulnerable and exposed to setbacks because of the way military, political, and economic elites increased their self-serving strategies during the Middle Periods. Overall, social upward mobility was markedly higher in the Islamic case, both within the ranks of the *ʿulama* and at courts. Yet clear differences from the European experience became most notable with regard to the organizational forms of the commoners' movements. This is evident through their understandings of the requisite disciplines (both individual and collective) and not least at the level of the overall institutional environment. In contrast to the mendicant orders' radicalization of the plea of urban commoners, the Sufi brotherhoods absorbed and reintegrated into mildly formalized dynamics and highly autonomous organizational grids the aspirations of the commoners for increased social space. Most importantly, such movements within the Islamic ecumene invested civic connectedness into translocal interconnectedness over long distances (by networking with far-distant places and groups) more than into locally entrenched forms of civic autonomy and local pride. Europe saw the emergence of municipal institutions within thriving urban settings which, as we saw, also captured the focus of the agency of the mendicant orders, in spite of the latter's social and geographical mobility. In the Islamic case, institutional malleability and translocal mobility trumped institutional autonomy and pride of place.

The differences appear clearly if we look at the most salient aspect of the wave of institutionalization of Sufism during the Later Middle Period. The new monastic orders in Europe contributed to a civic renaissance, sociologically, from within city life itself (because many members were of urban origin), but institutionally and symbolically from without (because the wall of the monastery remained external to the city wall). The Sufi orders instead merged almost symbiotically with urban associations and especially with the craftsmen guilds. They built multifunctional ties of trust underpinned by the authority of the masters of the brotherhoods—ties that could benefit both the *tariqa* activities and the everyday world of crafts and business (cf. Gerber 1994: 113–26).

In other words, the Sufi model did not suffer from any residual dualism between spiritual devotion and civic life and promoted a scalable formalization of the bond among brethren and between them and their masters. The resulting, mild formalization of relations could be calibrated according to needs and circumstances. Sufism also furthered the expansive dimension of the common affiliation, the key to the construction of the civic bond, by deploying its activities across distant territories. In contrast to such Islamic patterns, even the reformed monastic model in Europe continued to privilege a strict formalization of hierarchies and disciplines and reiterated a principled distinction (even after many monks became the leaders of a new cultural institution, the rising European university) between religious and civic bonds. In this sense, Sufism provided a permanent infrastructure of ties of trust, moral leadership, and a flexible discourse of justice reflecting a rigorous orientation to the ultimate truth. This was underpinned both by the authority of the masters of the brotherhoods and by the appeal of corresponding cosmological frameworks and was often corroborated by the healing capacities of Sufi leaders. This communicative infrastructure also included the channels through which commoners could represent their aspirations and grievances to local authorities within the *waqf* system (Levtzion 2002: 117). Most importantly, the Sufi path emphasized individual and collective bodily practices (breathing, chanting, dancing, also not excluding more eccentric-looking performances like snake charming, body piercing, etc., where usually the 'corporal' and the 'spiritual' dimensions densely intersect) in a variety of ways. This diversity reflected the higher degree of mobility, uncertainty, and connectedness characterizing the Islamic ecumene vs. the *respublica christiana* of Latin Christendom. The Islamic patterns resembled to some limited extent those enacted by the European *clerici vagantes*, who moved from city to city in their hunt for learning and a good life, often punctuated by eccentric behavior and transgressive practices. Unlike their Islamic counterparts, however, the wandering European knowledge-seekers remained rather on the margins of the mainstream movement.

Another element distinguishing European monastic innovators from the dynamism of Sufi brotherhoods was that the mendicant movements in Europe were able to turn local saints into symbols of civic allegiances. They did so by mediating between popular devotions and the Church's suspicion toward a bottom-up approach that challenged the centralized procedures of saints' canonization. The Sufi brotherhoods, instead, followed a straighter path: they instituted on their own a notion of saintliness that was more supple in institutional terms than the idea of the charisma of the chain of the *imam*s—the infallible guides of the community, the only legitimate heirs of Muhammad—the strict allegiance to whom happened to distinguish the Shi'a from mainstream Sunni trends. The Sunni insertion of prophetic charisma into a highly fragmented notion of authority did not recognize, in principle, authoritative sources external to the Qur'an and the *sunna* of the Prophet based on the teachings of the *hadith* corpus, i.e. external to a fluid and multifunctional notion of religious knowledge that could be disembodied and reembodied through a variety of paths, teachings, and practices.

Therefore the making of saintliness through movements and groups distinct from the colleges of teachers and the schools of jurists, while laying a claim to the preservation and transmission of Qur'anic piety, constituted a new, parallel form of authority that also claimed orthodox status and inclusion in the consensus. By catering preferentially to the commoners (via a mystical idea of the common man as the best aspirant to human perfection), organized Sufism accentuated a stress on the free human agent which was already inherent within Muhammad's preaching and in the Qur'an. On the other hand, the resulting Sufi notion of the saint culminated hierarchically in the idea of the *qutb*, representing the highest echelon of sainthood and the cosmic 'pole' of order—an ideal of perfection from which all existence, both cosmic and social, depended. In turn this idea retroacted on radical Sufi milieus of the Shiʻa like those called to life in the Sarbadar republic mentioned in the previous chapter. These milieus would become influential in inspiring the movement that would initiate the Safavid dynasty in Iran at the beginning of the modern era, as we will see in the next chapter (Hodgson 1974, II: 493–500).

Liminality, Charisma, and Social Organization

It is remarkable how, both in the Latin Christian and the Islamic Sunni cases, the activity of the spiritual groups cannot be considered a one-to-one 'super-structural' reflection of structural developments unfolding within the urban fabric of the economic and political spheres. The socio-cultural creativity of these groups consisted in a bottom-up building of trust and civic reason through common rituals and reflection, as well as counsel and authoritative (though not necessarily coercive) interventions (in the form of arbitrations, mediations, and the raising of claims) through the group leaders. In many ways, this activity reflected the extent to which the forces of civic inno-vation were acting in anti-structural, namely liminal, ways, before folding themselves into the institutional landscape and affecting it profoundly. This 'spiritual' ferment is ultimately identical to the liminal positioning and acting characterizing these movements. By invoking liminality I intend to stress that the sources of their innovative discourses and practices were located at a delicately yet also strategically positioned, liminal (i.e. marginal or 'borderline') point or stage with regard to society as a whole. They were thus protected from any easy assimilation into the centralized normative spaces identified with the legal charters of socio-political institutions. They could therefore develop visions and initiate ventures that altered the social fabric and contributed to define (and often renew) the civic nexus (see Eisenstadt 1985).

   The best example of such a liminal type of social insertion sidestep-ping assimilation into the central institutions and statutes was the perpetuation of a critique internal to the Franciscan movement, which was directed against any excessive involvement of the friars with material and political issues. The warning came from the groups that occupied a marginal position within the movement after its civic integration into urban life. These groups attempted to keep a role as the guardians of the social liminality intrinsic to Francis' example and message, which shunned the institutional power of authoritative intermediation and favored a direct link to and talk with others/Other, both to the divine and the brothers and sisters (Salvatore 2007: 123–31). Over time this blessed configuration of forces wherein friars played a role in the shaping of civic arenas evaporated, thus sterilizing the impact of their liminal location. Yet genealogically this type of liminality did not dissipate but happened to innervate the emergent discourse of the free and cooperative agent capable of engaging a variety of types of *alter* in an ideally power-free arena of communication and civic dialogue: what in due course, after several shifts, morphed into the Western idea of civil society whereby *ego* engages *alter* through an allegedly power-free moral sense (see Chapter 1). Symptomatically, however, as we saw, the outcome of the theory was not adequate to the liminal stage that had first facilitated the practices associated with the new space.

Liminality was already a key factor in the rise of prophetic discourse, including the initial vicissitudes and final success of Muhammad's reception and transmission of the new-old revelation and his sharing of the message with the embryonic community of the faithful in Mecca, surrounded by a hostile environment. The 'venture' of Islam (to refer again to an idea popularized by Hodgson in the title of his œuvre) originates in such a liminal space that springs up surprisingly and contingently from within the margins of Meccan social structure and ends up undermining it. The outcome of the liminal process was a thorough rewriting of the significance of the place (in this case Mecca) as the symbolic center of a new religious tradition and of what would become the Islamic ecumene. Liminality is a factor within all major transformations supported by spiritual quests, to the extent that such ventures are bent on the potential creation of new social spaces and cultural orders. One can interpret the just-analyzed religious movements and groups of the 12th and 13th centuries within Latin Christendom and their counterparts in the Islamic ecumene as probably the best examples of liminal groups affirming a distinctive social significance. At this historical stage and in both cases marginal forces initially occupying a low (and scarcely institutionalized) level within hierarchies of social and religious authority start to play a central role in them, by initiating a lengthy and steady—though in no way smooth—march into the institutionalized dimension of social spaces.

Not new was the liminal and in-between role played by these forces in restituting meaning, order, and coherence to social actors who can thus find better forms of cohesion and fresh social languages to build alternate loci of social power. The Axial Age itself reposed on the deployment of such liminal processes. What was new was that the emerging movements analyzed in this chapter, which in many ways replayed axial tropes of innovation, unfolded their mobilizing capacities from the margins or interstices of the socio-political order and acquired an unprecedented institution-building capacity that was carried forward into modern settings, as we will see, for the Islamic case, in the next chapter. This capacity was often, and paradoxically, deployed precisely through an act of distancing from existing institutional patterns if not through an overtly anti-institutional approach. This is due to the simple fact that being liminal requires almost by default an inoculation against the bonds and limits of institutional power (Szakolczai 2001: 361–2). The most spectacular instance of the liminal wave of the mendicant orders was the nurturing of a new power based on knowledge, namely the *universitas*, as a third power between *imperium* and *sacerdotium*, the temporal and spiritual institutions. The third power, soon to become an institution in its own right (what is still the 'university'), and significantly staffed with personnel of Franciscan and Dominican origin, was a type of power somewhat zeroing in to an almost pure notion of knowledge and its codified transmission.

While this case, and most notably the role of Franciscan friars, seems to provide the most solid benchmark of liminality suitable for comparisons, the liminality of the organized Sufism "of saints and brothers" (Green 2012: 71) was less explicitly anti-institutional, primarily for the simple reason that it did not face strongly self-entrenched institutions like the Latin Christian *imperium* and *sacerdotium*. Yet the Sufi instance is no less interesting from a sociological viewpoint for reflecting how the intra-institutional marginality of earlier Sufis, who partook in a variety of social loci within the Islamic ecumene, could be turned into extra-institutional strength. This was the case especially as far as both local, communal solidarity and long-distance connectedness were nourished by the flexible organizational form of the *tariqa*. The issue of liminality within Sufism can actually help shed light on a key concept of Weberian sociology that has been, however, thus far quite self-limiting in analytical terms and of little use in comparative perspective, as discussed in the two previous chapters. It is the relation between the sociologically opaque notion of charisma and charismatic leadership in periods of heightened transformation, on the one hand, and the ongoing need for a movement, group, or organization to stabilize mediation and adjudication in routine times—the Weberian question of the 'routinization' of charisma—on the other.

The discussion here should be considered complementary to our dealing with the issue of 'brotherhood' in the previous chapter. Weber is often considered the champion of a Eurocentric, rather evolutionist perspective that considers Western formal law the apex of a trajectory of rationalization without real equivalents in other civilizations. Yet we find in Weber one interesting escape from what he himself, far from triumphantly—indeed overtly pessimistically—called the "iron cage" of a one-directional modern rationalization process radiating from North-Western Europe, particularly due to the innovations promoted by the most radical versions and carriers of the Protestant Reformation. In a quite Vichian mood, he explicitly worked on possible common roots of divergent developments of patterns of rationalization: not just between West and East but also within what we call the West, which according to Weber does include, as we saw, Islam. A caveat for what follows: Weber never asserted that what should be dubbed rational from the viewpoint of the (at his time, in colonial and global terms) 'winning' Western trajectory is necessarily rational from other civilizational angles. According to Weber, the superior rationality of Western modernity was based on patterns of formal rationalization producing a powerful kind of instrumental rationality. He admitted, nonetheless, that the value-oriented rationality of religious and civilizational traditions (including those feeding in a metamorphosed way into Western modernity) cannot be diminished per se by the historic primacy of the modern Western 'exception.'

With this in mind, we can now enrich the Weberian excursus on the issues of 'charisma' and 'brotherhood' from the last two chapters with the question of the variable institutional outcomes of liminality introduced here. In Europe the new friars/brothers had at some point to face three alternatives. They consisted, respectively, in turning the new power acquired from their liminal space into a new institutional space, retreating into marginality, or coming to terms with the existing institutional landscape. Indeed while some components fully retreated from the institutional field (a step amounting to a dissipation or dilution of the original charisma), the two main outcomes were feeding into the new space of the *universitas*, as mentioned above, but also reconstructing the already existing monastic form of community life. This latter option was implemented by upgrading monasticism through ideas and practices promoting openness to the urban life of the commoners. The last two options represent two distinct outcomes of a Weberian routinization of charisma, namely the shaping of a brand-new institution or the folding of the new movement into an older institution.

In the Islamic world, instead, the organizational unit of Sufism, the *tariqa*, remained more malleable than the monastic form prevalent in Europe. It did not necessarily coincide with a self-enclosed religious brotherhood and not even with a lay confraternity like those promoted in urban contexts by the new monastic movements in Europe. A *tariqa*, which literally means a "way," remained basically a network of variably organized levels of master–disciple relations, kept together by strong congregational moments epitomized by the collective sessions of the adepts. It might appear as a puzzle—at least from a Weberian perspective—that the lower formalization and institutionalization of Sufi authority within a brotherhood tempered the challenging potential of its liminality. For sure, it also made it more suitable to absorb (and fulfil) generally Islamic institutional functions of mediation among individuals and between leaders and commoners.

In this sense, it was the different, inherently more flexible level of the majoritarian, Sunni shape of Islam that prevented Sufism from becoming more fully liminal and establishing self-perpetuating forms of monasticism. This type of outcome was not unknown to the spiritual ferments in Arabia that provided the immediate antecedent to Muhammad's preaching. In the Sufi case the charisma of individual saints, leaders, and masters was never completely absorbed into institutions and so 'routinized.' The resulting fluidity ensured that the passage from foundational and transformative momentums into everydayness would not be felt traumatically; moreover, charismatic effervescence was translated less into local institutions than into the translocal expansive impetus of a *tariqa*, as both the way and the network that embodied the charisma of the founder. So, as paradoxically as significantly, the lopsided Weberian view of the charisma of the leader that later becomes routinized in an institutional form is twice unsettled by the Sufi *tariqa*. Through the local and translocal spinning of the networks that constitute a *tariqa* it appears as if charisma were both born routinized and/or never been subjected to the type of dissipation, dilution, and absorption suggested by the idea of institutional routinization.

This comparative line of reasoning is well matched by some key elements in the approach of Ibn Khaldun, who at various stages of his life was also intensely involved with both Sufi spirituality and the attendant forms of sociability. Apart from Ibn Khaldun's appreciation of Sufism as the source of a type of intuitive knowledge that was also essential in his own method of socio-historical analysis, Sufi leaders appear in his theory as potential providers of lines of cohesion both among tribes and between the tribal and urban patterns of civility. As observed by Gellner,

> one and the same 'order' or 'brotherhood' will contain units of quite diverse kind, ranging from those approximating to a purely voluntary religious club or association to kin-selected hereditary tribal segments. Its diversity may be its strength.
>
> (Gellner 1981: 49)

Paradoxically perhaps (once more), even in the Khaldunian scheme Sufi authority seems to be the only one that works counter-cyclically, as a factor of cohesion not subject to either routinization–institutionalization or dilution–dissipation. Not by chance Ibn Khaldun compared Sufi leaders to the "men around Muhammad and the early Muslims" (Fromherz 2010: 124), as if they were the quintessential depositary of the permanent source code of specifically Islamic forms of socio-institutional charisma. The assimilation of the present to the past, far from being an essentialist reification of an authentic 'origin,' works in this case as an almost inverted kind of liminality. This anti-liminality is characterized by social ubiquity rather than by operating from the social and cultural margins. It allows for alternately implementing the requirements of organizational leadership either in terms of individual talent or of family and tribal ties (Gellner 1981: 49). Compared to Weberian presuppositions, it is as if the gulf between liminality and structure, between charismatic eruptions and institutional workings, were substantially narrowed if not erased by attaining an actual or symbolic closeness to what Islamic traditions considered the only foundational charisma in town, namely Muhammad's.

As a major corrective manœuver to Weber's approach, one should rather speak of a permanent circulation of mildly institutionalized forms of charisma as essential to the stability of the civic nexus. This is especially due to the high cyclicality of all other socio-political factors at work, particularly in the dynamic interaction between urban civilization and the nomadic sector (which as we know Ibn Khaldun credits with a civilizational impetus of its own, distinct from the urban one). What keeps the balance between the risk of overconcentration of charisma and the opposite danger of its evaporation is the existence of a unified yet highly competitive social economy of charisma. This economy cuts through urban and tribal processes and thus provides wide networks of connectedness, both among diverse locales and among a variety of key Islamic institutions (the guild, the *waqf*, the Sufi lodge, and even the college). Connectedness does not work here just as a social glue but also as a potential—even when latent—leverage on de facto political, hardly charismatic, sultanic authority.

This different ratio between fluidity and institutionalization of charisma made the leadership of the Sufi orders socially multifunctional and multivocal, as best witnessed by cases—most notably in the rise of the Ottoman house in the 13th century—where Sufi leaders played a salient role in the building of highly heterogeneous, tribally supported, political-military coalitions. This was not an isolated case, as it matched earlier formations like the *ribat* (a Sufi frontier center with military but also educational and retreat functions, often also including women as leaders) in the Maghreb and other similar frontier operations, such as in Buddhist-dominated Central Asia (Green 2012: 57). This role is at odds with the stress laid by some scholars on a growing gulf between clerics and warriors, and therefore between knowledge and power, in the Middle Periods (Moore 1997), allegedly in opposition to parallel developments in Latin Christendom, which even saw the rise of consecrated orders of monks-warriors (the most famous of which were the Templars).

On the other hand it was the flexible and overlapping organizational capacity of the brotherhood in an Islamic context that allowed at certain times and in given places the integration of *futuwwa*-based, i.e. rather chivalric, virtues into mainstream Sufism. This integration could be pushed to the point of transforming Sufism into the opposite of what it was under more standard circumstances, i.e. an almost official organization reflecting popular sentiments and supervised by the Caliph in person. This is what happened under the caliphal restoration of al-Nasir mentioned in Chapter 2: here we can rather see a similarity with mendicant orders and their frequent efforts to promote a sort of papal monarchy in Europe through the knowledge legitimacy accruing to the new learning institution that they massively colonized, namely the *universitas* (Arjomand 2004: 225–6). To sum up, it was the lighter weight itself of institutionalization and the absent or lower sacralization of the collective bond (see Chapter 3) which in the Islamic case made the distinction of institutionalized structure and liminal anti-structure no more than a soft dialectic, unlike in the European case where it deeply affected institutional change. On the other hand, this same type of dynamics rendered both the Sufi orders and the colleges of formal teaching managed by the *'ulama'* more strongly autonomous. This is true to the extent that they did not need to be fully chartered, as their European counterparts, in order to be functional and authoritative (Hoexter and Levtzion 2002: 11).

It would be a mistake, therefore, to see a polarization between, as it were, a well-structured world of the *'ulama'* and the 'rhizomatic' ramifications of the Sufis. In both sets of organizations, the ties between masters and disciples and the related networks prevailed over formal organization. If we then match organization with charisma—however redefined through our ongoing discussion—the organizational strength is located more on the side of the brotherhoods than of the colleges and legal schools (Gellner 1981: 50). This provides evidence for another difference: to the extent that organizations were not chartered, membership in them could not be 'voluntary' in the sense that prevailed in Europe—based on the long bow linking Aquinas' determination of *voluntas* as crucial to human freedom, through the voluntary and accountable character of associations under civil law, down to the activities and ethos of contemporary NGOs.

As a counterpart to *voluntas*, Islamic legal theory rather stressed the notion of *niyya*, understood as the rightly channeled intention of the agent. This construct seems to point out that the individual does not have to apply pure will to undertake drastic decisions such as opting in or out of organizations with clearly delimited membership and chartered borders, such as a monastic order or a professional gild. As being by default a member of an institutionally underdetermined *umma*, the individual is educated (more than simply born) into a network of social, educational, and charitable sites of adjudication and mediation and has to position herself accordingly to correctly formulated intentions. This activity seems to be inspired by modalities framed by the Aristotelian virtue of discernment or *phronesis*, which we already saw in Chapter 2 as providing a precedent to *fiqh*, i.e. Islamic jurisprudence (see Salvatore 2007: 142, 248). Such considerations should help immunize us against seeing the agent as by necessity alternately enveloped in a compulsory membership within the state (via citizenship) or voluntarily choosing membership of an association or a plurality thereof (via civil society). A non-voluntary, yet rational notion of the social agent, like the one we find in *fiqh* and in the prevailing patterns of civility within the Islam-Islamdom of the Middle Periods more in general, can dispense of both.

Municipal Autonomy vs. Translocal Connectedness

From here we can move toward revisiting the *vexata quaestio* of Weberian origin concerning the purported absence, within the Islamic ecumene, of municipal autonomies. In Weber's argument such autonomies are considered to be at the root of basically all modern Western institutions. As specified in the previous chapters, I seriously doubt that a one-sided parameter of modernity oriented to Western exceptionalism can provide universal standards predetermining a comparison of patterns of civility and autonomy. Indeed, if we start with the idea of 'municipal self-government' as the benchmark of comparison taken from Weber's type of the "European city," the conclusion can only be that the "Islamic city" was not an adequate match. This is due to its presumptive lack of precisely what characterized the excellence and uniqueness of the former: namely a principled and chartered autonomy from any overarching institution like the pope, the emperor, the king, the feudal lord, and the monastery—in spite of evident and continual links with (and dependences from) all of them.

A charter is here the legal instrument that determines rights and duties, spaces of (in principle) intangible freedoms and of (in principle) sovereign offices (within the chartered chain of command that enshrines legitimate power). The alleged source of the superiority of the European city, and thus of the entire fabric of modern Western institutions, was purportedly the strongly legalized frame of legitimacy, which its Islamic counterpart lacked even in those evident historic cases of self-government. Yet based on the previous analysis, one should be cognizant of the fact that the Weberian argument might be impaired by considering autonomy and legitimacy only under the umbrella of a specific type of chartered institution that is peculiar to the European development. Institutions do not need per se to be chartered and to rely on correspondingly consecrated offices to reflect autonomy and organize civility.

Said Arjomand, who dealt with the question at some length (Arjomand 2004), illustrates the issue of autonomy from a modified Weberian perspective, which includes a comparison with Europe's supposed monopoly on municipal autonomy. The background to Arjomand's argument is the Weberian notion of "*qadi* justice." This concept has become an epitome, on a general scale of comparison, of the circumstantial and non-formalized character of Islamic law as applied, which purportedly runs counter to the modern notion of right. The notion is also built on the (not entirely wrong) presumption that *qadi*s, i.e. judges, were community mediators and legal arbitrators rather than officials. Usually compared with their European counterparts to show the rather loose (and in this sense neither autonomous nor properly heteronomous) character of their legal mandate, *qadi*s were mostly recruited, like the more private practitioners of the art of delivering legal advices via *fatwa*s (the *mufti*s), from the *'ulama'* ranks. Since they were appointed by rulers, *qadis* were not, however, as autonomous community leaders as we would expect them to be, considering they belonged to the larger category of *'ulama'*. In this sense, the office of the *qadi* revealed a crack in the presumptive autonomy of the community in that it highlighted an at least partial dependence of their vulnerable office on scarcely legitimate rulers.

However, Arjomand argued that a fundamental degree of autonomy in the Islamic case was warranted by the fact that in several instances the *qadis*, though appointed by the government, applied a law that was predominantly based not on the law issued by the rulers but on principles of Islamic jurisprudence (Arjomand 2004: 244–5). This is an important argument because it affirms *fiqh* as the main idiom and token of civic autonomy in Islamic terms. *Fiqh* does not therefore institute heteronomy—i.e. in this case a dependence on an extra-social, divine will that can be arbitrarily and capriciously exploited by the rulers. It was indeed the case that *fiqh* was largely insulated from direct manipulation by the rulers, who often had to resort to a separate and hardly legitimate source of the law (often termed *qanun* particularly from the Later Middle Period onward) to justify their direct interventions in the legislating field. Such interventions were mostly motivated by the rulers' recognized prerogatives as the warrants of public order, as political and military elites. This is why in most cases during the Middle Periods such inroads into the legal field could never transcend the tautological function of a ruler to act on behalf of order and security (and its corresponding, limited legitimacy). In other words, there was no general and stable sense of legitimacy attached to the ruler's privilege to issue regulations exceeding the boundaries of *fiqh*, though there was a large degree of acceptance that this occurred for the reasons just mentioned.

In frequent comparisons, which Arjomand revisits, of the office of the *qadi* with, for example, the authority of the *alcalde* (indeed a name derived from *al-qadi*, meaning simply "the judge") in Christian Spain, and which was based on municipal law *(fuero)*, one should rather see proof of the fact that the *qadi* is also to be considered as an official autonomously applying the law. This insight comes from observing that the *qadi* was also entitled to exercise his function vis-à-vis subjects not belonging to the local community, Muslims and non-Muslims alike. Therefore the autonomy reflected by this function was not municipal in the strictest sense but actually much broader than that. Furthermore, it was open and interconnected to a wider ecumene recognizing the same type of legal idiom: something toward which municipal autonomy European-style, both in its legal and institutional dimension, is often inimical. As maintained by Hodgson:

> Without municipal autonomy, the cosmopolitan tendencies of the cities were accentuated. Internally, the city was socially fragmented; yet elements in one city became closely tied to other cities, and came to depend on the common norms of city life throughout Islamdom
>
> (Hodgson 1974, II: 66).

In this sense, while the institutionalized profile of the *qadi* as official is more tenuous than its European counterpart (coherently with the milder and non-chartered level of institutionalization of authority in the entire Islamic ecumene), the type of authority the *qadi* embodies is no less autonomous. At the same time his authority is both locally rooted (though less solidly than in Europe) and translocally extended (other than in Europe).

One can apply this type of comparative view to situations of even lower differentiation of authoritative functions and 'officialdom.' In contrast to self-governing communities with a given framework of legitimation in the communities depending on Christian rulers in Europe, Ibn Khaldun provides the example of informal urban *shura* ("deliberation") councils composed of a variety of assortments of 'patricians' and 'plebeians.' Such organs were often exposed to a certain degree of nomadic presence or intervention, as a consequence of the disintegration of centralized dynastic powers in the Maghreb during the Middle Periods. The councils provided services of judgment and adjudication to the local populations outside of any strongly formalized institutional framework, i.e. in the absence of an even tenuous formal dependence on the ruler, such as manifested in the procedures of appointments of members of the council (Arjomand 2004: 222). This type of civic authority, while operating de facto more than de jure, might appear as provisional or transitional from the viewpoint of Weberian bureaucratic rationality. Yet it should be better assessed and categorized, in a comparative perspective, in terms of its degree of autonomy, legitimacy, and effectiveness (all these being also Weberian categories) rather than by invoking rigid ideal-types that presuppose a given and purportedly optimal threshold of formalization of the law and institutionalization of authority as markers of a one-way process of 'rationalization' (Arjomand 2004: 220). Clearly the urban-nomadic nexus stressed by Ibn Khaldun already exceeds the all-urban, Occidental bias of the origin and scope of civility that provides the background to Weber's argumentation. Up to this point, Arjomand's modified Weberian perspective works pretty well.

Yet if we proceed beyond this point, such a perspective probably does not entirely capture the long-term originality of civility, connectedness, and governance in Islamic terms. As we have seen earlier in this volume, particularly when discussing the notion of charisma, one needs a more thorough questioning of Weberian categories. Weber's emphasis on the novelty of the type of social bond inherent in the urban autonomies of medieval Western-European ('Occidental') cities has been, indeed, critiqued and relativized for being too far-fetched (Arnason 2004: 19). This critique has often stressed that the emphasis on Occidental uniqueness revolves too singlehandedly on an idea of the urban bourgeois as a "person of property and culture" (Arjomand 2004: 217) who is anachronistically overcharged with a specific type of agency. We should be then ready to admit, as a result of our comparative considerations, that

> there was more urban autonomy and civic agency in the Islamicate context than Western comparative historians have mostly wanted to admit, but the legal framework and the political impact differed from the West in significant ways.
>
> (Arnason and Wittrock 2004: 7)

The investment into balanced though often unstable blends of practices and commitments in the Islamic case represented an important step in the construction of a combined ethic of personal responsibility and collective civility. This was also due to be revived as a key factor in later, modern (precolonial, colonial, and postcolonial) developments. Accordingly, Weberian categories should not necessarily be abandoned but instead reformulated and applied more flexibly within the comparative perspective. One should thus avoid invoking an Occidental exceptionalism as a normative yardstick and valorize instead the comparative advantages of adopting an Islamic perspective while determining what should be considered a benchmark of comparison.

As maintained by Arnason and Wittrock, who also refer to the argument of Arjomand (2004) we examined earlier,

> arguments about the presence or absence of certain preconditions are giving way to more complex models of common elements combined in different ways, with different weighting of factors involved, and thus resulting in different developmental paths.
>
> (Arnason and Wittrock 2004: 7)

While this approach can provide an Ariadne's thread for the comparative path that still needs to enliven the sociology of Islam, a bolder approach that puts a premium on an Islamic perspective can be developed by considering Gellner's understanding of the Islamic (Khaldunian) model of civility as a kind of Platonism 2.0 that develops and subverts, by way of an antithesis, the original Platonic vision of a rational republic governed by philosophers. According to Gellner, the idea of a rationally governed city or republic which for long remained a utopian horizon in Western thought and political imagination was effectively implemented, in a strongly altered form, within Islamic society (Gellner 1981: 17–28).

Gellner's idea is premised on splitting civility into two almost opposite components, namely the refined civilization of cultivated urban classes that favors pluralism and tolerance, and the civic virtue of puritan bourgeoisies that promotes cohesion. This distinction, which is familiar to Western political theory, is particularly important from a sociological viewpoint and should contribute to deflating the Weberian bias that favors a compact model of political autonomy and citizenship. Prior to the modern Westphalian state-society formations, efforts to match the two elements appeared too often caught in squaring the circle. In the Westphalian world, it was understood that the two components could be recomposed only through a top-down approach to government led by the knowledgeable— a remote possibility in the political world of the modern Leviathan. The spirit of revolution in the name of *demos* seemed at best able to secure an unstable balance between the two components of civility, whereby freedom and tolerance were permanently threatened by civic and republican zeal. This was the view, highlighted by Gellner, of a liberal 18th-century thinker like David Hume (1711–1776). It can be more generally evoked as the split between liberal and republican views of political modernity.

What is nonetheless interesting in Gellner's analysis is that, in the Islamic model, tolerant urban refinement and puritan civic virtue are not only equally present but also more neatly distinct than in Western cases (Gellner 1981: 7–16). Thus while in the Western trajectory the contrast between (religious) tolerance and (religious) zeal-*cum*-cohesion threatens the integrity of the standards of governance and participation, in the Islamic case the two components, precisely for being more clearly distinct, are integral to a much more dynamic sociological process, at first sight identifiable with the Khaldunian cycle. Within such dynamics, the former component represented by tolerance and freedom, and related to the kernel of civility proper, is on the side of the urban refined, while civic virtue is a product of tribal ethos and particularly of its spirit of cohesion that is the true source of collective, socio-political power, namely *'asabiyya*. This quite streamlined sociological process is made possible by the fact that, free from the Western biased view of civility as being the monopoly of the city, Ibn Khaldun could identify a civilization of the nomads as matching and confronting urban civilization. According to Gellner this was not an ideational difference but one allowed by the different configuration of forces in a semi-arid environment where the nomads have considerable autonomy and the peasants are either squeezed between them and the city or enjoy a much higher degree of mobility than in the West. This is true to the extent that peasants can within certain limits be assimilated into the nomadic component, both therefore representing the "countryside" as the counterpart to the "city" (Gellner 1981: 29–35).

What is remarkable is that, in the very moment that, as in the Islamic case, the countryside loses its solid anchorage in a land-bound peasantry (that in the Western model sees its dependence shifting from the feudal nobility to the urban bourgeoisie), the city itself is no longer what the West purports it to be almost by nature (not rarely by retrieving a surreptitious short-circuit with the Aristotelian *polis*, which we shunned as anachronistic), namely the stable and original source of civility. After all, a sensible reading of Weber's view of the exceptional character of the Western city leads us to admit that this is the outcome of a bundle of contingencies, not of a civilizational teleology (Turner 2013 [1987]: 53–73). Thus there is nothing intrinsic in civility and the civilizing process that binds them to the city. Islamic civility is both different and 'normal' in revealing this contingency, since, other than a civility rooted in the city 'in itself' (a Western exception or phantom), it can only acquire sharp and original contours in the context of dynamics that are both more stringent sociologically and open to variables and forces not confined to the city. How does this feature relate to Gellner's idea (perhaps initially intended as a provocation) that Islam provides a kind of Platonism 2.0? This sociological upgrading of a Platonism that fades off into utopia when confined within the Western city is allowed precisely by opening up the process to a wider civilizational dynamics. It is such a dynamics that endows the philosopher-king (which nobody could better represent than the already mentioned Ibn Tumart, the early 12th-century leader of the Almohads) with political and military support, originating in tribal cohesion, the proper source of the republican-puritan side of civility.

Several of the scholars from whose work I have drawn for the present analysis have placed the developments of the period treated here in the context of a hemisphere-wide "ecumenical renaissance" of the axial impulse of transformation of the knowledge–power equation, occurring at the beginning of the second millennium CE (see most explicitly Wittrock 2001; Pollock 2004). Yet as shown in the previous chapter, the Islamic ecumene is the hub itself of the wider Afro-Eurasian civilization and therefore of the latter's hemisphere-wide renaissance during an epoch coinciding with the Islamic Earlier Middle Period. Even if it did not teleologically pre-determine modernity, this process is particularly significant since it set key parameters for developments of the subsequent age. The institutional landscape in the various locales and macro-regions was a key propelling force to the ecumenical renaissance. Acknowledging the diversity of the social and institutional conditions for this hemisphere-wide renaissance as well as the originality and strength of its Islamic component is therefore a precondition for capturing its richness. Looking at this wider develop-ment helps us not to get trapped within the Weberian iron cage where modernization is a one-way road allowing human societies to abandon a low level of formalization of the law and a scarce differentiation between law and morality, on the one hand, and between office and charisma, on the other. In the Weberian narrative that provides the background storyline to the more recent modernization theory, formalization and differentiation are decisively accomplished, during this renaissance, only within Western Christendom. All other macro-regional and civilizational developments are basically downgraded to useful backgrounds for elegant comparisons, whose ultimate scope is nothing more than the affirmation of Western uniqueness. The comparative method is thus discredited.

As shown in the previous chapter, the practices associated with and covered by the *waqf* became the hub of the flexible institutional landscape of the Islamic ecumene. Perhaps the *waqf* was also the single Islamic insti-tution that was unequivocally based on a type of civil law that would stand Weberian tests of rationality. Surely one cannot separate this development from jurisprudential reflections that enriched a common legal and moral idiom and the associated methods of reasoning. Articulated by a variety of legal schools, Islamic approaches acquired an expansive hemispheric reach warranted by a flexible consensus moderately open to challenges and revi-sions. This process facilitated the emergence of a rich jurisprudential knowl-edge matching local practices but also connecting locales transregionally. Also due to this need to build up solid patterns of translocal connectedness and civility, law as practiced eschewed a too rigid formalization. Basically the idea itself of a codification of law was only acceptable to a very limited extent, lest it hampered the system at its fundaments through an anchorage in territorially delimited charters and personally anchored statuses. The corresponding, often intricate, transregional grids of the management of civility during the Middle Periods did not respond to a homogenizing, nor to a syncretizing, logic. They were part of a long-drawn-out process of balancing local customs with a moral idiom decisively modeled on *hadith*, i.e. on the exemplary virtues of Muhammad. This knowledge corpus was often filtered through the high culture of *adab* and via a variety of popular cultures and practices spanning a wide range between pious and transgressive, exoteric and esoteric, and markedly influenced by the teachings of traveling scholars and saints.

We should conclude the chapter by examining at a deeper level the rationalizing, and in this sense civilizing, potential of a malleable and multiversal type of law based on a mild, far from rigid differentiation between rules and rulings to be enforced and the moral norm. Without the need to dilute the issue into generic debates on normative pluralism, let us start by not succumbing to the easy temptation to see this normative dualism as an anomaly and a weakness in a theoretical and even comparative perspective. From a wider angle law is not just a facilitative instrument of 'strategic action' by individuals and groups based on a purposive rationality of sort but also reflects the communicative and connective scope of action. Law is here a reproductive force of the social bond that works through formulating rationally acceptable norms in a largely shared idiom. This process of formulation of valid law occurs both through conflict and consensus: i.e. the pursuit of specific interests is not unhooked from the daily management of identity, self-positioning, and a sense of collective pride and value.

Such a general view of the law is particularly well reflected by the approach followed by one of the champions of legal theory from Islamic history, Abu Ishaq al-Shatibi. Al-Shatibi, who lived in the Middle Periods (d. 1388), has not by chance inspired numerous modern Muslim reformers. He particularly excelled in clarifying the notion of the socio-legal actor, as well as the mechanisms of adjudication. This occurred particularly through his elaborations on the notion of *maslaha* ("common good," "public interest") which had been long considered pivotal by various Islamic schools of jurisprudence. A legal theorist and jurist belonging to the Maliki school and living in 14th-century al-Andalus (and therefore being not just a rough contemporary to Ibn Khaldun but also sharing largely in the latter's regional entanglements), al-Shatibi demonstrated how the *shari'a*, the ideal of Islamic normativity that provided orientation to the murky and muddy work of Islamic jurisprudence enmeshed with the regulation of everyday life, is essentially *ummiyya*. This latter term denotes various aspects of communication, including the general understanding of a word among the speakers of a particular language. It also embraces the level of conceptual apprehension that is shared by speakers of all languages, e.g. when utterances are successfully translated. This is a move that clearly envisions the norm as a socio-cultural, before 'moral,' idiom, i.e. as a system of signs and signposts that provides practical orientations to the social and legal actor (Masud 2000 [1995]: 176–80).

Khalid Masud, a leading contemporary scholar of Islamic legal theory and probably the main expert on al-Shatibi of our age (and also a prominent Muslim reformer), maintains that at the center of al-Shatibi's analysis we find an attention to how language works by facilitating an understanding of the law among commoners. The benchmark of understandability and so of effectiveness and legitimacy of the law is therefore not the specialized knowledge of the *'ulama'* or *fuqaha'* but of the average social and legal actor. The bottom line of the law's workings is as simple, in Islamic terms, as the exposure of a Muslim to the words of the Qur'an. Assuming these words had been unintelligible, we would have had no Qur'an, no Islam, no *fiqh* (Masud 2000: 169–81; see also Masud 2005). Most notably, and as a consequence of what we have just stated, al-Shatibi refuted the idea that the *shari'a* is normative only because it is incumbent on all Muslims to obey the commands of God, the supreme (and actually only) lawgiver. He stressed that the universal interests (which he defined through a catalogue of values that happened to closely overlap with those considered universal by Aquinas) are built on personal interests that push individuals to claim them as rights (Masud 2000 [1995]: 196–9). That is, the reality of rights depends on the capacity to claim them, which in turn rests on the ability to know and formulate them properly. It is the inner diversity itself of Islamdom as a social nexus and the variety of components of its patterns of civility that requires rights to be seen in this way: as originating from a general understanding that can be considered part of Islam itself (its core message) but inevitably expanding, and crystallizing, into a widening plurality of practices and interpretations.

The golden nexus between particular and public interests is thereby provided by the communicative process itself, which law reflects as much as institutes. One is not surprised, then, that while the legal and communicative process is universal, the type and level of institutionalization is subject to civilizational and cultural variations. It is remarkable that al-Shatibi worked to build a catalogue of local customs as a database to support his view that the agent apprehends normativity in action, based on her cultural background and linguistic and communicative skills. Clearly individual interests matter, yet only as formulated through an idiom that is able to reflect the values of a wider ecumene: in the Islamic case, through the conceptual grids of *fiqh*. Interests can be turned into rights, first, to the extent that their formulation as rights reflects the cultural values of the long-term egalitarian and cosmopolitan orientation of key urban strata exposed to the Irano-Semitic traditions, and, second, to the extent that they reflect local and contingent appropriations and enactments of normativity based on apprehended, and therefore specific, cultural and communicative codes. It is through this two-step process that a Muslim as a social agent becomes both the carrier of knowledge, religion, and culture in a given context, and the potential entrepreneur of long-distance connections, commercial or otherwise.

The idea of *maslaha* in this context is not just a legal device particularly dear to the Maliki school to which al-Shatibi (along with Ibn Khaldun) belonged but a necessary pillar of the social and communicative infrastructure of the ecumene. This gives *maslaha* a status well beyond that which other leading legal schools were formally ready to attribute to it. This is because, according to Masud, *maslaha* reflects the key principle for the protection of the individuals' capacity to enter agreements, before it protects the collective value of agreements themselves. In other words, there is not at play merely a vision of a friendly and irenic harmonization of interests vs. a coercive and confrontational one. While a towering scholar like Aquinas seemed willing to provide a normative theory of what it means to be a Christian as a social agent, al-Shatibi delivers a conception, steeped in the logic of communicativity and its contingency, of how action engenders normativity via cognitive, cultural, and communicative means.

Maslaha is here not just one additional source of norms but a meta-norm, an engine of rationalization of the norm, though one intended to be understood in a wider sense than in Weberian formalism or Western proceduralism. What is instituted here is not an instance of judgment, mediation, and arbitration through the consecration of an office based on a peculiar combination of sacralization and rationalization (the Weberian way, which we criticized at various points for its pretension to provide universal benchmarks of comparison). Neither is it a set of inalienable rights to be individually claimed or the legal mechanism to adjudicate them. To be instituted (in a sense that is different from how Weber reconstructs *Anstalt*, namely "institution") is process-bound agency itself, to the extent that it generates norms. In this sense, *maslaha* can both provide a cover for higher levels of formalism and proceduralism which are not fully alien to *fiqh*, to the extent that it reflects the *telos* of the shared normative idiom (*maqasid al-shari'a*, the objects of normativity), and can work against them if the *telos* is impaired. The Weberian, sharp differentiation between traditional value rationality and modern purposive rationality appears here as out-of-synch with a hemisphere-wide civilizing process. Accordingly, the bifurcation of the two types of rationality is only one possible outcome of the process, and not exactly one that favors inclusion and consensus. At the level of social interactions and transactions (*mu'amalat*) there are potentially no limits to the principle of rationalization of *maslaha*. Limits are set only at the level of *'ibadat*, namely the forms of cult that express the human surrender to God (without which there would be no Islam, which at root means precisely that).

The work of al-Shatibi can be compared to that of Aquinas, both thinkers standing out as leading representatives of the ecumenical renaissance which included Islamdom and Latin Christendom. They both worked to transcend the dichotomist polarization between *civitas terrena* ("earthly city") and *civitas Dei* ("godly city"), best epitomized by Augustine during Late Antiquity. The renaissance of the axial ethos to which they both contributed was more a precondition of modern forms of human action and civility than a sheer revival of the older axial spirit. It is fair to say that the Southern-Italian monk-theologian and the Andalusi jurist and theoretician of the law represent the culmination of a hemisphere-wide renaissance that reconstructed axial formulas in almost proto-sociological, and therefore potentially modern, fashions. But it is also possible to observe that as a representative of the Islamic philosophy of law—though not an uncontested one either in its time or in the modern era (see Opwis 2005)—and more generally as an Islamic theorist of the social bond and of the common good, al-Shatibi had the particular merit of sedating the risk of an excessive concentration of agency on a principled and sacred autonomy of the subject, while focusing on the intersubjective conditions that generate agency and its normativity. This excess rather characterized Christian Europe's genealogy of the subject of law and of the social agent, and was finally well reflected by Weber's sociology of law, formulated at the height of European global hegemony at the beginning of the 20th century.

Al-Shatibi's theory deserves our attention for its coherent sticking to an axially rooted, relational view of the agent as *ego* involved with *alter* on all nodal issues attending the construction and maintenance of the social bond: in a double sense, as a participant in, and as an observer and judge of, social interaction. This theory was perhaps not by chance produced toward the end of the Middle Periods during which the Islamic ecumene reached the zenith of its expansion. This was also when the far Western part of the ecumene, where al-Shatibi operated, was entangled in an ongoing conflict with the encroaching Latin Christian kingdoms on a variety of levels. Al-Shatibi's approach might be less cogent in purely theoretical and theological terms if compared to the masterful architecture of Aquinas' œuvre. Yet it possesses a greater potential for a socio-anthropological reconstruction of agency beyond civilizational divides, and therefore as representative of the wider, ecumenic, proto-global civilizing process. On the other hand, it cannot be denied that the Western trajectory of gradual reinvention of the autonomous foundations of civility and society, whose seeds are found in Aquinas' theory, created a new radical reflexivity about the material and immaterial conditions of constitution of the social bond, which were later inherited by Western modernity (Salvatore 2007: 178).

A comparative historical sociologist like Benjamin Nelson, who tried to reformulate the relations between Western Christendom and its exceptionalism, on the one hand, and the civilizations with which it interacted, on the other, was particularly keen to stress that the parting of the developmental ways between Latin Christendom and other civilizations occurred exactly in this period, namely during the European High Middle Ages, which corresponds to the Islamic Later Middle Period that followed the so-called Mongol invasion (Arjomand 2004: 213). Nelson also showed that the outcome of the process in Europe, which became fully manifest after the Protestant Reformation, is the turning of axial, 'tribal' brotherhood into the universal otherhood of inalienable rights (Nelson 1969 [1949]; see also Silver 1997). These can only be protected and adjudicated upon from the top down, i.e. no longer through a brotherly accommodation (if not harmonization) of minds and bodies.

This is not to say that al-Shatibi's theory photographed a stable idyll. As just stated, it was probably the ingenious snapshot of a vulnerable equilibrium that had been already gravely eroded by the end of the Middle Periods. As we will see in the next chapter, the end of the Middle Periods is also the time when Hodgson sees the maturation of seeds that prefigure the inception of an original, Islamic type of modernity. This will be soon (yet not so soon) thwarted by the much more spectacular and effective unfolding of Western modernity, also, if not especially, thanks to the new impulses generated by the dynamism of the new Atlantic routes from which Muslim actors were excluded. What is important to highlight is that, also following Nelson, the main issue at stake is no longer one of identifying common vs. diverging patterns of civility but rather intercivilizational exchanges and conflicts setting the West on its specific and hegemonic road to modernity (Arjomand 2004: 214–15). The clearer we are called to delineate the traits (rather than simply weighing off 'success' and 'failure') of such an Islamic modernity, in both its genesis and unfolding, the more the comparative perspective needs to be further refined by taking into account entanglements, dependences, reappropriations, and challenges.

References

Arjomand, Said Amir. 2004. "Transformation of the Islamicate Civilization: A Turning Point in the Thirteenth Century?" In *Eurasian Transformations, 10th to 13th Centuries: Crystallizations, Divergences, Renaissances*, edited by Johann P. Arnason and Björn Wittrock, 213–45. Leiden: Brill.

Arnason, Johann P. 2004. "Parallels and Divergences: Perspectives on the Early Second Millennium." In *Eurasian Transformations, 10th to 13th Centuries: Crystallizations, Divergences, Renaissances*, edited by Johann P. Arnason and Björn Wittrock, 13–40. Leiden: Brill, 2004.

Arnason, Johann P. and Björn Wittrock. 2004. "Introduction." In *Eurasian Transformations, 10th to 13th Centuries: Crystallizations, Divergences, Renaissances*, edited by Johann P. Arnason and Björn Wittrock, 1–10. Leiden: Brill.

Chittick, William C. 1992. *Faith and Practice of Islam: Three Thirteenth Century Sufi Texts*. Albany, NY: SUNY Press.

Eisenstadt, Shmuel N. 1985. "Comparative Liminality: Liminality and Dynamics of Civilization." *Religion*, 15: 315–38.

Elmore, Gerald. 1999. "Ibn al-Arabi's Testament on the Mantle of Initiation (al-Khirqah)." *Journal of the Muhyiddin Ibn 'Arabi Society*, 26: 1–33.

Friedrich Silber, Ilana. 1995. *Virtuosity, Charisma and Social Order: A Comparative Sociological Study of Monasticism in Theravada Buddhism and Medieval Catholicism*. Cambridge: Cambridge University Press.

Fromherz, Allen James. 2010. *Ibn Khaldun: Life and Times*. Edinburgh: Edinburgh University Press.

Gellner, Ernest. 1981. *Muslim Society*. Cambridge: Cambridge University Press.

Gerber, Haim. 1994. *State, Society and Law in Islam: Ottoman Law in Comparative Perspective*. Albany, NY: SUNY Press.

Green, Nile. 2012. *Sufism: A Global History*. Oxford: Wiley-Blackwell.

Hodgson, Marshall G.S. 1974. *The Venture of Islam: Conscience and History in a World Civilization*, I–III. Chicago and London: University of Chicago Press.

Hodgson, Marshall G.S. 1993. *Rethinking World History: Essays on Europe, Islam and World History*, edited, with Introduction and Conclusion, by Edmund Burke III. Cambridge: Cambridge University Press.

Hoexter, Miriam, and Nehemia Levtzion. 2002. "Introduction." In *The Public Sphere in Muslim Societies*, edited by Miriam Hoexter, Shmuel N. Eisenstadt, and Nehemia Levtzion, 9–16. Albany, NY: SUNY Press.

Levtzion, Nehemia. 2002. "The Dynamics of Sufi Brotherhoods." In *The Public Sphere in Muslim Societies*, edited by Miriam Hoexter, Shmuel N. Eisenstadt, and Nehemia Levtzion, 109–18. Albany, NY: SUNY Press.

Masud, M. Khalid. 2000 [1995]. *Shatibi's Philosophy of Islamic Law*. Kuala Lumpur: Islamic Book Trust.

Masud, M. Khalid. 2005. "Communicative Action and the Social Construction of *Shari'a* in Pakistan." In *Religion, Social Practice, and Contested Hegemonies: Reconstructing the Public Sphere in Muslim Majority Societies*, edited by Armando Salvatore and Mark LeVine, 155–79. New York: Palgrave Macmillan.

Moore, Robert I. 1997. "The Birth of Europe as a Eurasian Phenomenon." *Modern Asian Studies*, 31/3: 583–601.

Nelson, Benjamin. 1969 [1949]. *The Idea of Usury: From Tribal Brotherhood to Universal Otherhood*. Chicago and London: University of Chicago Press.

Opwis, Felicitas. 2005. "Maslaha in Contemporary Islamic Legal Theory." *Islamic Law and Society*, 12/2: 182–223.

Palacios, Miguel Asín. 1919. *La escatología musulmana en la Divina Comedia*. Madrid: Real Academia Española.

Pollock, Sheldon. 2004. "The Transformation of Culture-Power in Indo-Europe, 1000–1300." *Medieval Encounters*, 10/1: 247–78.

Rahimi, Babak. 2006. "The Middle Period: Islamic Axiality in the Age of Afro-Eurasian Transcultural Hybridity." In *Islam in Process: Historical and Civilizational Perspectives*, edited by Johann P. Arnason, Armando Salvatore, and Georg Stauth, 48–67. Bielefeld: Transcript; New Brunswick, NJ: Transaction (*Yearbook of the Sociology of Islam* VII).

Reichmuth, Stefan. 2010. "Murtadâ al-Zabîdî (d. 1205/1791) and his Role in 18th Century Sufism." In *Le soufisme à l'époque ottomane/Sufism in the Ottoman Era*, edited by Rachida Chih and Catherine Mayeur-Jaouen, 405–6. Cairo: Institut français d'archéologie orientale du Caire.

Salvatore, Armando. 2007. *The Public Sphere: Liberal Modernity, Catholicism, and Islam*. New York: Palgrave Macmillan.

Santoro, Emilio. 2003 [1999]. *Autonomy, Freedom and Rights: A Critique of Liberal Subjectivity*. Dordrecht: Kluwer.

Silver, Allan. 1997. "Two Different Sorts of Commerce: Friendship and Strangership in Civil Society." In *Public and Private in Thought and Practice*, edited by Jeff Weintraub and Krishan Kumar, 43–76. Chicago: University of Chicago Press.

Szakolczai, Arpad. 2001. "Eric Voegelin's History of Political Ideas." *European Journal of Social Theory* 4/3: 351–68.

Turner, Bryan S. 2013 [1987]: "State, Science and Economy in Traditional Societies: Some Problems in Weberian Sociology of Science." In *The Sociology of Islam: Collected Essays of Bryan S. Turner*, edited by Bryan S. Turner and Kamaludeen Mohamed Nasir, 53–73. Farnham and Burlington, VT: Ashgate.

Voegelin, Eric. 1997. *The History of Political Ideas, vol. II, The Middle Ages to Aquinas. In The Collected Works of Eric Voegelin, vol. 20*, edited and with Introduction by Peter von Sivers. Columbia, MO: University of Missouri Press.

Wittrock, Björn. 2001. "Social Theory and Global History: The Periods of Cultural Crystallization." *Thesis Eleven*, 65: 27–50.

PART III

MODERN ISLAMIC ARTICULATIONS OF CIVILITY

5

KNOWLEDGE AND POWER
The Civilizing Process before Colonialism

From the Mongol Impact to the Early Modern Knowledge–Power Configurations

As succinctly put by Hodgson, at the threshold of the modern era "Islam promised itself, not without reason, that it would soon be absorbing the whole world" (Hodgson 1993: 24). From this perspective, the famous question asked by Bernard Lewis (2002) *What Went Wrong?* (with Islam, and particularly the Middle East, vis-à-vis Western modernity, after such promising beginnings) appears embarrassingly anachronistic. We are not dealing here just with 'essentialism' but with the lack of a transparent method that can stand the test of a comparatively oriented historical sociology which takes entanglements and clashes for what they are, i.e. moments of larger processes responding to the complex unfolding of the knowledge–power equation governing human relations and the social bond. Lewis' analysis is neither based on a serious reckoning with Islam's long-term civilizational impetus on the one hand, nor on a lucid exploration of the complex character of modernity due to its specific twists of the knowledge–power equation on the other.

Against this biased simplification, Hodgson, who belonged to the same generation as Lewis but passed away prematurely in 1968, framed his research question in terms that considered the knowledge–power coordinates as enlivening the expanding and innerly diversifying Islamic ecumene prior to, if not at the very moment of, the Western colonial impact. This inner-Islamic expansive dynamics ended up succumbing to the Western hegemony in the modern era due to the latter's overwhelming strength,

The Sociology of Islam: Knowledge, Power and Civility, First Edition. Armando Salvatore.
© 2016 John Wiley & Sons, Ltd. Published 2016 by John Wiley & Sons, Ltd.

but we as observers and analysts can only determine this outcome ex post, without indulging in anachronistically itemizing purported deficits and reasons of inner decay, in the orientalist way. What is unacceptable in this approach is not so much a lack of recognition of the vitality of the Islamic ecumene prior to the Western colonial impact; we certainly have to suppose that orientalists in general know the history and the texts, though they have to be selective and are inevitably biased in what to focus on, due to their narratives of golden eras and decays of what they tend to see as airtight civilizations and as their 'original' and often 'essential' characteristics. The real problem with the orientalist approach is in its frequent, not to say invariable, trivialization of the complex antinomies of the knowledge–power equation within Western modernity, Enlightenment included, which orientalists tend to uncritically adopt as a self-evident benchmark of comparison (an excellent example is Radtke 1994). Hodgson, instead, took into account from the beginning the variables of Western exceptionalism in conjugating knowledge with power in ways that proved irresistible for at least two centuries, as well as the process through which this exceptionalism disrupted the Islamic hemisphere-wide hegemony. Strengthened and legitimized by this sophisticated approach, Hodgson analyzed the Islamic civilizational multiverse, its relative strengths and weaknesses, in their own terms, including a diagnosis of its balance sheet at the time of the modern colonial impact of the West, by adopting parameters that could well suit a serious comparative perspective.

The passage from the early modern power apogee of Islam to an incumbent crisis was neither sudden nor of such a kind as to be easily grasped by any major actor before the rapid ascension of European colonial power apparatuses had already visibly and incontrovertibly taken hold. The more pervasively the new European colonial power manifested itself, the less plausible it became to describe the disturbances in the hegemonic balance between Western and Islamic empires in terms of an Islamic civilizational rise or decline. The change occurred within the mutual impact of the knowledge–power equation between the two sides. Colonialism affected not only the way colonies were ruled and their economies managed but also the socio-political knowledge disciplines of the respective colonial 'motherlands.' As we will see in the next chapter (and further articulate in possible follow-up volumes), this process led to an unprecedented rearticulation of the entire knowledge–power equation. Knowledge was deployed by European states and capitalist enterprises to increase the capacity to discipline and mobilize populations, and to control and manage territories.

Power became ever more pervasive thanks to the rise and, during the 19th century, academic institutionalization of a vast array of old and new knowledge disciplines. The term discipline characteristically reflects both the methodical accumulation and selection of valid knowledge in Europe, and its systematic implementation for the sake of the organizational and economic advancement of national societies. The process unfolded through the promotion of new types of institutional subjects and their respective 'offices': from the modern hospital through the modern prison to the modern university. They were the outcome of a metamorphosis from their premodern counterparts and channeled their underlying knowledge mandates into a machine accumulating the power of control and surveillance. In previous chapters and in what follows, I have preferred to refer to the sociology of Norbert Elias rather than to the seminal work of Michel Foucault to explain this process since Foucaultian references taken alone risk authorizing unilateral neo-Westernist angles (as in postcolonial studies) that are relatively impermeable to the consideration of Islamic perspectives in their own right.

Notwithstanding the uniqueness of what Hodgson called "the great Western transmutation," major changes were simultaneously unfolding in the central, Islamic side of the hemisphere. This process created new fractures at the passage from the Later Middle Period to early modernity, not least because of the effects of the long wave of the Mongol conquests. Part of the upheaval was due precisely to the power gaps increasingly opened within the social fabric of an ecumene that, due to the expansive entropy of the Middle Periods, was far from being strongly institutionalized and centralized. As consistently pointed out by Arnason, the intensifying of a civilizing process works against building civilizational monoliths and rather favors a diversification of patterns of civility (e.g. Arnason 2001; 2003). In this sense, to revisit Hodgson's quote from the beginning of this chapter, it was the success itself of a multiversal, more than of a universal, type of civilizing process that made Islam at the dawn of the modern era potentially powerful, yet in a quite entropic way—therefore also markedly vulnerable to the new articulation of the knowledge–power equation radiating from the European Westphalian and colonial orders, which reflected the emergence of a strong Western exceptionalism based on strongly disciplinary centralizations and the systematic elimination of power gaps within society.

Against the background of this unprecedented global transformation centered on European power which Hodgson dubbed, in a rather old-fashioned and certainly reductive way, as heralding the "technological age," we should remember that the particular strength of Islamic civilization at the inception of the modern era did not suddenly evaporate at the moment that newly emerging colonial powers affirmed their lead in long-distance maritime trade and discoveries. Such advances occurred particularly thanks to the opening of transatlantic routes and the creation of colonies in the East and West of the enlarged globe, initially aided by private enterprises launched and implemented on an unprecedentedly large scale. In the process, the European religious, cultural, and linguistic fragmentation counted less than the European colonial articulation of knowledge and power. No doubt the birth of a new epoch of exceptional European undertakings has constituted, in both historical and conceptual terms, the common core of modernity. This in turn has entailed the implosion of traditional forms of social cohesion and the start of a process of deep, socio-cultural transformation that continues to spread throughout non-European societies, often captured by the fuzzy idea of 'globalization.' It should be remarked, however, that both so-called postcolonial and other branches of cultural and historical studies have stressed the extent to which, during the colonial epoch and in its aftermath, the colonized peoples were not just passive victims or onlookers. Accordingly, one should carefully account for their specific contributions, resistances, and appropriations of the vast process that particularly sociologists of earlier generations have often subsumed under the no less one-sided category of 'modernization.'

Set against the complexity of the process, Bernard Lewis' earlier-mentioned view and more generally the orientalist paradigm of postulating an inherent tension between Islam and modernity appears gravely lopsided in both ideological and methodological terms, well beyond the generic accusation of 'essentialism.' In contrast, Hodgson's approach, though in need of revision and updating, is particularly insightful in addressing the tension between an incipient kind of Islamic modernity and its succumbing to the hegemonic Western one. It has the merit of rejecting the dominant narrative of a Western monopoly on the birth of modernity from its inception, based on reductive and homogenizing assumptions about linear alignments of Reformation, Enlightenment, and commercial and industrial revolutions in Western Europe. This view, which orientalists have shared with a variety of historians and social scientists but which they have often subjected to further trivializing twists, obscures the tensions and antinomies underlying the process and, by extension, the elements of potential strength and coherence of other concomitant programs and visions in the non-Western, including Islamic, world. In other words, the undeniable, exceptional success of European and more generally Western patterns of articulating the knowledge–power equation cannot be considered a token of their inherent and transhistorical superiority, allegedly representing the only and original matrix of what we call modernity or the apex of human civilization.

Here the task on which we have embarked, to explain how a structural differentiation among various spheres of life developed across the Islamic ecumene through a variety of complex societal and historical trajectories, acquires a strategic value within the program of the sociology of Islam. The task includes demonstrating the dynamism, originality, and diversity of the trajectories of the Islamic ecumene well into the modern era, without neglecting the inner attritions and self-limitations that inevitably result from expansive processes. Set in the framework of the need to reconceptualize modernity by taking into account a variety of historical entanglements, in this chapter I pursue an investigation of the complex ways through which early modern, Muslim societal formations interacted with the acceleration of the European civilizing processes. I also explore how in return these formations contributed to creating new global configurations and institutional orders, which we conventionally identify with (early, colonial, and postcolonial) modernity.

One should start by acknowledging how the specific ways of blending power and knowledge (via strategic action or cultured life conducts) which constitute a civilization continued to bring fruits well into the modern era and its strategic dilemma which were faced by the three major, different, yet equally flourishing, empires of the Islamic ecumene: the Ottoman, in a large area covering Anatolia, the Near and Middle East, North Africa, the Balkans, and other East-European regions; the Safavid, on the Iranian plateau and historically related and geographically adjacent regions; and the Mughal, in South Asia. To these we could add a fourth, the Central Asian Uzbek Empire. Their models of state centralization, control of territories and populations, and styles of ruling had a varying degree of affiliation to the Mongol notions of centralized military rule. These empires showed quite different capacities to resist the climax of upheaval—starting in the 17th and accelerating in the 18th century—during which Western Europe turned around the power balance with the Islamic ecumene and gained a hegemonic position over both the Euro-Mediterranean area and along the maritime routes of the Indian Ocean. From those locations European powers continued to make further inroads, all the while benefiting from the influx of resources and the perfecting of colonizing techniques across the transatlantic routes that led to the Americas. This was particularly evident in the British military encroachment on the territories controlled by the

Mughal Empire, and, at the end of the 18th century, in the French response in Egypt and Syria that led to Napoleon's occupation of the area. This endeavor was significant also due to the spirit of knowledge enterprise that accompanied the military campaign (Cole 2007). In the Ottoman and in the Iranian cases, the long-term, relative strength of their socio-political formations could also be measured by the long-drawn-out resistance of the centers of their empires to the ongoing process of Western colonial encroachment. The dual process of encroachment and resistance only exhausted its impetus between the two world wars of the 20th century, namely at the historical juncture when European, though not Western, hegemony started to crumble. As we will see in the next chapter, the colonial turn dramatically affected the inherited patterns of civility in the Islamic ecumene by enveloping them within an increasingly global civilizing process, without however reducing them to ashes.

The early modern flourishing of the three Muslim empires was to a large extent the result of a sustained intervention by rulers and elites on the potential strengths they inherited from the Islamic patterns of civility that had characterized the Middle Periods. This intervention mainly consisted in superimposing on the social and cultural solidity of such features a more solid system of governance than available in the previous era. This program was based on important innovations: a systematic valorization of the dynamism of composite, often multicommunal urban economies after the negative effects of the Mongol devastations had begun to recede (a valorization whose seeds were already planted during the Later Middle Period); new administrative patterns overlaying the earlier networks and flexible institutions with better legitimized and more effective mechanisms of control of territories and populations by the political centers, especially for the sake of the implementation of sound fiscal and military policies; and, ultimately, the appropriation (particularly in the Ottoman Empire that was also the inheritor of the Byzantine imperial tradition) of a more conscious capacity to use centralized power in order to allocate resources across space to a variety of constituencies (Salzmann 2004: 14).

The knowledge–power constellation of the early modern Muslim empires also helps us to situate in a longer-term perspective the remarkable, yet ambivalent, achievements of the Middle Periods. I refrained in the previous chapters from celebrating this epoch as simply and only an age of 'renaissance' pivoting on the Islamic ecumene, and therefore as the age of the 'rise of the commoner.' This is because while it is true that elites entered a much more intense relationship with peoples and strata hitherto considered as outside or on the margins of civilization (Arnason 2004: 35), it is also important to acknowledge that, particularly in the Later Middle Period, the quite open character of the cosmopolitanism of the Islamic semi-arid zone resulted in particularly acute processes of militarization of social relations (Hodgson 1974, II: 64). Such developments cannot be entirely imputed to the violent imposition of Mongol rule over vast Muslim territories, since they more generally represented the flipside of the openness of social relations and of the related degree of unpredictability of individual life courses. This political instability caused by the relative fluidity of status hierarchies often called for military interventions to reduce social uncertainty. We can say, therefore, that where the densely legitimized Islamic moral idiom and the related contractual patterns were not sufficient to settle disputes and create social coordination if not cohesion, the relatively easy recourse to, and widespread availability of, weapons did the rest to impose a certain degree of order, albeit on rather contingent bases. Characteristically, Sufism played a crucial role at both levels, the social and the political-military, and in key instances—as in the state-building confederation of forces and groups that brought to power the Ottomans and the Safavids— legitimized the cohesion of political-military formations and coalitions. In this way Sufi authorities circumvented the legalistic trappings inhibiting the *fuqaha'* from authorizing wars on fellow Muslims.

This constellation of forces at the passage from the Later Middle Period to early modernity justifies the Hodgsonian certification of a historic Muslim apogee of civilizational knowledge–power at the dawn of the new era. Nonetheless, the fact that this zenith was soon exposed to a serious and accelerating erosion because of the Western onslaught might in principle call into question the epochal partition itself between the ages of the 'middle' (Middle Ages, Middle Periods) and the idea of a universally, yet Europe-led, modern 'new beginning'. Blindly buying into paradigms of early modernity potentially risks confirming one-sided narratives about the predominantly, if not exclusively, West-European origins of the political and cultural project of modernity. It might also indirectly corroborate the concomitant, alleged unfitness for this 'age of the new' of Islamic civilization which, however rich in knowledge and power, did not survive intact the test of being subjected to the increasing pressure of modern Western power. On the other hand, however, speaking of an early modern Islamic hegemony, as did Hodgson, might be advantageous, since it provides at the same time a factual reminder and a precious theoretical provocation. We can now appreciate the narrative provided in the previous chapters, which showed the dynamism of the

Islamic Middle Periods in comparison to the European High Middle Ages in terms of urban economies and civilities, and highlighted the unique Islamic capacity of hemisphere-wide expansion and integration. Thanks to this background we can now provide a critical angle to rewrite 'early modernity' out of a teleology of Western supremacy that was also transported by the classics of sociology, and into a dynamics of constitution of 'global society' whereby Islam does not play a merely passive and/or reactive role.

More difficult to counter is the paradigm enshrined in the work of Max Weber, according to which at the dawn of the modern era the upheavals of Western Christendom, instead of precipitating this civilization into chaos, produced new cultured ways of manifesting the inner power of life conduct. This transformation was first evident in the emerging economic elites of bourgeois origin and their innerwordly asceticism conducive to a rationalization of the pursuit of worldly success. Second, this new "spirit of capitalism" was according to Weber matched by a rationalization of law and science that created the conditions of predictability and exploitability of emerging opportunities. This increasingly occurred under the control of a state bureaucracy which absorbed the earlier religious charisma of 'office.' Both in the economy and in politics Weber saw religious traditions metamorphosing into the source of unique Western codes and forms of modern life management. This Weberian paradigm has often been regarded skeptically within Western academia itself as the somewhat overstated peak of a more complex transformation of early modern religious radicalism into a broader social dynamism which put a premium on innovation over the continuity of traditions. Weber's move nonetheless had the merit of bringing to a higher level of theoretical coherence scattered instances of social, religious, and political change. Both supporters and detractors of this paradigm, which has accompanied (or haunted) the rise of Western social sciences in the last century, seemed equally focused on singling out the specific factors of the exceptional, modern Western metamorphosis against the background of a broader civilizational comparison with the non-Western world. The road not taken was seeing the West as integral to a wider Afro-Eurasian circulatory framework of exchange and change (for a critique in this sense, see Goody 2006).

In our attempt to advance the sociology of Islam in both a theoretical and a comparative perspective, the path we are certainly not taking while confronted with Islam's attrition with modern Western hegemony is the moot reiteration of the motive of a blockage of political and economic development brought about by an all-pervading doctrine of divine authority (most recently, Diner 2009 [2005]). According to this worn-out argument, this doctrine was deemed responsible for withholding a full legitimization of political power and so preventing both a modern state formation based on a radical differentiation of politics from a religious field and the constitution of a modern entrepreneurial and largely autonomous bourgeoisie. The more interesting question to raise in the case of Islam concerns rather the aborted, yet still latent, potential of a modern type of civic cosmopolitanism. Viewed from the perspective of the expansive dynamics of the Middle Periods, the three modern Muslim empires achieved a remarkable centralization of political power without however disrupting the integrative force of long-distance connectedness and networking. The rulers of the new empires could therefore put the prosperity of their populations quite near the top of their agendas of government (just below the obvious priority of the self-preservation of their power).

On the other hand, while political elites drew on a variety of religious resources of charisma to upgrade their rule from de facto to legitimate, they used this legitimacy (not unlike their early modern European counterparts) to make their rule as autonomous as possible from the unpredictabilities of the evolution of societal and civic forces. While the Safavid and Mughal rulers styled themselves as millennial, savior-like sovereigns (Moin 2012), the Ottomans added the caliphal title to their sultanic authority and, even more strongly, construed the latter as relying on a charisma potentially even higher than that of the Caliph. The Ottoman rulers opted to posture as the supreme warrantors of a justice that, as we will see, occupied the peak of a now virtuous circle, the 'circle of justice,' after successfully redeeming the vicious circularity of the Khaldunian cycle. In this sense, the new Muslim empires invested their power in a quite modern way into specific patterns of differentiation of state and religion, much to the advantage of the former, without however obliterating the principled autonomy of the latter.

Yet such new civilizational crystallizations could only partially capitalize on the civic impetus of the Middle Periods, when a cosmopolitan high culture thrived alongside a dense social autonomy, balancing horizontal cooperation and solidarity with hierarchy and command, as we have seen in the previous three chapters. This dynamic civilizational pattern had facilitated a diffusion of the piety-minded and populist ethos of Islam within the practices and cultures of lower strata across distant regions. However, at the moment of transition into the new, early modern era this dynamism became largely frozen into a new centrality of elites. These carriers of both power and knowledge, however concerned with the welfare of their populations, put an increasing premium on the prerogatives of their central courts. This transition did not make the civic dimension of the knowledge–power articulation of the Middle Periods suddenly and irremediably subordinated to the new centralistic mode of dynastic rule. For example, the *waqf*, even when subjected to the same centralization, continued to thrive on a broadly societal level. In some circumstances the *waqf* evolved to give every citizen the right to file a lawsuit in the name of a public interest: this occurred in the increasingly frequent court cases filed for improper management of *waqf* properties in the Ottoman Empire. Overall, the centrality of the *waqf* could be further promoted as fitting into a sustained centralization of rule entailing an organization and hierarchization of public offices. This process only stopped short of the type of full-fledged, Weberian, institutional conse-cration of office that we saw in the previous chapters as fundamentally alien to the Islamic articulation of the nexus between civility and institution. In the Ottoman context, *waqf* administration became more complex as well as ubiquitous, also enclosing numerous villages. Even if Ottoman rulers were now vested with a stronger legitimacy inherent in their office, they still preferred to provide basic services in the form of personal bestowal rather than through a faceless bureaucracy (Gerber 2002: 75–6). The intensive promotion of *waqf* by the imperial centers intensified through assigning a share of public revenues to religious foundations across rural regions. The process perfected a practice that has its origin with the Saljuq dynasty in the Earlier Middle Period but also folded it into the framework provided by the centralization processes that accompanied the apogee of Ottoman power in the 16th century (Barnes 1986; Isin 2011).

Thus, paradoxically, the societal and non-centralized meta-institution of the *waqf* proved malleable enough to support the power of centralized imperial formations, provided their centers were able to integrate and co-opt (while not fully curbing) the practical and symbolic autonomy of the *'ulama'*. The shift of the balance between city and tribe in favor of the former during the process of centralization contributed to buttress the centrality and prestige of the predominantly urban *'ulama'*. The new highest office in their hierarchy within the Ottoman Empire, the *şeyhülislam*, even included the prerogative to certify the unfitness of the sultan and authorize his depo-sition. While the *'ulama'* certainly provided the Ottoman ruling apparatus with an unprecedented legitimacy compared to historic Islamic standards, their central role in society at large (and with it their legal and moral idiom, the *shari'a*) received in turn an even stronger boost. Thus the *'ulama'* continued to perform a role at the ever more crucial (quintessentially modern) interface between the two distinct spheres identifiable as the society and the state, as these became much better differentiated than in prior epochs.

Based on such premises, we should focus on issues of both originality and comparability of the early modern configurations of Muslim power in the Islamic ecumene. Here early modernity can be conceptualized within overlapping socio-economic, socio-political, and cultural processes that differed from (in spite of densely interacting with) the European knowledge-power configuration that produced the modern Westphalian, and later colonial and secular, states. Opening up a theoretical and comparative vista on multiple modernities with the Islamic ecumene playing a central role encourages a shift of focus from a self-enclosed view of the rise of modernity as a European miracle toward a perspective on the ecumene-spanning (today we would say, global) origins of modernity as entangled in dense intracivilizational and intercivilizational circulatory dynamics. Far from providing a backdrop of deficits and decay to the triumphing Western modernity, early modern Islamic articulations of the knowledge–power equation decisively contributed to such dynamics. This is not too surprising, if we heed Hodgson's warning quoted at the beginning of this chapter and look at the shifting, overall power balance which at the beginning of the process still prized Islamic formulas and formations (see also Abou-El-Haj 2005 [1991]; Barkey 2008).

Developing and at the same time integrating Hodgson, this path of analysis provides an alternative to teleological views of Western exceptionalism and Islamic backwardness. This task includes evaluating the innovative dimension of the articulation of the knowledge–power equation within the formations that Hodgson not by chance dubbed the three "gunpowder empires" (the Ottoman, the Safavid, and the Mughal). We have here to do with patterns of, as it were, Islamic proto-modernity that flourished in particular during the 16th and 17th centuries. The task would then most delicately consist in evaluating the extent to which this type of modernity turned out to be a less than adequate response not to the challenge of its European counterpart but to the ideal of human connectedness, civic autonomy, and transregional interconnectedness that had flourished during the Middle Periods within the Islamic ecumene. This ideal had been constructed with crucial contributions from Sufism—and in fact the genesis and early development of the three empires owes a lot to Sufi-related forms of connectedness and (even military) organization. Not by chance the 16th century was likely the period of highest influence of the teachings attributed to the great Sufi master (*al-shaykh al-akbar*) Ibn al-'Arabi (see Chapter 4), whose tomb in Damascus the Ottoman sultan Selim I honored with a visit when he conquered the city in 1516. Nonetheless, the new imperial formations could not consistently live up to the ideal. Was this lack of consistency just the obvious reflection of the fact that the ideal had been formulated and practiced in a context where societies could enjoy a large degree of autonomy during the Middle Periods, while the new empires were bent on imposing on them largely new disciplines? We must postpone to a separate discussion in a later volume a more detailed examination of the question of whether and to what extent, in spite of differences and imbalances between European and Islamic states, the trajectories of the Ottoman and of the other early modern Muslim empires can be considered modern state formations in their own right. Here we must content ourselves with looking at the question from the viewpoint of the civilizing process that provides the necessary background to governance.

Taming the Warriors into Games of Civility? Violence, Warfare, and Peace

The Westphalian type of modern sovereignty in Western Europe created socio-political spaces capable of incorporating, disciplining, and empowering individual subjects who became connected to each other through organic patterns of solidarity based on a social division of labor, as defined by Durkheim. Solidarity so defined overcame the more transversal ties of connectedness of traditional societies based on a matrix of brotherhood (Salvatore 2011). Norbert Elias paid particular attention to early modern European court life as the privileged model of action, interaction, and performance producing increasingly stable patterns of coordination, whose latently violent dimension was increasingly restrained. The management of this dimension was concentrated in the hands of the symbolic hub of court games themselves, the sovereign monarch (Elias 1983 [1969]).

The juridical and political notion itself of sovereignty can hardly be understood without grasping this socio-cultural transformation: a major upheaval in the knowledge–power equation. The engine of the change, the civilizing process pivoted on the monarchic courts, provided the (at least initially) centralized hub of disciplining. It also represented the more general cultural model for taming the violence of the warriors, incarnate in the feudal class or nobility. It instilled in them a sense of participation in a wider power game initially restricted to court society but ultimately coinciding with society as a whole. This was a game of power not just in the sense of putting incentives on the acquisition of the skills to exercise power over others in micro-settings. It was also capable of singling out power as such from its cultural shell, which had traditionally defined the ethical scope of power and the proper modes of its exercise. As aptly described by Talal Asad:

> In this early modern world, the moral economy of the self in a court circle was constructed very differently from the ways prescribed in the medieval monastic program. Created and re-created through dramas of manipulative power, at once personal and political, the self depended now on the maintenance of moral distance between public forms of behavior and private thoughts and feelings [corresponding to a] radical reconceptualization of appropriate behavior into representations and of skill in manipulating representations, increasingly divorced from the idea of a disciplinary program for forming the self.
>
> (Asad 1993: 67–8)

This twist of the knowledge–power equation did not eliminate propriety and manners but rather put them at the service of an increasingly singular notion of power. Power could ultimately be aligned without residues with the knowledge of the modalities through which it was exercised both in interpersonal relations and in the art of governing social bodies. In this process cultured behavior and disciplined modes empowering the self to interact with others became the living school through which the subject, later to become the citizen, was incorporated in the organic social body. It also became the macro-engine for civilizing what would become the nation. Set against this Western model, we should explore the extent to which the early modern civilizing process in the Islamic ecumene privileged a different assortment of sites and processes through which power was rendered partly autonomous from civic and religious cultures and internalized by the individual via self-restraint. In the process individuals became increasingly entangled in new types of institutional formations, which, however, fell short of engendering the twin, radical individualization and institutionalization that characterized the European trajectories.

The question, of Eliasian origin, can be reformulated, from our analytical angle, as the issue of the match (or lack thereof) between a wider societal process of self-restraint in the use of violence, on the one hand, and the concentration of violence control within centralized institutions (both ideally and practically pivoting on the rulers' courts), on the other. Such courts in Europe became endowed, during early modernity, not only with the material (physical, organizational, and fiscal) resources to implement measures of centralization of government and control but also with a quintessentially modern kind of charisma that became manifest in the symbolic prerogatives of sovereignty. This charisma, released from the social ties and networks that produce it interactively (as we have seen in the previous chapters), contributed not only to a monological legitimation of modern power but also to the shaping of the subjects as microcosms of the same forms of power incorporated by the sovereign. Sovereign power became iconically vivid in the *Leviathan* of Thomas Hobbes, depicted on the frontispiece of that famous book as the *magnus homo* literally incorporating the individual bodies of the subjects in his own encompassing socio-political body (Hobbes 1996 [1651]). As a result, the subjects themselves became sovereign, yet in their 'inner forum', which was increasingly recognized, under the aegis of the Westphalian order, as an intangible realm free from the encroachment of any outside power, including the power of the sovereign. This construction was ultimately the source of the modern notion of individual rights, whose development did not contradict the strong power concentrated in the hands of the state but actually depended on the effectiveness of its perpetuation (see Koselleck 1988 [1959]).

The particular type of civilizing process as just defined is therefore not intrinsically inimical, or, inversely, favorable to militarization and the widespread use of violence. It is rather a reflection of the degree of concentration of violence control and of the capacity of key weapons-carrying subjects and groups to frame a decision on their use in terms of wider games of power transcending their original privileges linked to localized ('feudal') realms. These wider games of power are in turn supported by a knowledge of the rules of engagement, i.e. of engaging a wide assortment of socio-political others. The transformation of civility at this crucial historical turn represented by early modernity depends on the forms and degrees of codification and taming of potentially unrestrained violence, rather than on its quantifiable reduction. With the advancement of the civilizing process the opposite might actually occur in principle (and historically this was mostly the case), namely that the self-taming of warriors plays into the hands of the centers of power which are then able to redeploy largely legitimate violence with a higher power of destruction. This is measured not just in terms of the number of direct and indirect victims and the amount of suffering and destruction (as in the proliferating European and colonial wars that broke out from the 17th century onward, after the peace of Westphalia) but in terms of its negative impact on the potential of translocal societal integration beyond the borders set by Westphalian sovereign powers.

From this viewpoint, the rise of court-centered, modern sovereign states explains the increasingly debilitating pressure exercized on hemisphere-wide circulation and horizontal integration: not by chance the process coincided with the beginning of colonialism along the new Atlantic routes, simultaneously transposed onto the Indian Ocean and the continental networks of the wider Afro-Eurasian ecumene. The process of colonization marked an acceleration of the civilizing process along lines of rationalization and centralization of violence use. The economic and geo-cultural integration of the hemisphere-wide civilization was not the sole or main casualty of the new civilizing process. To suffer a lethal blow was the cultural mutuality and the communicative translatability of legal and moral idioms across the wider civilizational ecumene and the capacity of circulation of related forms of knowledge.

Framed in these terms, the modern Western twist of the civilizing process appears as a sociological determinant of colonialism itself and therefore as a key factor in the debilitation of the Islamic ecumene. However, as we warned earlier, it would be fatal to see the issue as a mere zero-sum game in the style of unsociological, hyper-Orientalist interrogations such as those condensed in a question like *What Went Wrong?* This is even more necessary since Hodgson himself, while criticizing this approach as particularly well represented in the work of leading orientalists like Gustave von Grunebaum and Hamilton Gibbs, singled out Bernard Lewis for actually being ready to acknowledge the factors of strength emanating from the early modern Ottoman model of court-centered administration of the empire (Hodgson 1974, II: 112). This observation should be read as amounting to the suggestion that orientalism, whose key categories Hodgson subjected to critical scrutiny long before Edward Said, can be potentially rescued from its own prejudices if helped with sound sociological tools of analysis. The problem with Lewis' acknowledgment of the strength of the Ottoman Empire among early modern Muslim state formations was that it derived from viewing it as an exception within the exception, namely as the ultimate limit of rational adjustment of governance within a historical, religious, and cultural environment, the Islamic one, allegedly hostile to the legitimacy of government.

The only way out from this kind of hyper-orientalism is to shift our focus back to the three early modern Muslim empires without exceptions and determine the points of their similarity and originality vis-à-vis the West-European developments. The first obvious specificity is that in the Muslim case the traumatic event that interrupted (not at once but over a long stretch of time) the controlled anarchy of the Earlier Middle Period was the so-called Mongol invasion. This was in reality a largely self-propelling movement of conquests conducted by Central Asian tribal confederations that, as we saw, Ibn Khaldun himself attempted to integrate into his more general sociology of civility and power focused on the interaction between nomadic forces and urban society. Indeed, while the cumulative effects of Mongol rule produced, at the dawn of modernity, the Timurid/Moghul (meaning Mongol) Empire in South Asia, the same sociological constellation was responsible for the rise of the two other empires that found themselves competing with the long wave of Mongol conquests, namely the Ottoman and the Safavid. In the Later Middle Period, through a singular fusion of Irano-Semitic egalitarian ethos and Inner and Central Asian nomadic warrior codes, and stemming from earlier patterns of Islamic brotherhood, an original type of Sufi-knightly culture with a strong state-building potential saw the light. This type manifested itself both in the Ottoman (at the beginning of the period) and the Safavid cases (at the end of the period), in spite of their finally diverging doctrinal outcomes. During early modernity this divergence ushered in a rivalry between an orthodox Sunni vs. a staunchly Shiʿa power, whose consequences have been carried over to the present day (Rahimi 2004: 85–102).

The state-building dynamics that were the outcome of the organized violence of the Sufi-knightly confederations produced a type of post-heroic civility that is different from, yet compares pretty well with, the Eliasian scheme illustrating the taming of the warrior ethos via the increasing confinement of their elites (the high nobility) to central courts. Thus what was originally the military nature of government in the three Muslim empires became increasingly 'civilized.' This is to be interpreted in the quite technical sense of configuring a de facto, if not de jure, autonomy of a civil, cultured bureaucratic elite also bent on producing and reproducing cultural and life-orientational codes inspired by the *adab* tradition and promoting its amalgamation with *shariʿa* normativity. This transformation unfolded most prominently in the Ottoman Empire, by far the longer-lasting of the three formations and the one more conspicuously and consciously engaged, as we will see, in finding ways to overcome and stabilize the Khaldunian cycle of power and civility: a crucial feature that makes this empire the quintessentially modern norm within the more general Afro-Eurasian norm represented by Islamic civility—rather than the exception within the exception as adumbrated by Lewis and cognate orientalists.

In parallel, the *pax mongolica* imposed by the successors of Genghis Khan (d. 1227) mid-way through the Middle Periods further encouraged long-distance, overland trade connections along with links with Muslim missionary activism. The Mongol leaders' attitude to Sufism was not quite linear, but it is known that Timur had a particularly strong relationship with the most mobile echelons of Sufi practitioners and leaders, namely those frequently identified as 'wandering dervishes.' This preference was almost a counterpoint to the Mongol's diffidence toward the semi-autonomous and more localized powers of the urban bourgeoisie (Hodgson 1974, II: 432). Not by chance the gradual islamization of the Mongols that started by the late 13th century with the conversion of their leader Ghazan Khan was largely due to the activism of the Naqshbandi Sufi order that expanded through vast domains in Central and South Asia between the Later Middle Period and early modernity (yet also due to the active contribution of rival Sufi brotherhoods that the Naqshbandis gradually weakened if not supplanted from the 14th century). As observed by Richard Foltz in his history of the religions of the Silk Road, hagiographies from the 16th and 17th centuries portray Sufi masters belonging to the Naqshbandi order as successfully islamizing the strategically located Tarim basin, in what is today the southern part of China's Xinjiang region (Eastern Turkestan). The Sufis in question combined pious deeds and armed operations in favor of pro-Muslim and against non-Muslim Turk, Mongol, and Chinese rulers (Foltz 2010: 101).

This larger development contributed to twist the cycle of violence and restoration of order that according to Ibn Khaldun characterized the rise and collapse of civility ('*umran*) through the combined force of centralizing factors of civilization (court culture) and decentralized ones (Sufi leadership combined with religious, cultural, and commercial circulation). Curiously, as previously noted, the Maghrebi scholar built up his theory while such developments were still unfolding in a different region to the one in which he lived, North Africa, which at his time was still suffering from the final spasms of the collapse of Muslim rule in al-Andalus. In light of these trends, we should reconsider and critically reformulate some insightful remarks by Ernst Gellner (1981), to whom we have previously referred. His approach to what he simply called *Muslim Society* (the title of his famous book) has often been dismissed in ways that had him as part of a sort of unholy trinity of agents of Islam's essentialization and bashing, along with Bernard Lewis and Samuel Huntington. I do agree that the two latter scholars are responsible for conveying a negatively lopsided image of Islamic civilization, and is it not my goal to engage in a wholesale rehabilitation of Gellner's often essentializing view of Islam. I rather aim to show that, while some of his conclusions bring him dangerously close to the views of Lewis and Huntington, other key features of his analysis of Muslim society are premised on an entirely different, sociologically sound, and theoretically inspiring approach. They are worth being discussed at some length as a resource for the sociology of Islam (a field to which, as he wrote in the Preface of his *Muslim Society*, he explicitly intended to contribute).

Basically Gellner singled out the importance of the Ottomans precisely for their capacity—after the emergence of some rather entropic political-military developments that were typical of the Later Middle Period—to interrupt the Khaldunian cycle and rebuild civility and governance on much more stable bases, thus turning centrifugal impulses into centripetal power. Let us for a moment remind ourselves that the weakness of Khaldunian civility and its dizzily cyclical spin was due to the fact that once in power, new dynasts were not able to install at their central courts a stable administrative and military elite. Providing stability requires that the government elite neither depends on the ruling dynasty or coalition (often of nomadic origins and therefore originally endowed with a strong sense of in-group cohesion) nor on the consensus or acquiescence of urban clerics, the 'ulama', holding (and mostly withholding from the rulers) the keys of legitimacy in Islamic terms. The Ottomans were able to circumvent this double dependence and build an autonomous power basis by bringing to a high level of sophistication the so-called Mamluk system (actually originating in the caliphal Abbasid court itself) of recruiting a non-tribal elite from outside the field of both rulers and ruled. This typically occurred through the acquisition of young recruits by way of taxation from non-Muslim populations, especially among Christians in the Caucasus or, in the Ottoman case, the Balkans. These youngsters underwent a rigorous training at court and became the backbone of the central administrative and military elite of the Ottoman Empire. It was not rare for a member of their group to reach the highest office of grand vizier, often the de facto holder of the loftiest power in the empire.

Interestingly, when faced with the need to find a match for this recruitment system by buttressing the charisma of the ruler, the Ottomans did not sacralize sovereign power as happened in Western Europe with the emergence of the modern Leviathan. They elaborated a theory of the supreme ruler as the enlightened guarantor of the previously mentioned 'circle of justice', outside of which the subjects of the empire could not prosper. Hereby prosperity (or civility, the Khaldunian *'umran* meaning both at the same time), guaranteed by political-military strength, was fundamentally measured by the possibility of entertaining the kind of connectedness and type of transaction (from economic to spiritual) that had characterized the expansion of the Islamic ecumene in the Middle Periods. Crucially, the doctrine of the circle of justice was explicitly intended by Ottoman scholars, courtiers, and top administrators (some of whom were eager followers of Ibn Khaldun in general and of the idea of the virtuous circle in particular) to represent the type of sound socio-political interconnectedness reached by the Khaldunian cycle at its highest point of effectiveness. This point was reached before civility started its new downward journey and the interconnections of the circle of justice broke down. In other words, it was the Ottomans' achievement to turn an inherently unstable cycle into a type of enduring socio-political balance that could be ideally mirrored by the circle. The circle of justice is finally turned from an unrealistic ideal into a consistent methodology of rule (while certainly retaining an appreciable component of ideological justification, which centralized rule now needed more than ever). Deepening his intuitive (and/or provocative) view of the birth of Islam as a Platonism 2.0, Gellner dubbed the system of Ottoman rule, through which an elite of professional administrators and commanders were trained at court after severing all their links to family, as a Platonism 3.0. This program effectively synthesized the (in principle) opposite imperatives of elite rule and good governance, based on a concern for the wellbeing of all the subjects of the polity (Gellner 1981: 76–7).

In the Ottoman case both crucial components of the engine of the European civilizing process—namely the neutralization of the warriors' violent power through a rationalization of court dynamics, and the sublimation of this evaporated power into a new charisma of the ruler—are present, but in attenuated forms. Specific to the Ottoman case is how this moderate charisma of wisdom, expressed by the ruler as the guarantor of the circle of justice, was strengthened, at a later stage, by an 'invention of tradition', through which the caliphal office, claimed by the Ottoman in earlier eras, was emphatically added to the sultanic prerogatives and in the late 18th century also enjoyed international recognition (thus becoming de jure 'Westphalian'). In reality, as also stressed by Hodgson, rather than simply as a sultan (the term in use for designating independent rulers from Saljuq times onward, in the Earlier Middle Period) the Ottoman ruler was mainly identified as the *padishah*. This term originated in Persian statecraft and therefore embedded an ancient, even pre-Islamic, type of charisma (Hodgson 1974, III: 1). Throughout the process through which the prerogatives of the ruler acquired a stronger Islamic connotation key components of the *'ulama'* ranks were coopted into the court and the high echelons of the administrative elite. The emerging *'ulama'* hierarchy culminated in the office of the previously mentioned *şeyhülislam*, whose prerogatives were continually increased and ever more tightly integrated in the central administrative and juridical apparatuses of the empire. This was a function without equal in previous forms of Muslim rule (the label was just occasionally used during earlier epochs as an honorific title for leading jurisprudents). As a segment of the elite, i.e. viewed from above, the entire layer of court-based or court-related high-ranking *'ulama'* happened to be called *ilmiyye*, as their credentials were grounded explicitly on knowledge. As such they matched the *kalemiyye* composed of increasingly professional, systematically trained bureaucrats, representing more directly the power of the pen of an earlier Persian tradition of statecraft, which no power in the Islamic ecumene, least of all the Ottomans, were ever willing to abrogate or supersede. Clearly, a double civilizing of the ruling (*askeri*: literally, military) class was accomplished, starting from its earlier, both Khaldunian and post-Mongol, basis of power-formation: through an appropriate combination of *adab* and *shari'a*.

We saw earlier that the type of knowledge subsumed under the label of *adab* did not clash with the core Islamic traditions based on Qur'an and *sunna*, but provided catalogues of the ethical and practical norms of good life not primarily controlled by the *'ulama'*, since cultivated by a class of literati in the framework of life at court. The *adab* tradition became central to Islamic civilization from early Abbasid times, even if detached from the core religious traditions of Islam. The idea of the circle of justice was considered a prime yield of the *adab* tradition. Indeed, the circle of justice was not just geared to a legitimization of the power of ruling and administrative bodies but was also understood as the source of a type of reflexive thought on the nature and delicacy of the social bond, which required a careful modulation of the mutual roles of subjects, the ruling class, and the sultan.

The circle of justice, in spite of providing a leitmotif of the court-based *adab* literature and the related Persianate tradition of statecraft, could also be referred back to the Khaldunian cycle. The vision of circular harmony guaranteed by the *padishah* impacted views of civility until it encountered, and largely matched, the Khaldunian lessons on the cyclicality of socio-political formations: the circle was then seen as the outcome of the taming of the cycle, by turning it from vicious into virtuous. This conjunction was in evidence in the critical pamphlets published during periods of intense transformation of the Ottoman Empire and in particular in the course of the crucial 17th century, which witnessed strong centrifugal forces determined by inflation, a fiscal crisis, and military overstretching.

By the 18th century the well-rooted but continuously reconstructed court tradition of *adab* happened to provide the background culture for building renewed formulas for an ethic of governance. This culture and the corresponding ethic were entertained among the members of the higher echelons of the bureaucracy, who matched their administrative competencies with the cultural taste and life style of literati. According to Şerif Mardin, we can detect in the evolution of *adab* (*edep* in Ottoman Turkish) the first seeds of a reformist culture among the members of the Ottoman *kalemiyye*. As a result of a looming sense of crisis in the once all-powerful empire, this group started to cultivate the self-understanding of a modern bureaucracy that must deal with increasingly demanding tasks in the management of territories and populations. This trend is not contradicted, as we will see, by the fact that the 18th century manifested a new and mounting pressure from European powers, including the Russian Empire. This pressure was felt in the context of measures that effected the loosening of control of territories and populations by the central Ottoman administration. In other words, even when responding to the intensifying encroachment of the West, the Sublime Porte drew on cultural resources of its own in dealing with emerging centrifugal tendencies caused by a realignment of policies and underlying coalitions more than by a simple implosion of central rule based on a fateful trajectory of, as it were, civilizational decay.

Gellner fails to sufficiently highlight a key nexus between the Khaldunian cycle and the circle of justice which proves how the Ottomans consciously reflected on the vulnerability of the former in order to take suitable measures to stabilize the latter. The teachings of Ibn Khaldun were among the favorite readings of the Ottoman ruling elite, including the *'ulama'*. This is also shown by the fact that the first five chapters of the *Muqaddima* were translated into Ottoman Turkish in the early 18th century by no-one less than the *şeyhülislam* of the epoch (Salzmann 2004: 76). Even more remarkable is that the scholars who translated Ibn Khaldun discussed and integrated his analysis by filling in the supposed gaps in his argument or even by deepening some themes, also in order to take into account historical developments that followed his life and work and the limitations of his own observations. Overall, the cumulative dealing with Ibn Khaldun by several Ottoman scholars constitutes a creative compendium that reflects the conception of society, history, and political legitimacy of significant segments of the Ottoman elite of knowledge and power (see Fleischer 1984; Yıldırım 2009; Yilmaz 2009).

A serious match to the study of the Khaldunian cycle and its proactive overcoming via new forms of civility and governance in the Sunni Ottoman Empire was the trajectory of Safavid Iran, which became the Ottomans' Shi'i challenger on their Eastern frontier. Even more markedly than in the Ottoman case, the Safavid state was itself the product of the incorporation of a combined military and spiritual movement which came to maturation during the last phase of the Middle Periods (Rahimi 2004). The stabilization itself of the dynasty and the empire was sanctioned by a public civility combining devotional and carnivalesque components, aided by the reenactment of a key Shi'i ritual like the Muharram (Rahimi 2011). More than the prevailing of the state over a Khaldunian cyclical civility, what is worth emphasizing here is an emerging, orchestrated dimension of civility constituted through the condensed symbolism of an etatized ritual. This is important to the extent that it shows the need for early modern Muslim empires to stabilize the Khaldunian cycle by enacting ritualized techniques of consensus that brought to the political centers key elements of the religious culture entertained by the masses, while sterilizing their potentially destabilizing and even heterodox impetus. Clearly, there is an evolving side of civility here at play which is no longer autonomous but dependent on politicized public ritual.

While the ritual stabilization of public civility in the Safavid case was achieved through making the capital Isfahan the symbolic and ritual hub of the new state, the older Ottoman Empire, which reached the apogee of its power in the 16th century, faced a more complex challenge the more it emerged as the champion of Sunni Islam. This predicament required tackling an issue of legitimacy that lay deeper than sheer symbolism and ritual, namely the institution of the Caliphate, whose erosion and collapse during Abbasid times had been responsible for opening up the Khaldunian cycle. The claim of caliphal prerogatives by the Ottoman sultan was originally covered by the official narrative of a direct transmission of the caliphal charisma via the last heir of the Abbasid on the occasion of the Ottoman conquest of Egypt at the beginning of the 16th century. Clearly this narrative, taken alone, was in itself insufficient to pinpoint the necessary legitimacy underlying the claim to the Caliphate. The Ottoman court had to face the challenge of ingraining the caliphal office into an already well-dressed mechanism of power and legitimacy pivoting on the circle of justice. This occurred without overcoming the traditionally ambivalent legitimacy of the office in the theology and *fiqh* literature. In this way, the caliphal title was highly unlikely to be redressed even by the *'ulama'* who were integrated at the court. This is why their cooptation into the restricted ruling elite did not affect their yet traditional type of knowledge production, relying on commentaries (*şerh*) and glosses (*haşiye*).

Not surprisingly, perhaps, due to the role that Sufism played in the rise of the Ottoman state, *tasawwuf* had a stronger legitimizing role at court than *fiqh*, even more so once Ibn Khaldun's theoretical and historical teachings had been folded into court culture, given the importance he also attributed to Sufism. Nonetheless, the inconclusiveness of the process of stabilizing the caliphal prerogatives into the legitimacy of Ottoman rule (a charisma that was supposed to radiate also beyond Ottoman boundaries, as evidently implied by the caliphal title) was part of a larger fluidity of the entire social and political theory supporting the Ottoman Empire, not unlike the other modern Muslim empires. Yet by this epoch fluidity is no longer the harbinger of advancements. Clearly impairing was the fact that these empires and their courts could never devise a clear-cut political myth comparable to Hobbes' construction of the Leviathan, which European powers matched with the juridical apparatus of the Westphalian order during the 17th century (Yilmaz 2009). This was the century when Ottoman rule started to be overstretched both externally and internally. Therefore the explicitly legal reappropriation of the political dimension of the title of Caliph by the Ottoman sultan in the late 18th century, occurring in a framework already marked by a European Westphalian hegemony (particularly via the peace treaty with Russia of 1774), manifested a quite defensive reflex toward the European power system in general and the Russian Empire in particular. The move cannot be considered a conscious attempt to catch up with European trajectories via the formation of a full-fledged Muslim Leviathan effected through stabilizing the religious charisma of the ruler as Caliph.

What is nonetheless important to stress in this context is that the direct or indirect role of Sufi orders and networks within the civic spaces of the Islamic ecumene did not evaporate at the stage of transition from the fluid politics of the Middle Periods to the imperial crystallizations of early modernity. The prestige of Sufi teachings reached its symbolic zenith when the

Ottoman sultan Selim I, after the conquest of Damascus in 1516, promoted and, in 1518, personally inaugurated a mausoleum and a mosque built on the tomb of Ibn al-'Arabi, who thus became a sort of unofficial patron saint of the Ottoman house (Sirriyeh 2005: 126). Overall the new epoch coincided with a stabilization and strengthening of the role of some Sufi *turuq* within the new power constellations. A quite wide opening of the spectrum of their orientations between orthodoxy and heterodoxy ensued, often changing direction depending on the ruling regime. The Ottoman–Safavid rivalry directly impacted this polarization to the extent that the Ottoman power happened to incarnate the Sunni way, although Ottoman society as a whole did not become monolithically committed to an orthodox type of pietism. Striking evidence for this is the fact that the Janissary corps, which originated from the system of slave recruitment and education at court on a military level, entertained close relations with the rather heterodox and Shi'a-influenced Bektashi order. Yet in any such early modern constellation Sufis had to reconstruct their role largely outside of the traditional web of interrelationships that had facilitated a tight overlapping of guild, *tariqa*, and even neighborhood authorities well into the Middle Periods (Zubaida 1995: 165).

Nonetheless, there is a level at which Sufism contributed quite deeply to define civility at the transition from the Later Middle Period to early modernity. It is the dimension given by the normative stigmatization of antinomian tendencies that prevailed among the most heterodox and deviant groups that started to proliferate particularly in the 12th and 13th centuries, in coincidence with the organizational consolidation of several *turuq* and partly in opposition to this latter trend. The most typical such group that happened to be the object of denunciations was the Qalandars. They were singled out not just for their lack of observance of *shari'a* norms but also for their intentional orientation to a life conduct severed from social obligations and the mutuality and self-control inherent in civility (Karamustafa 2007: 164–5). What is particularly remarkable is that by the beginning of the modern era both Ottoman writers and European travelers could synchronically build binary categories of normative civility based on its antithesis, namely abnormal and antinomian behavior, often identified with the most heterodox Sufis.

On the other hand, Ottoman society was still able to absorb and to some extent integrate such groups and tendencies within its fabric. The most relevant example was the one, just mentioned, of the Janissaries, whose combination of official role as a centralized military force and heterodox sympathies might have been potentially perceived as even more destabilizing but in reality was not. There were also frequent instances of antinomian groups continuing to benefit from *waqf* income endowed by no-one less that the sultan, or enjoying legal protection against stigmatization and attempts to deprive them of their endowed lodges. Indeed such groups epitomized even more than organized and orthodox *turuq* the idea of movement and long-distance connections, via their radical disconnection from locales. Such ambivalence was carried over from the Later Middle Period into the state formations of early modernity and fed into the dilemmas of centralization vs. decentralization of power that characterized the epoch.

The Long Wave of Power Decentralization

Even after the early modern consolidation of the power distribution across the Islamic ecumene into a limited number of centralized empires, the long-term wave of expansion of Sufi networks did not exhaust its impetus. It rather diversified its modes of ingraining into the process of building civic spaces. The expansion of transregional and hemisphere-wide networks based on major traditional Sufi *turuq* intensified, from North Africa to Southeast Asia, from West Africa to Eastern Turkestan/Western China. At the same time, more locally centralized brotherhoods came into being, implanting themselves at regional levels. The more regionally entrenched orders happened to be those better able both to suit the new structure of the big Muslim empires and to face, also on a military level, the beginnings of European colonial encroachment on their territories. Sufi leaders and groups often became integral to the core of the new, early modern, centralized imperial formations. Yet as a consequence of these processes, and until the European pressure became ever more tangible and direct (see Chapter 6), the previously mentioned merging of Sufi spirituality and warrior ethos that we saw as characteristic of the Later Middle Period (be it of a knightly-heroic, as in the Ottoman case, or of a millenarian-populist type, like with the Safavids) receded for a while. It was largely absorbed— though not without residue—into the centralized military organization of the Muslim 'gunpowder empires' (Rahimi 2004: 64).

However, a most remarkable novelty that came to maturation toward the end of the 17th century consisted in the rise of new activist, revivalist (or, as some authors stressed, "renewalist") Sufi aggregations, linking in original

ways inherited dimensions of Sufi thought and new approaches to recruitment, practice, and mobilization (Voll 1994 [1982]: 24–83). In other words,
the demilitarization of the Middle Periods did not translate into a demobi-
lization but rather into new organizational patterns that put a premium on
discipline and cohesion, which could also be remobilized in military terms
in the new imperial, and later, colonial, contexts. This development entailed
major shifts among some Sufi orders toward more formal and hierarchical
modes of organization, especially after the 18th century, i.e. in coincidence
with (or right before) the first signs of the impact of colonial forces. The
process bolstered their capacity to create new powerful forms of civility able
to push for social and even political change. Better codified vertical relations
between master and disciple were ever more solidly supported by codes of
virtuous disciplines based on the imitation of Muhammad. Particularly in
the Ottoman case, the integration of the upper layers of the *'ulama'* into
the institutional structure of the empire—with several leading *madrasas*
located in the center and fulfilling the task of training the legal cadres—was
matched by the remarkable institutional integration of selected Sufi orders,
particularly those close to the court milieus, and whose lodges (*tekkes*)
often contributed to legal teaching. On the other hand, the Sufis' organic
links to guilds and civic associations underwent a process of erosion, if not
dissolution. Overall, Sufism's relation to governance changed remarkably
while remaining institutionally ambivalent (Arjomand 2004: 226–9).

With regard to such developments, scholars like Fazlur Rahman (1979
[1966]: 206) and John O. Voll (1994 [1982]: 29) spoke of a distinctive "neo-
Sufi" associational pattern characterized by a new type of socio-political
activism. This new impetus was nurtured by a quite orthodox commitment
to Islam's potential for mobilizing various social groups in order to implement reformulated and updated Islamic ideals of social cohesion and justice.
Some such Sufi groups cultivated the study of *hadith* in ways that were quite
comparable to some of the new 'puritan' movements—like the 18th-century
Wahhabis from the Arabian peninsula—of a decidedly anti-Sufi inclination.
As evidenced by Peter Gran, the inherently decentralized nature of studies of
hadith and the latitude allowed within this scholarly branch to reinterpret
norms of social interaction, including those affecting trade and business,
appeared in some cases to ultimately promote the interests of a rising
commercial class (Gran 1998 [1979]). It would be far-fetched to see in "neo-
Sufism" a unitary, almost Weberian type of social movement, organization,
or even formation (due to the fact that the activism of these new movements

also included state-building capacities in semi-peripheral areas), almost representing a successful new combination of charisma and Khaldunian *'asabiyya*. Nonetheless, these new Sufi, early modern aggregations were probably the manifestation of a major change in the Islamic ecumene within a mutating, hemisphere-wide geopolitical setting. This happened just prior to the period, during the 18th century, when power balances started to be tangibly affected by the emerging European hegemony that was simultaneously tightening its grip on the Western hemisphere, the New World or the Americas.

This is why the phenomenon underlying so-called neo-Sufism should be carefully analyzed irrespective of its labeling, since it reflects an activist response to the long transition between early and colonial modernity. This transition took place during the period when Europe was just taking form as a new powerhouse, peaking with the peace of Westphalia in the middle of the 17th century. The European process was initially pushed by a sense of urgency to avoid a major political and civilizational collapse due to the fragmentation triggered by the Reformation and the Ottoman expansion, also dubbed the 'Turkish threat,' emanating from the 'terrible Turk.' The process culminated with the irresistible triumph of European powers around the end of the 18th century at all levels of the, by then, truly global denouement of the knowledge–power equation. This was the time when the Ottoman realm and the entire Asian space started to be seen as strictly subordinated to European developments in strategic and economic terms. Set against this background, and in spite of the fact that neo-Sufism can hardly reflect a power formation in its own right, the concept is important as a heuristic aid to determine the relations between the early modernity of the Islamic ecumene and the first phase of Europe-led colonial modernity (O'Fahey and Radtke 1993; Voll 2008). The notion of neo-Sufism can be useful in highlighting how, far from ineluctably succumbing to European colonialism, the Islamic ecumene was able to show, exactly in the interstices and intervals between the modernity of the Muslim empires and the modernity of the European colonial powers, a singular capacity of articulation of activist forms of sociability, civility, and mobilization.

Significant attempts to reconstruct viable Islamic traditions, especially in the field of the law, had already been promoted by a host of variously motivated Muslim leaders particularly during the 18th century and prior to the emergence of a reform discourse with clear contours in the public spheres of late-colonial states. The activities of these leaders spanned a variety of regions of the Islamic ecumene (Keddie 1994). Some of these regions were variably affected by the direct or indirect effects of the beginnings, especially from the 18th century, of the Western colonial expansion on an increasing scale. Such developments, including the activist profile of many Sufi orders, depended on a capacity to respond to the new conditions through original ideas. These were often the outcome of a combination of a selective drawing from inherited patterns and true innovation—a recipe that was to be taken over, with mixed success, by the reform (*islah*) wave in the late-colonial period. The quality of this first wave of innovative responses is such that reducing them to collaterals of a new activist brand of Sufism is a sure way to diminish their importance. This is an additional reason why neo-Sufism should not be taken as a comprehensive type but as an interpretive foil of a wider transition from early modern to colonial parameters of social organization and intellectual innovation.

The first towering representative of this trend was the Indian master Ahmad Sirhindi (1564–1624), who not by chance was named *mujaddid*, i.e. renewer, by his disciples. This title had a quasi-millenarian significance, since he was supposed to incarnate the charismatic leader charged with renewing Islam at the beginning of its second millennium. Sirhindi founded a new order, the Mujaddidiyya, which kept a Naqshbandi affiliation but drew its name from the renewalist ethos reflected by founder's epithet. Sirhindi particularly stressed the 'puritan' and *sunna*-oriented dimension of Sufism and laid a vigorous focus on the human virtues and spiritual qualities of Muhammad as the example to be followed by every Muslim. Sirhindi's leadership in his regional context and epoch has been disputed, particularly to the extent that it has been reduced by some observers to a mere resistance to the concomitant success of a top-down type of syncretic, anti-puritan reinterpretation of Sufism by his contemporary, no-one less than the great Moghul emperor Akbar (1542–1605) and/or to the Chishti order that prevailed in South Asia and regularly enjoyed the ruler's support. Akbar founded a kind of *tariqa* overlapping with court hierarchies and for which he served as both the master and the quasi-semi-divine, living, saint, thus also duplicating as the philosopher-king of the *falsafa* tradition (Hodgson 1974, III: 73–80). Akbar's son, the emperor Jahangir, put Sirhindi in prison and Jahangir's grandson, the emperor Aurangzeb, in spite of going down in history for reversing the religious pluralist climate of his illustrious predecessors and espousing a renewed Islamic orthodoxy, banned Sirhindi's writings from the reign altogether. Even if interpreted in oppositional rather than in proactive terms in its own South-Asian political and cultural context, Sirhindi's reform-oriented approach proved to be significantly innovative of Sufi and scholarly traditions across the Islamic ecumene.

This program was brought to a new level of sophistication via the scholarly redefinitions of key Islamic traditions by the leading, yet until recently understudied, thinker 'Abd al-Ghani al-Nabulusi (1640–1731). Al-Nabulusi lived through a particularly delicate and tense period, the late 17th- to early 18th-century crisis of the Ottoman Empire that was characterized by growing uncertainty and spreading effervescence. However, he was also frequently on the move for a *rihla* (a journey in search for knowledge), which allowed him to author a famous œuvre within the successful genre with the same name, delineating a chain of places visited and their significance in spiritual and knowledge terms (Sirriyeh 2005; Akkash 2007). This is why one should contextualize his own involvement in a more localized confrontation within the broader picture of what it meant to be a leading scholar of the age. He had to face a 'proto-fundamentalist' movement led by mid-level *'ulama'* in Istanbul and Anatolia who spurned a literalist approach to the reading of Islamic sources. The movement also spread into Syria, where al-Nabulusi operated, but through its very success elicited firm responses. The surrounding controversies took the shape of a 'cultural war' to define the real truth of Islam, a type of contention that we can reasonably deem as distinctively modern. Al-Nabulusi's first objection to the puritan movement was of the kind: how can such puritan literalists tell what is right from what is wrong and what is true from what is false, if they ignore what is in the heart of every single devout Muslim? (Tamari 2012: 103–5). Against them he stressed the malleability of *shari'a* and its opening to future possibilities and aspirations. Most importantly, he was able to combine a stress on civic responsibility with a reinterpretation of the teachings of Ibn al-'Arabi, which other thinkers (both Sufis and anti-Sufis) were at the time starting to stigmatize as the epitome of un-Islamic passivism and esotericism (a grave distortion that became ever more popular during the follow-up reform stage of the 19th and 20th centuries).

Yet as previously observed, the anti-Sufi puritan stream was singularly connected to some neo-Sufi developments, as both strands focused on the virtuous personality of Muhammad. The founder of the Wahhabi movement, Muhammad ibn 'Abd-al-Wahhab (1703–1792), gathered a following extending well beyond the regions of the Arabian peninsula where he was active (mainly Najd and Hijaz) and can today be considered the main source of inspiration for all puritan and 'fundamentalist' currents within modern Islam (provided we do not neglect the just mentioned, late

17th-century Ottoman precursors). Clearly what matters in this context of quite deep transformations of Islamic traditions are less the reasons for the polarizations between anti-Sufism and neo-Sufism (and within the latter the renewed strength of the orthodox Sufi orders and branches). Rather, what is most salient is the fact that cutting through most of these movements, the period witnessed an important revival of *hadith* studies, in the context of a heightened competition to find the best ways to virtuously imitate Muhammad. The significance of these studies can be summarized as reflecting the wish to focus on the centrality of life conduct and self-steering, a secure token of a deepening civilizing process. Such endeavors became increasingly central to the redefinition of the key link between intellectual production and civic activism. So interpreted, the revival of *hadith* studies can be considered a match for the flourishing literature on manners and etiquette that characterized both Europe and Japan around the same period (Elias 2000 [1939; 1968]; Ikegami 2005). The important difference with Europe (and a potential analogy with Japan) is that *hadith* studies could innovate while reconstructing, not abandoning, the discursive tradition of reflection on exemplary, normative conduct enshrined at the religious core of Islamic traditions. In this sense the modern Islamic literature on life conduct and propriety did not lead to a radical singularization of power and reputation within social games as happened in Europe.

This development reflected the enhanced emphasis on the imitation of the 'way' of Muhammad (*tariqa muhammadiya*), on his singular virtues. This emphasis, though not unknown to the Sufism of the Middle Periods, was strongly accentuated at the dawn of the modern era and became particularly widespread during the 18th century. Here the Islamic postulate (and imperative) of *tawhid* (acknowledging the oneness of God) is no longer just a medium to achieve an *unio mystica* with the divine but the channel through which one may access the essence of the Prophet's *sunna*, and so of Islam itself. The Islamic commitment is now reconceptualized as a wider social force guiding responsible subjects. Despite this remarkable development, to a large degree the individual responsibility to perform good deeds is still mediated by the master of the brotherhood. Nonetheless, by way of this remodulation of *tawhid* through a focus on life conduct and discipline, Islam is now able to provide a higher coherence to the infinite manifestations of human diversity (and, in this sense, to the valorization of individual paths), well beyond the regional differences and cultural plurality that accompanied Islam's expansion during the Middle Periods. Yet it cannot be overlooked that what we term fundamentalism was inevitably born within this widening spectrum of Islamic options. The emerging puritan/ fundamentalist current both promised a simple accomplishment of the imitation of Muhammad and indicated a way to process the anxiety resulting from observing the widening pluralization of Islamic ways. It was favored by the improved communication and enhanced competition between the increasingly better organized Sufi orders and particularly between their masters. The first tangible effects of European pressure on Muslim lands also added to the potential allure of the fundamentalist alternative, whose prototype is conventionally identified with the already mentioned Wahhabi movement, though it had a more transversal appeal cutting through the innerly differentiating Sufi landscape. This transversality became ever more evident at the passage from the 18th to the 19th century (Weismann 2001), marking the beginning (somewhat symbolized by Napoleon's occupation of Egypt and the Levant) of the most intense phase of European colonialism.

The rather decentralized nature of the study of *hadith* and the latitude allowed within this scholarly branch for the chance to reinterpret norms of social interaction, including those affecting trade and business, appeared in some cases designed to promote the interests of a rising commercial class. This *hadith* revival occurred during a period that saw a sharp reversal of the centralization wave experienced especially in the Ottoman Empire during early modernity, particularly in the 16th and, after a crisis at the end of that century, the 17th century. According to Peter Gran (1998 [1979]), the 18th century was particularly important from this viewpoint for representing a watershed that marked the beginning of a new type of globalization of markets and their attendant geo-politics. This process superseded the earlier hemisphere-wide integration with the Islamic ecumene at its core, and now linked both hemispheres through colonial enterprises matching capitalist interests and the expansive strategies of European powers. However, again according to Gran, this development can in no way be reduced to simply reflecting Western colonial advancements, along with their collateral effects on a now allegedly decaying Islamic ecumene. Albeit in a context of increasing fragmentation, Islamic intellectual and legal responses were proactive in that they reflected a surging commercial ethos and even an emerging, bourgeois-like culture. The Sufi revival, often linked to such *hadith* studies, and particularly the founding of new orders like the Khalwatiyya in Egypt which exalted individual asceticism over collective ecstasy, were also linked to the rise of literary salons sponsored by wealthy merchants. Here the cultivation and recitation of Sufi poetry became a new vehicle of reflection and subjectivity-building within the culture of the emerging strata that were benefiting from the decentralization process (Gran 1998 [1979]: 37–68).

Not by chance, and by several standards, the leading figure of the last part of this transition period was the South-Asian neo-Sufi Naqshbandi Shah Waliullah (1703–1762). Like Sirhindi, he came from an important part of the Islamic ecumene, yet one now most exposed to the encroachment of European colonialism in the continental part of the Eastern hemisphere (maritime routes and coastal bridgeheads had been subject to European pressure since early modernity). He lived through the traumatic period of collapse of the Mughal Empire and had therefore the chance to promote a project of reconstruction of a South-Asian Muslim identity and even unity at the intellectual level. More in general, he was the first leading promoter of a fully conscious, large-scale synthesis between the legal (or, more general, *hadith*-based) approaches and the Sufi way (including its most consequentially 'spiritual' and prestigious version, going back to Ibn al-ʿArabi). At the same time, Shah Waliullah was a champion of the eclectic merging of the teaching of all legal schools. This novel approach contributed to improving the daily work of legal adjudication in times of rapid change, an idea that was due to become a crucial touchstone for 19th-century urban reformers across the Islamic ecumene.

Most notably, Shah Waliullah refuted the conception of *shariʿa* as the commands of a master intent on testing his slave's loyalty and sense of obedience. Discussing by way of example the Islamic laws of marriage, he explained that Muhammad retained most of the pre-Islamic Arab practices such as engagement before wedding, dower, and wedding feast. Similarly, Muhammad confirmed the pre-Islamic penal practices, which Muslim jurists assimilated into Islamic law under the heading of *hudud* (penalties). For Shah Waliullah this step amounted to an unambiguous recognition that customs constituted the major social source of the *shariʿa*. He argued that *shariʿa* provisions were not issued for the sake of mere obedience for the simple reason that the law needs to perpetually envision human welfare as its inherent goal. He even explained prophecy and the revelation of divine laws as a process of reform designed to enhance human cooperation and well-being. According to Shah Waliullah, the prophets examined the laws in practice, retained most of them, and reformed those that could no longer produce social values and goods due to changes in practice. Such observations come close to a proto-sociological approach to prophecy and the law originating from it (Masud 2005: 166–7).

We can now better appreciate how in the course of the 18th century the revival and renewal often associated with Sufism could still be seen as part of a longer-term process of testing and opening up Islamic teachings on the basis of demands determined by evolving needs and matching practice. There wasn't yet a strong sense of discontinuity triggered by the challenge of Western modernity. The leaders of the renewal movements were only selectively associated with the processes of centralization and decentralization promoted or accepted by the ruling elites and their court personnel. On the other hand, they were mostly well conscious of the new power constellations and therefore brought into the knowledge–power equation a sense of realism and a capacity to read social realities and transformations probably unknown to earlier spirits, including those we have singled out as the leading personalities of the Middle Periods. Yet the inception of late-colonial modernity was to change the equation once more and quite deeply. Innovative responses were to be followed by an implosion of traditions and norms which did not entirely impair conscious change and proactive responses, but channeled through ever more narrow disciplinary paths determined by the Western colonial blueprints of civility.

References

Abou-El-Haj, Rifa'at. 2005 [1991]. *Formation of the Modern State: The Ottoman Empire. Sixteenth to Eighteenth Centuries*. Syracuse, NY: Syracuse University Press.

Akkash, Samer. 2007. *'Abd al-Ghani al-Nabulusi: Islam and the Enlightenment*. Oxford: Oneworld.

Arjomand, Said Amir. 2004. "Transformation of the Islamicate Civilization: A Turning Point in the Thirteenth Century?" In *Eurasian Transformations, 10th to 13th Centuries: Crystallizations, Divergences, Renaissances*, edited by Johann P. Arnason and Björn Wittrock, 213–45. Leiden: Brill.

Arnason, Johann P. 2001. "Civilizational Patterns and Civilizing Processes." *International Sociology*, 16/3: 387–405.

Arnason, Johann P. 2003. *Civilisations in Dispute: Historical Questions and Theoretical Traditions*. Leiden: Brill.

Arnason, Johann P. 2004. "Parallels and Divergences: Perspectives on the Early Second Millennium." In *Eurasian Transformations, 10th to 13th Centuries: Crystallizations, Divergences, Renaissances*, edited by Johann P. Arnason and Björn Wittrock, 13–40. Leiden: Brill.

Asad, Talal. 1993. *Genealogies of Religion: Discipline and Reasons of Power in Christianity and Islam*. Baltimore and London: Johns Hopkins University Press.

Barkey, Karen. 2008. *Empire of Difference: The Ottomans in Comparative Perspective*. Cambridge: Cambridge University Press.

Barnes, John R. 1986. *An Introduction to Religious Foundations in the Ottoman Empire*. Leiden: Brill.

Cole, Juan. 2007. *Napoleon's Egypt: Invading the Middle East*. New York: Palgrave Macmillan.

Diner, Dan. 2009 [2005]). *Lost in the Sacred: Why the Muslim World Stood Still*. Princeton, NJ: Princeton University Press.

Elias, Norbert. 1983 [1969]. *The Court Society*, translated by Edmund Jephcott. Oxford: Blackwell.

Elias, Norbert. 2000 [1939; 1968]. *The Civilizing Process*. Oxford: Blackwell.

Fleischer, Cornell. 1984. "Royal Authority, Dynastic Cyclism and Ibn Khaldunism in Sixteenth Century Ottoman Letters." In *Ibn Khaldun and Islamic Ideology*, edited by Bruce Lawrence, 4–68. Leiden: Brill.

Foltz, Richard. 2010. *Religions of the Silk Road: Premodern Patterns of Globalization*. New York: Palgrave Macmillan.

Gellner, Ernest. 1981. *Muslim Society*. Cambridge: Cambridge University Press.

Gerber, Haim. 2002. "The Public Sphere and Civil Society in the Ottoman Empire." In *The Public Sphere in Muslim Societies*, edited by Miriam Hoexter, Shmuel N. Eisenstadt, and Nehemia Levtzion, 65–82. Albany, NY: SUNY Press.

Goody, Jack. 2006. *The Theft of History*. Cambridge: Cambridge University Press.

Gran, Peter. 1998 [1979]. *Islamic Roots of Capitalism: Egypt, 1760–1840*. Syracuse, NY: Syracuse University Press.

Hobbes, Thomas. 1996 [1651]. *Leviathan*, edited, and with an introduction and notes, by J.C.A. Gaskin. Oxford: Oxford University Press.

Hodgson, Marshall G.S. 1974. The Venture of Islam: Conscience and History in a World Civilization, I–III. Chicago and London: University of Chicago Press.

Hodgson, Marshall G.S. 1993. *Rethinking World History: Essays on Europe, Islam and World History*, edited, with Introduction and Conclusion, by Edmund Burke III. Cambridge: Cambridge University Press.

Ikegami, Eiko. 2005. *Bonds of Civility: Aesthetic Networks and the Political Origins of Japanese Culture*. Cambridge: Cambridge University Press.

Isin, Engin F. 2011. "Ottoman Waqfs as Acts of Citizenship." In *Held in Trust: Waqf in the Muslim World*, edited by Pascale Ghazaleh, 209–29. Cairo: American University in Cairo Press.

Karamustafa, Ahmet T. 2007. *Sufism: The Formative Period*. Edinburgh: Edinburgh University Press.

Keddie, Nikki R. 1994. "The Revolt of Islam, 1700 to 1993: Comparative Considerations and Relations to Imperialism." *Comparative Studies in Society and History*, 36/3: 463–87.

Koselleck, Reinhart. (1988 [1959]). *Critique and Crisis, Enlightenment and the Pathogenesis of Modern Society.* Oxford: Berg.

Lewis, Bernard. 2002. *What Went Wrong? Western Impact and Middle Eastern Response.* Oxford and New York: Oxford University Press.

Masud, M. Khalid. 2005. "Communicative Action and the Social Construction of Shariʿa in Pakistan." In *Religion, Social Practice, and Contested Hegemonies: Reconstructing the Public Sphere in Muslim Majority Societies,* edited by Armando Salvatore and Mark LeVine, 155–79. New York: Palgrave Macmillan.

Moin, A. Azfar. 2012. The Millennial Sovereign: Sacred Kingship and Sainthood in Islam. New York: Columbia University Press.

O'Fahey, R.S. and Bernd Radtke. 1993. "Neo-Sufism Reconsidered." *Der Islam,* 70/1: 52–87.

Radtke, Bernd. 1994. "Erleuchtung und Aufklärung: Islamische Mystik und europäischer Rationalismus." *Die Welt des Islams,* 34/1: 48–66.

Rahimi, Babak. 2004. "Between Chieftaincy and Knighthood: A Comparative Study of Ottoman and Safavid Origins." *Thesis Eleven,* 76: 85–102.

Rahimi, Babak. 2011. *Theater State and the Formation of Early Modern Public Sphere in Iran: Studies on Safavid Muharram Rituals,* 1590–1641. Leiden: Brill.

Rahman, Fazlur. 1979 [1966]. *Islam.* Chicago and London: University of Chicago Press.

Salvatore, Armando. 2011. "Civility: Between Disciplined Interaction and Local/ Translocal Connectedness." *Third World Quarterly,* 32/5: 807–25.

Salzmann, Ariel. 2004. *Tocqueville in the Ottoman Empire: Rival Paths to the Modern State.* Leiden and Boston: Brill.

Sirriyeh, Elizabeth. 2005. *Sufi Visionary of Ottoman Damascus: ʿAbd al-Ghani al-Nabulusi, 1641–1731.* London and New York: Routledge.

Tamari, Steve. 2012. "The ʿAlim as Public Intellectual: ʿAbd al-Ghani al-Nabulusi (d. 1731 CE) as a Scholar-Activist." In *Intellectuals and Civil Society in the Middle East: Liberalism, Modernity, and Political Discourse,* edited by Mohammed Bamyeh, 93–109. London: I.B. Tauris.

Voll, John O. 1994 [1982]. *Islam: Continuity and Change in the Modern World.* Syracuse, NY: Syracuse University Press.

Voll, John O. 2008. "Neo-Sufism: Reconsidered Again." *Canadian Journal of African Studies,* 42/2–3: 314–30.

Weismann, Itzchak. 2001. *Taste of Modernity: Sufism, Salafiyya, and Arabism in Late Ottoman Damascus.* Leiden: Brill.

Yıldırım, Yavuz. 2009. "Ottomans' Interpretation of Ibn Khaldun: Translation of the Muqaddimah." Paper presented to the Second International Symposium on Ibn Khaldun, Istanbul, May 29–31.

Yilmaz, Hüseyin. 2009. "Ibn Khaldunian Responses to the Problem of Legitimacy in the Ottoman Empire." Paper presented to the Second International Symposium on Ibn Khaldun, Istanbul, May 29–31.

Zubaida, Sami. 1995. "Is there a Muslim Society? Ernest Gellner's Sociology of Islam." *Economy and Society*, 24/2: 151–88.

6

COLONIAL BLUEPRINTS OF ORDER AND CIVILITY

The Metamorphosis of Civility under Colonialism

The idea that the transformation in the organizational and disciplining modes of Sufism was only catalyzed by the colonial pressures of the West is anachronistic, as we have seen in the previous chapter. Yet it cannot be denied that there was a deepening of these trends during the colonial era. Some Sufi orders became capable, in various regions of the Islamic ecumene, of expanding their constituencies and participating in, or even leading movements of, (also armed) resistance against incipient colonial occupations, most notably in North and West Africa and in South and Southeast Asia. Building on the example and innovations of Shah Waliullah, from the late 18th century onward more activist and militant leaders became involved in a variety of contentions and some of their movements were also able to play a role in embryonic state-building in various parts of the Islamic ecumene. I am referring to personalities such as Usman dan Fodio (1754–1817) in Hausaland, within territories corresponding to today's Nigeria, Umar Tall (1794–1864) in West Africa, Imam Shamil al-Daghistani (1797–1871) in the Caucasus, Sayyid Ahmad Barelvi (1786–1831) in South Asia,

The Sociology of Islam: Knowledge, Power and Civility, First Edition. Armando Salvatore.
© 2016 John Wiley & Sons, Ltd. Published 2016 by John Wiley & Sons, Ltd.

particularly in lands corresponding to today's Pakistan, Ma Mingxin (1719–1781) in North-Western China, Tuanku Nan Tuo (1723–1830) in Western Sumatra, and Muhammad ibn 'Ali al-Sanusi (1787–1859) in Cyrenaica.

Muhammad ibn 'Ali al-Sanusi was a Sufi scholar and activist, disciple of the Moroccan shaykh Ahmad ibn Idris (1760–1837), the most brilliant representative of neo-Sufism in the Western part of the Islamic ecumene (O'Fahey and Radtke 1993). Al-Sanusi promoted a cluster of Sufi organizations characterized by the new activist and renewalist ethos largely opposed to Wahhabi puritanism but sharing with it an emphasis on life conduct and adding to it a capacity for organizing a mass following. Predominantly shaped within urban scholarly circles, al-Sanusi's scholarship was based on cultivating relationships with leading centers of Islamic reform like Cairo even while being located in peripheral Cyrenaica, whose importance his leadership enhanced for a while to a relevant semi-periphery (Vikør 1995: 81–9). He had the particular merit of laying the basis for an expanded elaboration on the notion of *ijtihad*, the concept of autonomous interpretive effort (sometimes hyped as 'free reasoning') of Islamic jurisprudence. His work on *ijtihad* suited a perspective that at first seemed to reenact, under deeply altered sociological and historical conditions, the urban-tribal nexus of Khaldunian memory. Al-Sanusi's activist scholarship paid attention to the importance of tribesmen at the same time as it focused on the salience of urban traders in inspiring innovative interpretations of the legal traditions and thus legal and practical solutions to new problems. *Ijtihad* so redefined as a simultaneously legal and intellectual tool allowed for targeted innovations and provided an engine to the spirit of activist reconstruction of the social bond championed by neo-Sufism also (though not exclusively) in the face of colonial threats and encroachments.

Al-Sanusi reorganized the social and economic life of Cyrenaica on the basis of a new *tariqa* carrying his name, the Sanusiyya, providing an intertribal system of solidarity based on the virtuous imitation of the Prophet. The system matched the study of *hadith* with a proactive stance toward social development and cohesion involving not only tribesmen but also urban merchants and rural communities. Therefore it was configured as an originally modern undertaking of society-building, rather than as a sheer attempt to build an imitatively modern nation-state. Equally seminal was the role played in Algeria against the French occupation by the Qadiriyya, one of the most ancient Sufi orders, under the leadership of 'Abd al-Qadir al-Jaza'iri (1807–1883). After he led a military rebellion, al-Jaza'iri was captured by the French and spent the rest of his life in Damascus as a scholar. His life course is highly indicative of the trajectory of 19th-century revivalist and reformist forces. The Qadiriyya became almost a prototype, throughout the Islamic ecumene, of a brotherhood capable of combining local popular religion with an organizational platform for renewalist and anti-colonial militancy.

Such personalities, which it would be reductive to simply label 'reformist', were equally interested in the conception of *maslaha* of al-Shatibi and in the notion of *siyasa shar'iyya* of another leading scholar from the Later Middle Period, Ibn Taymiyya (1263–1328). The concept of *siyasa shar'iyya* came to mark attempts to reconcile Islamic normativity (*shari'a*) and governance (*siyasa*). Neo-Sufi leaders and scholars were setting the necessary conditions for a framework of reform and renewal by selectively drawing from such traditional resources and concretely implementing the result of their new elaborations and syntheses within the modern confrontation with the colonial powers. The sufficient conditions for such a project were to emerge at a later stage in the late 19th century, when the reform discourse better articulated thanks to the intervention of personalities acting under the conditions of mature colonial states. Only at that later stage did Muslim leaders become able to channel their teachings with the aid of the media of modern public spheres and so to address expanding, educated audiences; only then, therefore, is it correct to identify this trend as 'reformist'.

On the other hand, while leaders like al-Sanusi and 'Abd al-Qadir based their role on an—as yet—quite traditional, sub-institutional, and rather informal type of networking and disciplining, another thinker active in the scholarly center of al-Azhar in Cairo realized the importance of providing an institutional basis to the necessary task of expanding on the scope of *ijtihad*. This is particularly well shown in the earlier mentioned, seminal work of Peter Gran. The crucial character here is the personality of Hasan al-'Attar (1766–1835). Gran focused on al-'Attar precisely since his life course reflected the important period of transition that led from the vitality of the economy and culture in Egypt in the decades immediately prior to the first case of a direct colonial intervention (consisting in the Napoleonic occupation of Egypt in 1798) to the decades when this initial impact started to make its effects increasingly felt both on Egyptian society and its institutions (notably with the modernizing policies of the early 19th-century Egyptian autocrat Mehmed Ali). Al-'Attar not only witnessed the passage between the two phases but also experienced the important lines of continuity that were laboriously maintained across the transition. This continuity needed to be adapted to the obvious discontinuity represented by the impact of the French military invasion and the subsequent massive presence of French scholarly personnel which deeply affected the Islamic knowledge field (Gran 1998 [1979]). Gran intended to defy, or at least deflate, the idea that colonialism per se represented the major watershed in the process of transformation. He argued instead that even during the phase of acute decentralization and fragmentation that peaked in the mid-late 18th century—and which Egypt shared with several other regions of the Ottoman Empire and of the wider Islamic ecumene—there were autochthonous social and cultural factors at work that revealed the largely autonomous character of the transformation. Such factors cannot be reduced to a merely revivalist resistance to the European colonial encroachment, despite the fact that the rising global hegemony of European powers was in itself a factor undeniably influencing (and frequently unsettling) autochthonous developments even prior to the hard, direct, systematically colonizing impact.

Before becoming, under Mehmed Ali, the head of the leading mosque-university of al-Azhar and editor of the first state administrative bulletin *al-waqai' al-misriyya*, al-'Attar gained prominence with his lessons, public lectures, and poetry recitation in Sufi *majalis* (plural of *majlis*: meaning literally "council," yet here translated by Gran as "literary salon"). This climate of cultural effervescence was visibly influenced by the writings of Shah Waliullah. In turn this revival was facilitated by the increasing wealth that the urban patrons of such gatherings accumulated thanks to expanding commercial relations in the Mediterranean, notably with France, and the decentralizing policies of the Ottoman Empire. These policies, whatever their motivations, opened up spaces of bourgeois autonomy from the ruler which are to some extent comparable to those that were developing in 18th-century Europe under the rubric of what we call the Enlightenment. Another scholar, Reinhard Schulze, commenting on such developments, launched the provocation of whether we should speak in this context of nothing less than an "Islamic Enlightenment" (Schulze 1990; 2015). This is perhaps a way to reverse the conventional orientalist narrative of a deep decline, if not outright collapse, of the Islamic ecumene and the Muslim empires in the century of the European Enlightenment: a narrative that even Hodgson, though with important caveats, entertained (Hodgson 1974, III: 176–222).

Sociologically speaking, the issue here, rather than being simply a matter of mechanic and compulsive comparison with European categories (such as 'Enlightenment'), is the question of capturing the specificity of the trans-formation ongoing in the Islamic ecumene before and during the European colonial impact, and the contribution of endogenous traditions and social forces to complex social change. Observing these processes can subvert the inherited orientalist views—still quite popular up until the 1980s if not even today—according to which the carriers of Islamic traditions just opposed a basically blind resistance to a change inexorably brought to the 'Muslim Orient' by the now ever more triumphant 'Christian (or post-Christian) Occident.' As observed by Gran and Schulze regarding the late 18th century and the transition to the colonial era (passing also through decisive semi-colonial or precolonial stages as in the case of most of the 19th century in the Egyptian case just mentioned), what counts more than anything else in these developments is the process of emerging forms of civility that are preeminently urban-centered. Yet these forms and patterns also extended to the countryside and to the nomadic sector through Sufi networks in ways that, to a large extent, overlaid Khaldunian patterns and affected precolonial, colonial, and, later, postcolonial state formations. Such forms of civility were able to overlay the micro-order defined by the relationship between master and disciple, which was central to traditional social institutions like the guilds and the Sufi orders and more generally to the civil matrix of the 'brotherhood' (see Chapter 2).

What is particularly interesting in Gran's contribution is that, while depicting such emerging urban cultures, he lays a particular stress on a further orientation following the renewal of *hadith* studies discussed in the last chapter. In this development the main emphasis was on individual choice and responsibility, reflecting rising bourgeois interests. According to Gran's narrative, the life and work of al-'Attar was influenced by a revival of *kalam*, namely dialectical theology, right after he had been strongly exposed to the rising popularity of *hadith* studies. The change occurred at the same time as the modernizing autocrat Mehmed Ali (1769–1849) came to prominence at the beginning of the 19th century. This cultivation of *kalam*, quite in contrast to *hadith* studies, put a premium on a top-down disciplining rationality and a corresponding social engineering necessary for the reforms in the agricultural, industrial, and military sectors promoted by Mehmed Ali. Such policies were also bolstered by the presence and work, in Egypt, of European technicians and utopian thinkers like the radically enlightened Saint-Simonians (Alleaume 1989), inspired by the teachings of Claude Henri de Rouvroy, Earl of Saint-Simon (1760–1825), who used to be credited as one of the precursors of sociology as an academic discipline. The Egyptian autocrat attracted followers of Saint-Simon to his country by investing in their role as advisors for his modernizing projects. However, the Saint-Simonians were also moved to participate in such developments by their own universalist élan envisioning human society as bound to a potentially unlimited progress to be achieved via the implementation of rational measures for the organization of production and the structuring of social life. In the light of Gran's interpretation, the role played by Europe at this stage was not one of exporting the Enlightenment to the East but of spreading eastward seeds of Enlightenment's visions that were not necessarily welcomed in the Europe of the post-Napoleonic restoration. Even without mentioning the Saint-Simonians, the interpretation that Gran facilitates of the wider process is that those seeds fell on an intellectual and social terrain that the Saint-Simonians, inevitably sharing in the European colonial imagination after Napoleon's occupation of the country, might have envisioned as yet conceptually virgin and therefore highly fertile. They were willing to ignore that, as stressed by Gran, the terrain had been already fertilized by endogenously dynamic intellectual and entrepreneurial practices in the previous, turbulent decades.

A structural discontinuity in the process of transformation emerges in spite of the efforts of characters like al-'Attar who worked to maintain some continuity across change. This is due to the fact that the more intently Islamic leaders and scholars attempted to recapture and reconstruct their traditions, the more dishearteningly they faced them in merely imploded forms, and partly—though limitedly—in institutional shapes already pre-determined by the European colonial encroachment (and related imagination). What radically changed the methods of dealing with the traditions in innovative ways was the new political reality of the colonial states and attendant conceptions of power now incorporating knowledge by default. Gran invests this view in a comparison of Egypt not with other parts of the Islamic ecumene but with Italy's and Spain's responses to the Napoleonic occupations of their own territories (Gran 1998: xiv–xvi; Gran 2005). This type of comparison helps us more than Schulze's rhetorical provocation evoking an alleged Islamic Enlightenment. Gran's strategy shows us how colonial Europe, rather than suddenly benefiting from an inversion in its favor of the historic power balance with the Muslim world, altered and adapted to its hegemonic goals a global system that was already in place before the onset of modern forms of power and exploitation.

Particularly thanks to the developments of the Middle Periods well into early modernity, this system had been historically centered on the hemisphere-wide Islamic ecumene, which already encompassed ongoing dynamics of change and resistance to change. These ambivalent dynamics were well reflected by the fragile power balances of the modern Muslim empires mentioned in the previous chapter. From this perspective, the peripheralization of Egypt in the new colonial system hegemonized by

European powers is in principle on a par with the peripheralization of the parts of Europe which had once been the engine of its power (Italy during early modernity, i.e. the so-called Renaissance, and Spain as an initiator and leader of the colonization process itself, most notably in its transatlantic projection). This is due to the fact that one key feature of the alteration of the precolonial, proto-global system was the imposition of center–periphery dynamics and hierarchies that were also at work within the European core of the new system. Yet while examining this process we see, with Gran, that it does not simply confine the new peripheries (be they colonial or European) to historic insignificance. Rather, the way they responded to the new global centers both on a socio-economic and political-military level acquires a significance that cannot be squeezed into a one-sided narrative of 'decay' (the decline of the Ottoman Empire and of Islamic civilization but also the decay of Italian culture, the decline of Spanish power, etc.).

It is not surprising that the interpretive challenge launched by Gran and Schulze against the colonial and orientalist narrative of cultural, civilizational, and political decay elicited sharp responses from contemporary representatives of more established forms of orientalist scholarship. From the pages of scholarly journals devoted to the study of the Middle East and the Muslim world, two Dutch-based scholars, Fred De Jong (1982) and Bernd Radtke (1994), responded to Gran and Schulze and attempted to deconstruct their arguments. Such interventions are testament to the resilience of orientalist narratives of stagnation and decay in the Islamic ecumene. The common strategy of attack of the two established scholars was to show that the two (at that time) younger colleagues had read their own allegedly preconstituted (naively anti-orientalist) ideas of modern Islamic transformations into 18th-century Sufi texts. Yet according to this criticism those texts offered in reality nothing more than a repetition of older themes (like those enshrined in the heritage of Ibn al-ʿArabi discussed in the previous chapters) in—at best—just lightly shifting contexts: i.e. not only was there nothing really innovative in the texts but they were actually repetitive in the typical way of stagnating traditions. Not surprisingly, in both cases Gran and Schulze answered back by basically stressing that the analysis of texts can only be meaningful if situated in the context of wider socio-political processes of transformation, so that even older arguments and keywords can acquire fresh significations in such new settings (Masud and Salvatore 2009).

More generally, the challenge launched by Gran and Schulze reflected the assessment that not only the global rise of capitalism but also innovative political-intellectual currents like those subsumed under the European Enlightenment need to be placed in a wider socio-historical context. This context includes an ensemble of radical shifts within the global arena of economic, political, and cultural powers. The consequence is that country-specific trajectories of social and cultural transformations can only be understood as simultaneously integrated and dislocated across permanently shifting centers and peripheries, each with their own agencies and resources. This interpretive step was not intended to belittle the new imbalances of power found in the global arena in the colonial era but to circumvent the orientalist inclination for lazy (yet also self-serving) explanatory shortcuts like those prompting questions (and popularizing them as epoch-making) such as Lewis' *What Went Wrong?*

From this point of view, the Islamic 18th century, far from being the stagnant counterpart to a flourishing European Enlightenment, and though far from expressing an integrated and autonomous "Islamic Enlightenment" (Peters 1990), manifested nonetheless important innovative dynamics that deserve the attention of historians and sociologists of Islam. Without taking into account the wider context of such developments, namely the shift from a precolonial 'ecumenical' constellation to a colonial 'global' system and attendant changes in the articulations of the knowledge–power equation, scholars looking exclusively at texts are bound to remain trapped in their biased and simplified notions of tradition, modernity, and civilizational rise-and-decay. Such prejudgments are often naively hammered into simplified views of Western experiences and trajectories (e.g. unnuanced understandings of modernity, the Enlightenment or even just of the plain notion of socio-cultural change), if they result from ignoring (or at least shunning) the complexity of debates on contested concepts within Western philosophy and social sciences and consider uncontestable a methodological reliance on a flat, positivistic philology. This seems to have been the case with the orientalist challengers of Gran and Schulze. By insistently neglecting the socio-political context, a reiterated, lopsided, orientalist perspective loses any significant capacity to keep pace with current, more comprehensive general debates about the dynamics of tradition and the singularity and plurality of modernity, whereby the modern Western experience and hegemony are permanently challenged by non-Western predicaments and responses.

Thanks to Gran's analysis, Hasan al-'Attar becomes a paradigmatic character because his life and scholarship reflected exactly these types of multiple transformations and entanglements. An interesting aspect of al-'Attar's trajectory is that, while it is well documented that he was the teacher of

Rifa'a al-Tahtawi (1801–1873)—the first acknowledged Muslim 'reformer' in Egypt and one closely tied to the modernization projects of Mehmed Ali—he exerted some influence on the previously mentioned neo-Sufi leader, Muhammad ibn 'Ali al-Sanusi from Cyrenaica. This impact was particularly clear with regard to al-Sanusi's championing of new views of *ijtihad*. More generally, al-'Attar represents a prototypical case of how key urban reformers of the 19th century were apparently influenced by selective Sufi ideas even in the absence of solid organizational ties to any *tariqa* or Sufi master.

In the course of the century the reprimands of the heterodox practices of some Sufi orders became a leitmotiv of the writings of many urban reformers. This occurred under the increasing influence of resurgent Wahhabism, which was largely folded into the urban reform movement that came to be known as *salafiyya*. We might even start to see a red (though partly hidden) thread linking urban centers and tribal periphery/semi-periphery in ways that began to profoundly alter the type of relations exemplified by the inherited Khaldunian model of urban-tribal civility. Innovative Sufi practices in the semi-periphery, ranging from *ijtihad* through the improving of organizational patterns of brotherhoods and up to straightforward state-building activities directly opposed to colonial encroachment, now feed into the more strongly discursive and institutional arenas of urban reformers. Such arenas were more directly exposed to the influence of European powers in the context of an emerging 'transcultural' public sphere where the discourse of and on Islam acquired new traits and an unprecedented level of reification of basic concepts (starting from 'Islam' itself: W.C. Smith 1962: 80–118; Salvatore 1997: 47–54).

While the neo-Sufi innovations can be considered the necessary condition for sowing the seeds of modern Islamic forms of civility, the urban reformers' entanglements with colonial economies and powers created the sufficient ones (Salvatore 1997: 41–61). To be sure, those reformers who attacked Sufism stigmatized types of practices which most neo-Sufi leaders also shunned, like saint worshipping, shrine and grave visits, and above all what appeared to them as an abominable display of superstition and promiscuity at Sufi saints' festivals. Yet many postindependence Muslim reformers, like the Egyptian head of al-Azhar 'Abd al-Halim Mahmud (1910–1978), saw in the Sufi teachings a resource, and not a hindrance, for encouraging a new ethos of participation in the civic life of the nation (Aishima 2016). What is common to different stages and locales of this transition is that the engine of the idea of civility is shifted from a master's guidance to more impersonal mechanisms of inculcation of a collective commitment. At a more restricted administrative level, the transition calls for legal reforms formalizing both personal accountability and individual rights. It might be tempting here to reproduce a dichotomy (which is orientalist to some extent but can also be detected in sociological trivializations of Weber's own research questions) between charismatic and scriptural authority. This dichotomy remains such even if reformulated as a shift or evolution from seeking guidance from a master toward acquiring orientation in one's own life through a direct individual reflection on Sufi texts surrogating the Sufi practices and experiences they are supposed to cover.

Yet a sociological snapshot of the complex transformations of the 19th and 20th centuries would reveal more blurred lines between the two ideal types of authority just sketched, a question that will need further elaboration in the subsequent volumes of the trilogy. Briefly, in this complex and long-drawn-out process of transformation some Sufi *turuq* and the public discourse they produced acted as key laboratories of the wider civilizing process during the transition to colonial influence and rule in the course of both the 18th and 19th centuries. They did so by laying down the tracks for a deep metamorphosis of models of subjectivity and patterns of intersubjectivity, the two main components of civility. The transition raises fundamental questions concerning the extent to which the emerging patterns of civility significantly eroded, if not destroyed, the broad social autonomy that had characterized the Islamic ecumene up until early modernity. The alternate interpretation would be that the new patterns of civility rather transformed the ecumene under the umbrella of new general notions of order. According to this more refined interpretation, these formulas of civility were carried into the ecumene by European powers and were now variably internalized by key social actors (particularly the new urban Muslim reformers but also, before them, neo-Sufi leaders) intent on resisting this hegemony or turning it to their advantage.

Probably the only sensible way to approach the issue starts with renouncing the presumption of a zero-sum game between social autonomy within the Islamic ecumene, on the one hand, and control by precolonial, colonial, or postcolonial powers and institutions, on the other. This is well exemplified by the important case of Egypt. Here an essential condition of success for the program of the new autocrat Mehmed Ali was to curb the autonomy not just of the Mamluk households that had dominated society and politics even after Egypt's annexation to the Ottoman Empire in the 16th century, but also, to a large extent, of the *'ulama'* themselves. He carried forward his ambitious designs through different stages during the entire first half of the 19th century and even posed a military threat to the center of the Ottoman Empire itself. It was as much an autochthonous program as one reflecting colonial ideas of rational order. As in the scholarly trajectory of al-'Attar, continuities are overlaid by discontinuities. Most crucially, the program entailed taking away from the *'ulama'* the virtual monopoly they had held for centuries on the educational field and the legal system. Mehmed Ali was a determined and powerful autocrat, who quite consistently interpreted and implemented the modernizing imperatives of the age. In order to avoid falling prey to European colonialism he had to play by its rules.

Clearly, the implementation of such a program could not be smooth. While Mehmed Ali could get rid of the Mamluks in one single day, he could not rule over Egyptian society without securing a fair degree of cooperation by the *'ulama'*. He thus needed to intervene not only on the power relations between them and the government but also on their profile and skills as scholars, as producers of knowledge. What changed there was the relation between knowledge and power, what we have termed the knowledge–power equation. In many ways, we can consider this stage as the beginning of a process that continues to this day, in the era of the Arab Spring and its disappointing aftermath during which authoritarian governments have been reinstituted in partly new guises (Salvatore 2015). The process entails a permanent, even deepening dilemma for Muslim modernizers: namely to try to fit into global norms of civility and governance while evading the most deleterious consequences of the new order, which weigh most harshly on the parts of the global system confined, both economically and politically, to periphery status. Contextualized in a longer-term perspective, it is not surprising that the new Egyptian autocrat's other major task, in sociological terms, at the beginning of the 19th century was working out how to take appropriate measures to optimize his relations with the commercial and intellectual middle classes (including the more orthodox among the Sufi *turuq*) which had been thriving especially in the second half of the 18th century, while pursuing his policies to promote industrial and commercial state monopolies.

The dimension of the process most relevant from our perspective of privileging the knowledge–power equation is the extent to which the policies of the new autocrat and his court contributed to a deep metamorphosis of social disciplines and patterns of civility. This metamorphosis took place through the shaping of new channels of mutual fertilization between knowledge and power and is particularly evident in the case of the above-mentioned disciple of al-ʿAttar, shaykh Rifaʿa al-Tahtawi. Al-Tahtawi benefited from a program of government grants to travel to France to gather useful experience for supporting Mehmed Aliʾs program of modernization and, among other things, translated from French into Arabic the Napoleonic Code, the prototype of European civil codes tied to the evolution of Westphalian states. He thus happened to play a proactive role in the reform process. Along with other contemporaries, who came from the ranks of the *ʿulamaʾ* of the mosque-university of al-Azhar, he contributed to legitimize a process of differentiation of the functions of the legal system fitting the requirements of the modernizing state and the idea of a "new order." It would take several more decades and the transition of Egypt into a state of full colonial subjection during the second half of the 19th century to accomplish the process. The differentiation clearly damaged the previous centrality of legally trained *ʿulamaʾ* (traditionally known as *fuqahaʾ*) within the system and more generally put an end to their virtual monopoly over the educational sector (Gran 1998 [1979]; Mitchell 1991 [1988]; Gesink 2010).

Another major domain where state agents and social actors converged in affecting the patterns of civility was the field of control of the population, particularly of the urban poor. With regard to this area of endeavor, one should signal the process through which the function of the traditional (and traditionally well-functioning), largely autonomous institution of the *waqf* was altered in order to affect change. This transformation concerned in particular the management and the very conceptualization of poverty, which entailed a potential political virulence through the risk of urban riots that could follow a shortage of provisions of bread and other basic foods at prices accessible to the lowest social echelons. An additional factor of political virulence was simply that urban poverty became more widespread in the modern era. This was an immediate consequence of the new type of social division of labor caused by the growth of the commercial and industrial sectors. The problem was tackled through channeling, coordinating, and implementing measures (in a much more systematic way than under traditional, largely decentralized *waqf* regimes) to target the poor, within what was by then ever more clearly singled out as the sector of 'charity' (which as we know is largely synonymous with 'non-profit').

'Charity' is certainly a word charged with a specifically Christian meaning, which evolved over time in the shadow of the progress of modern industrial (and colonial) society. The delimitation of a field of charity out of the encompassing significance and centrality of the virtue of *caritas* in Aquinas (see Chapter 4) occurred most notably by its understanding as "benevolence" in 18th-century England (MacIntyre 1988: 232) and there-fore as an outgrowth of the 'moral sense' underlying 'civil society' (see Chapter 1). Charity thus became a sector calling for targeted measures, guided by a focus on the 'poor' as a specific social category facilitating manip-ulative interventions by state authorities. Some historians (most notably Mine Ener: 2003) have over the last two decades begun to explore the metamorphosis of charity in an Ottoman context of transition (including Egypt) from early modernity to the colonial era. This field of study suggests the importance of framing the issue at stake in terms of a metamorphosis of the civilizing process, or of the production of new patterns of civility.

The governments of the era, particularly the Ottoman one, were acutely aware of the importance of population control as being integral to the broader process of monitoring and disciplining their subjects in capillary ways. Population control was also a domain of increasing importance in terms of measuring the government's capacity to reaffirm its strength vis-à-vis traditional social autonomies. While such autonomies were a powerful yet also protean vector of civility, the control of especially urban populations and of the urban poor (notably via preemptive measures of public health) could no longer be entrusted by governments to basically autonomous mechanisms of regulation and compensation like those enshrined in the *waqf*. It might be a bit far-fetched to conceptualize this concern in full-fledged Foucaultian terms, i.e. by seeing a thoroughly intrusive process of creating new categories of subjects to be taken care of and so to be subjected to surveillance by new or strongly reformed institutions (as, in the West, the hospital, the prison, and the poorhouse). Yet it is quite plausible to frame the process in the more flexible Eliasian terms sketched in previous chapters (and that we will revisit in Chapter 7) as feeding into an accelerated (and now increasingly centralized) civilizing process. Such terms spelled out by Elias' theory of the civilizing process allow us to preserve the view of a higher degree of societal autonomy of such a process in the Ottoman and more generally in the Islamic cases in the longer term, and in spite of such centralizing interventions. What needs to be highlighted with regard to the late Ottoman Empire is that the simple yet powerful variable represented by the rise in population density within urban centers through population growth and migration from the countryside increased the pressure to formulate tighter codes of social intercourse, on which state authorities could then intervene with new manipulative intents and effects. The extent to which such processes also promoted new forms of self-control of the kind emphasized by Elias eludes us thus far.

Yet a further indicator of this considerable shift is that from the 18th century onward, and especially during the 19th century, the idea of the 'fraudulent poor' took shape, so that begging was now licensed by public authorities. This particular field within the management of doing good to others, which was the generalized paradigm of the *waqf* institution, was thus taken away from what earlier was its almost exclusive supervision by autonomous or semi-autonomous *waqf* administrators. The field began to be subjected to an increasingly centralized steering, based on the distinction by state authorities between the good and the bad poor, which in turn resulted in intense efforts to monitor the urban poor. Correspondingly, a civic norm of social obligation to help the good poor (to the exclusion of the bad) emerged, clearly delimiting the sphere of toleration of what by now were considered deviant behaviors among groups now explicitly identified as the riskiest sectors of the populations (Ener 2003). In the process, the urban poor became not just a potentially negative variable to be factored in by governments but also a classificatory resource within a new public sphere pivoting on the priority of creating docile subjects and policing rebellious ones. What is interesting is that this twist in the civilizing process was achieved not through suppressing but in large part via reformulating traditional notions and practices linked to the *waqf*, which were now strongly controlled by the governments (Assi 2008).

It is at this juncture that a quite well-integrated discourse on charity emerged, bearing stark resemblances to the one that took shape in England at about the same time. The discourse stressed religious inclusiveness, belonging, and even tolerance, yet in a frame of disciplining and policing. It is through the centralization of charity that a discourse pitting good ('civilized') against bad ('uncivilized,' fraudulent) indigent subjects saw the light. This change did not amount to a weakening of the *waqf* institution per se. At the beginning of the 19th century the pious foundations were still quite rich but no longer mainly responsible for the poor. The *waqf* itself became the hub of what was now, as we stressed, merely a 'sector' of social governance, though one to be singled out for its strategic relevance: not just for immediate political reasons but for providing the institutional cover to a wider discursive field to set standards of civilized behavior and responsibility. What now helped in identifying charity as a field of practice covered by a strong, officially propagated discourse was the establishment of a tighter notion of personal accountability. This was intended to offset the risk that the *waqf*, being in the hands of specific families and groups (those from which the foundational acts originated and/or those who had traditionally administered them), could reflect arbitrary reasons and preferences. A similar development was observable in Egypt when, during the 19th century, the country underwent a long transition from Ottoman domain, through being virtually independent and powerful, to becoming a British protectorate. Here the urban poor likewise became a resource in line with the type of utilitarian discourse that was famously propagated in early 19th-century England by the social reformer Jeremy Bentham. Within this frame, doing good to others in the form of 'benevolence' allowed for selective, intrusive, and potentially 'productive' interventions into the affairs of what is now a collective category from among the 'others', increasingly understood as an urban crowd to be controlled.

A collateral effect of the process is related to the fact that the religious dimension of the *waqf* started to be seen in a more restrictive, and no longer widely social and connective, sense. This development occurred in parallel with the prevalence of a view of secularization often taken from the European historical experience. In Europe, however, the primary meaning of secularization as confiscation of property of the Church referred to a sphere that pertained to a specific (ecclesiastical) institution and did not possess a fragmented yet capillary grid of control and management like the *waqf*. The twisted way through which a notion of secularization inherited from the specific European context affected the civilizing process and the governance of social relations in an Islamic context, particularly in Egypt, has been particularly well explained by Talal Asad:

> In 19th century Arabic in Egypt the verbal form for secularization, *'almana*, was restricted to a legal sense indicating transfer of property – as in the Reformation sense of *saecularisatio* … Thus the process of 'secularization' was rendered *tahwil al-awqaf wa al-amlak al-mukhtassa bi al-'ibada wa al-diyana ila al-aghrad al-'alamiyya* – literally, 'the transfer to worldly purposes of endowments and properties pertaining to worship and religion.' One problem with that was that a *waqf* (normally translated as a 'religious endowment') might have a 'religious or devotional purpose' (if it was a mosque, say), but more often than not it had no such purpose (as in the case of agricultural lands), or, more commonly, several purposes, 'religious' and 'nonreligious' (hospitals and schools, for example). *Waqf* (plural *awqaf*) was simply the sole form of inalienable property in the *shari'a*.
>
> (Asad 2003: 207)

In a parallel development, the organic relationship between the production and transmission of knowledge in *madrasa*s, and its funding provided by the *waqf*, started to be gravely eroded (Hefner 2007). Yet it would be wrong to see the process as simply a rapid and drastic transfer of control from society to the state over what now became key sectors of public policy like the provision of public welfare, health, and education. Once more, and not entirely unlike with modernization in Europe, the process also amounted to the creation of an intermediary space between the state and what was now increasingly singled out, both socially and legally, as the realm of the (increasingly nuclear) family, the locus where subjectivities are first formed. We see here, as also theorized by Hegel (see Chapter 1), a metamorphosis and at the same time a recuperation of traditional institutions as intermediary associations whose voluntary bases were ever more emphasized during the modernization process. Only at a later stage, within an Islamic ecumene increasingly fragmented into colonial states (and which over the last couple of decades we have ever more frequently designated with the weak and essentialist formula of the 'Muslim world'), was the process crowned with the adoption of civil codes. Their grammar designed the new social space linking the individual, the family, and the associational world. During the long 19th century (roughly identified with the period that saw the onset of colonial power in the Ottoman region after the Napoleonic occupation of 1798 and lasting until the sunset of the most aggressive stage of colonialism with World War I) we can hardly detect a linear, evolutionary process or an organic metamorphosis of the grammar of social connectedness. Until the beginning of the era of Muslim reform and the corresponding rise of modern, media-based public spheres (in the last third of the 19th century), we rather observe an overlaying of traditional, socially autonomous institutions subject to the type of implosion we have just observed in the case of the *waqf*, with mechanisms and procedures directly managed by the state.

In Egypt as elsewhere in what was left of the Islamic ecumene, traditional spaces and institutions were not erased but superimposed by what at first were not full-fledged, new institutions but rather provinces of a discourse and practice about a 'new order.' This was imagined on the basis of utopian or technocratic (or combinations thereof) colonial visions, of which the Saint-Simonians represent the earliest but also the most recognizable and radical version—irrespective of whether such a new order was conceived as immediately emanating from the vocabulary and imaginary of European regimes of the modern (Rabinow 1995) or was mediated with the help of endogenous concepts. This discourse of order, which backed emerging forms of civility, could not fully replace inherited yet flexible institutions and forms of sociability and identity (from the *waqf* to the *turuq*). Nonetheless, it immediately affected the formation of collective identities and so favored a social division of labor compatible with increasingly global rationalities of triumphant capitalism. This process in turn favored a strong role of emergent national bourgeoisies in the colonies, as both the beneficiary of the process at an economic level and as resistant to colonialism at a political level. Such developments indicate a rather Durkheimian twist of the civilizing process, putting a premium on collective representations of strong identities and covering up a social division of labor centered on the leadership of an emerging bourgeoisie of sorts, though inevitably not a copycat of European precedents of bourgeoisie-led modernization. In Egypt as elsewhere, increasingly explicit civilizing discourses with strong educational components and addressed to the emergent category of the 'people' acquired a political-intellectual tenor and ingrained into a coherent and hegemonic discursive framework under what by the last third of the 19th century became the ever more ubiquitous banner of "reform" (*islah* in Arabic).

Nonetheless, the imperatives to accommodate socio-economic development, cultural advancements, and the application of science in traditional and new professions (from the physician to the engineer) ensured that the process could already move forward at an accelerating pace in the first part of the 19th century in some key locales and regions within the Ottoman Empire and the larger 'Muslim world.' This process unfolded in Egypt during the reign of Mehmed Ali, through the thick grid of military, administrative, and economic reforms that he designed and implemented and which were roughly matched by the slightly later reforms known as *tanzimat* imposed in the center of the Ottoman Empire. In the process, the residual spaces of social autonomy were enlisted to contribute to the wider acceleration and stronger centralization of the civilizing process. Yet more than mediating between the family and the state, as in the Hegelian model, such intermediary institutions (as, for example, the mosque-university of al-Azhar) became a favorite terrain of experimentation for exactly the new discourse of order and civility that redefined the state and the family as clear-cut sources of authority, based on an emerging, increasingly sharp dichotomy between the private and the public spheres. In institutional terms, tradition was not crushed by but rather exposed to a process of self-implosion, and yet in this imploded form became a resource for the civilizing process, mostly as a provider of collective identities (Mitchell 1991 [1988]).

It is difficult to assess with any great precision the extent to and pace at which a corresponding shift from social autonomies toward both individual subjectivities and collective identities took place. It is probably easier to observe how the practices related to traditions of embodiment, like those providing glue to Sufi brotherhoods and the guilds, gave way to disembodied forms of belonging, identity, and self-policing (Pinto 2004). In parallel, one can trace the trajectory through which these disembodied forms of self-steering, which enfeebled the authority of the brotherhood masters and the attendant grids of vertical and horizontal relations, were defined as tools of governance both by emerging elites formed in new state schools and by transversal segments of traditional elites who were yet the product of the precolonial educational paths.

Court Dynamics and Emerging Elites: The Complexification of the Civilizing Process

While the process in Egypt was particularly turbulent and led to the imposition of a direct British colonial control over the country in the 1880s, in the center of the Ottoman Empire it was as complex, but slightly more linear. What needs to be stressed, as was by the leading Turkish historian Ilber Ortaylı (1983), is that the 19th century, described by him as "the longest century of the empire," was an intensely creative period and not one of prolonged agony—as it would appear if we were to take at face value the empire's nicknames in Europe, namely 'the sick man upon the Bosphorus' or even 'the sick man of Europe.' Unlike in Egypt, where an increasingly institutional rupture with the Ottoman Empire and its symbols of power and legitimacy unfolded during the entire 19th century, in the center of the empire, in spite of all upheavals and false starts with reform, a much stronger sense of continuity with the early modern framework of legitimacy was preserved through the various corrective interventions conceived and implemented by the ruling elites. This continuity (which Hodgson did not hesitate to dub conservatism) provided a sense of almost positivistic linearity to the long-term civilizing process, in spite of its sharp acceleration in the epoch of reforms. Most importantly, the main vehicle of legitimacy in the process, well through the period of the *tanzimat* conventionally identified with the years between 1839 and 1876 (during which printed administrative bulletins first saw the light), was the upgrading of the culture of *adab* (see Chapters 3 and 5) into the matrix of a rather self-sustaining project. This consisted in reconstructing from the top down viable patterns of civility and belonging across an ever more differentiated grid of social classes and groups. The vast array of measures affecting such fields as the military, finance, the law, the institution of schools for the education of civil servants, and the launch of identity cards or papers exemplifies the extent to which the practical dimension of reform was matched by the even stronger dimension of its collective representation. This is also why a fuller grasp of the process will only be made possible by framing it in the context of the emergence of a modern public sphere (which will be dealt with in a future volume).

The implication of this complex picture is that we cannot reduce the reform trajectory of the late Ottoman Empire to the defective agency of a state operating as a mere machinery for the rationalization of society in a desperate attempt to catch up with European standards. Even the idea of social engineering, which became increasingly popular among the Ottoman reformers situated at the highest echelons of the bureaucracy, needed to be anchored within a sphere characterized by a culturally specific ethos and a symbolic representation of organic forms of social solidarity. As we saw in Chapter 5, the cultivation of the *adab* tradition had become particularly intense in the Ottoman Empire at the dawn of the modern era. It provided the background culture to the scribal class which, especially from the 18th century onward, assumed the profile and reflected the ambitions of an increasingly modern bureaucracy. If we count *adab* as integral to Islamic traditions at large (those related to Islam as a civilization more than to its specifically religious teachings and norms) and essential to the dynamism of Islam-Islamdom delineated by Hodgson, we can detect a longer line of cultural continuity providing a background to the *tanzimat* reforms. This continuity lasted at least until the sultan and caliph Abdülhamid operated a shift, from the last quarter of the 19th century, toward specifically pan-Islamic (if not proto-Islamist) slogans and motifs. In this sphere emerging out of a sense of civilizational continuity, facilitated by the late adoption of the printing press on a mass scale, a recombination of the previously rival traditions of the *ilmiyye* of religious scholars and the *kalemiyye* of civil bureaucrats generated an original public culture. It was this culture and its public sphere that provided the background to the mature reform project of the late 19th and early 20th centuries (Mardin 2006a).

It has been observed that the specific wave of the Ottoman reform movement that was launched under the banner of *tanzimat* and which took off in the late 1830s was framed in the pragmatic and even positivistic language of the newly instituted Translation Office (*Tercüme Odası*, literally 'Translation Room') that became the hub of the emergent Foreign Ministry, which later added an office for correspondence in French with the European ambassadors (Findley 2012: 186). In other words, the language of the reforms originated from a capillary work of translation and communication on the basis of European concepts. As stressed by Şerif Mardin, the reform approach bore substantial resemblances to the theory and practice of the 18th-century Austro-German cameralists. These were bureaucrats or scholars who shunned the sophistications of modern social and political theory (including those examined in Chapter 1), and even more the conceptual battlegrounds of the Enlightenment vanguards, and favored a program for promoting civility via the art of administration, for which they acted as advisors to rulers and administrative bodies (Mardin 2006a: 125). This approach apparently suited the needs of the Ottoman bureaucracy, nurtured by their court culture of literati, also due to the principled neutrality of such Austro-German doctrines on matters of religion. It was also preferred due to the fact that Vienna had been one of the capitals where young *kalemiyye* members had been sent as travel grant recipients since the late 18th century (Mardin 2006b), unlike Paris, preferred by the Egyptian autocrat Mehmed Ali, as in the previously examined case of al-Tahtawi. At the same time, the reproduction of religion in the center of the Ottoman Empire continued to be based on a separate branch of knowledge administered by the *'ulama'*. This branch continued to provide the curricula to most schools as well as the essential personnel to the legal system and to the pious foundations that funded the bulk of public services under the previously mentioned, altered, framework of governance. While it is true that successive reform packages during the *tanzimat* era intervened in the realm of education and in the legal field and thus took power away from the *'ulama'*, the reform process unfolded without ever seriously questioning in principle the source of their authority located in the type of knowledge they administered.

However, as also maintained by Mardin, it would be moot just to look at this particular period of reforms and its methods independently from the larger dynamics of the "Ottoman century." In the largest cities of the empire a sophisticated cultural network saw the light which started to transform the relation between the ruling class and the subjects which had characterized Ottoman society from the beginning of the modern era. By the end of the century, a new Ottoman elite had taken full shape under the influence of a worldview mainly transmitted through the new state schools. These schools became key touchstones in the process, to the extent that they contributed to equipping bureaucrats with all required competences—be they military, administrative, or medical—to steer the reform project and the underlying civilizing process. Mardin actually decries the fact that at the beginning of the 20th century both the project and the process were finally folded by the Young Turk elite into a roughly Durkheimian doctrine of civility quite rigidly inspired by a view of society as an organic whole based on a rational division of labor. While such ideas were not entirely new to the larger process, the fact that they now became the explicit and increasingly exclusive ideological justification of the reform project accentuated the gulf between the culture of the high echelons of state elites and what they now increasingly looked down on as "the backward ways of the folk." This approach de facto destroyed all residual margins of integrity and legitimacy earlier provided by the theory and practice of the circle of justice (Mardin 2006a: 293–4). The Ottoman case allows us to conceive of the transformations of *adab* as the cultural engine of a civilizing process in the sense highlighted by Norbert Elias: initiated in court milieus but with the potential to reach down the social ladder by way of social differentiation and a sense of cultural distinction. Such views were compatible with a modern populist understanding of belonging and citizenship, which was most coherently developed and put to practice after the collapse of the Ottoman Empire, during the Turkish Republic.

As a first marker of difference toward Egypt and other Arab parts of the empire, we have noted that during most of the 19th century several Ottoman reformers came out of the Istanbul-based Translation Bureau. This fact created a much higher level of interpenetration between state reform and the intellectual dimension of the reform project in the Turkish case. In spite of the positivistic twists and the populist outcome of the upheavals of the "Ottoman century," the culture of bureaucratic reformers was not completely neutral toward specific traditions. The work of leading and largely independent Ottoman reformers like Namik Kemal (1840–1888) and Ziya Pasha (1825–1880) cannot be understood without placing their discourse in the framework of the longer-term tradition of *adab*, which allowed them to defend Islam as compatible with modern systems of government and organization of society. References to the *shariʿa* no doubt contributed to the reform project and to the civilizing process by providing key content to legal codification (notably in the form of civil and criminal codes), and by capitalizing, as it were, on the implosion of its underlying, traditional institutional network (based on the *waqf* and the *madrasa*s and supported by the disciplines of Sufism). Yet the *adab* tradition was at the forefront in powering the process by providing the know-how necessary to propagate and inculcate the values and disciplines required by the reformers/administrators/intellectuals.

We see how singularly willed combinations of *shari'a* and *adab* characterized the emerging forms of civility in the Islamic ecumene in the colonial era. As a result, these forms were comparable with, yet not reducible to, those that have become the object of Elias' theorizing with regard to Europe. Indeed the recombination of the two traditions, *adab* and *shari'a*—courteousness and normativity, whose sum is civility—was a development not limited to the center of the Ottoman Empire. Going back to the Egyptian case, the discourse of reform (*islah*) was developed within a field of permanent tension between the notions and rationalities included and permanently redeployed within Islamic traditions and the modern norms and disciplines of a centralizing state. It is to be remarked that, somewhat at the confluence of both civilizing streams (administrative measures and public discourse), the process was named *tamaddun* in Egypt by some leading reformers. Its meaning is precisely "civilizing," but almost in the sense of "citifying," i.e. indicating the dynamics of becoming urban or acquiring urban manners, the skills of a citizen. It is under the banner of *tamaddun* (a keyword that, it should be observed, explicitly reflects, on a linguistic level, the process-like character of the transformation) that *adab* acquired a meaning closely matching what we mean by civility. *Adab* was now ever more clearly understood as an ensemble of moral dispositions entailing not only appropriate manners of conduct but also a mastery of the self, to be further manifested via a sensibility toward shifting social circumstances in differentiated urban contexts: a kind of complex, highly social *savoir-faire* (Farag 2001).

Though still far from articulating a coherent notion of citizenship, a protean discourse on *adab* as communicative civility and social commerce proliferated within the Egyptian pedagogical and moral literature of the late 19th and early 20th centuries. It provided key ideas to the articulation of a modern, coherent, and self-enclosed notion of "society" that, though not unknown as an Arab keyword within Islamic traditions (e.g. it was used by Ibn Khaldun), had not worked hitherto as a central concept and guidance to action. Drawing on manuals of personal and social ethics published during this period, Iman Farag has shown how the traditional concept of *adab* was rethought in relation to projects of moral reform and mass education attendant upon such an emergent idea of society. More specifically, by designating traditionally conceived models of self-cultivation to be emulated, the concept of *adab* evolved into defining a unitary, homogeneous—though internally differentiated—and largely autonomous field of morality. It even bore some traits of a "moral science," according to the positivistic climate within which this literature flourished and which in Egypt was even more influential than it was in the center of the Ottoman Empire. This rather scientificized humanist discourse (the groundwork to what would soon be sociology) unsettled, expanded, and reordered traditional (including religious) notions and virtues, and in particular their hierarchies:

> The subject is man first and foremost: his positive and negative duties in concentric circles that begin with God, pause at the nation, and end with humanity, passing through duties to oneself – emotion, the body, reason – one's family, friends, peers, even superiors and inferiors.
>
> (Farag 2001: 96)

Opening up to ideas of participation in a modern and increasingly open public sphere, *adab* became the foundation stone for the articulation of a modern yet original conceptualization of social intercourse. Yet we have detected an additional layer to *adab* that developed at this stage. While initially reflecting a classic notion envisioning models of cultivation of the self, in the course of the reform process the concept gave rise to a moral sense similar to the one augured and theorized by the Scottish theorists of civil society (see Chapter 1). In other words, civility defined not just etiquette and exteriority but also an interior capacity to provide orientation and a sense of discernment to the self and to the subject's skills in connecting to the other. This is where *shari'a* reenters the civility field as best illustrated by 'Abdallah al-Nadim (1845–1896), a committed Muslim activist and a contemporary of the leading reformer Muhammad 'Abduh, but also one major disseminator of *adab*. He defined moral virtue not just in terms of the normative system of *shari'a* but as tied to economic development and "industriousness" (Gasper 2001: 79). The accompanying restraint from religious zeal that characterized the *adab* propagated by even a combative Muslim reformer like al-Nadim did not, however, diminish the emphasis on the centrality of religious norms. While in the first half of the 19th century al-Tahtawi could still be seen as a champion of the disciplining impetus of an autarchic yet modern state formation, al-Nadim was able to build up his role as a leading public educator by acknowledging the Western challenge. At the same time, he developed a consciously antagonist stance toward colonial Europe based on a reformed and reforming, civic type of Islam. He also considered the *khutba* (the Friday sermon) and the training of preachers equipped to deal with the actual problems of the community as fundamental to the Islamic reform project (Gasper 2011: 87). Al-Nadim stands out as one major disseminator of *adab* intended as civility, a notion transcending tact, good manners, and based on a mastery of the self and of social circumstances, and even resting on the idea of social commerce between Egyptians and foreigners. Therefore the concept also reflected an ethic of respect for the sensibilities of the members of other autochthonous, non-Muslim religious communities (particularly Christians and Jews). Clearly the involvement of *shari'a* in such a radically renewed discourse of civility purported big changes for the conceptions and implementations of Islamic normativity, which we can only address to a quite limited extent in the rest of this chapter and volume.

Suffice here to say that the autonomization of a modern field of morality bound to the wider civilizing process did not automatically undermine traditional disciplines and practices. Rather it displaced the relative impact of the latter on the reformers' reconstruction of a Muslim self. It also enhanced the awareness of the importance of situating the focus on subjectivity and identity within the crystallizing constraints of the nation-state in the making, thereby creating a tension between being a Muslim subject and a member of the nation (in due time 'citizen'). The dimension of 'invention of tradition' embedded in the public sphere of civility and *adab* superimposed the reformers' intervention upon still effective lines of tradition. This relation was also a process of "translation" and therefore incorporated both internal and external (i.e. colonial) relations of power (Asad 1993: 171–99), something of which the most acute spirits among the reformers—such as al-Nadim—were well aware.

Overall, while the process of implosion of tradition was slower and less linear at the institutional level (and autonomy was partly retained as a resource for governance), it was easier for the emerging elites to manage at the representational and normative level. As has been famously argued by Timothy Mitchell, it was at such levels that a "new order" was implanted (Mitchell 1991 [1988]). The process configured a dimension of change that we can dub the implosion of Islamic normativity. In the process, the *shari'a* was actually propped up, discursively and symbolically, as a normative tool for disciplining and civilizing the subjects and citizens. However, this ended up severely eroding its moorings in traditional institutions of teaching and adjudication, within the wider system centered on the *waqf* which traditionally provided funding and infrastructure for the educational sector.

The project of Islamic reform that took an increasingly clear shape in Egypt as elsewhere in the Muslim world in the last third of the 19th century was the main tool for capitalizing on this implosion of the institutional underpinnings of the *shari'a*. It was tightly bound to the construction of a type of subjectivity fitting into the remarkable turn taken by the civilizing process under the aegis of colonialism. The process did not amount to a unilateral bending of Islamic normativity toward a type of self-governance geared toward Western conceptions of autonomy and agency (Gasper 2001: 76). On the other hand, it cannot be denied that such conceptions were integral to the colonial hegemony of Western Europe, and particularly of Britain, which in the reform epoch emerged as the main colonial patron of Egyptian administrative reforms. To understand both the potential and the limits of the reform project and its relation to Western blueprints of a "new order," which should be analyzed in more depth in a future volume explicitly dedicated to the state, the law, and the public sphere, we need here briefly to address the level of discourse at which it was deployed and the notion of discursive tradition underlying the work of *islah*.

This keyword means, indeed, redressing and restoring more than reforming. As a discursive hub, this important idea was never a mere response to the social turbulences that made Egypt vulnerable to falling prey, in the last third of the 19th century, to the direct political and economic control of European colonial powers. On the other hand, in spite of a principled autochthony of the discursive elaboration of the reform project (also in terms of emerging class interests of the social carriers of the discourse, as we will see in the next volume), one cannot underestimate a growing colonial pressure on the terms themselves of the reform discourse. Reformers in Egypt, as elsewhere in the Muslim world, were often impelled to reformulate the knowledge–power equation according to new rules reflecting both the imperatives of colonial governance and the (either conscious or compulsive) anti-colonial resentment that tended to narrow the range of their options. Reform had to cope with the powers, discourses, and institutions carried over by Western colonial modernity, whose spokespersons purported to represent the only possible avenue of human progress and to embody the singular form of worldly civilization.

In the emerging reform discourse, a correct moral disposition emanating from an allegedly "civilized" (*mutamaddin*) subject was considered necessary for the proper exercise of practical knowledge. Ultimately (and paradoxically), the prototypical non-urban subject, the *fallah* ("peasant"), became the foil of both the limits and the potential of collective emancipation under the banner of a civilizing blueprint (Gasper 2008). The *fallah* was adopted as a privileged target by the reform discourse not only for his purported ignorance but also for the fact that ignorance led him, according to reformers, to conceive of his interests in backwardly narrow ways. The message of the reformers was that sheer interest could not provide a sufficient legitimacy to the increasingly sophisticated civilizing project propagated by the educated urbanites. Self-interest became the marker of an "uncivilized" behavior that needed to be eradicated via education. The fact that the key channel for these educational endeavors was the printing press shows how much the issue was one of representation of the peasant condition as the indicator of a civilizing gap, more than of the actual education of the peasantry. But this is also why the "civilizing process" (*tamaddun* in the new print Arabic) was explicitly related to a developing sense of interconnectedness: for the reformers, the peasants were those most in need of *tamaddun* since mostly "oblivious to the wider world in which they lived and unaware of the existence of the sociopolitical body to which they belonged" (Gasper 2008: 106).

The development highlighted by Michael Gasper is probably a specific variant—in an environment where the city–countryside dynamics were decreasingly affected by a nomadic component, which in Egypt had been historically weaker than elsewhere in the region—of a wider process unfolding in the geopolitical realm long hegemonized by the Ottoman Empire. We can say therefore that the reform discourse and program transcended the simple adaptation of the tradition of *adab* to envelop the modernizing and rationalizing imperatives of the colonial "new order." It resulted in a reinscription of the idea itself of social cohesion (or of the social bond at large) into the emerging consciousness of a sort of 'iron cage' of colonial civility, out of the earlier, more complex, but also better balanced, tension between city, countryside, and desert or steppe within precolonial realms of the Islamic ecumene.

Class, Gender, and Generation: The Ultimate Testing Grounds of the Educational-Civilizing Project

In the educational discourse of al-Nadim, a central place was taken by his explicit and insistent call to the educated class, consisting in exhorting them to systematically instruct peasants about the requirements of collective life in contemporary society. This putative educational program embraced the skills that were deemed necessary to accumulate and protect wealth, reflecting the imperative of collective prosperity, and, as the result of the entire process of stimulating a patriotic ethos, the priority of protecting the "homeland" (*watan*) and the "people" (*sha'b*). This proto-nationalist, yet islamically connoted, approach was needed, according to al-Nadim, in order to inculcate a novel spirit in the peasantry, who would then, thanks to a hard and conscious work ethic, contribute to the nation's prosperity by being recruited, almost conscripted, into society. Clearly, this idea was linked to the massive conscription of peasants in the new Egyptian army that was implemented more than half a century earlier by Mehmed Ali (Fahmy 1997). From the viewpoint of the reform discourse, that measure had been merely a preliminary step to make peasants conscious of being obliged to their homeland. What al-Nadim and other reformers envisioned and propagated was clearly not just a self-propelling, civilizing process but rather a coherent, top-down, educational project (Gasper 2008).

A class dimension was evidently central both to the underlying civilizing process and to the strategy adopted by the representation of the educational project. The extent to which both the process and the project fed into the growing self-awareness of a bourgeois class of mixed urban and rural origin favored a mutual convergence between the *islah* discourse and the administrative reforms, without the former fitting into the latter as a hand into a glove. The reform discourse, situated at a delicate junction between Islamic traditions and modern state-building in a context of colonial dependence, incorporated a notion of the "general public" (*al-sawad al-a'zham*) to be educated (Gaspar 2001: 75). Hereby recurrent references to the peasants as the most recalcitrant, yet to be civilized part of the population in the society or nation in the making played a crucial role.

Among all key categories used by the discourse, *tamaddun* suggested a steered and willed civilizing process tied to urban life and singling out the virtues of the educated population, as opposed to the purported ignorance of the rural, uneducated *fallahin*. This was no pure moralizing discourse, since schools (both real and virtual, i.e. staged through fictive pedagogical sessions published in the press), clubs, and associations of various kinds, including charitable ones, were called to implement the educational-civilizing project (or at least pretended to do so). These fora were deputed to inculcate the dispositions that would help Egyptians reverse what many reformers explicitly saw and denounced as the decline of their society. This capacity was to be achieved through the acquisition of adequate knowledge and education. The knowledge–power equation was altered accordingly. Knowledge was now primarily identified with the capacity to know one's own and thereby the community's interests. Religious knowledge and the *shari'a* retained a considerable importance, but as tributary to a broader knowledge reconceived both in utilitarian and moralistic terms. This view was additionally sustained by a proto-sociological vision of increasingly objective social relations, or interdependencies, resulting from the way in which the educated subjects were expected to enter into relationships with each other (Gasper 2001).

The ignorance imputed to the peasants for their allegedly distorted religious practices went hand in hand with the denunciation of their deficient public demeanor and their lack of skills in bringing up their own children. In this sense, the purported backwardness of their farming techniques could not be redeemed in isolation from the cultural forces allegedly retarding the development of the once proud Muslim homeland. In this context, the key traditional method of knowledge transmission and adjudication known as *taqlid* was singled out as the type of blind "imitation" that dries up the potential dynamism of religious traditions and impairs subjects in the necessary tasks to meet the daily relational challenges within society and the market. Al-Nadim's calls responded to such criteria and represented the epitome of a growing array of tracts, from popular to scholarly, exemplifying how educated and soberly religious subjects should struggle for a continuous improvement of their selves and the collective body of society. They were encouraged to do so by cultivating rightly conceived knowledge and mastering those skills that befit the public interest, including the intricacies of contract law and mortgages (Gaspar 2001).

The emergent public sphere that extolled the knowledge-based virtues of these educated and civilized subjects provided coherence and agency to the clearly gendered profile of the male, literate, urban intellectual who was now defined almost entirely in contrast to his nemesis, namely the superstitious and gullible peasant. Often of wealthy rural origins, several types of public intellectuals had an immediate stake in such processes of discursive rationalization, e.g. for being agricultural landowners. However, as they themselves insisted, sheer interest could not be the sole basis of such a civilizing project. The twin precolonial traditions supporting the civilizing process, namely normativity (*shari'a*) and courteousness (*adab*), were thus increasingly squeezed into the double track of discipline and distinction, two combined civilizing vectors in permanent tension with each other. The disciplining element can be assimilated here to a genuinely modern notion of diffuse power based on acquiring the knowledge about how to behave in any circumstance of social intercourse, both with peers and superiors. Unlike the connectivity of *shari'a* as envisioned by an author like al-Shatibi (see Chapter 4), which activates agency and detects accountability without overburdening the agent, discipline functions now by shaping autonomous, i.e. self-regulating, subjects (irrespective of whether and when they acquire the legal status of 'citizens'), while potentially embracing the whole population, 'society', or 'nation'. Distinction is made by marking the cultural distance that still has to be covered by lower classes in the process of generalization of norms of morality and civility and so supersedes the ritual techniques of coping with a variety of discrete others that were closely linked, within court cultures, to the appreciation of what is beautiful. Therefore class cleavages (but also clashes among fractions of the bourgeois elite with different sources of income, links to state power, and cultural outlooks) are justified on the basis of gradients tabling civility vs. the absence (or deficit) thereof. In other words, class matters, but through the lens of a cultural discourse of civility.

The rationality embedded in this eminently cultural process based on a skilled modulation of discipline and distinction by self-steering subjects mainly resides in the competence to anticipate effects through an increasing internalization of constraints. Education to anticipate the social impact of one's individual behavior via a type of knowledge that immediately feeds into social power provides the basis for the type of normativity that supports a modern public sphere: it feeds into the general competence to recognize needs and solutions while being invested into specific social fields. This approach reflects a concern for fitting differentiated rationalities (e.g. working as a law professional or being voluntarily engaged in what now takes the form of a charity sector targeted to the poor, the needy, and the uneducated) into unitary modes and codes of conduct. These in turn match both the prerequisites of the integrity of personality and agency and the views of the common, public good to be pursued by largely autonomous citizens (Eickelman and Salvatore 2002). Individualization and the shaping of civilized selves responds to the necessity of building up competences to act within different social fields (see Farag 2001). The citizens should prove able to recognize both the specific rules of a situation and the general, public interest to which civilized conduct is addressed. The public sphere appears to be as reliant upon collective reasoning as it is dependent upon a process of civilized anticipation of social, including sector-specific, situations, encounters, transactions.

Therefore we can preliminarily define the discourse of reform itself as simultaneously a reflection and an engine of the civilizing process: it generated comprehensive models of morality, at the same time as it created avenues of intervention within discrete fields of social activity and sustained their sectorial rationalization. The discourse legitimized and provided the apparatus for the diffusion of a civilizing process consisting in the rationalization of the state-bound steering capacities targeting society as a whole, as well as for the definition of rational rules suitable to special fields of social activity and economic production (in this period still mainly agriculture). Elias' notion of the civilizing process has here the merit of matching the increasing interdependence entailed by the differentiation of modern life and the related social division of labor, on the one hand, with the self-constraint that goes along with them, on the other. It helps explain the formation of codes of conduct and their additional turning into signs of social and cultural distinction. However, Elias' approach was limited by a lingering positivism (or incipient behaviorism). After emphasizing the importance of the literature codifying civility out of courtly manners and into a world of socially differentiated groups that became gradually hegemonized by the emerging bourgeoisie, Elias did not take sufficiently into account how discipline and distinction depend on discourse.

This cumulative process, including its discursive prism (or engine), is a complex mirror of social rationalization, a notion once at the center of Weber's sociology, including the sociology of religion, which cannot however be reduced to any generally valid, universal formula or algorithm of 'modernization.' Accordingly, rationality is measured by the capacity to constrain oneself according to the demands of increasing specialization and interdependence. The process is reflected in the differentiation and control of outer gestures that occurs according to the specificity of circumstances. It is also tuned into a homogenization of rules of conduct under the scrutiny of a 'general public.' The tension between specialization and generalization is a major characteristic of the civilizing process and provides a legitimate alley for a reentry of religious discourses (as historic, 'axial' tokens of general rules) into the ever more intricate social game. Implemented through an early inculcation of rules via education, self-control is increasingly interiorized and steered by binary religious codes splitting behavior into publicly allowed and prohibited (Elias 2000 [1939; 1968]: 355). As frequently stressed by Johann Arnason, the Eliasian model underestimates the extent to which a civilizing process has to rely on a culturally specific discourse, whose reembedding within wider social dynamics is exemplified by the Egyptian case just described. Here time-honored notions of normativity (*shariʻa*) and courtesy (*adab*) supporting the civilizing process within Islam/Islamdom did (and do) not seem bound to disappear.

Yet the tension between discipline and distinction also creates a discursive inconsistency hardly captured by Elias' theory, as when the *fallah* is depicted as in dire need of redemption from his ignorance through the help of proper religious, legal, and technical teaching, while in reality he is deemed as inherently unredeemable. These discursive breaches are precisely the factors that help to keep a tense and fragile balance between discipline and distinction and allow a reentry of the traditional doublet of normativity and courteousness (*shari'a* and *adab*) in shapes that do not fit colonial civility without attritions. It is such attritions—which depending on circumstances might appear as latent, interstitial, or destabilizing—that show how the knowledge–power equation is not unequivocally streamlined through a singularization of power in the form of diffuse social empowerment. The ambivalent modules of inclusion-exclusion that set the stage for the new shape of the civilizing process continue to exert pressure on either side of the unstable equilibrium. Nowadays the *fallah* appears on Egyptian TV—including commercials—in all facets again: as already redeemed and made fit to share in the project of national progress by contributing to it a unique token of authenticity, as yet on the way to redemption, or as irredeemably stupid and destined to be cheated. The ongoing misalignment between the specialization and the generalization of norms corresponds to the unsettled tension between discipline and distinction as vectors of the civilizing process. The *sui generis* rationalization that Weber imputed to modernity can only be understood as thriving in the intervals that are continually produced within such fields of tension. Not even discourse can smooth them out conclusively and persuasively.

A gender component was from the beginning integral to the reform blueprint and to its underlying tension between discipline and distinction, particularly via the often stated goal of the education of girls belonging to various social classes. The focus on the gender dimension partly functioned to make invisible the class divisiveness of the discourse. The "virtual school" for girls set up by 'Abdallah al-Nadim in the form of imagined dialogues published in his journal *al-Ustadh* in the 1880s puts him in a highly ambivalent relationship with the later reformer Qasim Amin (1863–1908) and even more with the first Egyptian feminist Huda al-Sha'rawi (1879–1947), who are considered the pioneers of the discourse on the emancipation of the Muslim woman in Egypt (Herrera 2002). Al-Nadim's goal was to address girls from both urban and rural backgrounds and from different social classes, and not by chance in some of the writings devoted to this goal he used a colloquial form of Arabic. His intentionally educational discourse looked to elicit in the Muslim girls a traditional sense of obligation as future wives and mothers in the context of emerging forms of nuclear family fitting a national project of prosperity and independence.

Al-Nadim thus became the champion of a type of education designed to provide not just the discrete tools for a program addressed to young women but also to build the type of subjectivity itself deemed necessary to conduct household activities in a context where the nuclear family provided both a microcosm and a laboratory for the work-in-progress on the nation. Through one of his fictional characters, named Zakia, al-Nadim lampooned "the girls who dress like foreigners and walk on the streets with clothes meant for the house, just like the foreign women." He also added: "We shouldn't go out without covering ourselves, and we shouldn't go to gatherings at the theater or to parties where there would be men whom we don't know" (Herrera 2002: 12). In other passages, he tried to define the dress code—whose traditional origin and further development are far from unequivocal in the Middle East, and certainly go back to pre-Islamic times—as originating from a more narrowly defined religious duty. We see in this kind of writing how the enforcement of a dress code evidencing the alleged modesty and virtuosity of an educated Muslim woman is from the beginning a delicate part of a reform discourse that strongly essentializes the traditional complexity of *shari'a*. While being a sort of 'preemancipatory' approach to reforming female subjectivities, al-Nadim's school prefigures the view of a good Muslim woman that was to be later rearticulated—under different social and historical circumstances—by the movement of the "new veiling" that started to be publicly visible in Egypt, as elsewhere in Muslim-majority societies, during the first half of the 1970s (Zuhur 1992).

While a clear-cut assessment of this type of discourse as strictly gender-specific remains difficult, it is evident that al-Nadim was developing here another key concept of the reform project, namely *tarbiyya*, a prime weapon within the discursive arsenal of several reformers, foremost his contemporary Muhammad 'Abduh (1849–1905). Its meaning comes close to "raising and instructing," thus configuring a tool for channeling and disciplining the energies of the youth to shape the future of society. The concept also helped pinpoint the highly paternalistic coordinates of the incipient nationalist discourse, undoubtedly rooted in a neopatriarchal interpretation of the civilizational program. This type of discourse laid the groundwork not just for the construction of the category of the 'Muslim youth' but also for the promotion of the need for a new culture of schooling. This culture was to accompany, inspire, and legitimize the founding of teaching institutions outside the educational sector hitherto controlled by the *'ulama'*. It is therefore too simplistic to dub the new schools as just 'modern'—unless we identify modernity with the strict combination of Taylorian organizational methods and Victorian morality which became hegemonic in the second half of the 19th century in the colonial metropole.

Typically and not surprisingly, a key node of the discourse on educating the youth was the emerging pattern of the ideal nuclear family. In many ways, the essentialized framing of the question of the woman's status in Islam was part and parcel—or most often the foil itself—of this broader project. The idea was particularly well developed among the urban reformers inclined to favor a Western type of schooling and the corresponding adoption of forms of intercourse modeled on the way colonialism carried over the image of the Western nuclear family and of its inner roles. As Lila Abu-Lughod has put it:

> It was not insignificant that the 'new' wife and mother was now to be in charge of the scientific management of the orderly household of the modern nation, as well as the rearing and training of the children who now were seen as the future citizens of the modern nation.
>
> (Abu-Lughod 1999: 28)

Given this colonial framing of the discourse on the family and the moral training of mothers, such a Western-style bourgeois domesticity was tightly linked both to the colonial programs and to the incipient Egyptian nationalist resistance to it. This model took shape at the same time as British colonists used the discourse stigmatizing polygamy, veiling, and other household practices concerning women as incompatible with the promoted civil bourgeois ethos, which worked prima facie as a justification for colonial rule over a Muslim society (Pollard 2005). This development shows both that the gender question was a key marker of civility in the colonial situation and that mobilization against colonial rule among the emerging nationalist elites subscribing to the reform discourse embraced the same patriarchal and colonial model of civility, only to reverse the power relations between colonizers and colonized. Therefore, and paradoxically, this strategically delicate subfield of the reform discourse, far from being gender-specific, is rather gender-neutral. The paradox reveals the encompassing power of the civilizing dimension underlying the colonial situation, irrespective of its political bending by representatives of different, partly overlapping and partly clashing, interests.

In a concurrent work, Wilson Chacko Jacob (2011) has spelled out the effects of the process on patterns and models of masculinity and youth. Masculinity here is probably a better token of gender-specificity as it became a privileged dimension for the construction of the subjectivity of that self-consciously cultured segment of the bourgeoisie that mediated between the reform discourse and the emerging urban, increasingly nationalist, middle stratum. This socio-cultural layer happened to be designated as *afandiyya*, denoting the social standing and connoting the everyday culture associated with the state bureaucracy, its professions, and its educational reform-orientedness (Ryzova 2014). One visible result of this group-formation was a sort of *afandi* masculinity that had to differentiate itself from Western colonial models while using the material infrastructures (clubs, sports, scouting, fashion) and the immaterial images of the body vectored by colonialism. The *afandiyya* became gradually distinguished from the intellectual current that, at the turn of the 20th century, came to represent a deepening of the more specifically Islamic dimension of the reform discourse, labeled *salafiyya*. This label originates from the emphasis laid on the exemplary normative patterns embodied by the "reputable ancestors"—*al-salaf al-salih*—foremost Muhammad and his companions: a formula that had become popular since the earlier-mentioned revival of *hadith* studies of the immediately precolonial period.

However, Jacob also shows how in the process a residual non-bourgeois dimension of masculinity survived as a sort of purported, authentic other-hood, via a rejuvenation of the *futuwwa* whose prominence we observed in the Middle Periods of Islamic history as a form of youth urban organization that enshrined notions of spiritual chivalry and support of the weak. We also saw how this type of brotherhood could be the source of norms of social power and civility largely escaping the supervision of the *'ulama'* and therefore becoming potentially disruptive of the social bond and its under-lying Islamic moral idiom (see Chapter 2). Not surprisingly, in the new colonial and nationalist conjuncture, the discourse on *futuwwa* revealed anxieties about the emerging bourgeois order and the attendant civilizing process. It reflected the transgressive side of tradition that the discourse of reform was not able to tame and put to profit for the emerging elites of the nation, while it also fell out of range of the increasingly 'puritan' radar of the *salafiyya* discourse. At the same time and exactly for these reasons, the *futuwwa* discourse also represented a reservoir of authenticity. Authenticity was both ineliminable and ultimately desirable from the viewpoint of the reform project: it revealed that any reconstructed masculinity could not be integrally bourgeois, civilized, and modern, but also had to enact (unlike and even opposite to the discourse on femininity) a hard core of non-functional identitarian resilience and resistance (Jacob 2011: 229–61).

References

Abu-Lughod, Lila. 1999. "Feminism, nationalism, modernity." Interviewed by Aysha Parla, *ISIM Newsletter*, 2: 28.

Aishima, Hatsuki. 2016. *Public Culture and Islam in Modern Egypt: Media, Intellectuals and Society*. London: I.B. Tauris.

Alleaume, Ghislaine. 1989. "Linant de Bellefonds (1799–1883) et le saint-simonisme en Égypte." In *Les Saint-Simoniens et l'Orient: Vers la modernité*, edited by Magali Morsy, 113–31. Aix-en-Provence: Edisud.

Asad, Talal. 1993. *Genealogies of Religion: Discipline and Reasons of Power in Christianity and Islam*. Baltimore and London: Johns Hopkins University Press.

Asad, Talal. 2003. *Formations of the Secular: Christianity, Islam, Modernity*. Stanford, CA: Stanford University Press.

Assi, Eman. 2008. "Islamic Waqf and Management of Cultural Heritage in Palestine." *International Journal of Heritage Studies*, 14/4: 380–5.

De Jong, Fred. 1982. "On Peter Gran, Islamic Roots of Capitalism: Egypt 1760–1840. A Review Article with Author's Reply." *International Journal of Middle East Studies*, 14/3: 381–99.

Eickelman, Dale F. and Armando Salvatore. 2002. "The Public Sphere and Muslim Identities." *European Journal of Sociology*, 43/1: 92–115.

Elias, Norbert. 2000 [1939; 1968]. *The Civilizing Process*. Oxford: Blackwell.

Ener, Mine. 2003. *Managing Egypt's Poor and the Politics of Benevolence, 1800–1952*. Princeton, NJ: Princeton University Press.

Fahmy, Khaled. 1997. *All the Pasha's Men: Mehmed Ali, His Army and the Making of Modern Egypt*. Cambridge: Cambridge University Press.

Farag, Iman. 2001. "Private Lives, Public Affairs: The Uses of Adab." In *Muslim Traditions and Modern Techniques of Power, Yearbook of the Sociology of Islam*, edited by Armando Salvatore, 95–122. Hamburg: Lit/New Brunswick, NJ and London: Transaction (*Yearbook of the Sociology of Islam* III).

Findley, Carter V. 2012. *Bureaucratic Reform in the Ottoman Empire: The Sublime Porte, 1789–1922*. Princeton, NJ: Princeton University Press.

Gasper, Michael. 2001. "'Abdallah Nadim, Islamic Reform, and 'Ignorant' Peasants: State-Building in Egypt?" In *Muslim Traditions and Modern Techniques of Power, Yearbook of the Sociology of Islam*, edited by Armando Salvatore, 95–122. Hamburg: Lit/New Brunswick, NJ and London: Transaction (*Yearbook of the Sociology of Islam* III).

Gasper, Michael. 2008. *The Power of Representation: Publics, Peasants, and Islam in Egypt*. Stanford, CA: Stanford University Press.

Gesink, Indira Falk. 2010. *Islamic Reform and Conservatism: Al-Azhar and the Evolution of Modern Sunni Islam*. London: I.B. Tauris.

Gran, Peter. 1998 [1979]. *Islamic Roots of Capitalism: Egypt, 1760–1840*. Syracuse, NY: Syracuse University Press.

Gran, Peter. 2005. "Egypt and Italy, 1760–1850: Towards a Comparative History." In *Society and Economy in Egypt and the Eastern Mediterranean, 1600–1900: Essays in Honor of André Raymond*, edited by Nelly Hanna and Raouf Abbas, 11–40. Cairo and New York: American University in Cairo Press.

Hefner, Robert W. 2007. "Introduction: The Culture, Politics, and Future of Muslim Education." In *Schooling Islam: The Culture and Politics of Modern Muslim Education*, edited by Robert W. Hefner and Muhammad Qasim Zaman, 1–39. Princeton, NJ: Princeton University Press.

Herrera, Linda. 2002. "The Soul of a Nation: Abdallah Nadim and Educational Reform in Egypt (1845–1896)." *Mediterranean Journal of Educational Studies*, 7/1: 1–24.

Hodgson, Marshall G.S. 1974. *The Venture of Islam: Conscience and History in a World Civilization*, I–III. Chicago and London: University of Chicago Press.

Jacob, Wilson Chacko. 2011. *Working Out Egypt: Effendi Masculinity and Subject Formation in Colonial Modernity, 1870–1940*. Durham, NC: Duke University Press.

MacIntyre, Alasdair. 1988. *Whose Justice? Which Rationality?* London: Duckworth.

Mardin, Şerif. 2006a. *Religion, Society and Modernity in Turkey*. Syracuse, NY: Syracuse University Press.

Mardin, Şerif. 2006b. "Continuity and Change in the Modernization of Turkey." In *Contemporary Islam: Dynamic, not Static*, edited by Abdul Aziz Said, Mohammed Abu-Nimer, and Meena Sharify-Funk, 101–6. London and New York: Routledge

Masud, M. Khalid and Armando Salvatore. 2009. "Western Scholars of Islam on the Issue of Modernity." In *Islam and Modernity: Key Issues and Debates*, edited by Muhammad Khalid Masud, Armando Salvatore, and Martin van Bruinessen, 36–53. Edinburgh: Edinburgh University Press.

Mitchell, Timothy. 1991 [1988]. *Colonising Egypt*. Berkeley, CA: University of California Press.

O'Fahey, R.S. and Bernd Radtke. 1993. "Neo-Sufism Reconsidered." *Der Islam*, 70/1: 52–87.

Ortaylı, Ilber. 1983. *İmparatorluğun En Uzun Yüzyılı* [The Longest Century of the Empire]. Istanbul: Hil Yayınları.

Peters, Rudolph. 1990. "Reinhard Schulze's Quest for an Islamic Enlightenment." *Die Welt des Islams*, 30/1: 160–2.

Pinto, Paulo G. 2004. "The Limits of the Public: Sufism and the Religious Debate in Syria." In *Public Islam and the Common Good*, edited by Armando Salvatore and Dale F. Eickelman, 181–204. Leiden and Boston: Brill.

Pollard, Lisa. 2005. *Nurturing the Nation: The Family Politics of Modernizing, Colonizing, and Liberating Egypt, 1805–1923*. Berkeley and Los Angeles: University of California Press.

Rabinow, Paul. 1995. *French Modern: Norms and Forms of the Social Environment*. Chicago: University of Chicago Press.

Radtke, Bernd. 1994. "Erleuchtung und Aufklärung: Islamische Mystik und europäischer Rationalismus." *Die Welt des Islams*, 34/1: 48–66.

Ryzova, Lucie. 2014. *The Age of the Efendiyya: Passages to Modernity in National-Colonial Egypt*. Oxford: Oxford University Press.

Salvatore, Armando. 1997. *Islam and the Political Discourse of Modernity*. Reading: Ithaca Press.

Salvatore, Armando. 2015. "A Public Sphere Revolution? Reconsidering the Role of Social Media in the 'Arab Spring.'" In *Routledge Handbook of the Arab Spring: Rethinking Democratization*, edited by Larbi Sadiqi, 343–53. London: Routledge.

Schulze, Reinhard. 1990. "Das islamische achtzehnte Jahrhundert. Versuch einer historiographischen Kritik." *Die Welt des Islams*, 30/1: 140–59.

Schulze, Reinhard. 1996. "Was ist die islamische Aufklärung." *Die Welt des Islams*, 36: 276–325.

Smith, Wilfred Cantwell. 1962. "The Historical Development in Islam of the Concept of Islam as an Historical Development." In *Historians of the Middle East*, edited by Bernard Lewis and P.M. Holt, 484–502. London: Oxford University Press.

Vikør, Knut S. 1995. *Sufi and Scholar on the Desert Edge: Muḥammad b. ʾAlī Al-Sanūsī and His Brotherhood*. Evanston, IL: Northwestern University Press.

Zuhur, Sherifa. 1992. *Revealing Reveiling: Islamic Gender Ideology in Contemporary Egypt*. Albany, NY: State University of New York Press.

7

GLOBAL CIVILITY AND ITS ISLAMIC ARTICULATIONS

The Dystopian Globalization of Civility

As the analysis from the previous chapters shows, it would be misleading (while taking into account the exploration of 'civil society' in Chapter 1), to consider civility a mere late-comer in the long genealogy of buzzwords produced within the centuries marked, first, by an Anglo-Scottish, and later, by an Anglo-American, intellectual hegemony over the determination of the essential vocabulary and grammar of society and politics (Salvatore 2007: 215–41). Both the theoretical and the historical explorations of the previous chapters have suggested the extent to which the idea of civility, whatever its specific, local expressions, can be seen as demarcating a field of intertwined grids of concepts and practices. It should not be concealed, however, that attempts at a unitary, universal definition of civility reducing the complexity of the conceptual grammar continue to pop up (e.g. see Boyd 2006). The inescapable diversity of patterns of civility results from the fact that the determination of the socio-political field, however debatable, needs to reflect specific and sometimes competing ways of covering the relationship among individuals and larger groups, both within discrete locales and in the so-called global village.

In this chapter we should complete the work of understanding civility both in its global deployment and in its specifically Islamic articulations. It is important, however, not to fall prey to the temptation, and related illusion, of seeing civility as a *passe-partout* for capturing a smooth and long-term development characterized by essential models and defective imitations. The discussion, in Chapter 1, of the nearly contemporary Neapolitan

The Sociology of Islam: Knowledge, Power and Civility, First Edition. Armando Salvatore.
© 2016 John Wiley & Sons, Ltd. Published 2016 by John Wiley & Sons, Ltd.

alternative to the Scottish Enlightenment provided by Vico (1999 [1744]) has been in the chapters that followed used to help show how the trajectory of the civilizing process in the Islamic ecumene cannot be constructed as a defective form of a universal model originating in the West. As we saw from Chapter 2 onward, the Islamic perspective seems to be characterized by a high, and increasing, degree of cosmopolitan circulation and transborder connectedness, which constituted the benchmark of civility within the Afro-Eurasian civilizational area until early modernity (Bamyeh 2000; Duara 2015). Boundaries have been continuously created and challenged within the arena of transregional movements and exchanges occurring during the longer-term civilizing process. The ongoing mediations and contestations of such boundaries can only be covered by a larger concept of civility that selectively redeploys key elements of more classic notions and avoids strict adherence to the modern hegemonic modeling that gravitates around the highly ambivalent notion of 'civil society.'

Emerging contemporary patterns within the multiverse that once deserved to be labeled the Islamic ecumene might be seen as retrieving—at least in part and certainly not without ambiguities—some of the paradigms that preceded the Westphalian turn in Europe and the ensuing global hegemony of the West. This is particularly the case for transnational Islamic movements, whose contemporary variants should be analyzed in a future volume. The current situation in North Africa and in the Middle East (particularly in Libya, in the former mandates of Syria and Iraq, and in Yemen) indicates that contemporary patterns are no longer indissolubly bound to the political and cultural project of the nation-state (Eisenstadt 1998), an indissolubility yet purported within those Western historic conceptions of civil society which were revived in the early 1990s. This potential disconnection of civility from Westphalian regimes and its frequent turning into its opposite (most typically confined to the 'uncivility' of 'failed states') can also be observed where what is left of ethnically bound nationalism is invested in fiscally disarticulated and ideologically impoverished forms of neo-patriotism, as in the banners that have been often raised during the Arab Spring and in the follow-up restorations of autocratic forms of government.

The unstable understanding of civility that we gain from the experience of the early 21st century not only modifies some key elements of the Western historic ideas of civil society but also exposes them to global critique, distancing, and reappropriation in ever new guises. Civility is therefore not a miraculous key for transcending unilaterally (both political and conceptual)

Western hegemonic notions and practices, and for attaining a facile consensual view of the essential traits of the global civilizing process. Civility is
rather interesting, both theoretically and empirically, precisely for its resistance to being folded into a fully globalist and conceptually universalistic
normalization. Without indulging in the frenzied game of sharply defining
and redefining civility, we should in this concluding chapter elaborate a sustainable review of Elias' basic insights into the ambivalent concept of the civilizing process mentioned at various points in this volume (Elias 2000 [1939;
1968]). Accordingly, within the sociology of Islam I have developed, civility
has been, and will continue to be, investigated as the outcome of a variety of
factors of knowledge and power inherent in the social bond. Such combined
factors work as a self-propelling force for taming violence and increasing
coordination among individual subjects. This coordination occurs via a
cumulative dynamics of self-control and self-policing reflected in etiquette
and formalized codes more than in a proper ethic. Too often, as also represented by the grammar of the Scottish moralists, this process is reduced to an
inner steering of the self deriving from an evanescent 'sense' or 'sentiment'
of the self for the other, more than being based on interactive dynamics
(see Chapter 1). The notion of civility that emerges from this Eliasian
review avoids an excessive emphasis on subjective factors and focuses
instead on a rather intersubjective, even impersonal, joining of knowledge
and power.

In her remarkable study of patterns of civility in early modern Japan, Eiko
Ikegami has provided a precious precedent for how civility, while taking
into account Western experience and theory, can and should be understood
from non-Western cultural and civilizational angles which have disposed
of any aspiration or 'dream' (remembering Mardin's assessment quoted in
Chapter 1) of 'civil society.' Ikegami states: "Sociologically, civility might be
thought of as a ritual technology of interpersonal exchanges that shapes a
kind of intermediate zone of social relationships between the intimate and
the hostile" (Ikegami 2005: 28). Interestingly, when faced with the task of
providing concrete examples of a type of trust-building civility not primarily
bound to state power and/or court culture, Ikegami mentions the case of
Maghrebi Jewish trading networks in the Mediterranean and in the Indian
Ocean. These networks were active during the Earlier Middle Period and
were as such integral to the 'maritime Silk Road' that played a crucial role
with the Islamic ecumene. Ikegami refers to a strand of sociological research
that can be considered a spinoff of Shlomo Dov Goitein's famous historical

work on the documents from the Cairo Geniza (see Cohen 2006). More in general, this strand of study reflects a growing awareness that civility depends on cultural patterns and traditions (Davetian 2009).

From such reflections one can try to approach a more truly transversal view of the complexity of patterns of civility. This step needs to take into account the variance of the knowledge–power equation underlying the variety of networks at play, also depending on the alternate involvements of state power in the civilizing process. Elias investigated civility through examples drawn from Western Europe, particularly by looking at the political neutralization of a long-recalcitrant nobility through its integration into the sophisticated social and cultural games of power centered in early modern royal courts (Elias 1983 [1969]). The outcome of the process affected patterns of self-restraint that could gradually trickle down from the upper class to a variety of subjects and social groups. The first of such groups was the bourgeoisie that in its upward socio-economic trajectory never ceased to look at the nobility as a model of social behavior and taste. This is the process through which aristocratic cultures are absorbed into an all-encompassing game of power that is ultimately managed by an increasingly centralized state. Ideally, according to Elias, the state is able to integrate all emergent forms of social power into its authority in ways that ultimately make the transition from Leviathan to *demos* in the European cases (which we mentioned in Chapter 4 and will revisit in this chapter) much more of a socio-cultural than a political process. If and how this really happens is obviously dependent on specific circumstances that are also subject to cultural variations and (most crucially for the topic dealt with in this volume, yet neglected by Elias) to the inherited religious conceptions embedded in a given articulation of the knowledge–power equation and generating a corresponding meta-institutional potential.

The aspect of Elias' work that privileges a kind of top-down civilizing process encompassing the masses by disciplining every individual into a self-steered subject has often been assimilated into the later teachings of Michel Foucault, in spite of the fact that the latter's explicit remarks on civility appear marginal to his overall œuvre. Yet it is important to recall that according to Elias the first meaning of civilization (as a process) and civility (as a pattern but also as a socio-political discourse on the value of civilization) pointed to the "modes of behavior considered typical of people who are civilized in a Western way," starting from what we call "manners" (Elias 2000 [1939; 1968]: ix). This definition might seem highly reductive not only for its explicit Occidental bias but also because it seems to trivialize most of what we have been saying thus far about civility. Based on that, the outer shell of social behavior and composure, i.e. manners, only matters as part of a much more complex and substantial process (see particularly the references to the late Scottish Enlightenment and to Adam Smith in Chapter 1). This process consists of creating and managing social connectedness without recourse to material violence (as actually practiced, or also as threatened) or with only a modicum of it. It is also useful to keep in mind that Elias, originally writing in the late 1930s (i.e. when Western colonial power was still intact), spelled out transparently that the idea of civility reflects a centrality and hegemony of the "Western way." As he exemplified right at the beginning of the Preface to his *magnum opus*, this centrality is also if not primarily a matter of viewpoint sustained by adequate power: the power of the angle determined by the modern, and surely powerful, Western self-understanding of what counts as a civilized way or, particularly, in French, *civilité* (Elias 2000 [1939; 1968]: ix).

Although Elias' notion of the civilizing process starts from a focus on "manners," it further develops into capturing a much more encompassing process. The outcome of the process appears as an impersonal and potentially universal mechanism of coordination of individual actions providing stability to the social bond, in spite of the contentiousness and fragility of the underlying games of self-composure and other-conditioning among the social players. It is indeed important that the theory of Elias was developed not by bracketing out conflict but by integrating it into civility. Remembering this aspect is particularly crucial since the idea of civilization today risks being ever more associated with the inheritance of Western predominance based on the above-mentioned Westphalian, colonial state system. This inheritance of 'strong states,' allegedly reflecting a generalized and conscious renunciation of gratuitous violence, is often dichotomously opposed to a violent, 'uncivilized' socio-political behavior leading to radicalism and extremism, if not to terrorism, and ultimately to 'failed states.'

Stressing contentiousness and conflict as part of civility is also an antidote to an overly culturalist reading of the factors (as, for example, those identified by Weber in the role played by what he calls the cultural elites) that are conducive to establishing a balance between inner conduct and outer enforcement of rules. Within European modernity this balance was increasingly managed by state instances and, according to Foucault, was the result of the state's takeover and remolding of the Christian pastorate's techniques of disciplining (Foucault 2007). It is quite well known that Foucault's approach to "the technologies of the self" quite intrinsically resulted in a long-term genealogy of the Western knowledge–power equation centered on building individual subjectivities. As we have seen, Elias' notion of, and approach to, the civilizing process also shows similar bias and needs critique and integration. Some such critiques have been formulated in the last couple of decades but are as yet in their infancy (somewhat occluded by the Huntingtonian vulgate on civilizations and their clash: Huntington 1996). However, as also shown by the earlier quote from Eiko Ikegami's work on civility in early modern Japan, which intentionally competed with Eurocentric definitions, Elias' work can provide a fair, initial, transversal reference prism for reflection leading to a pluralization and complexification of the process. This is an important alternative to the streamlining of the process into an exclusive genealogy of the 'subject' (with its invariably Western traits) that we see in Foucault's œuvre.

The main merit of Elias' approach is to reveal from the outset, more clearly than Foucault was able to do, that the European global hegemony both captured and disseminated ideas and practices of building the self from the inside out in ways that could be integrated in ever more penetrating mechanisms of control and surveillance. However, and though this might have been neglected by Elias, the process could also empower the controlled subjects to contest, modify, and appropriate the resulting hegemonic modes. As such, Elias' theoretical proposition is a welcome complement to the one, illustrated in the Introduction, associated with civilizational analysis. Johann Arnason, the leading scholar of sociologically informed civilizational analysis, has had the merit of integrating Elias' work on the civilizing process within this branch of study and simultaneously diluting the danger of squeezing it into rigid 'Weberist' straitjackets (Arnason 1997; 2003). Particularly since the 1990s, also thanks to the intervention of scholars engaged in the sociology of Islam like Bryan Turner and Georg Stauth, the knowledge–power equation has been initially identified with the axis of thought linking Nietzsche, Weber, and Foucault (Stauth and Turner 1988; Stauth 1993; Szakolczai 1998). Yet a parallel, corrective trend has shifted the attention to how the work of Norbert Elias can make the analysis of the mutual entanglements of knowledge and power and their relation to civility less Western-centered and Christocentric than is the case within a Weberian sociology of religion and/or a Nietzschean or Foucaultian genealogy of the subject (see in particular Stauth 1993: 39–42). This volume has intended to contribute to making this latter trend more robust and better integrated within the sociology of Islam.

In order to better understand how the work of Elias, in spite of being explicitly centered on Europe, can moderate the Eurocentric iteration of the centrality of the Western subject we need to gain some sense of historical perspective concerning the mutual influences among some of the key authors here referenced. Not surprisingly, Weber provided an important background to Elias' work. However, and not entirely by chance, it was Jaspers—later to become the theorist of Axial Age civilizations (see Introduction)—who initiated Elias to Weber (Szakolczai 2000: 8). Elias' interest in civility as particularly centered on court-like social games of power led him to make Weber's ideas of modernity as rationalization more complex and sophisticated. The result is the theorization of a peculiar type of rationality that encompasses integrated bodily and psychological factors, affecting an actor's capacity to deal with the uncertainty about the moves of the interactants. These factors equip the actor to learn from, and elaborate upon, the communicative codes resulting from these interactions as ways to channel and reduce actual uncertainty, as well as the individual anxiety and stress it produces. Rather than on a bourgeois or professional ethos of a Weberian kind, this rationality depends on a strong interdependence among, potentially, all kinds of social interactants. For Elias, this type of interaction is epitomized by the power games and the associated codes of behavior taking shape in early modern European courts, but is also subject to a deep and continual metamorphosis at the moment civility slips into the hands of theoreticians and practitioners variably linked to the emergent bourgeoisie.

What is noteworthy is that both the strategic games and the mannerist codes depend not just on the intersubjective competences of the subject but on games of visibility and on the appreciation of the subject in the eyes of others, which provide the source and benchmark of individual reputation. As we saw in Chapter 1, these were also the key factors stressed by Adam Smith. It is ultimately the capacity to master the codes resulting from exposure, self-esteem, and competition which allows a subject to gain the credentials for belonging to 'good society.' Its token is behavior (or, if we prefer a pregnant Weberian concept, "life conduct") based on reason, reflection, and calculation, wrapped in strategic games of visibility, reputation, and power, where knowledge plays a particularly salient role at the crucial interface between theory and practice. We saw that what is lost in most reconstructions of Western trajectories of such a civilizing process (including in the French and German cases studied by Elias) is the art of channeling and refining one's dispositions precisely by putting aside the eyes of the others and by heeding the eye of the Other (i.e. God or transcendent equivalents thereof). The transversal and transcultural rebalancing of Elias' ideas on the civilizing process, to which our exploration of the Islamic ecumene has intended to contribute, will need to remedy to this Eurocentric, purportedly 'secular' loss of the higher complexity of the individual's motivational prism.

What needs to be preserved and cultivated among Elias' key teachings notwithstanding the necessary work of deprovincializing their exclusive Western focus is the idea that the process of rationalization underlying the civilizing process is deeply marked by ruptures, unequal levels of knowledge of the rules, and resistances to them. It is inevitably also a conflict-laden development, whereby conflict is due to accelerate the more the process facilitates the integration of new actors (or new social groups like the workers and other popular classes) into the game via sharing in—but also altering—the code that governs it. Popular, mass, and 'pop' cultures can both transgress and reinforce the code by making it accessible to wider sectors of the population (Stauth and Zubaida 1987). Interdependence in the Eliasian sense can hardly be equated to social harmony and organic cohesion. Nonetheless, in the process the measure of actual, externalized, visible violence is reduced even concomitantly with the deepening of the con-flicted dimension of the process. Violence is increasingly internalized and absorbed by the individual social actors, via their reflection, calculation, and strategic reasoning. The process is not incompatible with the concomitant release of actual, organized violence by state apparatuses on larger scales, as occurred in the history of Western colonial enterprises but also within social conflicts in the metropoles. Yet the civilizing process is a primarily sociological rather than political occurrence that relentlessly individuates and ambivalently empowers the subjects to share in the social game, even from subordinate positions. Our refinement of the concept has occurred by integrating into it Islam's historic (and highly variable) knowledge–power equation, particularly as it manifested itself through its meta-institutional fertilization of flexible institutional loci like the brotherhoods and the pious endowments (the *waqf*).

Drives, fears, and control of affects figure prominently in Elias' theory, and this can be explained without necessarily invoking Freud and psychoanalysis, which no doubt were important early references for the German sociologist. Modulation of emotions and affects occurs through interdependence and games of power. These games do not depend on the strictly individual modularity of the agency of members of a liberally oriented civil society, as purported by Gellner (see Chapter 1). The long-term process of habitual internalization of power via knowledge of codes and etiquettes is not steered by a central instance, in spite of the fact that according to Elias within European modernity the process ultimately feeds into state governance by facilitating the formation of largely self-steering and self-restraining subjects. The civilizing process is far from linear, and it is not irreversible. As warned by Vico, who anticipates (and partly subverts) Elias, civility can easily and unexpectedly turn into a new uncivility, spurred however not by wild and unrestrained sentiments but by an excess of calculation and reflection (Vico 1999 [1744]: 185–93). What is supremely clear is that Elias' view of civilization as a process is not normative but describes and to some extent measures the degree of interdependence that is reflected by societal relations and so reveals the complexity (and often the antinomian shades) of the social bond. For the actor, the external other is rarely either an unreserved friend to be fully trusted or an enemy to be strenuously combatted—while the internal or internalized other (whether in the shape of a transcendent Big Other or in psychoanalytically twisted forms) continues to hold the higher civilizing potential over the individual.

This notion of the civilizing process, which spells out and, above all, dynamizes civility, is particularly precious for indicating the simultaneous working of external factors facilitating self-restraint and intersubjective exchange on the one hand, and the inner, individual (and only in this sense 'moral') construction of the citizen—so to speak from the inside out—on the other. The process includes two aspects: the intersubjective dimension of civil relations and the subjective attitude through which individual membership in a group is constructed through proper conduct via self-scrutiny and self-policing. To establish a priori which of the two dimensions comes first would just reiterate the dilemma of the chicken and the egg. Being civil means being social in concordance with formal and informal rules that allow for no more than a moderate and strictly codified recourse to outright, publicly ascertainable violence. The extent to which the subject internalizes such modes and rules of self-restraint is intimately related to the interaction with other subjects, which is largely determined by traditional teachings and practices of cultivation (for an early attempt to use Elias to interpret such developments in an Islamic context, see Hofheinz 1992–3; 1996). In this sense, we can reappraise the type of knowledge intervening in the process as constituting a specific cognitive prism for learning and habitualizing the mechanisms of affect control. Knowledge is here not just the source of the social know-how needed by self to engage other but also, and concomitantly, the engine of a mechanism of internalization and externalization of power. The civilized self exercises power in the framework of the interaction with other by bringing to fruition a type of knowledge that is primarily interactive and social. Through this work, the inherent contingency of human relations is made more predictable and governable.

Civility so defined needs to be shielded from any triumphalist perspective that might depict it as the Holy Grail allowing us to unlock both processes of integration and contention within global society. To this end, it is useful to elaborate upon a view recently provided by Slavoj Žižek, who injects dynamism into the understanding of how the Western dream of civil society gives way to civility. The gifted thinker and noted provocateur suggested that while the fall of the Berlin Wall revived the utopia of civil society, 9/11 killed it again. Yet while civil society died as utopia, its shadow, namely civility, survived its death and morphed into a quite dystopian, yet politically powerful, idea—the more powerful since deeply ingrained in the long trajectory of the European rise to world hegemony and in the accompanying alleged 'civilizing mission' (Žižek 2010: 324). The yet inchoate nature of a global civility is no longer held up by a solid Western hegemony supported by the normative matrix of the state-society complex framing ordered templates of citizenship, to which notions of civil society contributed at several turns of modern history. More than that, there was never a one-to-one relationship between Western Westphalian and colonial hegemony, on the one hand, and global civility, on the other, since civil society, the certified harbinger of civility, was mostly enclosed within nation-state borders and did not even bridge the relations between motherland and colonies (as dramatically staged by the American Revolution). The 'no longer' of the match between globality and civility which transpires through Žižek's diagnosis is nonetheless the possible symptom of a kind of nostalgia for the colonial age, which paradoxically even postcolonial studies contribute to nourish. Since non-Western postcolonial elites have been enthroned by their anti-colonial struggles, it is not surprising that global revivals of civil society might fit into the stabilizing, yet mystifying, discourse that celebrates postcoloniality. The same observation should apply whenever calls for a global civil society are supported by raising the banner of resistance to 'neoliberal globalization.' Overall, utopian 'civil society' and dystopian 'civility' are two sides of the same coin.

Therefore the long-term trajectory of exit from Western hegemony does not seem to authorize a view of civility as the neat reflection of either Western power or resistance to it. In spite of the evidence I have provided of how the process depends on a shift of interpretive perspectives, and while trying to avoid understanding it in terms of hegemonic decline or colonial nostalgia, the impulse to building and propagating a normatively laden, globally valid notion of civility that we inherit from colonialism cannot be entirely dismissed as a vacuous ideology, since it is still ubiquitous in the form of a shadow or ghost, as Žižek stressed. Ghosts can suffuse reality. Post-9/11 developments seem to infuse the ghost of civility with the organizational form of international NGOs often acting in support of humanitarian wars, or to turn the shadow of civility into the inducement of market-oriented forms of electoral democracy that never match the hard political reality on the ground. This is too often determined by the logic of the War on Terror and the concomitant dissipation of the nation-state form in large areas of North Africa and the Middle East (for an earlier diagnosis, see Salvatore 2011: 808–10). Such strictures have been confirmed by how the West's initial support of the relatively fair electoral process in Egypt which followed the ousting of Mubarak was swiftly replaced by the Western acceptance (and later active support) of the military coup that explicitly revived the rhetoric of the War on Terror. This support coincided symptomatically with the regime's promise to promote a civil, i.e. not political, form of Islam amid a climax of repression against all forms of opposition well beyond the Islamist camp.

The tension between the erosion of the Western global power and its lingering cultural hegemony should not be entirely surprising. It is nevertheless paradoxical that civility could only claim a global, normative status in the short-lived revival of civil society of the late 20th century. This was the stage when the demise of the Cold War was propagated as the end of history, as if fixing forever the triumph of Western values. In order to better understand this tension and the associated paradox one needs to consider the trajectory of the rise of the West to world hegemony. This trajectory led through various steps to the building of cohesive national formations in Europe and in selective settler colonies, which thrived and expanded via the formation and transformation of colonial empires. Unlike the historic Islamic expansion, this remapping of civilization was characterized by a sharp discontinuity between 'motherland' and 'colonies.' This split occurred not just in territorial but also in purportedly cultural terms: "as if the world were divided in two," as felicitously photographed by Timothy Mitchell with regard to the globally hubristic imagination increasingly nurtured by colonial Europe in the second half of the 19th century, at its apex of power, while staging the first streak of "world" exhibitions (now better known as expositions), which were not by chance labeled as "universal," and where the colonized "Orient" was staged with intensifying sophistication (Mitchell 1991 [1988]).

We have seen in this volume that there are clear historical antecedents to the paradox that civility as the ghost of civil society matters even if, or perhaps exactly because, it has become, with the eclipse of the Western-turned-universal dream of civil society, both normatively imploded and discursively invasive. By keeping such complex historical background in mind, we have started to revisit the issue of civility from the viewpoint of its dispersion in a globalizing framework, via the lengthy dilution of its dependence on a Westphalian frame that includes the state, more specifically the nation-state, as the disciplinary armory of society. Within this process the grave erosion of the fiscal integrity of several nation-states (if not of the Westphalian system of sovereignty as such) is revealed by the spiral of sovereign debts that has been just peaking in recent years. This erosion goes hand in hand with the possibility, which easily turns into a necessity, that governments and their media apparatuses might revive the specter of national authenticity and self-sameness—something that often occurs without the resistance, if not with the complicity, of new media, including social media. The authentic nation-state must be defended by all means against internal and external enemies. The narrative of the War on Terror, connected as it is to the dystopian twist of civility after 9/11, could be interpreted as the most recent (if not the last) lifeline grabbed by the agonizing legitimacy of Westphalian formations, a process finding its epicenter within the most fragile parts of the Muslim-majority world, once the hub of the entropic dynamism of the Islamic ecumene.

These spasms of postcolonial governments discursively reaffirming their sovereignty in spite of their increasing dependence on being bailed out (both financially and geo-strategically) by powerful external sponsors (like Egypt with Saudi Arabia and the UAE) should be related to the larger process that world historian William McNeill recognized as a long-term civilizational inertia occurring within the Afro-Eurasian landmass and the modern drives to break it. This inertia consisted in a sustained crossborder connectedness and circulation (of people, goods, ideas, techniques, diseases), which was then resisted, with the consolidation of the Westphalian system, by the setting up of borders in the name of ethno-nationalist closure. Ethnic identities preexist the modern state but the modern state claimed pride and legitimacy for them. The argument of McNeill stresses that ethnic closure cannot erase the ultimately irresistible translocal and transregional connectedness of the ecumene, supported by a steady circulation that cannot be limited to goods and capitals and which by necessity embraces people and ideas. His argument also suggests that the irresistible steadiness of connectedness and circulation is what ultimately initiates and supports the longer-term civilizing process across various epochs. This type of process renders the sovereign claims authorized by self-enclosed bureaucratic rationalities and territorial borders ever more vulnerable in the long term (McNeill 1983).

Modern European states, while imposing new types of border and being able to filter out circulation to their economic advantage, remained unable to regulate transborder connectedness without residues, while promoting a peculiar type of civilizing process. This process rests, up to the present, on forms of symbolic and material demarcation (first, the state borders; second, the initially sharp dichotomy between being a citizen and a non-citizen) that are even stronger than those existing in prior systems of regulation as well as mild restriction of circulation that responded to non-Westphalian notions of sovereignty, like the one, centered on the Islamic ecumene, which we have started to explore in this volume. The strengthening of already flourishing long-distance trade within the modern capitalist economy and the concomitant colonial hegemony of European powers has created the impression that the Westphalian interstate order provided the ultimate normative and institutional infrastructure to Europe's and the West's global (political and cultural) dominance supported by liberal, and more recently neoliberal, norms. Several actors, stakeholders, and observers even became convinced that state power was ultimately both the agent and the result of an almost unlimited colonization of spaces through expanding networks of control over populations and territories. The transatlantic expansion and colonization that made up the 'West' contributed to this perception of limitlessness (and to the latent, indeed religious, understanding of sovereignty as omnipotence) more than the European colonial enterprises in the Old World were able to do.

Diversifying Civility as the Outcome of Civilizing Processes

Yet there is a radical difference between this type of dynamics, which relies on the accumulation of information and sustains it with ever more sophisticated forms of organized and legitimate violence, and the more porous type of connectedness of the long-term networks of long-distance trade and enterprise that existed and thrived prior to European modern colonialism.

Such networks supported a type of civilizing process whose importance is mostly underplayed since it unfolded prior to the emergence of modern capitalism and was often perceived, from the viewpoint of the Westphalian order, to be furthering instability and even anarchy. This type of premodern and early modern, certainly precolonial, civilizing process, with the Islamic ecumene at its center, was largely self-sustaining. It was 'entropic' to the extent that it did not depend on the need to store, process, and centralize information for the sake of maximizing surveillance, control, and regulation (Bamyeh 2000). In many ways, the notion itself of information (and, more specifically as a function of state sovereignty, 'intelligence') nurtured by the colonial process was intimately tied to the specific, emerging forms of state power and interstate regulation of conflict. This primacy of information occurred optimally by promoting a type of knowledge in principle independent from cultural traditions and the social connectedness they presuppose; a type of knowledge that is itself, almost by default, power, if not its core. This zeroing of knowledge on power might seem to herald the end itself of the historic civilizing process, which was intrinsically built on balancing knowledge and power as mutually autonomous factors of social and political life. Instead, by looking at the metamorphosis of the knowledge–power equation through the conceptual tools inherited from Elias, as I attempted to do, we should rather see that the novel system altered and hijacked the older, longer-term civilizing process without (yet) extinguishing it. In spite of hubristic ideas envisioning power as becoming fully independent from cultural factors (almost a socio-political 'singularity'), power could never entirely absorb and subdue knowledge and its relative autonomy.

Not surprisingly, a new pattern of mutual permeability and permutation of knowledge and power emerged that could only be promoted within the skewed civilizational vision that deviated and redirected the civilizing process. The cultural dimension of the peculiar civilizational breakthrough that occurs first in the shadow of Leviathan and then via colonialism rests on a spatiotemporal reconstruction of the globe by the new European hegemonic powers based on ranking non-European others according to often racialized criteria of civilizational distinction. The result is that the Westphalian rearticulation of civility could only be affirmed via a type of global ordering that overdetermines ethnic identities even in the delimitation of *demos* (Bamyeh 2000: 92–3). While precolonial civility was based on a fragile balance of social connectedness, individual autonomy, and cultural distinction among social layers, the modern civil society matrix in a nation-state framework has not been able to safeguard this balance over the long term on the global stage. The defective universality of European and Western hegemony is highlighted by such recurrent imbalances. These are frequently revealed by an oscillating emphasis on restricted citizen rights and universal human rights, entitlements and humanitarianism, closure and access.

This hegemonic yet never truly universal strand of civilization as globalization has been instrumental to the singular European construction of lopsided visions of 'one world.' Whenever we say 'global,' this peculiar vision still lurks behind it. In the colonial and postcolonial worlds, non-state patterns of solidarity have often been able to negotiate their alternate insertion into the Westphalian system, but their chances have generally improved with the weakening of both the fiscal autonomy of the nation-state and its iconic self-legitimization via orchestrated rituals of domestic and international politics. The contemporary reopening of the definition of civility, and the possibility with it to show the importance of hitherto marginal practices often linked to religious traditions, is potentially favored by the erosion of the nation-state as an organic socio-political body, first as reflected by Leviathan, then by the idea of democratic collective autonomy, or simply *demos*. The *demos*, originating from ancient Athenian democracy, happened to become the "people" of constitutional preambles, which were supposed to wrest sovereignty out of the hands of the Leviathan. In this way the people's sovereignty and the rule by the *demos*, namely (now modern) democracy, were legitimized and enshrined in constitutional charters.

In the colonial and postcolonial eras this post-Westphalian leitmotiv consisting in the shift from absolutism to democracy has also animated movements and groups explicitly invoking Islamic frameworks of solidarity and governance (and often dubbed from the late 1970s, succinctly yet simplistically, as 'Islamists'). Such groups have often sought to benefit from the positive trade-offs between nationalism and transnationalism without having to subscribe to normative standards and collective identities that do not secure the cohesion of their constituencies, nor the preservation of inherited notions of good life. Yet as we have seen in the previous chapters, the long-term transregional deployment of the Islamic ecumene precedes the Western-centered globalization initiated by colonialism. The historic integrity of the Islamic ecumene was not completely destroyed by Western colonial hegemony and by the subsequent postcolonial states. These imitated, though not organically, the Westphalian framework of sovereignty and solidarity enveloping the state-society complex, mostly through recourse to one, often authoritarian, variant from within the package of developmental ideologies. These loosely covered the idea of people's sovereignty within socio-economic fabrics that had been subject to colonial dependence, if not outright depredation.

In what is now the 'Muslim world,' the postcolonial successor to the Islamic ecumene, state elites, often of military origin, have in most cases kept Islamist groups at bay through various repressive measures (as, for example, in Turkey and Indonesia until the late 1990s, in Tunisia until 2011, and in Egypt until the present day), and have in some other cases intermittently coopted the most docile among those groups (e.g. in Morocco and Jordan). Concomitantly, they have selectively borrowed bits and pieces of their visions (see, for example, the Salafi leanings of the postcoup Egyptian president al-Sisi). The postcolonial twist and fate of what Hodgson dubbed "the *shar'i* opposition" (i.e. oriented to Islamic normativity, the *shari'a*) to established powers could not be fully normalized within this pseudo-Westphalian mix of developmentalism and authoritarianism. Neither can all movements attempting to revive Islamic normativity and therefore called Islamist be suspected wholesale and by default of representing nothing more than a docile adaptation to neoliberal frameworks. Hodgson reminds us that the precolonial antecedents to an Islamic transnational mobilization were not restricted to big traders and elite scholars but also included more autonomous, lower-ranking scholars, Sufis, and pilgrims. In the post-colonial era this precedent legitimizes a plural and potentially democratic rearticulation of both solidarity and governance across the divide too often artificially constructed between secular and Islamist forces. The factors that periodically prevent the crossing of this divide should be discussed in a future volume.

The inherent ambivalence of the purported yet impossible universality of Western-style, modern, state-bound civility should be read alongside the old, rather aseptic metaphor of the world as a 'global village.' Precisely because it has been overused and abused, this image has the advantage of revealing a contradictory significance of, simultaneously, the civilizing process and globalization. The 'village' metaphor points out that the civi-lizing process, in its primary meaning of making individuals and groups fit for city life (as clearly distinct from the community life of rural villages), reflects a crucial tension. It is the tension between globalization, which supposedly expands the connective and associational bonds far beyond the geographically constrained and legally protected space of the city, and the more localized processes consisting in the making and spreading of organized life. Such processes necessarily emerge from communal, neigh-borhood, and affinity ties, especially where the historic umbrella of a rule of law warranting the respect of contractual relationships is absent or weak. On the other hand, however, the civilizing process as the continual engine of the inevitably shared, global modern condition remains to be accounted for from every culturally specific civilizational locale. This means that the civilizing process, whatever its global import, must have tangible underpinnings in a wide variety of localized patterns of civility. As a consequence, the Westphalian idea of monopolizing violence and matching it with inherited forms of social autonomy imposes an improbable homogenizing straitjacket on the inevitable diversity of the global civilizing process, which works differentially and unevenly with regard to the modern unfolding of states and capitalist economies.

In this sense, the civilizing process and the consequent emergence of patterns of civility, if applied to a variety of civilizational environments, no longer appears as a one-way, cumulative and teleological process of singularization of power, i.e. as a one-directional engine for enshrining power into the singular authority of a fully legitimized ruler, be it autocratic or democratic. The process produces a certain habitus that first grows up in determined settings if not within closed arenas (prototypically, the royal court), and then spreads out in unequal yet ultimately encompassing (and therefore potentially democratizing) ways. Civility is a modality of the *ego-alter* relation that modulates contiguity and distance, the sharing of (material or immaterial) values. As stressed by Arpad Szakolczai (2011), in spite of the fact that the most visible aspects of civility seem to be limited to formalisms, mannerisms, and etiquette, it also requires a degree of grace in mastering the codes.

The resulting process is then open-ended not just in terms of the degree of civility achieved but also of its type and patterns. It ends up depending to a much larger extent than admitted by Elias on the dynamics of development and contestation of the shared idioms provided by religious and cultural traditions, which usually associate grace and beauty in social relations to (strictly or largely) religious values, along with their contestations and transformations (Arnason 1997: 53–4; 362). For example, grace and its transmission is involved both in the social mode represented by *tasawwuf* (Sufism) and in the exemplary narratives of *hadith*. These are two of the Islamic meta-institutional matrices that we have first identified in the Introduction and in Chapter 1, and then seen at work in the diversified trajectories of the Islamic ecumene in the historical chapters of the volume. Opening up Elias' view of the civilizing process to crossfertilizations actually helps to show how the counterpart to the outer manners within civility is not an inner forum of morality as purported by several champions of post-Reformation Enlightenment (from Hutcheson to Kant) but graceful habits which are formed through the working of cultural, educational, and religious traditions. As we have seen in this volume, in the Islamic case a more 'secular' match to religiously defined grace (as within the perimeter of Islamic normativity) has been the courtly culture of *adab*, which was however decisive in defining standards of beauty. Such standards by necessity provided orientation to grace as practiced. Islamic patterns of civility owed much to this original combination of religious normativity and courtly aesthetics.

As also adumbrated by Ikegami in her choice of wording and examples to define civility, the civilizing process, and the social relevance of the formation and transformation of patterns of civility understood as the outcome of the process, do not need to be necessarily seen, as by Elias, as a trickle-down mechanism integrating wider sectors of society (starting with the emerging bourgeoisie) into the culture of the elites. Therefore it is not necessarily a process progressively expanding into a state formation. As the outcome of a variety of formulas of the knowledge–power equation, civility is no longer a mere function of a one-sided evolutionary trajectory of state modernization but a relatively open modality of the social bond that can be variably associated with state power and legal regulation. Civility as a prism for taming violence by putting aside the differences that may unleash conflict might appear at first sight as a ruse of power. Yet in a broadened cross-civilizational view, knowledge keeps a particularly strong leverage on power by mediating between it and largely autonomous forms of social organization, like those associated with Sufism and more in general with the organizational matrix of the brotherhood. This, as we saw, is a crucial locus of sociability and civility that can, under given circumstances, contribute to a state-building process and, in contemporary settings, feed into waves of transnational mobility and migration.

The Sufi example highlights how the notion of civility needs to cover the dynamics of social interaction that cannot be caged within localized institutional constraints since they tend to spill over into wider translocal, even trans-social, types of connectedness. The organized Sufism originating and thriving in the Middle Periods, while highly constructive of the social bond, cannot be reduced to a localized pattern of interaction. The matrix of brotherhood plays a role in transcending the initial localization of the bond and can even exemplify broader patterns of civility crossing conventionally localized, national, and societal borders, including canonized modes of self-construction enshrined in modern educational models, which often favor a strict functionalization of the self for the building of collective identities and solidarities. Understood through the prism of its translocal potential, civility is an obvious key to overcoming a socio-centric approach modeled on the nation-state. This is the 'methodological nationalism' that has dominated the social sciences since their inception (be it declined functionally as by the sociologists Parsons and Luhmann or normative-constitutionally, as by the social philosopher Habermas). Civility is thus not merely a dystopian ghost of the fading civilizing mission of the West but a transversal tool to better appreciate civilizational, intercivilizational, and transcultural dynamics.

In this regard, one should consider that Johann Arnason's work, while integrating Elias' perspective into a global civilizational analysis, has tended to fold the cultural traditions innervating civility into a hermeneutic plane of exploration. Religious traditions themselves have been thus integrated into civilizational analysis as the interpretive and evaluative prisms supporting and enabling human agency. One of the main reasons why Arnason leaned on this hermeneutic side of culture was probably to counter Eisenstadt's contrary tendency to anchor culture on the functionalist side, coherently with his previous allegiance to modernization theory (Adams, Smith, and Vlahov 2011). I would be tempted to use here the metaphor of a 'quantic' reorientation of the approach to civility, which in analogy to the quantic turn in theoretical physics and its uncertainty principle accepts the basic indeterminacy of action's degree of dependence on a protean and potentially ubiquitous force that a host of scholars still define as 'culture.' All branches of sociology directly or indirectly inspired by Weber have kept a degree of determinacy of action through culture, however defined. My suggested move beyond culture might help transcend any residual culturalist temptation within the sociology of Islam bent on reducing the field to the application of standard methodologies of the sociology of religion to Islamic contexts or to 'Muslim actors' on the basis of the consideration of Islamic 'cultural determinants' (even with all due adaptations, e.g. by appreciating that Islam is not just religion in a modern, Christian, or post-Christian sense). This move might prove effective to the extent that culture can be downsized to a rather weak, intermediate plane determining, through the influence of forms and codes, the spectrum (or superposition) of possible actions within a given field. In this optic, each discrete action is inescapably determinable only ex post: most specifically (and here too one can retrieve a metaphorical analogy with the quantum turn in physics), only after it has been observed. Making civility the outcome (almost the valve of escape) of the knowledge–power 'quantic' indeterminacies and disturbances that constitute the social bond (in all its fragility) can prove to be useful for practicing the sociology of Islam in a transcultural perspective.

This suggestion works toward helping overcome the 20th-century's dichotomy between functionalism and culturalism in sociology and the social sciences at large. It should leave the determination of notions of agency, interpretation, and intentionality out of the general theory, and consign them to the analysis of given fields of elaboration on knowledge within specific cultural traditions, as well as to the exploration of their connections. It is knowledge itself, within a given cultural or religious tradition, which determines the inherent indeterminacies at play within discrete, 'quantic' fields of social power. A social field can no longer be imagined as a Newtonian homogeneous space responding to comprehensive laws. The knowledge factor within a given tradition can determine action through the discrete dispositions, and corresponding moves, possessed by the actors and inspired by the underlying traditions. All we can do is try to filter out the perspective, or perspectives, resulting from the articulation of knowledge by the plurality of actors of a given social field or social nexus, like Hodgson's Islamdom.

In spite of all suggested revisions and corrective manœuvers, a diluted Weberian perspective and the corresponding ad hoc semi-orientalization of Islam continue to impair a plural articulation of civilizational analysis. The shift of perspectives that I have proposed is, however, not quite of a 'Copernican revolution,' as it might have seemed by the extent to which I argue that Weber's "son of the modern European cultural world" (Weber 1986 [1920]: 1) is no longer at the center of the civilizational universe. The shift does not recenter the perspective on a new privileged observer but rather dispels the illusion of a homogeneous universe and opens up to a multiverse. Here, however (to spell out the astrophysical metaphor), not just galaxies and stars but also black holes determine the dislocation of civilizational matter. However, black holes, far from representing just odd discontinuities or perilous decays of matter, are ultimately the units that guard the constitutive codes of the multiverse.

Making this latter metaphor more explicit, Islam could be seen not as a singular civilizational constellation but as a supermassive civilizational black hole, which, located at the center of a galaxy, absorbed and concealed a vast array of surrounding civilizational matter, thus desingularizing their components through the whirlpool of matter but also recreating a basically immaterial singularity at its own internal bottom. In parallel, one should raise the question of whether the making of Islam as a singular civilization,

Oriental or otherwise, by European Orientalists and comparative scholars of 'world religions' (or, at least, its semitization, in parallel with the hellenization of Christianity; Masuzawa 2005: 179–206), was itself a reflex of the rise to global hegemony of the son of the modern European civilization. This question could collaterally help bring thirty years of suggestive, yet largely inconclusive, 'Orientalism debate' into sharper focus. The main implication is that the matter, or, if you prefer, the quantum fields of civilizational analysis, which we can conceptualize around two main parameters, like knowledge and power, are plausible objects of enquiry, while its resulting units, i.e. 'civilizations,' are much more elusive as objects per se, except as contingent constellations reflected by hegemonic discourse. In this sense, while Islam in the precolonial era (yet well into early modernity) could still be interpreted as a desingularizing force, the mother of all singularities is given by the civilizational acceleration and condensation represented by Western Christendom's transitioning into modernity. This singularity only makes sense from the observational vantage point and hegemonic position of Weber's son of Western civilization. From this perspective, the myth of the clash of civilizations is the master narrative disguising this singularity and covering an argument according to which the lack of an endogenesis of modern institutions in the Islamic world is explained in terms of a civilizational deficit (either because of defective, dark matter or of poor acceleration).

This supposed Islamic shortfall allegedly consists in the purported incapacity of renewal of the best assets within the heritage administered by Muslim cultural elites. The argument ultimately stresses a corresponding failure by Muslim political elites to institutionalize patterns of civility and modern governance in the Westphalian framework of a nation-state. This argument has been echoed by several commentaries on the deep roots of the phenomenon of the rise of the Islamic State (IS) in territories corresponding to post mandate Iraq and Syria. The discourse legitimizing the mandates after World War I assumed that the European colonial powers were entrusted with the administration of provinces of the dismantled, former Muslim empire of the West (the Ottoman Empire), already dubbed 'the sick man of Europe,' until solid national elites were to be formed and able to take over. The follow-up discourse, which has been ongoing for more than one century, grappled with the fact that this supposed maturity never came, as finally, allegedly proven by the rise of the IS. The chain of Western colonial and neocolonial interventions should be correspondingly seen— so the storyline goes—as part of the attempted solution incarnate in the mandates and their postcolonial successor states. The discourse excluded the possibility that the purported solution (diagnosing the Ottoman Empire as irredeemably sick and envisioning the cure of the mandates) was actually the ever more burning problem, a real ticking bomb that finally exploded, with no solution in sight within the parameters of the Westphalian system. Yet the ongoing argument from within this system purported (and continues to do so in more politically correct, though increasingly hesitant, tones) that the roots of the problem were to be found within the culture (including, if not mainly, the political culture) of the fading empire, with Islam at its center, and now of its successor states (failed or otherwise) and societies.

As an essential conceptual hub of this discourse, the capacity of sociocultural self-renewal itself was de facto considered a Western monopoly. This argument was based on the view that only in the West did the subject become autonomous in a way that satisfied the requirements of governance within first the absolutist, then the liberal, and at the latest stage democratic, nation-states (von Grunebaum 1964). The obsessive refrain on the civilizational deficit of Islam, which is presupposed in the myth of the clash of civilizations (Bottici and Challand 2010), is therefore the necessary flipside of the affirmation of a unique Western cultural singularity. This uniqueness is seen as rooted in the capacity of Western hegemony to power up the cultural factors presupposed by modernity through a model of subjectivity essentially bent on self-renewal and institutional change. This step occurs through bending the knowledge–power equation entirely in terms of the self-empowerment of modern Western man. This is no longer the carrier of a specific culture or tradition but rather the harbinger of a global civilizing mission. The basic flaw in the argument consisted in the fact that in order to capture the complexity of an accelerating universe dependent on quantum fields, one still relied on a Newtonian conception of homogeneous space and uniform laws: in this case, the laws of the Westphalian system.

From Islamic Exceptionalism to a Plural Islamic Perspective

It is the sociology of Islam that, relying on critical and theoretically informed historical scholarship like Hodgson's, helps not only to highlight the dynamism of the Islamic ecumene but also, and in the same move, to expose the aporias of the argument on the cultural superiority of such an allegedly 'postcultural' West. This move was more than adumbrated by Hodgson, who was uniquely well positioned to pay an adequate tribute to the originality of Islam's venture into human history. He laid the seeds for such a shift of perspectives not as a simple anti-orientalist provocation but as the opening of a hitherto unexplored critical angle on the world-historical development of global civility. This step has the potential to help transcend the comparative approach itself to religions and civilizations. As maintained by Edmund Burke III, "Marshall Hodgson clearly saw that Islamic history was a strategic point from which to undertake a critique of the discourse on Western civilization" (Burke III 1993: xv). But even this assessment is somewhat reductive, as the potential of Hodgson's approach is not just one of critique but of rethinking basic paradigms. This strategy addressed not only the mutual positioning of Europe and the Muslim world but also helped explain how the Islamic trajectory can provide an exceptionally precious perspective on how global history itself is charted and innervated. A coordinated investment into such an Islamic perspective has helped build on the strengths of Hodgson's work in the light of the more than forty years of scholarship that have lapsed since his premature death. Following the tracks of Hodgson's meticulous and ingenious, yet unfinished, work on Islam (see Arnason 2006), we have encountered his Islamdom not as a mirror-like reflection of Christendom but as a quite transcivilizational type of ecumene (Salvatore 2010). This view of an Islamic transcivilizational ecumene is a double-edged sword for civilizational analysis: on the one hand it can provide the parameters of what a civilizational formation is in terms of the knowledge–power equation better than any Weberian kind of Western exceptionalism (however revised or made politically correct); on the other it is inevitably bound to transcend the notion itself of a civilizational formation, so restituting the inherent 'quantic' fluidity of the underlying equation and the inevitable contingency of any civilizational crystallization.

Hodgson's approach entailed a sustained criticism of the provincialism of Western orientalist views on Islam. Such views privileged not only the Mediterranean projection of Islamdom, most notably because of the long-drawn-out rivalry between the emerging powers of Western Christendom and the Ottoman Empire but also the resulting perception by the former of an almost existential 'Turkish threat', which was so central to the fears of early modern Europe and its emerging print-based public spheres. These orientalist views also revolved incessantly on Islam's Arabian origin. The result was to disregard the key fact that, in the unfolding of a dynamic trajectory of development of Islam as a transcivilizational ecumene and of corresponding modes of civility, and quite from the beginning, it was not just Islam's expansive flourishing but also its intrinsic vitality that presupposed intense crosscultural borrowings with other civilizational realms (Hodgson 1993: 104). It is also important to add, following Hodgson, that the implications of these wider Afro-Eurasian entanglements became ever more visible after Islam's inception and fully transparent in the postcaliphal era. So rather than the Hijaz, the cradle of Islam should be seen as the wider 'Nile-to-Oxus region.' In the words of Hodgson: "when Islam was announced there, the new doctrine did not seem strange" (Hodgson 1993: 105). This is because it was quite well aligned with the aspirations earlier developed across what Hodgson identified as the Irano-Semitic civilizational realm.

Since this potential only came to full fruition in the postcaliphal, postclassic era, a characterization of Islam as a transcivilizational ecumene (which I consider a Hodgsonian concept, though he never used this exact wording) has the advantage of allowing us to bypass all debates and polemics on the foggy origins of Islam and the process of consecration of Muhammad as the last prophet. On a civilizational level, that beginning only counts for legitimizing the later formation of a repertoire of mildly institutional patterns of regulation of a vast array of social arrangements and modes of connectedness and communication, from educational dynamics through 'spiritual' character-training to commercial relations. Yet such patterns only crystallized (all by keeping a transformative dynamics) during the epoch that Hodgson called the Middle Periods of Islamic history, stretching from the 10th to the 15th centuries CE. In this volume I have explored in particular three main meta-institutional matrices that bundled together patterns of civility: the *waqf* ("pious endowment"), the *tariqa* (literally "way," "brotherhood") of Sufism, and the set of normative ideals and practices which gradually, and fully by the Earlier Middle Period, were subsumed under the cover idea of *shari'a* via the authentication of sayings of Muhammad and his companions (*hadith*).

Undoubtedly the *hadith*, which is the body of exemplary discourse underlying Islamic normativity, is understood as a reflection of the virtues of Muhammad and his pristine community, which provided the exemplary model to the later expanding ecumene in the form of Muhammad's *sunna*. But the body of *hadith* was built over time through complex and sophisticated procedures that put a premium on participation and competition among the carriers of a variety of pious and often also less-than-pious and/or mundane concerns. The process involved a variety of groups, schools, and milieus sharing in this expanding knowledge field (Melchert 2002). As paradoxical as it may sound, *hadith*, which became a performative more than a merely normative corpus, worked as a crucial vector for transcivilizational fertilization, by helping Muslim actors interface with other traditions. This process was facilitated by the extent to which the methodologies of *hadith* selection and certification relied on a networked culture of circulation (Şentürk 2005) and unfolded as a genre of formalized conversation and expressivity (Aishima 2011: 208–68). Such a method of production and dissemination of *hadith* can even be taken as the exemplary foil of Islam's overall venture. The *hadith* corpus developed the integral charisma of Muhammad in ways that make the historic secular question— which arose in the European Westphalian context—of a separation of religion from the body politic little suited to explain Islam's own dynamics of inner unfolding and differentiation. This was to become a European, early modern problem due to the unprecedented virulence of the Wars of Religion and the way powerful state actors therein constructed religion as a separate force, only to instrumentalize it politically to unprecedented levels (see Salvatore 2013). The rich development and wide range of application of *hadith*, which in the long term shunned a centralized canonization and use restriction, promoted the building of expansive patterns of connectedness. Here religious practice originating from the prophetic example provided the source of a locally differentiated, yet translocally shared, mildly normative idiom, while never entirely coinciding with that idiom. We have here a process of differentiation of codes both *within* and *from* religion, more than a differentiation *of* religion as an altogether separate field of human activity characterized by 'belief.' The latter, as just stressed, originated in early modern Europe through the agency of sovereign states placing strict limits on the intersubjective dimensions of religious practice and sociability.

Particularly the geographic centrality of Islamdom within the Afro-Eurasian landmass was matched by a sense of unique cultural salience. Hodgson often liked to see this relevance as originating from what he saw as a "cultural pressure" determining a mild level of homogenization of normative idioms over long distances in the wider civilizational area. The pressure to create such a homogenization remained steadfast in spite of a steady centrifugal push working against a rigorous territorialization of governance and control. Such a communicative success of Islamic idioms relied on a unique mix of what Hodgson saw as a quite apolitical cosmopolitanism and a highly social egalitarianism (Hodgson 1993: 97). This impetus could even extend into a sort of populism *ante litteram* (a term used by Hodgson in the 1960s, without the negative connotations it acquired more recently) offsetting the absence of a permanent legitimization of a fully sovereign, charismatic type of state of the kind that developed in Western Europe as a successor to the fragile medieval paradigm of the *respublica christiana* (see Chapter 4).

These populist premises configured a kind of super-*shari'a*, i.e. a more broadly civil, meta-normative benchmark rather than a strictly normative set of applicable rules. This standard often pivoted upon a value that several schools of jurisprudence articulated through rather flexible visions of the "common good" (*maslaha*) and that was articulated by integrating a diverse range of locally variable customary norms. This combined meta-normative approach and flexible articulation of discrete rules interacted (and sometimes clashed) with a more strictly legalistic view of normative sources, first of all, the Qur'an and *hadith*. The latter phenomenon, however, was most often a token of the identity and power of specific sectors of the *'ulama'* class, their social moorings, and their educational mandate, more than a standard imposing rigid parameters of normative regulations. The intrinsic limit to the rigidification of norms originated from the necessity itself to make the scholarly knowledge of the *shari'a* porous to popular practice. In other words, excesses in the self-privileging of the positions of power of the *'ulama'* through the medium of their normative knowledge constantly risked making this knowledge sterile as a source of power by losing touch with the concerns and grievances expressed through popular forms of knowledge and related practices. These often reflected patriarchal structures but also expressed critiques of unjustified and exploitative hierarchies. The posturing of the *'ulama'* as the guardians of the norms was successfully challenged during the Middle Periods, when among the commoners who could gain access to literacy a desire to share in the active consumption, if not in the production, of knowledge arose and made itself felt. Both Islamic normativity and its flipside in the form of millennial expectations frequently encouraged the manifestation of popular desires for justice. What Hodgson intended by "populist" points to a capacity—indeed, a necessity—among the main producers of knowledge to keep a living nexus with such popular practices and aspirations.

This is why the potential strength of the long-term expansive pressure delineated by Hodgson with regard to the Islamic ecumene could be interpreted as a 'multiversal' sublimation of the more identity-based tendencies of Islamic normativity (its legal-moral code proper, the kernel of what was only gradually identified as the divine norm or the *shari'a*). This strength resulted from a magnification of the power of ethical prophecy that had characterized the Irano-Semitic civilizational realm from earlier epochs (i.e. from the onset of axial transformations). Even if little explored, I would hypothesize that the long-term combination of homogenizing and pluralizing tendencies at the normative level lay in the mutual interfacing of patterns of imitation of prophetic virtue (via *hadith*) and attempts of accommodation and construction of locally acknowledged balances of social forces (via practices inspired by *maslaha* and the role played by customary law). An excess of emphasis on *maslaha*, which would become a favorite weapon of several modern reformers, was however shunned, as it would have entailed the risk of providing a blank check for power holders and their arbitrary decisions. This would have been detrimental to the prerogatives of the carriers of knowledge, thus putting in jeopardy the fragile equilibrium underlying the knowledge–power equation.

The European Orientalists' privileged focus on Islam's origin, quite neatly mirrored by some brands of 20th-century and contemporary Islamic fundamentalists, looks past the key issue discussed here. It ignores the fact that while the Islamic integration of the Nile-to-Oxus region could occur on the basis of patterns of relative continuities with the regional traditions, the subsequent leaps into the heartland of Sanskritic and Hellenic civilizational circles, which turned the core of Islamdom into a much wider Balkans-to-Bengal ecumene, entailed a more genuine transcivilizational integration. This process, in turn, presented the risk of a serious erosion of the normative kernel of the civilizational glue. Yet this kernel did not disintegrate. It is through the process of expansion which preserved such a kernel that the originality and impetus of Islam's soft institutionalized toolkit of legal means and moral codes (going well beyond conventional views of the *shari'a*) came to full fruition (see Chapters 2, 3, and 4). On the other hand, this malleable normative framework also showed its limits as a long-term integrative solution exposed to ever new tests and challenges in different epochs and locales (see Chapters 5 and 6). Yet the issue was never, as we saw, Islam's relation to modernity per se.

The Islam/Islamdom complex proved itself capable of simultaneously drawing from, or being attracted by, such distant repertoires as Roman law, Indic mysticism and charisma, Central Asian (therefore non-Arab) codes and practices of nomadic rulership, and more ancestral, non-axial rituals based on mobile equilibriums between patriarchal and matriarchal elements (to which we should also add, to a quantitatively minor yet strikingly significant extent, Sinitic patterns of cosmic and moral order). From a phase of culmination of this capacity reached in the Later Middle Period, it could only be subject to erosion, which precipitated into a crisis with the emergence of a powerful catalyst such as the overwhelming colonial challenge of Western Christendom. This power imposed itself in the guise of partly competing, partly coordinating, modern Westphalian state formations increasingly engaged in a continental and colonial race linking the old Afro-Eurasian landmass with the New World of the Western hemisphere. Yet there was nothing intrinsically decaying in the multileveled and entropic expansion of the Islamic ecumene, nothing that condemned it to a certain collapse.

The knowledge–power equation of the Middle Periods, which the new, early modern configuration of centralized Muslim empires did not entirely neutralize, showed an astounding degree of fluidity. Yet surprisingly, perhaps, it also set the highest standard of mutual permutability between knowledge and power ever reached for Afro-Eurasian civilizational integration. As a result of our sociological and historical exploration, we cannot consider as normal (and normative) a type of civility that can only bind knowledge and power via cultured habitus according to specific recipes, like the formulas enshrined in Elias' yet Eurocentric view of the civilizing process. These formulas only stand out for being conducive to the degree of corporate centralization of governance that bestows a sacral aura on the Westphalian state. The alchemy of knowledge and power that synthesizes civility may shun such a high threshold of formal institutionalization, corporate legitimization, and corresponding sacralization. In this volume I have endeavored to show how an Islamic perspective can reorient the Eliasian idea of the civilizing process. This perspective provides insights into the interplay between the civilizing process and the modes through which religious traditions innervate modern patterns of civility. Through the sociology of Islam, a plural Islamic perspective gains original contours reflecting the search for a type of modernity that is eccentric with regard to the mono-civilizational axis of the Western-led, global civilizing process. Through its decentered character, this perspective has helped us better grasp the diversity, contestability, and, to a certain extent, malleability of the 'ghost' of global civility.

References

Adams, Suzi, Karl E. Smith, and George Vlahov. 2011. "Introduction: Arnason's Social Theory." *European Journal of Social Theory*, 14/1: 3–8.

Aishima, Hatsuki. 2011. *The Production and Consumption of Islamic Knowledge in Contemporary Egypt: The Revival of the Intellectual Legacy of 'Abd al-Halim Mahmud (1910–78)*. PhD thesis, Faculty of Oriental Studies, University of Oxford.

Arnason, Johann P. 1997. *Social Theory and Japanese Experience: The Dual Civilization*. London: Kegan Paul International.

Arnason, Johann P. 2003. *Civilisations in Dispute: Historical Questions and Theoretical Traditions*. Leiden: Brill.

Arnason, Johann P. 2006. "Marshall Hodgson's Civilizational Analysis of Islam: Theoretical and Comparative Perspectives." In *Islam in Process: Historical and Civilizational Perspectives*, edited by Johann P. Arnason, Armando Salvatore, and Georg Stauth, 23–47. Bielefeld: Transcript; New Brunswick, NJ: Transaction (*Yearbook of the Sociology of Islam* VII).

Bamyeh, Mohammed A. 2000. *The Ends of Globalization*. University of Minnesota Press.

Bottici, Chiara and Benoit Challand. 2010. *The Myth of the Clash of Civilizations*. London: Routledge.

Boyd, Richard. 2006. "The Value of Civility." *Urban Studies*, 43/5–6: 863–78.

Burke, Edmund III. 1993. "Introduction: Marshall G.S. Hodgson and World History." In *Rethinking World History: Essays on Europe, Islam and World History*, edited, with Introduction and Conclusion, by Edmund Burke III. Cambridge: Cambridge University Press.

Cohen, Mark R. 2006. "Geniza for Islamicists, Islamic Geniza, and the 'New Cairo Geniza'." *Harvard Middle Eastern and Islamic Review*, 7: 129–145.

Davetian, Benet. 2009. *Civility: A Cultural History*. Toronto: University of Toronto Press.

Duara, Prasenjit. 2015. *The Crisis of Global Modernity: Asian Traditions and a Sustainable Future*. Cambridge: Cambridge University Press.

Eisenstadt, Shmuel N. 1998. "The Construction of Collective Identities. Some Analytical and Comparative Indications." *European Journal of Social Theory*, 1/2: 229–54.

Elias, Norbert. 1983 [1969]. *The Court Society*, translated by Edmund Jephcott. Oxford: Blackwell.

Elias, Norbert. 2000 [1939; 1968]. *The Civilizing Process*. Oxford: Blackwell.

Foucault, Michel. 2007. *Security, Territory, Population: Lectures at the Collège de France, 1977–1978*, translated by Graham Burchell. New York & Basingstoke: Palgrave Macmillan.

Hodgson, Marshall G.S. 1993. *Rethinking World History: Essays on Europe, Islam and World History*, edited, with Introduction and Conclusion, by Edmund Burke III. Cambridge: Cambridge University Press.

Hofheinz, Albrecht. 1992–93. "Der Scheich im Über-Ich oder Haben Muslime ein Gewissen?" *Wuqûf*, 7–8: 461–81.

Hofheinz, Albrecht. 1996. *Internalising Islam: Shaykh Muḥammad Majdhūb, Scriptural Islam, and Local Context in the Early Nineteenth Century Sudan*. PhD thesis, University of Bergen.

Huntington, Samuel P. 1996. *The Clash of Civilizations and the Remaking of World Order*. New York: Simon and Schuster.

Ikegami, Eiko. 2005. *Bonds of Civility: Aesthetic Networks and the Political Origins of Japanese Culture*. Cambridge: Cambridge University Press.

Masuzawa, Tomoko. 2005. *The Invention of World Religions: Or How European Universalism Was Preserved in the Language Pluralism*. Chicago: University of Chicago Press.

McNeill, William H. 1983. *The Pursuit of Power*. Chicago: University of Chicago Press.

Melchert, Christopher. 2002. "The Piety of the Hadith Folk." *International Journal of Middle East Studies*, 34/3: 425–39.

Mitchell, Timothy. 1991 [1988]. *Colonising Egypt*. Berkeley, CA: University of California Press.

Salvatore, Armando. 2007. *The Public Sphere: Liberal Modernity, Catholicism, and Islam*. New York: Palgrave Macmillan.

Salvatore, Armando. 2010. "Transnational Islam in a Post-Westphalian World: Connectedness vs. Sovereignty." In *World Religions and Multiculturalism: A Dialectic Relation*, edited by Eliezer Ben-Rafael and Yitzhak Sternberg, 145–57. Leiden: Brill.

Salvatore, Armando. 2011. "Civility: Between Disciplined Interaction and Local/Translocal Connectedness." *Third World Quarterly*, 32/5: 807–25.

Salvatore, Armando. 2013. "Beyond the Political Mythology of the Westphalian Order? Religion, Communicative Action, and the Transnationalization of the Public Sphere." In *Rethinking the Public Sphere through Transnationalizing Processes: Europe and Beyond*, edited by Armando Salvatore, Oliver Schmidtke, and Hans-Jörg Trenz, 91–106. Basingstoke: Palgrave.

Şentürk, Recep. 2005. *Narrative Social Structure: Anatomy of the Hadith Transmission Network, 610–1505*. Stanford, CA: Stanford University Press.

Stauth, Georg. 1993. *Islam und Westlicher Rationalismus: Der Beitrag des Orientalismus zur Entstehung der Soziologie*. Frankfurt und New York: Campus.

Stauth, Georg and Bryan S. Turner. 1988. *Nietzsche's Dance: Resentment, Reciprocity and Resistance in Social Life*. Oxford: Blackwell.

Stauth, Georg and Sami Zubaida, eds. 1987. *Mass Culture, Popular Culture, and Social Life in the Middle East*. Frankfurt am Main: Campus/Boulder, CO: Westview.

Szakolczai, Arpad. 1998. *Max Weber and Michel Foucault: Parallel Life-works*. London: Routledge.

Szakolczai, Arpad. 2000. *Reflexive Historical Sociology*. London and New York: Routledge.

Szakolczai, Arpad. 2011. "Civilizing Processes and Accelerating Spirals: The Dynamics of Social Processes, after Elias." *CAMBIO. Rivista sulle trasformazioni sociali*, 1/2: 177–84.

Vico, Giambattista. 1999 [1744]. *New Science: Principles of the New Science Concerning the Common Nature of the Nations*, 3rd ed., translated by David Marsh. London: Penguin.

Von Grunebaum, Gustave E. 1964. *Modern Islam: The Search for Cultural Identity*. New York: Vintage.

Weber, Max. 1986 [1920]. *Gesammelte Aufsätze zur Religionssoziologie*, I. Tübingen: J.C.B. Mohr (Paul Siebeck).

Žižek, Slavoj. 2010. *Living in the End Times*. London: Verso.

CONCLUSION

Overcoming Eurocentric Views: Religion and Civility within Islam/Islamdom

In this volume, I have provided an analysis of how the sociology of Islam as a field and as a project needs to investigate—in a comparative framework enriched by views of entanglements and dense interactions with other civilizational realms—the distinctive Islamic approach to building patterns of life conduct and sociability that can be subsumed under the rubric of 'civility.' This process does not occur in isolation from highly variable and often flexible institutions of governance. However, specific investigations of the level of governance and of the dimension of statehood should be ideally dealt with in a follow-up, second volume. The scope of this introductory book has been to present a trajectory of developments in Islamic history and society articulating—in often original and mostly malleable ways— the civilizational equation of knowledge and power. Such developments unfolded through a variety of interactions between commoners and elites across urban, agrarian, and nomadic milieus.

The introductory tour-de-force here attempted has by necessity simplified a host of questions that will need to be explored in their many facets in future volumes. However, this summary of interim results and the accompanying inventory of research questions yet to be sketched and tackled will benefit from first summarizing some key arguments of Marshall Hodgson's *The Venture of Islam*, due to its invaluable contribution for inspiring the project of the sociology of Islam. In the light of Hodgson's work, Islam embraces a rich ensemble of religious, juridical, and literary traditions that

The Sociology of Islam: Knowledge, Power and Civility, First Edition. Armando Salvatore
© 2016 John Wiley & Sons, Ltd. Published 2016 by John Wiley & Sons, Ltd.

enlivened a steadily expanding transcivilizational commonwealth located at the very center of the Afro-Eurasian landmass (the Eastern hemisphere). Hodgson more specifically intended to show through the example of Islam that a civilizing process needs a cumulative, broadly cultural, and more specifically religious tradition on which to rely. This process is instrumental in demarcating specific ideals of life conduct and ensuring that the 'high,' lettered traditions of cultural elites are not disconnected from more popular practices. The case of Islam/Islamdom is important for showing the extent to which, while relying on knowledge, a civilization also depends on power. This is particularly evident in the process of crystallization of patterns of civility within collectivities that include key urban components and their complex interactions with the countryside. This is the case even if such urban developments involve—quite evidently within Islamic history right from its onset—an intermittent but often decisive role of nomadic groups.

On the theoretical level, my reconstruction of a feasible, open program for a sociology of Islam inspired by Hodgson, but also renewing and enriching his conceptual apparatus, has been thus far twofold. First, I have focused on the human endeavor to build, inhabit, and shape the civil world and the underlying social bonds, as they are fine-tuned to the twin need of taming violence and promoting cooperation. For this step it was useful to analytically separate two main factors, namely knowledge and power, and their respective social carriers. In this volume I have dealt in particular with the carriers of knowledge. We have seen how their interaction with the power holders produces not only distinctive institutions but also legitimate degrees of institutionalization of formal relations. Such congruous levels of institutionalization leave open a broad range of informal or semi-formal arrangements which stop short of sacralizing those institutions per se. Second, I have begun to dynamically illustrate this endeavor as a civilizing process based on patterns of what I have called 'civility,' which I considered the most relevant, certainly the most visible, outcome of the knowledge–power equation. This second conceptual vector has been merely put to initial use and will need to be deepened in future investigations.

Yet the attentive reader might still be tempted to ask: What is the final place of culture in this complex picture? Culture is notoriously a fuzzy keyword whose vagueness many sociologists have struggled to reduce if not to overcome, while too often ending up overdefining it. I have proposed to see culture as intervening in the civilizing process as a mediator between knowledge and power and therefore as a prism for habitualizing civility. On the other hand, the focus on civility can also relieve us of the need to invoke culture as an intervening variable or prism in its own right. Most important is the understanding that knowledge and power can be analytically distinguished (and mainly referred to separate sets of elites, as Axial Age theory suggests), whereas in the actual social process they are increasingly bound together. This is particularly true in societies that have faced the challenge of colonial modernity. While in general terms knowledge defines power and power presupposes knowledge, colonial modernity has manifested the disciplinary potential of bundling power and knowledge in original, potent ways which have unsettled their more traditional balance and have pivoted the equation quite firmly on its power variable.

The rich, theoretically informed approach of Marshall Hodgson has proven to be helpful particularly after it has been debated among historians, social scientists, and civilizational analysts during the last couple of decades. The discussion, which is far from over, has most crucially focused on the way cultural and religious traditions are supposed to innervate the broader civilizing process through which individuals are shaped and societies take form. Ultimately by reframing and upgrading the Hodgsonian approach through sociological arguments, this book has intended to challenge the well-entrenched paradigm of identifying Islam with Oriental despotism: a red thread running through the Western political and intellectual traditions since the 18th century and that often provides a sense of identity and exclusiveness to the West as the original and ultimate locus of democracy and accountability. Since the Enlightenment, this view of Islam has provided a convenient antithesis to modern Europe's liberal and republican politics, with its morally autonomous individuals and politically disciplined, but also conscious, citizens (Arjomand 2004b). Self-entrenched and self-serving paradigms of modern civility, resting on one-sided views of the normative ways to relate knowledge to power, have been at the root of this deep-seated perception. The comparative approach adopted by the program of the sociology of Islam and introduced in this volume, particularly if enriched by a view of transcivilizational entanglements, immunizes us against the distortions of an ever more outdated, yet resistant, Eurocentrism and contributes to building a richer analytic terrain.

This type of approach which still benefits from, yet also transcends, a comparative perspective is an important condition for allowing a more balanced study of Islamic manifestations of civility through social movements and associational life, religious discourses and institutions, governance and public scrutiny across various historical epochs: precolonial, colonial, and postcolonial. Viewed from an Islamic perspective influenced by the work of

Hodgson and aided through Arnason's appraisal of the latter, the exclusive and exemplary character of the Western civilizing process as it emerges from the oeuvre of Elias and related works might appear in a different light. This shift of perspective out of a Western axis creates new angles on the relations between Western Christendom and Islam/Islamdom before and after the irruption of modernity on the global scene. It also encourages a redefinition of modernity, an essential theme for sociology. Such a move also facilitates shedding light on the specificities of Islamic civilization as a civilization *sui generis*. The particularities of Islam/Islamdom contribute not just to pluralize the notion of civility but actually to push forward the theoretical boundaries of this concept, by putting a premium on transborder connections and crosscivilizational dynamics.

One of Hodgson's key arguments was that the dynamics of construction of the social bond intrinsic to the civilizational visions of Islam resisted the formation of a fully sovereign state and responded to egalitarian and cosmopolitan (and to some extent 'populist') presuppositions. Such presuppositions helped in specific contexts to pursue a universal sublimation of the more particularistic tendencies of Islamic normativity. This occurred thanks to Islam's capacity to magnify the power of ethical prophecy characteristic of the Irano-Semitic civilizational realm. The result is that while other civilizations entrenched their power centers and the supporting identities (also when nourished by overlapping religious teachings and spiritual paths) on specific macro-regions, Islam kept its civilizational impetus much more fluid. This was due both to the prevalence of centrifugal dynamics (before and after the era of the Mongol conquests) and the expansiveness of the normative appeal of its religious and moral idiom.

This is why the opening of an Islamic perspective right at the core of this kind of 'postcomparative' civilizational analysis has the potential to unsettle the inherited views on civilizational transformations and intercivilizational encounters. These views have too often, directly or indirectly, served the need to retroactively explain the hegemonic rise of the singular type of Western, transatlantic modernity. This hegemony offset the primacy and centrality of Islam within the Afro-Eurasian civilizational landscape and set purportedly universal benchmarks of civility. Nowadays the older Eurocentric perspective risks being revived with just tenuous adaptations and hardly any critical reflections, in order to take into account the rise of China and India as new superpowers. As suggested in the Introduction, the field of postcolonial studies seems paradoxically to confirm this centrality of the West and neglect Islam's original pattern of transcivilizational dynamics.

Our alternate perspective is not a way to replace the Western self with the Islamic other but a much more radical shift from universe to multiverse, from the homogeneity of axial space toward its subjection to 'quantic' leaps determined by a resilient, yet open-ended, civilizational mapping like the one characterizing Islam's expansive venture across various epochs.

If we acknowledge as inevitable this turbulence that questions the stability and identity of all civilizational formations, Western-biased comparative civilizational analysis is profoundly altered though not exhausted. With this recognition we face the necessity not so much of rejecting such notions as civilizations, formations, or even modernities, but rather of rewriting them from a perspective, the Islamic one, which far from being peripheral, should qualify as central, in the *longue durée*, to the global civilizing process. This centrality is primarily due to Islam's emergence at the core of the Afro-Eurasian civilizational realm in the crucial period located between the axial and the modern breakthroughs. Yet this centrality was not completely offset by Islam's subsequent, increasingly eccentric (yet close to the center), repositioning vis-à-vis the West's rise to world hegemony (Salvatore 2011a). Once we recognize the centrality of this Islamic perspective, the knowledge–power equation of civilizational analysis can yield a more truly plural, though also tensional, view on civility. Thus from such a perspective oriented to the centrality of long-term Islamic trajectories a radical singularization of power from its cultural bases (a key touchstone of the civilizing process as elucidated by Elias and other authors by reference to the modern West) appears less necessary for the survival and thriving of the cultural and religious traditions innervating the process. Such a full autonomization of power from the parameters nurtured by cultural traditions would have been rather counterproductive for building an expansive Islamic ecumene.

This process was fed by transcivilizational encounters more than by a sheer optimization of knowledge resources for a type of governance entrenched in, simultaneously, municipal and national communities like those that characterized Western Europe's trajectory into modernity. No doubt in the case of Islam/Islamdom the civilizing rationale, the engine itself of the civilizing process and the underlying formulations of the civilizational equation, both at the micro- and macro-levels, differed from that of the West (as well as, although we could not deal with it in this volume, from that of China). Particularly in Chapters 2 and 3 I provided evidence of how the Islamic perspective is rather pivoted on a translocal and multicentered type of civility. Yet in order to understand how these Islamic dynamics have been much better aligned with long-term civilizational developments of the Afro-Eurasian civilizational realm we also needed to examine what rendered eurocentrically biased the municipal view of city-centered civility that occupies a central space in Weber's sociology and more generally in the Western historic self-understanding (and self-conceit) as a superior civilization.

It remains a fact of intellectual history that Islam's historically and civilizationally eccentric positioning vis-à-vis Western-centered modernity has been the object of lopsided representations by a wide array and subsequent generations of Western orientalist, neo-orientalist, and post-orientalist scholars (see Salvatore 1997; Masud and Salvatore 2009). They have tended to misrecognize Islam's unique character as, simultaneously, a civilizational insider and outsider within global modernity. Marshall Hodgson's provocation, mentioned in the Introduction, on the diagnosis of an Islamic civilizational hegemony by a Mars visitor at the dawn of modernity well reflects the need for this shift of perspectives. It also shows how resolutely investing into an Islamic perspective inevitably induces a conceptual estrangement in the reader who is permanently exposed to Western-centered narratives. The fact that Islam continues to appear as eccentric to the hub of the global civilizing process cannot be logically inferred from characteristics of Islam's own vectors and matrices within the civilizing process, which we analyzed both historically and conceptually, but depends on the rise of the West and particularly on its transatlantic and colonial expansion. This unprecedented development on a global scale put (ever more traumatically) to rest the civilizational centrality of Islam in the Eastern hemisphere. This centrality had been a given until early modernity, wherein "the greater part of the key historic lands of citied culture … , from Athens to Benares, were under Muslim rule" (Hodgson 1993: 98).

The way out of such aporias starts by questioning the hegemonic discourse that propounds standardized, dichotomous models of normal and progressive kinds of modernity and civility resisted by stagnant traditions: as if there had been, in spite of all colonial and imperial rivalries, a basically homogeneous Western civilizing mission embracing the entire globe and facing an amorphous inertia of backward, premodern cultures. The idea of one single homogeneous conception of modernity has become increasingly untenable since the demise of modernization theory. As argued by the historical-comparative sociologist Björn Wittrock, we would be theoretically shortsighted if we were to see a high degree of institutional homogeneity even within the civilizational area that happened to be designated, ever more clearly during the modern age, as Europe. This objection certainly disproves the idea of modernity as the outcome of a multicivilizational convergence on a new, worldwide civilization erasing all cultural differences and producing homogenizing notions of knowledge, power, and civility. Nonetheless, there is some truth in the view of modernity as a global condition, regardless of the wide varieties in the articulations of the knowledge–power equation (Wittrock 2000: 58–9). Diverse patterns of modernity articulate this equation in variable ways but modernity remains nonetheless a global singularity restricting the range of variability of the equation.

Yet this singularly profiled, however globally extended, condition, no matter how deeply influenced by Western hegemony, can never be its mirror-like reflection, as if there were an overwhelming global civilization where the *telos* of every locale would be to clone a bundle of genes from the Western original stock. The globalization of a singularity is subject to sharp variations and also surprises. On the other hand, one cannot dismiss out of hand that we might be in the process of approximating something like a global civility precisely through the increasing interconnections among varieties of modernity. This might be happening in the wake of overlapping civilizing processes reflecting diverse cultural traditions and the differential way in which they are impacted by modernity as a global condition. Islam itself has been a historical vector of the globalizing influences of transborder processes of civility. Therefore we should be able to identify the main points of friction in the process of formation of global civility, including the ways in which several non-Western trajectories and forces (yet also some originating or unfolding in the West itself) make the likely outcome of the process quite different from a Western-centered cosmopolis. The principle of order of global civility cannot be universal, since the criteria of insertion of actors and groups into its turbulence are cemented by specific patterns of connectivity of the social bond more than by a renewal of the model of the *polis* on a global scale. One should carefully assess what makes such a global civility desirable and functional to hegemonic forces (nowadays no longer merely the hegemonic Western powers but also China as the rising alternate hegemon) from a modern, systemic viewpoint, on the one hand, yet subject to contestations, compromises, and civilizationally specific articulations, on the other.

From an angle that puts a premium on an Islamic perspective, global civility becomes the cipher of a social bond that cannot be reduced to the primacy of a singularized power and of the political field per se. By adopting civility as a prism not just for comparison but also for analyzing entanglements, we circumvent the Western-centered assumption of a world revolving around politics defining the arena that inherits the dynamics of the small and circumscribed, ancient, Greek *polis*. Truly, the dimension of civility in social interaction, which feeds into a theoretically informed sociology of Islam, has recently been brought to the fore due to its association with expectations of democratization processes in Eastern Europe and other regions of the world, including the Middle East, since the early 1990s. Yet the idea itself of a political development of sorts along the lines of a purported 'transition' to democracy based on the flourishing of a 'civil society' proved to be overblown, since it reflected unrealistic and to some extent hypocritical Western norms, if not outright bias (Salvatore 2011b).

A primary reference to civility as the outcome of culturally and religiously specific civilizing processes rather than as the mere renunciation of violence within a democratic civil society spares us the pain of ever and again falling back onto the uniqueness of the Western and European historical experiences, or rather of the West's lopsided self-understanding (and self-celebration). The main goal of this volume (and of the trilogy it hopes to inaugurate) has been to explore the extent to which the history and the present of an internally diverse, civilizational constellation— wherein various aspects of Islam as religion, culture, and civility play combined roles—justifies and legitimates a more comprehensive and less Western-centered view of civility. This is a civility that needs to be explored historically and hammered out conceptually, without being reduced, almost by default, to ultimately normative, well-rounded 'models' of civil society (Salvatore 2011a).

The Institutional Mold of Islamic Civility: Contractualism vs. Corporatism?

Our understanding of the sociology of Islam also requires a quite conscious and energetic process of emancipation from European philologists' obsessions with 'authentic' origins. The problematic character of this view lies not only in the mirage of authenticity, nourished by the craft itself of philologists whose professional task (and no doubt merit) is to restore a text to its purported authorial originality—by literally liberating it from what are seen as undue accretions and contaminations (which often are part and parcel of the life of a text). Questionable is also the idea itself of 'origin,' which has experienced a quite strong appeal in Western cultural history, while being subject to unacceptable reductionisms (Esposito 2012 [2010]:

45–142). A process of emancipation from a philological or civilizational trivialization of the idea of authentic origins has been nurtured, thanks to Hodgson, by the attention we have been able to pay to the cumulative trajectory of Islam's venture into world history and global society, and most notably to the expansion and entropy marked by the Middle Periods, the 11th to 15th centuries CE. Not by chance has this epoch played a crucial role in this introductory volume.

As repeatedly stressed by Hodgson, the meaning and role of the Islamic civilization as a multiverse within the wider expanse of the Afro-Eurasian ecumene should be seen as the partial exception to the hegemony of agrarian aristocracies that stretched through the two millennia that separate the axial (in the middle of the first millennium BCE) from the modern (in the middle of the second millennium CE) breakthroughs. The vigorous rise and expansive flourishing of Islam during at least one millennium and its direct or indirect impact on self-entrenched civilizations should be interpreted on the basis of its capacity to relativize the attachment to given locales and to promote a flexible, urban-nomadic, cyclical duopoly limiting (though in no way neutralizing) aristocratic power in the areas under Islam's influence. This capacity reveals the specificity of the Islamic social institutions analyzed in this volume and their dependence on movement more than on origin. This specificity is based on the operation of a type of civic and public space that had both a local rooting and a translocal projection, even when it was deployed within territorially well-demarcated political formations. The civic space hosted—but also placed incentives on actors to engage in—a continuous negotiation and interpretation of a variety of stakes. A rather overlapping consensus among rival juridical and theological schools (and Sufi orders) promoted those interests that could be considered legitimate. Out of this consensus, elaborate, variable, but also contentious, discourses on (and practices of) the common good gained ever clearer contours.

In this context, Hodgson has spoken of an Islamic moral-contractualist vs. a European formal-corporatist view of the civic space and of the underlying patterns of formation and legitimation of the social bond (Hodgson 1993: 149–58). This question both rounds up our concluding reflections here and opens up the transition to the next set of topics to be dealt with in some detail in a dedicated future volume, namely the state, the law, and the public sphere. Particularly during the epoch that witnessed the most dramatic expansion of Islam across Afro-Eurasian depths, the Middle Periods, the vitality of the Islamic ecumene was characterized by a mercantilist spirit that favored a type of contractualism that did not need a strong state. Here Hodgson's view shows that to construe an Islamic exceptionalism on the basis of a purported deficit in institutionalizing autonomous collective bodies (with the alleged damage consisting in missing the benefits of municipal autonomies and of a state-civil society symbiosis) is a dubious operation, a truly 'orientalist' one turning specific civility patterns into a civilizational deficit.

Indeed, Hodgson stressed that it was precisely thanks to the absence of municipal autonomy that the cosmopolitan tendencies of Muslim cities were particularly accentuated. Internally, the city was socially fragmented; yet social groups in one city became closely tied to their counterparts in other cities. As a result, they came to depend on the common norms of city life throughout Islamdom, which were a combination of *shari'a* (Islamic normativity) and *adab* (the rules of courtly behavior, 'courtesy,' inspired by a sense of what is proper and beautiful). The ratio of mutual influence between the two components of civility often depended on whether an urban center was more mercantile oriented or rather tied to the ruling courts and their economies. In other words, Islamic contractualism and cosmopolitanism could only thrive together because flexible urban powers needed no statutory incorporation of civility into municipal autonomies or other encompassing charters. In some key passages of *Economy and Society* that we have revisited, Weber himself suggested, albeit in a not too linear manner, that the phenomenon of incorporation is theological and sacramental or even magical before it is political and juridical (Weber 1980 [1921–22]: 420–37). Such a model of incorporation can be quite unattractive for a society culturally controlled by unconsecrated guardians of a moral law enacting rulings that facilitate contractual relationships and other transactions.

While the *waqf* and its civil law stopped short of envisioning incorporation for the reasons just explained, a neo-orientalist view took this self-immunization precisely as the mother of all deficits of the Islamic civilization, the key reason for incapacities or delays in producing the entire assortment of modern economic, social, and political institution: from entrepreneurial capitalism through NGOs to rational bureaucracies, all of which variably but securely rely on the juridical pattern of incorporation (Kuran 2001; 2011). This bias, which will be examined in more detail in the next volume dedicated to law and the state, has a textual basis in the Weberian corpus which is as crudely crystalline as it is spectacularly nourished by orientalist clichés: it is where Weber indicts the lack of incorporation reflected by the *waqf* for being the outcome of an "old-oriental" heritage and the token of Islam's taking the opposite way to the "medieval Occident" (Weber 1980 [1921–22]: 437).

Hodgson had the additional merit of not being tempted to depict such distinctively non-sacral patterns of Islamic civility in excessively harmonious (or 'holistic') terms. He rather underlined the tensions between multiple rationalities within the Islamic cultures and practices rooted in, and radiating from, West-Asian urban civilization. In particular, he focused on the not necessarily smooth interaction between individualism, contractualism, and moralism. While moralism prevents a fully formal consecration of the law and acts as an anti-corporatist shield (Arjomand 2004a: 214), Islamic law facilitates social mobility. The downside of the process is that this morally based law might appear inimical to solid institution-building. Neglecting the publicly institutionalizable dimension of the law left many areas of human interaction unmarked, particularly those where coercion and its legitimacy might have undergone a clearer specification. These gray zones of normativity could therefore become easy prey for the Caliphs or whoever else aspired to incarnate postcaliphal authority. The latter option, eagerly practiced by the 'ulama', had as a consequence to keep suspended, if not hostage, the potential (albeit rarely activated) moral judgment of the custodians of the norm over the legitimacy of those in charge of public order and governance, i.e. the rulers.

On the other hand, precisely because deprived of a public institutional foothold, contractualism needed the backup of moralism. This predicament in turn legitimized cyclical upsurges of activism and puritan movements, whose initiators felt empowered by wielding the moral norm (the recurrent 'revivalist' mode, which the colonial and modern circumstances exacerbated but did not first create). It is of crucial importance here, nonetheless, not to equate such a vulnerability with an Islamic tendency to privilege uniformity over pluralism. Hodgson stressed exactly the opposite when he wrote:

> Islam has proved consistent with quite different social forms and standards from those of the Irano-Semitic core area in the Middle Periods. Accordingly, we must see Islamicate contractualism not as the result of Islam but as largely a tendency parallel to that of Islamic moralism itself, though perhaps unrealizable without the support of Islam.
>
> (Hodgson 1993: 139)

In this sense, the moralism-contractualism doublet is largely the operational dimension of the Islam-Islamdom complex, with individualism (and the corresponding social mobility) becoming their collateral effect. The conceptual reevaluation of Sufism itself, which was also a major achievement of Hodgson, should then be placed largely within this often productive tension between moralism and contractualism and with regard to the patterns of civility it produced. The Sufi brotherhoods namely acquired prestige not just because of the authority and respectability of their masters but because they "answered perfectly to the contractualism of the sharia law" (Hodgson 1993: 117). This mechanism explains the success of the three meta-institutions we singled out following Hodgson: *waqf*, *tasawwuf*, and *hadith* (more than *shari'a* as such, as implementable law, an aspect that will be explored in the next volume). Aided by the contractual-moral tenor of civility writ Islamic, each of these meta-institutional matrices (alone or in mutual combinations) produced organizational patterns, which nonetheless never exhausted the creative potential of the religious ideas underlying those matrices. For example the *khanqah*, the material place ("lodge") that hosted the activities of a local branch of a Sufi *tariqa*, should be seen as a contingent, concrete organizational crystallization of *tasawwuf*, and the *madrasa*, similarly, appears as a crystallization of *hadith*—both institutions needing the fiscal support and legal protection of the *waqf*.

Said Arjomand has criticized Hodgson's Islamic "invariant contractual-ism" for mirroring the lack of historicity of Weber's "Western rationalism" (Arjomand 2004a: 215). However, contractualism is duly contextualized by Hodgson within the urban and mercantile nexus of Islamdom, as the examples just mentioned also show. He did not refer to contractualism in the same way Weber referred to rationalism. The US historian attempted to stress the social cohesiveness and the civic spirit of Islam/Islamdom which secured the alignment between an articulate moral idiom and its variable, concrete organizational forms, depending as they did on contingent assign-ments and agreements. It is in this dynamic and shifting context, and not as the projection of a Weberian ideal-type of sorts, that Islamic contractualism works. One might feel perplexed by how such a contractualism was posited by Hodgson but kept unrelated to the integrative politics of the Caliphate and attempts to revive its charisma, whose importance Arjomand was eager to highlight. Yet Hodgson convincingly demonstrated (and the literature on the matter produced after him largely corroborated his findings) that both Sufi brotherhoods and guilds, apart from the aborted caliphal revival of the time of al-Nasir whose importance Arjomand rightly emphasized, were more enduringly functional to the patterns of civility supported by contractualism than any reconstructed political authority could prove to be. The reasons for Weber's ahistorical construction of Occidental rationalism reside in a singular obsession with the uniqueness of the West and with its allegedly ineluctable fall into the 'iron cage' of modernity (cf. Stauth and Turner 1988; Salvatore 1997). Hodgson's move was a shift of perspectives that can also help sociology and social theory to get rid of this obsession. In this volume I have tried to follow through his bold but lucid intuition.

Whether Hodgson's soft generalizations are suitable as a theoretical contribution to the sociology of Islam should also be judged by their conditional capacity to integrate the continually resurfacing notion of tradition, a concept that Hodgson only tackled rather superficially. The concept of tradition, which might possess a religious, piety-oriented core, also embraces a much wider set of patterns of connectedness and coordination of action than those related to the individual cultivation of virtue by specific groups of 'virtuosos' (another Weberian abstraction that is not very helpful here). Originating from the work of Alasdair MacIntyre, such a complex notion of tradition shows sociological significance; I have dealt with it from an explicitly sociological perspective in an earlier work (Salvatore 2007). Tradition is still essential to the knowledge–power equation to the extent that it represents the intersubjective and communicative mechanism that produces and reproduces knowledge, including specific types of religious knowledge, and thus empowers the practitioners of the tradition as largely autonomous socio-cultural agents.

There is no need to play down the fact that specifically religious dimensions of Islamic traditions are particularly salient due to the Irano-Semitic presuppositions that put a premium on the civility-friendly potential of urban piety. This step, however, should not be performed by singling out preventively what is religious from what is not ('secular' or 'profane') in the social bond but by carefully assessing, as we attempted to do, the role of religion's meta-institutional capacities. One of the key failures of Weber's sociology of religion, which the sociology of Islam should vigorously dis-inherit, is its inability to distinguish between religion as a civilizational premise and as an institutional sphere, between meta-institution and institution. In the sociology of Islam the meta-institutional dimension is far more relevant as it emanates from the religious ideas of exemplary prophecy. These ideas were first enshrined in the *hadith* corpus, then mildly institutionalized through the incentives to do good to others (both to fellow members of the ecumene and to unmarked travelers or 'strangers') via the *waqf*, and finally crowned by the spiritual cultivation of ultimate truth through *tasawwuf*. All these three dimensions of Islamic traditions are also, and quite inevitably, intensely social, no less than they are religious. This is why the sociology of Islam is also a way to deprovincialize the sociology of religion and reproblematize the scope of religion in a perspective that embraces historical and conceptual entanglements more than sheer comparisons. Absorbing religion into the core of a meta-institutional framework reflected by traditions and associated practices is also a good way to make sure that religions are understood as neither power-neutral nor power-blind. Religious traditions inevitably provide orientation to the shaping of power patterns and to the legitimacy (or lack thereof) of the ruling class. The principled openness of a tradition vis-à-vis power creates frequent occasions for contesting authority. The common practitioners of a tradition might protest the extent to which power is not endorsed by legitimate authority, or authority is usurped via the sheer exercise of untamed power.

Therefore a key level on which the sociology of Islam could expand on Hodgson's analysis has been and will continue to be in the attempt to assess which kind of institutional formulas were produced as the outcome of the ongoing knowledge–power equation, the attendant level of formalization of institutions, and the underlying legitimation of this formalization (or, inversely, and quite evidently and interestingly in the Islamic case, the immunization against an excess of blanket legitimization through full-fledged formalization). Ultimately it is Hodgson himself who provides key elements for treating the meta-institutional dimension, which is integral to a tradition, as a sociological wild card, more than just as the outer shell of the workings and élans of inner piety mediated by the civilizing process. It would run counter to Hodgson's praise of the originality and creativity of the Middle Periods to treat, for example, the large-scale and long-distance institutionalization of Sufi *turuq* effected in the epoch (and based on networked patterns) as a Weberian case of routinization of a type of charisma which in earlier times was mainly nourished by intensely personal piety. The solidification of the *turuq* rather marked a stage of institutional initiation of charisma itself, the charisma of the masters and their simultaneously horizontal networks and vertical hierarchies. The most charismatic Sufi leaders (both in terms of their teachings and of their organizational success) are largely from the Middle Periods, and particularly from the 12th and 13th centuries, as also Hodgson did not fail to stress. This view is well matched by the revision and critique that Shmuel Eisenstadt (who pioneered the interdisciplinary reformulation of the Axial Age approach in a series of conferences that hosted historians, philologists, and sociologists since the end of the 1970s) made of the Weberian dichotomy between pristine and routinized charisma (Eisenstadt 1968). Without his premature passing, Hodgson might have been a key interlocutor of Eisenstadt.

Yet it is also fair to admit that, at the life and career stage he prematurely left us, Hodgson had remained stuck half-way in the historical analysis of the Islamic meta-institutional matrices. He could not explicitly reconstruct or summarize the way in which they provided the crucial nexus to a particularly elastic, far from self-enclosed, relation between the religious and civilizational dimensions in Islam (the linkage itself between Islam and Islamdom). Bryan Turner delivered a quite early critique of Hodgson's approach that is very relevant in this context (Turner 2013 [1974]: 76–8). We may reformulate this critique here in the following terms: Hodgson, who unlike Turner was not a sociologist, relied on a too rigid dichotomization between inner consciousness and piety, on the one hand, and outer social configuration of public religion, on the other. Consequently, he was not sufficiently well equipped to single out the key channels through which Islam's institutional openness and creativity unfolds between the private and public spheres. A theoretically more conscious reliance on the notion of tradition—e.g. as elaborated by MacIntyre (1988) and Asad (1986)—has been helpful in starting to fill these gaps.

As discussed throughout this volume, Hodgson emphasized the importance of the mercantile class, itself closely linked to (if not overlapping with) the layer of specialists that ran the colleges and administered the *waqf* (the so-called *'ulama'*, the intellectual core of the larger stratum of the notables or *a'yan*). He also saw this urban class as having always been the engine of the egalitarian cosmopolitanism that characterized the Irano-Semitic civilizational realm, thus being at least semi-autonomous vis-à-vis the agrarian aristocracies. Such margins of autonomy were particularly broad if compared to their counterparts within other areas of the Afro-Eurasian realms of citied agrarianate civilizations. They further increased as Islam expanded into new regions. Yet as already prefigured by Ibn Khaldun, the limiting factor of this autonomy lay rather in the dependence of Muslim urban classes on nomadic pastoralists. In the post-Mongol era, however, this limitation was largely overcome by the centralizing arrangements of the early modern Muslim empires. In the Ottoman case, the new configurations of social power allowed for a stronger integration of the higher echelons of the urban classes, including the *'ulama'*, into the central administration and court politics. Integral to this process was also a partial but significant folding of *'ilm* into *adab* (or *ilim* into *edep* in the Ottoman case).

The reason why Ibn Khaldun's approach is not the ideal aid for conceptualizing the institutional linkage between the religious and the civilizational dimensions of Islam lies with the basic institutional pessimism frequently attributed to him. What can help correct this, and should be further deepened, is a reframing of the relation between the three dimensions of Islam at large: religious, civilizational, and, at their confluence, meta-institutional/traditional; or, to give them a name: Islam, Islamdom, and the Islam/Islamdom nexus and node. Their particularly adaptable interplay and their dynamic outcome in the shape of distinctive and often diverse institutional configurations allow us to see in a new light the frequently invoked Khaldunian idea of a cyclical pattern accompanying the life of Islamic institutions. Such a view should help overcome what often amounts to a bias that conveys the image of Islam as lacking the capacity to consecrate stable patterns of political (and, relatedly, economic) development, a cliché that is often, albeit superficially, referred back to Ibn Khaldun's idea of the socio-political cycle and its seemingly sterile spiral. The idea of a lack of institutional stabilization of the cycle generates the familiar pitfall of attributing deficits and delays to an undifferentiated Islamic culture, in comparison with various other and allegedly much more dynamic civilizations, not only the West. The prejudice was not completely absent in Hodgson, yet it was handled in ways that at least avoided a typical bottleneck in the argumentation.

The Hodgsonian version of the cyclical model is therefore redeemable through analytical and theoretical resources ultimately drawn from his own historical reconstructions. In Hodgson's elaboration the cycle was not necessarily a symptom of a lack of virtuous institutionalization and legitimization of collective bonds, but became open-ended and potentially expansive thanks to the ongoing dynamics of the Islam-Islamdom nexus. The cycle (and its underlying nexus) facilitated translocal connections, be they at the level of long-distance trade or through the deployment of Sufi orders and networks across the Afro-Eurasian depths. Hodgson provided a profound understanding of the fact that, thanks to the large autonomy of religious elites, their interests, and ideas, the cycle was not idle and repetitive but included an ongoing differentiation and complexification occurring inside the socio-religious sphere itself. This process was furthered by the divergent options between law-minded piety, on the one hand, and personal piety oriented to a cultivation of the match between microcosm and macrocosm (the more philosophical and/or Sufi-oriented styles), on the other (often evoking a mesocosm/*barzakh*, or *mundus imaginalis*/*'alam al-mithal* in-between).

A plurality of religious and other registers often virtuously coexisted within the same personalities or even groups. This diversity became even more socially and culturally creative when such styles entered relations of open antagonism. Clearly this is an important marker of a largely autonomous civility, a sphere which cannot be reduced to a simple source of challenge to given, and weak, political rule. The narrow, Khaldunian cycle that entwines the religious mobilization and the political domination of tribal warriors would, from such an angle, be an actual instantiation (though not the most virtuous one) of a much larger, potentially expansive cycle that embraces not only the relationship between religion and politics and between scholars and warriors but also their mutual and inner differentiation. The specific Khaldunian cycle cannot be considered representative of the larger one since it was confined to a particular region and a specific epoch (Ibn Khaldun's more immediate historical and geographical background: the Later Middle Period and North Africa). It was a much broader development that facilitated the formation of both powerful translocal networks and, at the transition from the Middle Periods to the subsequent epoch, strongly centralized empires of a new, rather modern type—one of which at least, the Ottoman one, embodied a reflexive and practical turn of the Khaldunian cycle and its ultimate overcoming via a legitimate and even 'charismatic' type of rule.

From the Postcolonial Condition toward New Fragile Patterns of Translocal Civility

The events associated with and the developments issuing from the so-called Arab Spring have impacted strongly, yet ambivalently, on the perspective that relativizes and potentially decenters Western hegemonic notions of civility. The question should be reassessed, once more, in a broader theoretical and, as it were, tensional perspective which takes into account the specific postcolonial predicament of the Muslim world vis-à-vis Western hegemony. Yet as stressed by Talal Asad, this shift of perspective should not be restricted by the old motive of anti-Western resistance but should rather pay attention to "new institutional and discursive spaces (themselves not immutably fixed) that make different kinds of knowledge, action, and desire possible." He also warned that one should not remain caught in the polarization between two standard ways of accounting for the emergence of such new spaces, namely "either … as evidence of 'a failure to modernize properly,' or … as expressions of different experiences rooted in part in traditions other than those to which the European-inspired reforms belonged, and in part in contradictory European representations of European modernity" (Asad 2003: 217).

It is too early to conclude that contemporary, emergent transnational forms of Islamic civility exalt movement and dispersion and shun institutionalization, or at least contribute to lowering its threshold. Civility in the era of the War on Terror must still respond to Westphalian paradigms of sovereignty. For now these standards, far from disappearing, are metamorphosing in parallel with the expanding extraterritorial prerogatives of the global hegemon. The inevitable postcolonial predicament of Muslim-majority societies should not, however, distract us from seeing within Islamic history, in the longer term, trajectories of formation of distinctive yet open-ended patterns of civility. The adoption of a knowledge–power grid of analysis by the sociology of Islam shows the potential to reveal the twists and turns of this trajectory across epochs and regions, including the era marked by the rise of colonial modernity and the beginning of relations of dependence on the West. Following Johann Arnason, I have adopted such a long-term perspective by elaborating theoretical insights in conjunction with a constructive reframing of Marshall Hodgson's historical approach to both Islam's venture and to its encounter with Western-centered modernity.

Clearly deep-seated geo-cultural biases have converged to aggravate the limitations of restricted, Eurocentric angles. Their combination particularly affected the late Weber's attention to, and contemporaneity with, the late Ottoman Empire, which he saw as almost the prototype of a declining society affected by defective governance, at the very moment it desperately tried to catch up with European standards of modernity. Yet coincidently, and quite inconsistently, Weber derived the sociological characteristics of Islam almost exclusively from its Arabian origin, by reducing Islam to a "warrior religion." This view in turn largely depended on the 19th-century European characterization of Islam as a particularistic Semitic religion, which took form in the framework of both Oriental Studies and in the emerging field of the comparison of world religions (Masuzawa 2005: 179–206). This is why Weber willingly ignored, as also stressed by Arnason, that the issue of 'formation' (which is as much civilizational as it is political) is particularly crucial in the case of Islam. What makes it difficult to grasp based on Western sociological categories, which tend to conflate formation with full-fledged institutionalization of civilizational visions, is that in the case of Islam expansion and formation almost coincide to produce distinctive modes of civility.

When it comes to more recent transformations, especially those interconnected with the global rise of Western power, there is no denying that the Islamic ecumene did not match other non-Western responses to the West's political and economic hegemony. This is true at least in the sense that, in spite of an intense phase of admiration for Japan's trajectory by reformers of the late Ottoman Empire and Egypt, there has been no specifically Islamic parallel to the East Asian reinvention of both modern capitalism and the modern state—if not during the last three decades as a quite promising (if not fully successful) Islamic variant within an East/Southeast-Asian developmental model, particularly represented by Malaysia and Indonesia. This predicament also shows the risk of automatically transposing the historic civilizational model onto a late-modern context without further reflections on the interplay between the religious and civilizational dimensions and the specificity of the institutional factor (whose salience was magnified within modern transformations and colonial constraints) at the confluence of both.

This situation is closely related to the fate of nation-state institutions in a colonial and postcolonial context. Nationalism in the Muslim world has a long history of problematic and unsettled relations with Islam. Now in the 21st century the redefinition of the inherited relationship between the religious, the civilizational, and the institutional levels is presenting particularly complex problems to nationally framed Muslim-majority societies and corresponding Westphalian state formations (or imitations and adaptations thereof). Invoking the normative force represented by a nation-state-related constitutional framework is quite inescapable for the great majority of modern and contemporary socio-political actors. This framework is indeed still capable of shaping and polarizing the most crucial contemporary debates and contests. Yet it would be difficult to argue that the expansive Islamic entropy of egalitarian cosmopolitanism is just a relic of history. It can be revived in new forms that deserve a careful analysis to which I wish to contribute in a future volume, ideally the third of the trilogy inaugurated by the present one. The revitalization of Islam's historic transregional, and also transcultural, impetus also occurs thanks to the new type of connectedness and networking allowed by new and social media (Salvatore 2013). This predicament reflects an unfinished and particularly conflict-ridden process of transposing a complex religious and civilizational legacy into a modern institutional and constitutional framework. Yet this interpretive challenge makes a comparatively enriched approach to the history of Islam and the theoretically matching tasks of the sociology of Islam even more necessary and potentially fruitful.

In spite of a host of questions that still need to be addressed, one should not miss the chance to explore in the future whether there is a potential for a (hypermodern?) return to the ethos of the Middle Periods, where membership of a group was often left under-defined across the myriad organizations like Sufi orders, youth chivalry brotherhoods, guilds, and tribal confederations. Yet at the moment, and perhaps paradoxically, it is the shift from the last wave of the "Western dream" of civil society (Mardin 1995) in the 1990s to the much more sobering discourse on civility (in the frame of the securitization implemented by the War on Terror and cognate campaigns) that contingently legitimizes deinstitutionalized or under-institutionalized Islamic practices seeking a transnational frame of reference. Such wider patterns of civility facilitate local and translocal connectedness and make them potentially more tangible than any militarized parole or residual utopia. They deserve not only to be carefully studied (investigations certainly abound, ranging from transnational women's groups all the way to jihadist networks) but also to be adequately understood in theoretical terms and related to broader themes in the social sciences.

As shown in this introductory volume, such widely diverging forms of connectedness and mobilization do not respond to a homogeneous normative basis but reflect overlapping patterns of civility (and the always present danger to turn them into their opposite, namely uncivility) bearing a family resemblance to those associated with the Eliasian model of the civilizing process. Correspondingly, the types of civility consecrated 'on high' (both through securitization and via Western-controlled NGOs) are absorbed down the hierarchy of the world system and interfere with more mobile patterns of connectedness and mobilization at both local and translocal levels. These are nurtured by resilient, often merely imagined— rather than duly transmitted—institutional ideas (not least the one of the Caliphate: Hassan 2009). Yet they do not necessarily clash with the global normative frameworks and can sometimes even benefit from them (as in the case of the deregulated micro-entrepreneurship of the Anatolian province that provides the main infrastructures to a modern Islamic ethos in the Turkish case).

In this unstable context, the kernel of civility as legally and morally framed self-restraint, and therefore as a key presupposition of cooperation and connectedness, can easily slip into an imaginary of uncivility and attendant practices, depending on who formulates the political agenda and based on whose priorities. Yet even when faced with violent and resentment-fuelled responses, one should never lose sight of the fact that Islamic imaginaries are highly diversified. Though mostly articulated from radically weakened positions on a global scale, they should never be reduced to a mere anti-Western, anti-modern, ultimately anti-global resistance. They present us with a variety of articulations of the global game of matching conflict and cohesion through civility. Postcolonial patterns of civility, including the slippery plane where civility turns into uncivility, are as complex as they are difficult to interpret. This is due to their highly ambivalent relation to subsequent waves of Western-led economic globalization, the latest of which is usually associated with the implementation of what is commonly defined, with a theoretically unsavoury conceptual shorthand, as a neoliberal global order.

The process no doubt contributes to enfeeble the already weak legitimacy of postcolonial states into which the Islamic ecumene has been fragmented during the colonial era. It therefore favors transnational reconstructions of the knowledge–power equation which variably retrieve, albeit in shortened forms, memories of long-term Islamic patterns of civility and trajectories of expansive translocal connectedness within and across networks supporting knowledge production and dissemination, trade, and the formation of often transversal loyalty patterns. Viewed from an Islamic perspective (or, better, as is increasingly the case, through a plural set of not necessarily bundled Islamic perspectives), the Western exceptional path within Afro-Eurasia, now peaking in an ambivalent hegemonic gasp under the neoliberal banner, appears ever more characterized by complex, contradictory, even antinomian tendencies. The main antinomy is given by how the new regulative powers of supranational institutions supported by cosmopolitan visions, far from carrying a legitimacy derived from a smooth evolutionary path marked by a progressive rationalization of global relations, are ever and again challenged by the resilience of subsystems of sovereign nation-states. As shown by the heritage of the mandates of the League of Nations in the Middle East, this system works ever more as the multiplier of unredeemable conflicts and as the revealer of the weakness of that type of Western-rooted cosmopolitanism (though not of cosmopolitan ideas as such) now often used as the cover and alibi for global ('neoliberal' or otherwise) blueprints.

Not surprisingly, perhaps, the best alternate frame that comes into consideration via the adoption of the proposed Islamic perspective is a critical adaptation of the idea of "multiple modernities" proposed by such different authors as Shmuel N. Eisenstadt (2000) and Charles Taylor (2004) since the 1990s. This approach facilitates looking into transformative trajectories within non-Western civilizational realms where the break of modernity with tradition is not as allegedly radical as in Western experiences and where a stronger continuity of civilizational mapping is kept alive. This is due to an inherently different articulation of the knowledge–power equation and its transformations. It also results from the constraint to respond to Western hegemony by having recourse to local, regional, and civilization-specific traditions both popular and, within limits, useful. Ultimately the multiple modernities approach suggests that the building of successful institutions of control and discipline as well as the liberation of modern creative forces in the economy and within cultural production do not necessarily require the adoption of package-like notions of modernity based on *one*, stereotypical and largely mythical (if compared to the reality and diversity of the Western experience itself), European model. The approach also allows for non-Western civilizations to be considered more than just potential providers of fragmented civilizational ingredients to standard cultural recipes of modernity. The diversity of civility and of the underlying articulations of the knowledge–power equation accrues to the generative sources that facilitate the investment of selective components of multiple traditions into potentially original varieties of modernity and so link a diverse civilized past to a complex sustainable future.

References

Arjomand, Said Amir. 2004a. "Transformation of the Islamicate Civilization: A Turning Point in the Thirteenth Century?" In *Eurasian Transformations, 10th to 13th Centuries: Crystallizations, Divergences, Renaissances*, edited by Johann P. Arnason and Björn Wittrock, 213–45. Leiden: Brill.

Arjomand, Said Amir. 2004b. "Coffeehouses, Guilds and Oriental Despotism: Government and Civil Society in Late 17th–Early 18th-Century Istanbul and Isfahan, and as Seen from Paris and London." *Archives Européennes de Sociologie/European Journal of Sociology*, 45: 23–42.

Asad, Talal. 1986. *The Idea of an Anthropology of Islam*. Washington, DC: Center for Contemporary Arab Studies, Georgetown University.

Asad, Talal. 2003. *Formations of the Secular: Christianity, Islam, Modernity*. Stanford, CA: Stanford University Press.

Eisenstadt, Shmuel N. 1968. "Introduction: Charisma and Institution Building: Max Weber and Modern Sociology." In *Weber on Charisma and Institution Building*, edited and with an Introduction by Shmuel N.Eisenstadt, ix–lvi. Chicago and London: University of Chicago Press.

Eisenstadt, Shmuel N. 1986. "Introduction: The Axial Age Breakthroughs: Their Characteristics and Origins." In *The Origins and the Diversity of Axial Age Civilizations*, edited by Shmuel N. Eisenstadt, 1–25. New York: SUNY Press.

Eisenstadt, Shmuel N. 2000. "Multiple Modernities." *Daedalus*, 129/1: 1–29.

Esposito, Roberto. 2012 [2010]. *Living Thought. The Origins and Actuality of Italian Philosophy*, translated by Zakiya Hanafi. Stanford, CA: Stanford University Press.

Hassan, Mona F. 2009. *Loss of Caliphate: The Trauma and Aftermath of 1258 and 1924*. PhD thesis, Department of Near Eastern Studies, Princeton University.

Hodgson, Marshall G.S. 1974. *The Venture of Islam: Conscience and History in a World Civilization*, I–III. Chicago and London: University of Chicago Press.

Hodgson, Marshall G.S. 1993. *Rethinking World History: Essays on Europe, Islam and World History*, edited, with Introduction and Conclusion, by Edmund Burke III. Cambridge: Cambridge University Press.

Kuran, Timur. 2001. "The Provision of Public Goods under Islamic Law: Origins, Impact, and Limitations of the Waqf System." *Law and Society Review*, 35/4: 841–97.

Kuran, Timur. 2011. *The Long Divergence: How Islamic Law Held Back the Middle East*. Princeton, NJ: Princeton University Press.

MacIntyre, Alasdair. 1988. *Whose Justice? Which Rationality?* London: Duckworth.

Mardin, Şerif. 1995. "Civil Society and Islam." In *Civil Society: Theory, History, Comparison*, edited by John Hall, 278–300. Boston: Polity Press.

Masud, M. Khalid and Armando Salvatore. 2009. "Western Scholars of Islam on the Issue of Modernity." In *Islam and Modernity: Key Issues and Debates*, Edinburgh: Edinburgh University Press, edited by Muhammad Khalid Masud, Armando Salvatore, and Martin van Bruinessen, 36–53. Edinburgh: Edinburgh University Press.

Masuzawa, Tomoko. 2005. *The Invention of World Religions: Or How European Universalism Was Preserved in the Language Pluralism*. Chicago: University of Chicago Press.

Salvatore, Armando. 2007. *The Public Sphere: Liberal Modernity, Catholicism, and Islam*. New York: Palgrave Macmillan.

Salvatore, Armando. 2009. "Tradition and Modernity within Islamic Civilisation and the West." In *Islam and Modernity: Key Issues and Debates*, edited by Muhammad Khalid Masud, Armando Salvatore, and Martin van Bruinessen, 3–35. Edinburgh: Edinburgh University Press.

Salvatore, Armando. 2011a. "Eccentric Modernity? An Islamic Perspective on the Civilizing Process and the Public Sphere." *European Journal of Social Theory*, 14/1: 55–69.

Salvatore, Armando. 2011b. "Civility: Between Disciplined Interaction and Local/Translocal Connectedness." *Third World Quarterly*, 32/5: 807–25.

Salvatore, Armando. 2013. "New Media, the 'Arab Spring,' and the Metamorphosis of the Public Sphere: Beyond Western Assumptions on Collective Agency and Democratic Politics." *Constellations*, 20/2: 217–28.

Stauth, Georg and Bryan S. Turner. 1988. *Nietzsche's Dance: Resentment, Reciprocity and Resistance in Social Life*. Oxford: Blackwell.

Taylor, Charles. 2004. *Modern Social Imaginaries*. Durham, NC: Duke University Press.

Turner, Bryan S. 2013 [1974]. "Conscience in the Construction of Religion: A Critique of Marshall Hodgson's *The Venture of Islam*. In *The Sociology of Islam: Collected Essays of Bryan S. Turner*, edited by Bryan S. Turner and Kamaludeen Mohamed Nasir, 75–89. Farnham and Burlington, VT: Ashgate.

Weber, Max. 1980 [1921–1922]. *Wirtschaft und Gesellschaft: Grundriß der verstehenden Soziologie*, edited by Johannes Winckelmann, 5th ed. Tübingen: J.C.B. Mohr (Paul Siebeck).

Wittrock, Björn. 2000. "Modernity: One, None, or Many? European Origins and Modernity as a Global Condition." *Daedalus*, 129/1: 31–60.

INDEX

The Sociology of Islam: Knowledge, Power and Civility, First Edition. Armando Salvatore
© 2016 John Wiley & Sons, Ltd. Published 2016 by John Wiley & Sons, Ltd.